Multiethnic Education

Multiethnic Education

Theory and Practice

Second Edition

James A. Banks
*University of Washington,
Seattle*

Allyn and Bacon, Inc.
Boston London Sydney Toronto

Series Editor: Susanne F. Canavan
Production Administrator: Annette Joseph
Production Coordinator: Susan Freese
Editorial-Production Service: Wordsworth Associates/Grace Sheldrick
Cover Administrator: Linda K. Dickinson
Cover Designer: Christy Rosso

Library of Congress Cataloging-in-Publication Data

Banks, James A.
  Multiethnic education.

  Includes bibliographies and index.
  1. Minorities—Education—United States.   2. Intercultural education—United States.   I. Title.
LC3731.B365   1988   371.97   87-17573
ISBN 0-205-11169-6

Printed in the United States of America

10   9   8   7   6   5   4   3   2   1   92   91   90   89   88   87

To Lula, Cherry Ann, Rosie Mae, and Tessie Mae,

important women in my life,

and to Angela and Patricia,
with the hope that this book
will help to make their adult world
better than ours

Overview

vii

PART V
Teaching and Instruction 203

Contents

PART II
Conceptual Issues   55

PART V
Teaching and Instruction   203

12 Teaching Decision-Making and Social Action Skills   205

13 Reducing Prejudice in Students: Theory, Research,   223
and Strategies

Preface

In response to the ethnic revival movements that emerged in the 1960s, educators and policy makers in many parts of the world have implemented programs and practices designed to respond more adequately to the needs of ethnic and immigrant groups and to help these groups become more structurally integrated into their societies. These various programs and practices are characterized by many different goals and strategies and are supported by diverse and often conflicting philosophical positions. Programs related to ethnic education are often conceptualized differently and known by a variety of names, including *multiracial education*, *multiethnic education*, and *multicultural education*. *Multicultural education* is the most widely used term in the United States, the United Kingdom, Canada, and Australia. *Intercultural education* is the most frequently used term in European nations, including France, Germany, the Netherlands, and Switzerland.

Despite educators' attempts to implement sound programs in multiethnic education, there are, as in any emerging field, conceptual inconsistencies, philosophical conflicts, and widespread disagreement about what should be the proper role of public and state schools, colleges, and universities in the ethnic education of students. Educators and social scientists with diverse and conflicting ideological positions are proposing a wide range of educational reforms and programs related to ethnic and cultural diversity.

The debate about multiethnic education has intensified since the first edition of *Multiethnic Education: Theory and Practice* was published. Since that time a neoconservative movement and a quest for increased nationalism in several Western nations have arisen and challenged the need to make education more consistent with the ethnic realities in Western societies. However, the large number of immigrants who entered the United States and the significant number of racial incidents several Western nations experienced in the late 1980s indicated the persistence of issues and problems related to race and ethnicity in Western societies.

Multiethnic Education: Theory and Practice, second edition, is designed to help preservice and inservice educators clarify the philosophical and definitional issues related to pluralistic education, derive a clarified philosophical position, design and implement effective teaching strategies that reflect ethnic diversity, and prepare sound guidelines for multiethnic programs and practices. *Multiethnic Education* describes actions that educators can take to institutionalize educational programs and practices related to ethnic and cultural diversity.

Readers acquainted with the first edition of *Multiethnic Education* will notice that this second edition has been substantially revised and reorganized. Much of the text was rewritten to make it more consistent with current theory and research and to make the inclusion of four new chapters possible. Chapters 2, 6, 9, and 13 are new to this edition. Since the first edition was published, I have studied and worked in multiethnic education in several nations, including Canada, the United Kingdom, Australia, the Netherlands, France, and Sweden. Most of the issues, concepts, and theories discussed in this second edition are manifested in these nations as well as in the United States. I have broadened the perspective of this edition by using examples from the United States and other nations.

Multiethnic Education: Theory and Practice is divided into five parts. Part I discusses the history, goals, and practices in multiethnic education. Multiethnic education is conceptualized as a process that has the potential for spearheading substantial curriculum reform.

Conceptual issues and problems related to education, ethnicity, and cultural diversity are the focus of Part II. Major concepts, such as ethnic group and culture, are discussed and defined. The major research and programmatic paradigms related to ethnicity and education are also described. The philosophical and ideological issues related to ethnicity, education, and citizenship are discussed in the chapters in Part III.

Part IV focuses on the curriculum. Major topics in this part include the efforts made to reform the curriculum in the last two decades, the limited extent to which curriculum reform has occurred, the nature and goals of the multiethnic curriculum, and how the curriculum can be reformed to reflect the ethnic characteristics of students.

The teacher is the most important variable in multiethnic education. Part V presents strategies, knowledge, and guidelines designed to help teachers implement multiethnic education in the classroom. Planning units that focus on social issues, reducing prejudice in students, language diversity, and curriculum guidelines are discussed in Part V. The final chapter, which describes curriculum guidelines, also summarizes some of the major issues, problems, and recommendations presented in *Multiethnic Education: Theory and Practice*. The Appendix consists of an inventory that will help educators determine the extent to which their institutions reflect the ethnic diversity within their society.

Acknowledgments

I would like to thank several colleagues who helped with the preparation of this edition. Ricardo L. Garcia contributed Chapter 14. Geneva Gay co-authored Chapter 4. I wrote Chapter 15 with the following colleagues: Carlos E. Cortés, Geneva Gay, Ricardo L. Garcia, and Anna S. Ochoa. James Lynch, Dean of the Faculty of Education at Sunderland Polytechnic in the United Kingdom, reacted to several drafts of the outline and prepared thoughtful comments on five of the chapters. David Spain, an anthropologist and colleague at the University of Washington, prepared helpful comments on Chapter 5. I would like to thank the following individuals for preparing prepublication reviews of the manuscript: Edith King (University of Denver) and Philip T. K. Daniel (Northern Illinois University). Even though all of the comments on the manuscript were helpful and informative, I assume total responsibility for the contents of this book.

I am grateful to the National Academy of Education for a Spencer Fellowship that supported my research for three years. Many of the concepts I formulated during these years are incorporated into this and the previous edition. My present and former graduate students at the University of Washington listened to and reacted to many of the ideas in this book as they were formulated and refined.

I wish to thank Cherry A. Banks, President of Educational Materials and Services Center in Edmonds, Washington, for stimulating and supporting my intellectual growth for almost two decades, for thoughtful and helpful reactions to the ideas in this book, and for ably preparing the index.

My daughters, Angela and Patricia, have taught me a great deal about the essence of life and given me renewed faith that humankind can create a better world.

I would like to thank the following organizations, publishers, and individuals for permitting me to draw freely from the publications noted that I authored:

Academic Press, Inc., and Geneva Gay, for (with Geneva Gay), "Ethnicity in Contemporary American Society: Toward the Development of a Typology," *Ethnicity*, Vol. 5 (September 1978), pp. 238–252.

The Association for Supervision and Curriculum Development, for "Curricular Models for an Open Society," in Delmo Della-Dora and James E. House, eds., *Education for an Open Society* (Washington, D.C.: Association for Supervision and Curriculum Development, 1974), pp. 43–63; and "The Emerging Stages of Ethnicity: Implications for Staff Development," *Educational Leadership*, Vol. 34 (December 1976), pp. 190–193.

Cassell, for a section from one of my chapters in James A. Banks and James Lynch, eds., *Multicultural Education in Western Societies* (London: Holt, Rinehart and Winston, 1986), pp. 10–25.

The Centre for the Study of Curriculum and Instruction, The University of

British Columbia, for "Reducing Prejudice in Students: Theory, Research and Strategies," in Kogila Moodley, ed., *Race Relations and Multicultural Education* (Vancouver: Centre for the Study of Curriculum and Instruction, the University of British Columbia, 1985), pp. 65–87.

The Faculty of Education, University of Birmingham (England), for "Ethnic Revitalization Movements and Education," *Educational Review*, Vol. 37, No. 2 (1985), pp. 131–139.

Heldref Publications, for "Pluralism, Ideology and Curriculum Reform," *The Social Studies*, Vol. 67 (May–June 1967), pp. 99–106.

Howard University Press, for "Shaping the Future of Multicultural Education," *Journal of Negro Education*, Vol. 48 (Summer 1979), pp. 237–252.

Longman, Inc., for a figure from my book (with contributions by Ambrose A. Clegg, Jr.), *Teaching Strategies for the Social Studies*, 3rd ed. (New York: Longman, Inc., 1985), p. 435.

The National Council for the Social Studies, for "Cultural Democracy, Citizenship Education, and the American Dream," (Presidential Address), *Social Education*, Vol. 47 (March 1983), pp. 231–232; "Should Integration Be a Societal Goal in a Pluralistic Nation?" in Raymond Muessig, ed., *Controversial Issues in the Social Studies* (Washington, D.C.: National Council for the Social Studies, 1975), pp. 197–228; "Ethnic Studies As a Process of Curriculum Reform," *Social Education*, Vol. 40 (February 1976), pp. 76–80; wth Carlos E. Cortés, Geneva Gay, Ricardo L. Garcia, and Anna S. Ochoa, *Curriculum Guidelines for Multiethnic Education* (Washington, D.C.: National Council for the Social Studies, 1976).

The University of Chicago Press for "The Social Studies, Ethnic Diversity and Social Change," *The Elementary School Journal*, Vol. 87 (May 1987), pp. 531–543.

Multiethnic
Education

PART I

History, Goals, and Practices

Chapter 1 is a review of some of the major historical events related to ethnicity in U.S. society and the Western world since the turn of the century. It describes the development of educational reform movements related to pluralism within an historical context. The intergroup education movement of the 1940s and 1950s, ethnicity and education in various Western societies, and the new immigrants in the United States are discussed.

Chapter 2 describes the ethnic revival movements that have emerged in various Western societies since the 1960s. It also presents a typology that classifies the major phases of ethnic revitalization movements, particularly as they have developed in the United States and the United Kingdom.

In Chapter 3 the historical development of multiethnic-multicultural education is described. The nature of multiethnic education, its goals, problems, and current practices are discussed, as are the promises of multiethnic education. Multiethnic education is viewed as a process of curriculum reform that has the potential for spearheading change in the total educational environment.

1

The Historical Development of Multiethnic Education

The Rise of Nativism

Most of the European immigrants who came to North America before 1890 were from nations in Northern and Western Europe, such as the United Kingdom, Germany, Sweden, and Switzerland. Although conflicts developed between these various immigrant groups, the English were dominating social, economic, and political life in North America by the 1700s. As the twentieth century approached and new waves of immigrants began to arrive in the United States from Southern, Central, and Eastern Europe, the immigrants from Northern and Western Europe began to perceive themselves as the "old" immigrants and rightful inhabitants of America. They saw the new immigrants as a threat to American civilization and to the American democratic tradition. Sharp and often inaccurate distinctions were made between the "new" and "old" immigrants. A movement called *nativism* arose to stop the flood of "new" immigrants arriving in America.[1] The nativists pointed out that the new immigrants were primarily Catholics, whereas the old immigrants were mainly Protestants. A strong element of anti-Catholicism became an integral part of the nativistic movement.

Because of their Catholicism, cultural differences, and competition for jobs with the "old" immigrants and native-born Americans, the new immigrants became the victims of blatant nativism. A suspicion and distrust of all foreigners became widespread near the turn of the century. The outbreak of the Great War in Europe in 1914 greatly increased the suspicion and distrust of immigrant groups in the United States and further stimulated nativistic feelings and groups. Nativism swept through the United States during the Great War. Nativists argued for one-hundred percent Americanism and said that America should be for "Americans." The new immigrant groups tried desperately but unsuccessfully to prove their national loyalty to the nativists.

Nativism and Education

The public schools, colleges, and universities usually perpetuate the dominant ideologies and values that are promoted and embraced by the powerful groups within society.[2] Reflecting the prevailing goals of the nation as articulated by its powerful and economic leaders, the schools and colleges promoted and embraced Americanization and blind loyalty to the nation and also showed a distrust of "for-

3

eigners" and immigrant groups during the turn of the century and World War I periods. The teaching of German and other foreign languages was prohibited in many schools. German books in school libraries were sometimes burned. Some schools prohibited the playing of music by German composers in music classes and in school assemblies.[3] In this atmosphere of virulent nativism, government-sponsored propaganda, and emphasis on blind patriotism and Americanization, the idea of cultural pluralism in education would have been alien and perhaps viewed as seditious and un-American.

The Melting Pot

The assimilationist ideology that was pervasive near the turn of the century and during World War I was embodied and expressed in the play *The Melting Pot.* This play, written by the English-Jewish author Israel Zangwill, opened in New York City in 1908. It became a tremendous success. The great ambition of the play's composer-protagonist, David Quixano, was to create an American symphony that would personify his deep conviction that his adopted land was a nation in which all ethnic differences would mix and from which a new person, superior to all, would emerge. What in fact happened, however, was that most of the immigrant and ethnic cultures stuck to the bottom of the mythical melting pot. Anglo-Saxon culture remained dominant; other ethnic groups had to give up many of their cultural characteristics in order to participate fully in the nation's social, economic, and political institutions.[4]

However, as Chapter 7 points out, cultural influence was not in one direction. Although the Anglo-Saxon Protestant culture became and remained dominant in the United States, other ethnic groups, such as the Germans, the Irish, Indians, and Blacks, influenced the Anglo-Saxon culture as the Anglo-Saxon culture influenced the culture of these groups. However, the Anglo-Saxon Protestant culture has had the most cogent influence on U.S. culture.[5] This influence has been in many cases positive. The American ideals of human rights, participatory democracy, and separation of church and state are largely Anglo-Saxon contributions to U.S. civilization.

The American school, like other American institutions, embraced Anglo-conformity goals. Two major goals were to rid ethnic groups of their ethnic traits and to force them to acquire Anglo-Saxon values and behavior. In 1909 Ellwood Patterson Cubberley, the famed educational leader, clearly stated a major goal of the common schools:

> Everywhere these people [immigrants] tend to settle in groups or settlements, and to set up here their national manners, customs, and observances. Our task is to break up these groups or settlements, to assimilate and amalgamate these people as part of our American race, and to implant in their children, as far as can be done, the Anglo-Saxon conception of righteousness, law and order, and popular government, and

to awaken in them a reverence for our democratic institutions and for those things in our national life which we as a people hold to be of abiding worth.[6]

The Call for Cultural Pluralism

In the early years of the twentieth century, a few philosophers and writers, such as Horace Kallen, Randolph Bourne, and Julius Drachsler, strongly defended the rights of the immigrants living in the United States.[7] They rejected the assimilationist argument made by leaders such as Cubberley. They argued that a political democracy must also be a cultural democracy and that the thousands of Southern, Eastern, and Central European immigrant groups had a right to maintain their ethnic cultures and institutions in American society. They used a "salad bowl" argument, maintaining that each ethnic culture would play a unique role in American society but would also contribute to the total society. They argued that ethnic cultures would enrich American civilization. They called their position *cultural pluralism* and said it should be used to guide public and educational policies.

The arguments of the cultural pluralists were a cry in the wilderness. They fell largely on deaf ears. Most of America's political, business, and educational leaders continued to push for the assimilation of the immigrant and indigenous racial and ethnic groups. They felt that only in this way could they make a unified nation out of so many different ethnic groups with histories of wars and hostilities in Europe. The triumph of the assimilationist forces in American life was symbolized by the Immigration Acts of 1917 and 1924.

The Immigration Act of 1917, designed to halt the immigration of Southern, Central, and Eastern European groups, such as Poles, Greeks, and Italians, required immigrants to pass a reading test to enter the United States. When this act passed but failed to reduce the number of immigrants from these nations enough to please the nativists, they pushed for and succeeded in getting another act passed, the Immigration Act of 1924. This act drastically limited the number of immigrants that could enter the United States from all European nations except those in Northern and Western Europe. It ended the era of massive European immigration to the United States and closed a significant chapter in U.S. history.

Ethnic Education between the Two World Wars

Mainstream American leaders and educators generally ignored the voices advocating pluralistic policies in the early years of the twentieth century. However, because of the tremendous value and cultural diversity within the United States, rarely is there consensus within our society on any important social or educational issue. Consequently, while those who dominated educational policy usually embraced the assimilationist ideology and devoted little time and energy to the education of the nation's ethnic minority groups, other American leaders, researchers, and educators engaged in important discussions about the education of the nation's ethnic minorities, formulated educational policy related to ethnic groups, and did important research on American ethnic communities.[8] Ironically, however, often the policy formulated by those deeply concerned about the education of ethnic minorities was assimilationist oriented. This indicated the extent to which the assimilationist ideology had permeated American life and thought. However, there were always a few educational leaders who advocated pluralism.

Policies and programs in ethnic education did not suddenly arise during the ethnic revitalization movements of the 1960s and 1970s. These developments gradually evolved over a long period. It is true, however, that they became more intense during various historical periods, usually because of heightened racial consciousness and concern stimulated by events such as racial conflicts and tensions. The evolutionary character of ethnic education in the United States will be illustrated by a brief discussion of the educational policies related to American Indians, Black Americans, and Mexican Americans between the two great world wars. The education of other ethnic groups, such as Jewish Americans, Italian Americans, and Puerto Rican Americans, could also be used to illustrate the evolutionary nature of ethnic education. However, the choice of these first three ethnic groups can in part be justified by the fact that educational policy and programs related to them have stimulated enduring and controversial discussions and programs for most of the present century.

American-Indian Education

How American Indians should be educated has evoked a continuing debate since the late 1800s.[9] Since the 1920s, educational policy for American Indians has vacillated between strong assimilationism to self-determination and cultural pluralism. The landmark Meriam Report, issued in 1928, recommended massive reforms in American-Indian education.[10] The Report recommended that Indian education be tied more closely to the community, the building of day schools in the community, and the reformation of boarding schools. It also recommended that the curriculum in Indian schools be changed to reflect Indian cultures and the needs of local Indian communities.[11] The 1969 Senate Report on Indian Education, called the Kennedy Report, stated that many of the reforms recommended by the Meriam Report had not been attained.[12]

Black-American Education

Developments in the education of Black Americans were both active and controversial in the decades between the war years. Carter G. Woodson, a Black historian who received a doctorate from Harvard in 1912, did seminal research and work on Black history and Black education. Woodson founded the Association for the Study of Negro Life and History in 1915.[13] This organization was founded to sponsor and encourage research in Black history and to disseminate this research to scholars and teachers in Black schools and colleges. The Association started two important publications that are still published: the *Journal of Negro History* and *The Negro History Bulletin*. Woodson began Negro History Week in 1926 to commemorate milestones in Black history.

Black educational policy became very controversial within the Black community. Booker T. Washington and William E. B. DuBois set forth sharply contrasting views about directions for Black education. Washington, a former slave and the most influential Black leader of his time, believed that Black students needed a practical, industrial education.[14] He implemented his ideas at the Tuskegee Institute in Tuskegee, Alabama. DuBois, the noted Black scholar and educational philosopher, felt that a "talented tenth" should be educated for leadership in the Black community. The "talented tenth," he argued, should study the classics, political philosophy, and other academic subjects.[15]

Mexican-American Education

During the 1930s and 1940s, considerable attention was focused on the education of Mexican Americans by scholars and educators concerned with their educational plight. Most educators during this period, according to Carter and Segura, saw the school as an agency for the acculturation of Mexican-American students.[16] Betty Gould, for example, recommended what she considered effective methods for the acculturation of Mexican-American students in her 1932 thesis, "Methods of Teaching Mexicans."[17] Carter and Segura described Mexican-American education during the 1930s:

> School programs for Chicano children during the 1930s emphasized vocational training and manual-arts training; learning of English; health and hygiene; and adoption of American core values such as cleanliness, thrift and punctuality. Segregation, especially in the early grades, was regularly recommended and commonly established. It was inexplicably argued that Americanization could best be accomplished by keeping foreigners out of contact with Americans.[18]

The voices speaking for the education of Mexican Americans during the 1930s and 1940s, however, were not unanimous. George I. Sánchez, a pioneer Mexican-American educator and scholar, urged educators to consider the unique cultural and linguistic characteristics of Mexican-American students when planning and implementing educational programs for them.[19]

The Intergroup-Education Movement

Social, political, and economic changes caused by World War II stimulated a curriculum movement related to cultural and ethnic diversity that became known as intercultural education or intergroup education. World War II created many job opportunities in northern cities. Many Blacks and Whites left the South during the war years in search of jobs. More than 150,000 Blacks left the South each year in the decade between 1940 and 1950 and settled in northern cities. In such northern cities as Chicago and Detroit conflict developed between Blacks and Whites as they competed for jobs and housing. Racial conflict also occurred in the Far West. Mexican Americans and Anglos clashed in serious "zoot-suit" riots in Los Angeles during the summer of 1943. These racial conflicts and tensions severely strained race relations in the nation.

Racial tension and conflict were pervasive in northern cities during the war years. In 1943, race riots took place in Los Angeles, Detroit, and in the Harlem district of New York City. The most destructive riot during the war broke out in Detroit on a Sunday morning in June, 1943. More southern migrants had settled in Detroit during this period than in any other American city. The Detroit riot raged for more than thirty hours. When it finally ended, thirty-four persons were dead and property worth millions of dollars had been destroyed.[20] The Detroit riot stunned the nation and stimulated national action by concerned Black and White citizens.

A major goal of intergroup education was to reduce racial and ethnic prejudice and misunderstandings.[21] Activities designed to reduce prejudice and to increase interracial understanding included the teaching of isolated instructional units on various minority groups, exhortations against prejudice, organizing assemblies and cultural get-togethers, disseminating information on racial, ethnic, and religious backgrounds, and banning books considered stereotypic and demeaning to ethnic groups. A major assumption of the intergroup-education movement was that factual knowledge would develop respect and acceptance of various ethnic and racial groups. Unlike the ethnic-studies movement of the late 1960s, however, the emphasis in the intercultural-education movement of the 1940s and 1950s was neither on strong cultural pluralism nor on maintaining or perpetuating strong ethnic loyalties.

Two important national projects were implemented to actualize the goals of intercultural education. The Intergroup Education in Cooperating Schools project, directed by Hilda Taba, was designed to effect changes in elementary and secondary schools.[22] The other project, the College Study in Intergroup Relations, was sponsored by the American Council on Education and directed by Lloyd Allen Cook.[23] The College Study project was the first cooperative effort in the United States to improve the intercultural component of teacher education. Twenty-four colleges with teacher-education programs participated in this project from 1945 to 1949.

The Intergroup-Education Movement Ends

The intergroup-education movement and its related reforms failed to become institutionalized within most U.S. schools, colleges, and teacher-training institutions. This statement should not be interpreted to mean that the movement did not benefit our society and educational institutions. Cook has noted the tremendous impact that the College Study projects had on the individuals who participated in them. The action and research projects undertaken in the College Study contributed to our practical and theoretical knowledge about race relations and about intervention efforts designed to influence attitudes and behavior.[24] The basic idea of the College Study was a sound one that merits replication: teacher-training institutions formed a consortium to develop action and research projects to effect change.

It is also true that many individual teachers and professors, and probably many individual school and teacher-training institutions, continued some elements of the reforms related to intergroup education after the national movement faded. By the 1960s, however, when racial tension intensified in the nation and race riots again sprang up, few U.S. schools and teacher-education institutions had programs and curricula that dealt adequately with the study of racial and ethnic relations. However, most all-Black schools and colleges were teaching Black studies and were responding in other ways to many of the unique cultural characteristics of Black students.

As we consider ways to institutionalize reforms related to multiethnic education, it is instructive to consider why the reforms related to intergroup education failed to become institutionalized in most U.S. schools and colleges. The reforms related to the movement failed to become institutionalized, in part, for the following six reasons:

1. Mainstream American educators never internalized the ideology and major assumptions on which intergroup education was based.

2. Mainstream educators never understood how the intergroup education movement contributed to the major goals of the American common schools.

3. Most American educators saw intergroup education as a reform project for schools that had open racial conflict and tension and not for what they considered their smoothly functioning and nonproblematic schools.

4. Racial tension in the cities took more subtle forms in the 1950s. Consequently, most American educators no longer saw the need for action designed to reduce racial conflict and problems.

5. Intergroup education remained on the periphery of mainstream educational thought and developments and was funded primarily by special funds. Consequently, when the special funds and projects ended, the movement largely faded.

6. The leaders of the intergroup-education movement never developed a well-articulated and coherent philosophical position that revealed how the intergroup-education movement was consistent with the major goals of the American common schools and with American Creed values.

Assimilation Continues and Helps to Shape a Nation

Despite the intergroup-education reforms of the 1940s and 1950s, assimilationist forces and policies dominated American life from about the turn of the century to the beginning of the 1960s. The assimilationist ideology was not seriously challenged during this long period, even though there were a few individuals, such as Marcus Garvey in the 1920s, who championed separatism and ethnic pluralism.[25] These lone voices were successfully ignored or silenced.

Most minority as well as dominant group leaders saw the assimilation of America's ethnic groups as the proper societal goal. Social scientists and reformers during this period were heavily influenced by the writings of Robert E. Park, the eminent American sociologist who had once worked as an informal secretary for Booker T. Washington.[26] Park believed that race relations proceeded through four inevitable stages: *contact, conflict, accommodation,* and *assimilation.*[27] The most reform-oriented social scientists and social activists embraced assimilation as both desirable and inevitable within a democratic pluralistic nation such as the United States.

The American assimilationist policy shaped a nation from millions of immigrants and from diverse American-Indian groups. The United States did not become an ethnically Balkanized nation. This could have happened. The assimilationist idea also worked reasonably well for ethnic peoples who were White. However, it did force many of them to become marginal individuals and to deny family and heritage. This should not be taken lightly, for denying one's basic group identity is a very painful and psychologically unsettling process. However, most, but not all, White ethnic groups in the United States have been able, in time, to climb up the economic and social ladders.

The New Pluralism

The assimilationist idea has not worked nearly as well for ethnic peoples of color. This is what Blacks realized by the early 1960s. The unfulfilled promises and dreams of the assimilationist idea was a major cause of the Black civil rights movement of the 1960s. By the late 1950s and early 1960s, discrimination in such areas as employment, housing, and education, combined with rising expectations, caused Afro-Americans to lead an unprecedented fight for their rights, which became known as the Black civil rights revolution.

Many Blacks who had become highly assimilated were still unable to participate fully in many mainstream American institutions. Blacks were still denied many opportunities because of their skin color. They searched for a new ideal; many endorsed some form of cultural pluralism. An idea born during the turn of the century was refashioned to fit the hopes, aspirations, and dreams of disillusioned ethnic peoples in the 1960s.

Blacks demanded more control over the institutions in their communities and also demanded that all institutions, including the schools, more accurately reflect their ethnic cultures. They demanded more Black teachers and administrators for their youths, textbooks that reflected Black culture, and cafeteria foods more like those their children ate at home.[28]

Educational institutions, at all levels, began to respond to the Black civil rights movement. The apparent success of the Black civil rights movement caused other alienated ethnic groups of color, such as Mexican Americans, Asian American, and Puerto Ricans, to make similar demands for political, economic, and educational changes.

Mexican-American studies and Asian-American studies courses that paralleled Black studies courses emerged.[29] The reform movements initiated by the ethnic peoples of color caused many White ethnic groups that had denied their ethnic cultures to proclaim ethnic pride and to push for the inclusion of more information about White ethnic groups in the curriculum. This movement became known as the *new pluralism*. In a sense, the Black civil rights movement legitimized ethnicity, and other victimized ethnic groups began to search for their ethnic roots and to demand more group and human rights.

The New Immigrants

Since the Immigration Reform Act of 1965 became effective in 1968, the United States has experienced its largest wave of immigrants since the turn of the century. Nearly 80 percent (78.6 percent) more immigrants entered the United States in the decade between 1971 and 1980 than had entered in the years between 1951 and 1960.

Not only has the number of immigrants entering the United States increased by leaps and bounds since 1968, but the characteristics of the immigrants have also changed dramatically. In the decade between 1951 and 1960, most of the immigrants to the United States came from Europe (about 59.3 percent). However, between 1971 and 1980, Europeans made up only 18 percent of the legal immigrants who came to the United States. Most immigrants during these years came from Asian and Latin-American nations, such as the Philippines, Korea, China, Mexico, and Cuba.[30] A significant number of people from the war-torn nations of Indochina sought refuge in the United States when communists gained control of their homelands. By 1985 more than one million Vietnamese, Laotians, and Kampucheans were living in the United States.[31]

The wave of new immigrants to the United States from non-European nations and the relatively low birthrate among Whites compared to that of most ethnic minority groups are having a significant impact on U.S. society, particularly on its demographic characteristics. The new wave of immigrants to the United States has hastened the decline in the relative proportion of the White population in the United States. This decline began as early as 1900. Between 1900 and 1980 the White proportion of the U.S. population declined from 87.7 percent to 83.1 percent. During the same time, the proportion of non-Whites in the United States increased from 12.3 percent of the population in 1900 to 16.9 percent in 1980.[32] These demographic changes would be even more dramatic if the percentage for non-Whites included the 8.1 million Hispanics classified as White in 1980.

The new immigrants, along with the diversity of indigenous U.S. ethnic groups, are having a tremendous impact on the nation's schools. Ethnic minorities made up the majority of the school enrollments in twenty-three of twenty-five of the nation's largest cities in 1984.[33] It is estimated that by 1990 30 percent of all of the students in the U.S. public schools will be ethnic minorities. In some urban school districts, more than fifty different languages are spoken.

Even though the characteristics of the students in U.S. schools are changing substantially, conflict often develops between the home and the school and between teachers and students. The schools have been reluctant to adapt their curricular and teaching styles to make them more consistent with the needs of ethnic minority students. In many schools that have multiethnic populations, the curriculum, teaching, and motivational techniques remain Anglo-centric.

Racial and ethnic problems are major sources of conflict in many U.S. schools, particularly in urban areas. Disproportionality in achievement, discipline, and dropout rates among mainstream and minority students is a significant source of tension in most urban school districts. The parents blame teachers and administrators; the school blames the home and the student's culture.

As long as the achievement gap between Blacks and Whites and Anglos and Hispanics is wide, ethnic conflicts and tension in schools will continue. Improving the academic achievement of ethnic minority students and developing and implementing a multicultural curriculum that reflects the cultures, experiences, and perspectives of diverse ethnic groups will help reduce the racial conflict and tension in U.S. schools.

The Response to the New Immigrants

During the early 1980s, net legal immigration to the United States was about 750,000 persons per year. About 800,000 immigrants came to the United States in 1980.[34] These figures do not include the large but unknown number of illegal (i.e., undocumented) immigrants who entered the United States during this period. It has been estimated that at least a half million illegal immigrants came to the United States each year during this time.

The large number of legal and undocumented immigrants who entered the United States during the early and mid-1980s, like large waves of immigrants in the past, evoked concern among many U.S. citizens that the nation was being overpopulated by immigrants from poverty-stricken nations who lacked the skills, attitudes, and knowledge to participate effectively in U.S. society.

A large number of the new immigrants spoke Spanish and Asian languages. Particularly in regions in which large numbers of Hispanic immigrants settled, such as California, Florida, and Texas, acid controversies developed over their rights to have bilingual education in the schools and public documents in their native languages. Many new immigrants advocated bilingual education in the schools and wanted ballots and other official documents in their native languages as well as in English. Many U.S. citizens argued that the immigrants should learn English — and only English — as quickly as possible. English was established as the official language in seven states — Georgia, Kentucky, Indiana, Illinois, Nebraska, Virginia, and California. A movement was also undertaken to make English the official language of the United States.

A major debate occurred regarding how the United States could and should restrict the large number of undocumented immigrants who were entering the nation. Some employers welcomed the undocumented immigrants because they worked for very low wages. However, many Americans believed that the number of illegal immigrants entering the United States each year created problems for other workers and for the nation's public institutions. There was little agreement about how the number of undocumented immigrants could be reduced.

In 1983, Senator Alan K. Simpson of Wyoming and Representative Romano L. Mazzoli of Kentucky introduced a bill designed to curb the number of illegal immigrants in part by imposing civil penalties and fines for employers who knowingly hired them. The bill evoked considerable controversy within the Congress and the nation. After several years of a vigorous and often acrimonious debate, the bill finally became law on November 5, 1986. Some of the bill's more controversial provisions were removed before it was enacted. Known as the Immigration Reform and Control Act of 1986, it imposed severe penalties on employers who knowingly hire illegal immigrants. The act also included an amnesty program that allowed a large number of illegal immigrants living in the United States to obtain legal status if they could prove they had been living in the United States since January 1, 1982.

The New Nationalism

During the 1960s and 1970s events such as the civil rights movement, ethnic revival movements, the quest for women's rights, and the Vietnam War challenged many U.S. values and demanded that U.S. ideals and realities become more consistent. The development of ethnic studies programs, affirmative action initiatives, and renewed efforts to desegregate the nation's public schools were direct results of the social movements of the last two decades.

The social movements during the 1960s and 1970s not only resulted in some significant reforms in U.S. society, but they also helped usher in a neoconservative movement designed to slow the pace of reform to reduce perceived polarization, and to promote national identity and what became known as the *new national-*

ism.[35] After two decades of reform that focused on diversity and equality and after the national trauma that resulted from the Vietnam War, many Americans believed that the nation needed to close ranks, celebrate its strengths, and emphasize cohesion and nationalism. This attitude was symbolized in 1986 during the celebration of the one-hundredth birthday of the Statue of Liberty in New York Harbor. There was a great deal of adulation about the virtues of U.S. society and the need to promote nationalism and a national identity during this celebration. The new nationalism quest often became identified with the new right movement that emerged in the 1980s. This movement was often radically conservative, and it unabashedly advocated an extreme form of Americanism reminiscent of the nativistic movement at the turn of the century.

Multiethnic Education in Other Western Nations

The ethnic revival movements in the United States echoed throughout the world as groups such as the Jamaicans in the United Kingdom, the Australian Aborigines, and the Moluccans and Surinamese in the Netherlands demanded more social, political, and educational equality in their societies. European nation-states such as the United Kingdom, the Netherlands, and France have long been characterized by ethnic and cultural diversity. The diversity within these nations was enriched considerably during the post–World War II period because many immigrants from their former colonies came to these nations in search of a better life.[36]

Large numbers of West Indians and Asians from India and Pakistan emigrated to the United Kingdom in the years after World War II. Indonesian Dutch and Moluccans, as well as immigrants from Surinam and the Antilles, settled in the Netherlands during this same period. Many of the immigrants in France came from Algeria, Morocco, and Tunisia, as well as from the Asian nations of Cambodia, Laos, and Vietnam. In addition to the emigrants from their former colonies, many immigrants in nations such as the United Kingdom, the Netherlands, and France come from other parts of Europe, especially from Southern and Eastern Europe. Emigrants from Portugal, Spain, Greece, Yugoslavia, and Poland often go to France and other Western and Northern European nations seeking work. Germany has a large number of immigrants from Turkey. Foreign workers from Yugoslavia, Greece, and Turkey also go to Sweden seeking work. The largest immigrant group in Sweden are Finns.

Large numbers of immigrants also settled in Australia and Canada during the postwar period. In 1981, about 25 percent of the population of Australia had been born in foreign countries; another 20 percent had at least one parent born in a foreign country. The largest percentage of foreign-born persons in Australia in 1981 were from the United Kingdom and Europe (37.7 percent), followed by Italy (9.2 percent), Greece (4.8 percent), Yugoslavia (5.0 percent), and Germany (3.7

percent). There was also a significant number of people born in Turkey and Vietnam.[37] In addition to the two major cultural groups, the British (more than 9 million) and the French (more than 6 million), a range of other cultural and ethnic group live in Canada, including the Native peoples (the Indians and the Métis), the Portuguese, Italians, Indo-Pakistani peoples, Chinese, and Blacks.[38]

Ethnic minority groups in these various lands, including the United Kingdom, France, the Netherlands, Australia, and Canada, face problems similar to those faced by their counterparts in the United States. They often achieve less well in school than do mainstream students because of language problems, poverty, and the conflict between their cultures and the culture of the schools. When multicultural education first emerged in the European nations in the 1970s, the problem of immigrant and ethnic youths was viewed primarily as a language problem. It was generally believed that these students experienced problems in the school primarily because of their language and dialect differences. Consequently, most of the first programs formulated in Europe to help immigrant youths increase their academic achievement focused on helping them learn the dominant language of the national society.[39]

With the experience of more than a decade of dealing with the educational problems of ethnic and immigrant groups, combined with the insights and knowledge from nations such as the United States, Canada, and Autralia, multicultural theorists in Europe now view the problem of educating ethnic and immigrant groups as much more complex than merely teaching them the national language. Factors such as racism, cultural conflict, teacher expectations and attitudes, and the need to reform the total school environment to make it more reflective of the ethnic and cultural diversity within the society are important theoretical and policy issues in multicultural educational reform in Europe as well as in Canada and Australia.[40]

Summary

A large wave of immigrants from Southern, Central, and Eastern Europe entered the United States between 1890 and 1917. The Europeans who already lived in the United States during this period were primarily from Northern and Western Europe. Because of their cultural differences, Catholicism, and competition for jobs with native-born Americans, a nativistic movement arose to halt the immigration of the "new" immigrants. Nativism became widespread throughout the United States and influenced the nation's institutions, including the schools. The outbreak of World War I in Europe greatly increased nativistic expressions within the larger society and the schools. The schools tried to make the immigrants one-hundred percent Americans and to exclude all elements of "foreignness" from the curriculum.

A few philosophers and writers, such as Horace Kallen, Randolph Bourne, and Julius Drachsler, defended the immigrants' rights, stating that cultural democracy should exist in a democratic nation such as the United States. The arguments of these writers, however, influenced few American leaders.

Most institutions within American society, including the schools, remained assimilationist-oriented between World War I and II and devoted little serious attention to the educational needs and problems of ethnic minority groups. However, a number of American educational and scholarly leaders formulated policy and programs for educating ethnic minorities during this period. The educational developments in American-Indian, Afro-American, and Mexican-American education between the two wars illustrate the evolutionary nature of ethnic education in the United States.

The intergroup-education movement grew out of the social developments that emerged in response to World War II. Conflict and riots developed in U.S. cities as Blacks and Whites and Anglos and Chicanos competed for housing and jobs. The intergroup-education movement tried to reduce interracial tensions and to further intercultural understandings. Developments in intergroup education took place at the elementary, secondary, and college level. The intergroup-education movement, itself only mildly pluralistic, did not seriously challenge the assimilationist ideology in American life. When the ethnic revitalization movements of the 1960s and 1970s and related educational-reform movements emerged, the intergroup-education movement had largely faded.

Since 1968, the United States has experienced a major wave of new immigrants primarily from nations in Latin America and Asia. These new immigrants have had a major impact on the social, economic, and educational institutions in the United States. While schools and other social institutions are trying to respond to the needs of these groups—sometimes reluctantly—a renewed movement toward nationalism is advocating national cohesion and identity rather than diversity.

Other Western nation-states, such as the United Kingdom, France, Canada, and Australia, have also become more ethnically diverse since World War II. The ethnic minorities within these societies face problems similar to their counterparts in the United States. Multicultural education has emerged within these nations to respond to the unique needs, problems, and aspirations of ethnic minorities.

Notes

1. John Higham, *Strangers in the Land: Patterns of American Nativism. 1860–1925* (New York: Atheneum, 1972).

2. Michael B. Katz, *Class, Bureaucracy, and Schools: The Illusion of Educational Change in America*, expanded edition (New York: Praeger Publishers, 1975).

3. Wayne Moquin, ed., *Makers of America: Hyphenated Americans, 1914–1924*, volume 7, (Chicago: Encyclopaedia Britannica Educational Corporation, 1971), p. 107.

4. Maldwyn Allen Jones, *American Immigration* (Chicago: University of Chicago Press, 1960).

5. Edward C. Stewart, *American Cultural Patterns: A Cross-Cultural Perspective* (LaGrange Park, Ill.: Intercultural Network, Inc., 1972).

6. Ellwood P. Cubberley, *Changing Conceptions of Education* (Boston: Houghton Mifflin, 1909), pp. 15–16.

7. Horace M. Kallen, *Culture and Democracy in the United States* (New York: Boni and Liveright, 1924); Randolph S. Bourne, "Trans-National America," *The Atlantic Monthly* 118 (July 1916); Julius Drachsler, *Democracy and Assimilation* (New York: Macmillan, 1920).

8. See Meyer Weinberg, *A Chance to Learn: A History of Race and Education in the United States* (New York: Cambridge University Press, 1977).

9. Estelle Fuchs and Robert J. Havighurst, *To Live on This Earth: American Indian Education* (Garden City, N.Y.: Doubleday, 1973).

10. Lewis Meriam, ed., *The Problem of Indian Administration* (Baltimore: Johns Hopkins University Press, 1928).

11. Margaret Szasz, *Education and the American Indian: The Road to Self-Determination, 1928–1973* (Albuquerque: University of New Mexico Press, 1974).

12. *Indian Education: A National Tragedy–a National Challenge.* 91st Congress, 1st Session, Report of the Committee on Labor and Public Welfare, Special Subcommittee on Indian Education, U.S. Senate. (Washington, D.C.: U.S. Government Printing Office, 1969).

13. See, for example, Carter G. Woodson and Charles H. Wesley, *The Negro in Our History* (Washington, D.C.: The Associated Publishers 1922); and Carter G. Woodson, *Mis-Education of the Negro* (Washington, D.C.: The Associated Publishers, 1933).

14. See Booker T. Washington, *Up from Slavery: An Autobiography* (New York: Doubleday and Company, 1901); and Louis R. Harlan, *Booker T. Washington: The Making of a Black Leader, 1856–1901* (New York: Oxford University Press, 1972).

15. W. E. B. DuBois, *The Souls of Black Folk* (New York: Fawcett Publications, Inc., 1961). (Published originally in 1903.)

16. Thomas P. Carter and Roberto D. Segura, *Mexican Americans in School: A Decade of Change* (New York: College Entrance Examination Board, 1979).

17. Betty Gould, "Methods of Teaching Mexicans" (Master's thesis, University of Southern California, 1932).

18. Carter and Segura, *Mexican Americans in School,* p. 17.

19. George I. Sánchez, *Forgotten People* (Albuquerque: The University of New Mexico Press, 1940); George I. Sánchez, ed., *First Regional Conference on the Education of Spanish-Speaking People in the Southwest. Inter-American Education Occasional Papers,* no. 1 (Austin: The University of Texas Press, March, 1946).

20. James A. Banks and Cherry A. Banks, *March toward Freedom: A History of Black Americans,* rev. 2nd ed. (Belmont, Cal.: Fearon-Pitman Publishers, Inc., 1978), p. 103.

21. Hilda Taba, Elizabeth Hall Brady, and John T. Robinson, *Intergroup Education in Public Schools* (Washington, D.C.: American Council on Education, 1952).

22. Ibid.

23. Lloyd Allen Cook, ed., *College Programs in Intergroup Relations* (Washington, D.C.: American Council on Education, 1950).

24. Lloyd Allen Cook, "Intergroup Education," *Review of Educational Research* 17 (1947), pp. 266–278.

25. John Henrik Clarke, ed., with the assistance of Amy Jacques Garvey, *Marcus Garvey and the Vision of Africa* (New York: Vintage Books, 1974).

26. "Robert Ezra Park 1864–1944," in Lewis A. Coser, *Masters of Sociological Thought*, 2nd ed. (New York: Harcourt Brace, 1977), pp. 357–384.

27. Stanford M. Lyman, *The Black American in Sociological Thought: A Failure of Perspective* (New York: Capricorn Books, 1972), p. 27.

28. Stokely Carmichael and Charles V. Hamilton, *Black Power: The Politics of Liberation in America* (New York: Vintage, 1967).

29. John H. Burma, ed., *Mexican-Americans in the United States: A Reader* (Cambridge, Mass.: Schenkman Publishing Company, 1970); Emma Gee et al., ed., *Counterpoint: Perspective on Asian America* (Los Angeles: Asian American Studies Center, University of California, 1976).

30. U.S. Bureau of the Census, *Statistical Abstracts of the United States*, 1985, 105th ed. (Washington, D.C.: U.S. Government Printing Office, 1985), p. 86.

31. Robert W. Gardner, Bryant Robey, and Peter C. Smith, *Asian Americans: Growth, Change, and Diversity* (Washington, D.C.: Population Reference Bureau, 1985).

32. Jamschid A. Momeni, *Demography of Racial and Ethnic Minorities in the United States: An Annotated Bibliography with a Review Essay* (Westport, Conn.: Greenwood Press, 1984), p. 20.

33. American Council on Education, "Minority Changes Hold Major Implications for U.S.," *Higher Education and National Affairs* (March 9, 1984), p. 8.

34. Momeni, *Demography of Racial and Ethnic Minorities*, p. 13.

35. Peter Steinfels, *The Neoconservatives: The Men Who Are Changing America's Politics* (New York: Simon and Schuster, 1979).

36. James A. Banks and James Lynch, eds., *Multicultural Education in Western Societies* (New York: Praeger, 1986); Lotty V. D. Berg-Eldering, Ferry J. M. De Rijcke, and Louis V. Zuck, eds., *Multicultural Education: A Challenge to Teachers* (Dordrecht, Holland: Foris Publications, 1983); Aaron Wolfgang, ed., *Education of Immigrant Students: Issues and Answers* (Toronto: The Ontario Institute for Studies in Education, 1975); Peter Batelaan, *The Practice of Intercultural Education* (London: Commission for Racial Equality, 1983).

37. Des Storer, editor-in-chief, *Ethnic Family Values in Australia* (Sydney: Prentice-Hall of Australia, 1985), p. 3.

38. Kogila A. Moodley, "Canadian Multicultural Education: Promises and Practice," in Banks and Lynch, *Multicultural Education in Western Societies*, pp. 51–75.

39. James A. Banks, "Multiethnic Education across Cultures: United States, Mexico, Puerto Rico, France, and Great Britain." *Social Education* 42 (March 1978), pp. 177–185.

40. Banks and Lynch, *Multicultural Education in Western Societies*; V. D. Berg-Eldering, De Rijcke, and Zuck, *Multicultural Education*; Andrew Sturman, *Immigrant Australians and Education* (Hawthorn, Victoria: Australian Council for Educational Research, 1985); Brian Bullivant, *The Pluralist Dilemma in Education: Six Case Studies* (Sydney: George Allen & Unwin, 1981).

2

Ethnic Revitalization
Movements and Education

Educators in the various Western nations have created a range of programs and activities to respond to the ethnic revitalization movements that have arisen since the 1960s. These programs and activities differ widely in nature and scope and are known by a variety of names, including *multiethnic education*, *multiracial education*, and *multicultural education*. However, they are all designed to help students from diverse ethnic, racial, cultural, and social class groups experience educational equality and increase their academic achievement. In each of the Western nations in which ethnic revival movements have arisen, such as the United States, Canada, Australia, and the United Kingdom, students from certain identifiable ethnic, racial, and cultural groups are not achieving on parity with students from dominant and mainstream groups. In addition to being ethnically and culturally distinct, most of these students are poor. In this chapter, I limit my observations primarily to the United States and the United Kingdom, two nations that have important educational reform movements and a rich literature on multicultural education.

Ethnic Revitalization: A Phase Typology

In both the United States and the United Kingdom, multicultural education has created tremendous debate over goals. However, the two nations appear to be in different phases of ethnic revitalization and consequently in different stages of debate. This chapter describes a typology that attempts to outline the major phases of the development of ethnic revitalization movements in Western societies. The typology is a preliminary ideal-type construct in the Weberian sense and constitutes a set of hypotheses based on the existing and emerging theory and research and on my study of ethnic behavior in several Western nations. Because it is drawn primarily from ethnic events in the United States, it might be less generalizable in other nations. Observers in other nations must determine the extent to which the typology is valid in their societies. However, I do try to interpret current events in the United Kingdom using the typology. It is presented to stimulate discussion and analysis and to help educators better interpret ethnic events in Western nations.

I am conceptualizing ethnic revitalization as consisting of four major phases: a precondition phase; a first or early phase; a later phase; and a final phase (see Table 2.1). The typology is an ideal-type construct and should be considered as

Table 2.1.   Phases in the Development of Ethnic Revitalization Movements

The Precondition Phase	*The First Phase*
This phase is characterized by the existence of a history of colonialism, imperialism, racism, an institutionalized democratic ideology, and efforts by the nation-state to close the gap between democratic ideals and societal realities. These events create rising expectations among victimized ethnic groups that pave the way for ethnic protest and a revitalization movement.	This phase is characterized by ethnic polarization, an intense identity quest by victimized ethnic groups, and single-causal explanations. An effort is made by ethnic groups to get racism legitimized as a primary explanation of their problems. Both radical reformers and staunch conservatives set forth single-causal explanations to explain the problems of victimized ethnic groups.
The Later Phase	*The Final Phase*
This phase is characterized by meaningful dialogue between victimized and dominant ethnic groups, multiethnic coalitions, reduced ethnic polarization, and the search for multiple-causal explanations for the problems of victimized ethnic groups.	Some of the elements of the reforms formulated in the earlier phases become institutionalized during this phase. Other victimized cultural groups echo their grievances, thereby expanding and dispersing the focus of the ethnic reform movement. Conservative ideologies and policies become institutionalized during this phase, thus paving the way for the development of a new ethnic revitalization movement.

dynamic and multifaceted rather than as static and one-dimensional. The divisions between the phases are blurred rather than sharp. One phase does not end abruptly and another begins; rather, the phases blend and overlap. As with any ideal-type typology, the phases approximate reality rather than directly describe it. No actual ethnic movement exemplifies each characteristic of the four phases.

Ethnic Revitalization: The Precondition Phase

Ethnic revitalization movements usually arise within societies that have a history of imperialism, colonialism, and institutionalized racism. Groups with particular ethnic, racial and cultural characteristics are denied equality and structural inclusion into the nation-state. These societies also have a national democratic ideology stating that equality and justice should exist for all individuals and groups within the nation-state. The first phase of revitalization begins when the nation-state takes steps to close the gap between its democratic ideals and the inequality institutionalized within it.

The attempt to improve the conditions of victimized groups — usually stimulated by action taken by these groups — creates rising expectations and hope and causes these groups to perceive their condition as intolerable. The ethnic revitalization movement is born out of the hope and rising expectations created by the nation-state when it attempts to eliminate some of its most blatant forms of institutionalized racism and discrimination. The desegregation of the armed forces and state universities after World War II and the *Brown* vs. *Board of Education* Supreme Court decision (1954), which made de jure school segregation illegal, were key events in the United States that stimulated the birth of the civil rights movement.

Ethnic Revitalization: The First Phase

In the first phase of ethnic revitalization, positions are sharply drawn and ardent, single-causal explanations tend to predominate, controversy is acrimonious, and the debate tends to take the form of "us and them" — you are either for us or with them. Racism is usually the major issue in the debate during the early stages of ethnic revitalization because it has usually not been previously acknowledged as an important component of the society. It is during the early stages of ethnic revitalization that groups that perceive themselves as oppressed or as victims of racism force the dominant society to acknowledge that racism is institutionalized within it.

The debate between radical reforms and conservative defenders of the status quo remains stalemated and single-focused until the existence of racism is acknowledged by the dominant group and meaningful steps are taken to eliminate it. Until this acknowledgement occurs in official statements, policies, and actions, radical reformers continue to perceive racism as the single cause of the social, economic, and educational problems of excluded ethnic groups. Radical reformers will not search for or find more complex variables that explain the problems of victimized ethnic groups until mainstream leaders acknowledge the existence of institutionalized racism. In other words, instituionalized racism must become legitimized as an explanation, and serious steps must be taken to eliminate it, before an ethnic revitalization movement can reach a phase in which other explanations will be accepted by radical reformers who articulate the interests of groups that are victims of institutionalized racism.

During the early phase of ethnic revitalization, ethnic groups, in their efforts to shape new identities and to legitimize their histories and cultures, often glorify those histories and cultures and emphasize the ways their people have been oppressed by the dominant group and mainstream society. This early combination of protest and ethnic polarization must be understood within a broad social and political context. Groups that perceive themselves as oppressed and that internalize the dominant society's negative stereotypes and myths about themselves are likely to express strong in-group feelings during the early stages of ethnic revitalization. They also attempt to shape a new identity. During this phase the group is also likely to reject outside ethnic and racial groups, to romanticize its past, and to view contemporary social and political conditions quite subjectively.

An ethnic group in the early stage of revitalization is also likely to demand that the school curriculum portray a romanticized version of its history (to compensate for past omissions and errors) and to emphasize how the group has been victimized by other ethnic and racial groups. Extremely negative sanctions are directed against members of the ethnic group who do not endorse a strong "ethnic" position. Consequently, little fruitful dialogue is likely to take place either within or between different ethnic groups. Members of both the "oppressed" and the "oppressive" groups remain ardent in their positions during the first phase of revitalization.

Educational institutions tend to respond to the first phases of ethnic revitalization with quickly conceptualized and hurriedly formulated programs designed primarily to silence ethnic protest rather than to contribute to equality and the structural inclusion of ethnic groups into society. In both the United States and the United Kingdom, many early programs related to ethnic groups were poorly conceptualized and implemented without careful and thoughtful planning. Such programs are usually attacked and eliminated during the later phases of ethnic revitalization, when the institutionalization of ethnic programs and reforms begins. Their weakness becomes the primary justification for the elimination. When such programs were attacked and eliminated in the United States, many careful and sensitive observers noted that they had been designed to fail.

The Rise of Anti-Egalitarian Ideology and Research

The ideology and research radical reformers develop during the early stage of ethnic revitalization do not go unchallenged. An ideological war takes place between radical reformers and conservatives who defend the status quo. While radical and liberal reformers develop ideology and research to show how the ethnic groups' major problems are caused by institutionalized racism and the wider society, anti-egalitarian advocates and researchers develop an ideology and research stating that the failure of ethnic groups in school and society is due to their own inherited and socialized characteristics.

Both radical and conservative scholars tend to develop single-causal theories and explanations during the early phase of ethnic revitalization. The theories and explanations developed by radical theorists tend to focus on racism and other problems in society, whereas those developed by conservative researchers usually focus on the characteristics of ethnic students themselves, such as their genetic characteristics and their family socialization.

In the United States the most popular anti-egalitarian theories focused on the genetic characteristics of Black and lower-class students; these theories were developed by such researchers as Jensen, Shockley, and Herrnstein.[1] Jensen argued that the genetic characteristics of Blacks was the most important reason that compensatory educational programs, designed to increase the IQ of Black students, had not been more successful. Shockley developed a theory about the genetic inferiority of Blacks that was less accepted by the educational community than was Jensen's. Herrnstein's controversial article, which argued that social class reflects genetic differences, appeared in the *Atlantic Monthly*, a widely circulated and highly respected popular magazine. Herrnstein's views evoked more controversy than did Jensen's, perhaps because he argued that social class rather than race was related to heredity.

Radical reformers use the research and theory developed by anti-egalitarian researchers as evidence to support their arguments that racism is pervasive and institutionalized within the society and that it has permeated much of the research done at some of the nation's most prestigious universities. The anti-egalitarian research developed in the United States was done by faculty members at several of the nation's most respected and prestigious universities. Jensen, Shockley, and Herrnstein taught at the University of California at Berkeley, Stanford University, and Harvard University, respectively.

Ethnic Revitalization in the United Kingdom

In recent years, events in the United Kingdom have exemplified many characteristics of the early stage of ethnic revitalization. Views and opinions about ethnic and racial issues are highly polarized. Single-causal explanations frequently dominate discussions. The radical reformers and their conservative critics often stridently state their divergent views and positions. The British radical reformers see drastic reconstruction of existing institutions as the only viable way to give victimized ethnic groups equality and justice. The radical reformers often dismiss reformist approaches, such as multicultural education, as a palliative to keep excluded and oppressed groups such as Blacks from rebelling against a system that promotes structural inequality and institutionalized racism.

The current ethnic revitalization phase in the United Kingdom highly resembles the phase that existed in the United States during the late sixties and seventies, when the ethnic protest movement first emerged. It is understandable why the first phase of ethnic revitalization is currently manifested in the United Kingdom. Even though Blacks have been a part of Great Britain for a large part of its long history, they did not immigrate to Britain from Commonwealth nations in significant numbers until after World War II. Only after the West Indians and Asians immigrated to Britain in significant numbers did institutionalized racism began to be nationally recognized as an important part of British society and culture.

The early phase of ethnic revitalization is usually characterized by strong rhetoric as well as by violence in the form of riots and rebellions. A series of race riots and rebellions occurred in the United Kingdom from early 1980 to July, 1981.[2]

Ethnic Revitalization: The Later Phase

During the later phase of ethnic revitalization, ethnic groups search for multiple rather than single causes for their problems; racism as an explanation becomes legitimized but recognized as only one important cause of the problems of ethnic groups; ethnic rhetoric and polarization lessen; and ethnic groups form coalitions and jointly articulate their grievances.

During the first phase of ethnic revitalization, many researchers and intellectuals who feel committed to ethnic equality but who do not agree with radical reformers on many issues do not freely express their views in public forums because they fear being called racists. These individuals begin to express their views and opinions freely during the later phase of ethnic revitalization. This now becomes possible because emotions cool, thus enabling individuals who disagree to engage in fruitful dialogue without accusations and epithets.

In the United States a group of conservative intellectuals has emerged who argue that they are committed to ethnic equality and that their views represent another valid way for ethnic groups to attain structural inclusion. In general, these intellectuals favor few government intervention programs and encourage ethnic groups to establish businesses and compete in the market economy of the United States. This group of intellectuals, the neoconservatives, has been highly visible and influential in the national press and has evoked tremendous controversy, especially among ethnic scholars and leaders.[3] Only a few of these scholars, however, are ethnic minorities.

Nation-states facilitate the movement from early to later phases of ethnic revitalization by making symbolic concessions to ethnic groups, such as Black Studies programs, the hiring of ethnics in highly visible positions, the establishment of affirmative action policies, and the creation of a middle-class ethnic elite that serves as visible proof that "ethnics can make it." The ethnic elite plays a very important role in moving the nation-state from the early to the later phase of ethnic revitalization. They develop counterarguments to radical reformers, teach balanced and scholarly ethnic studies courses, and search for complex explanations for the causes of the social, economic, and political problems of ethnic groups.

Ethnic Revitalization: The Final Phase

During the final phase of ethnic revitalization, many of the reforms born during the early and later phases become institutionalized within the schools and other institutions. Other groups that perceive themselves as oppressed also begin to echo the grievances of ethnic groups and thus broaden the scope of the reform movement. Women, handicapped persons, and other groups articulate their problems and make their special case for entitlements. Conflict tends to develop between these groups and ethnic groups because they compete for the same scarce resources.

Institutions such as the state and federal government and universities and schools begin to view these groups as a collectivity and to respond to their needs with single programs, projects, and legislation. When women and handicapped groups began to argue their case for inclusion into the school curriculum in the United States, schools created multicultural education, which combined content and information about these diverse groups into a single program. The United States federal government established affirmative action programs designed to help both ethnic minorities and women gain more access to jobs and education.

The final phase of ethnic revitalization is a process that does not end until diverse ethnic and racial groups experience structural inclusion and equality within the nation-state. Consequently, the final phase of ethnic revitalization has not ended in the United States because ethnic groups are still only partially included within the structure of society. Even when ethnic groups attain inclusion into institutions they do not necessarily experience equality. Many middle-class Blacks in the United States are discovering, for example, that when they gain access to mainstream American universities that they do not necessarily experience equality within them.

At the same time that the United States is experiencing the final phase of ethnic revitalization, social, political, and economic events are developing that are paving the way for a new ethnic revival that may have many of the same characteristics of the ethnic movement in the 1960s and 1970s. A conservative government and national atmosphere are engendering the kind of alienation, hostility, and poverty that give rise to ethnic revival movements. However, it is possible that future protest movements in the United States might be as linked to social class as they are to race and ethnicity. Many poor Whites in the United States are beginning to see how their social and economic fate is tied to that of poor Blacks and to other non-White ethnic groups. The current conservative movement in the United States is victimizing poor Whites as well as Blacks.

The current situation in the United States suggests that ethnic revitalization movements are cyclic rather than linear. Once an ethnic revival movement has occurred within a nation-state, social, political, and economic conditions tend to arise that give birth to new revivals. As ethnic revitalization movements reach their later and final phases—as in the United States today—events tend to evoke new ones. Ethnic revitalization movements will continue to reemerge in Western democratic societies until racial and ethnic groups attain structural inclusion and equality in their nation-states and societies.

Ethnic Revitalization: Educational Implications

To help nations move from early to later phases of ethnic revitalization, educational institutions at all levels should help ethnic and majority group students accurately interpret the current phase of the ethnic revival movement and respond to it in ways that will help ethnic students satisfy their psychological and academic needs.

During the early phase of ethnic revitalization, such as currently exists in the United Kingdom, the school should help legitimize racism as a valid explanation of societal realities in the nation-state. Educators who refuse to validate racism as an explanation or to take serious steps to eliminate it will extend the early phase of ethnic revitalization and alienate many ethnic students and radical reformers. Educators who insist, during the early stage of an ethnic revival movement, that the problems of ethnic groups are caused by more complicated variables than racism may be accurate in their views but are not dealing with the subjective reality of victimized ethnic groups. Racism is the most important or only significant variable for these groups because their daily experiences validate this reality. When educational and other institutions have validated racism as an important explanation of the problems of ethnic groups and have taken meaningful steps to eliminate it, then other causes of their problems can be legitimately explored and validated.

Multiple-causal theories that explain the problems of ethnic groups are developing and becoming legitimate in the United States. Even though racism is still regarded as an important and cogent variable in American society, a few Afro-American scholars, such as Wilson, Patterson, and Sowell,[4] are trying to determine how such variables as class, culture, and values influence the achievement and experiences of ethnic groups. However, these scholars' writings have created considerable controversy and debate within both the minority and majority communities. In general, their writings are less controversial among dominant groups than among ethnic minorities.

Cultural, National, and Global Identifications

Educational institutions can facilitate the movement of a society from early to later phases of ethnic revitalization by helping students develop clarified and reflective identifications with their cultural group, the nation-state, and the global community. Individuals who have clarified and reflective cultural, national, and global identifications understand how these identifications developed; are thoughtfully and objectively able to examine their cultural group, nation, and world; and understand both the personal and public implications of these identifications. The school should also help students develop the attitudes, knowledge, and skills needed to function in their cultural community, in the nation-state, and in the global community.

Traditionally, schools in modernized Western nations have tried to make students effective citizens of the nation-state by alienating them from their first cultures and communities. The school often taught students contempt for their family cultures.[5] It is difficult for students to develop positive attitudes toward other groups and a strong identification with the nation-state unless they have a clarified identification with their first cultures. Understanding and relating positively to self is a requisite to understanding and relating positively to other groups and people.

As important as it is for the school to reflect cultural democracy and to respect and understand students' cultures, it is also vitally important for all citizens within a nation-state—from each cultural group—to develop a reflective and clarified national identification and a strong commitment to the national political ideals. In the United States, these ideals include equality, justice, and human dignity. For national cohesion and unity, it is important for all racial and ethnic groups to share a set of overarching values and goals. However, it is essential that all ethnic and racial groups participate in the formulation of these overarching national goals and values. Otherwise, some groups will be alienated and will not have an allegiance to them.

It is essential that we help students develop clarified, reflective, and positive cultural and national identifications. However, because we live in a global world society in which the solutions to humankind's problems require the cooperation of all nations of the world, it is also important for students to develop global identifications and the knowledge, attitudes, and skills needed to become effective and influential citizens in the world community.

I believe that cultural, national, and global identifications are developmental in nature and that individuals can attain a healthy and reflective national identification only when they have acquired a positive and reflective cultural identification; and that individuals can develop a reflective and positive global identification only after they have a realistic, reflective, and positive national identification.

Individuals can develop a clarified commitment and identification with a nation-state and the national culture only when they believe they are a meaningful part of the nation-state and it acknowledges, reflects, and values their cultures and them as individuals. A nation-state that structurally excludes an ethnic group from full participation in the national society and culture risks creating alienation within that group and giving rise to new ethnic revival movements. Structurally including ethnic groups into the nation-state is the best way to reduce ethnic conflict and polarization and to help students attain the skills, knowledge, and attitudes they need to become effective citizens of their communities, nation-state, and the world.

Summary

Since the 1960s, a series of ethnic revitalization movements have arisen in the various Western nation-states that are characterized by ethnic and racial diversity, such as in the United States, Canada, the United Kingdom and Australia. This chapter presents a typology describing the major phases of ethnic revitalization movements, particularly as they have developed in the United States and the United Kingdom. The major phases of ethnic revitalization movements can be identified, even though they acquire unique and different characteristics in the various nation-states. Different nation-states are also in different phases of ethnic revitalization.

Nation-states can facilitate the movement from early to later phases of ethnic revitalization by implementing educational policies and programs that promote the integration of structurally excluded ethnic groups into the mainstream society. A curriculum that reflects the cultures, ethos, and experiences of the diverse groups within a nation will reduce ethnic polarization and weaken ethnic revival movements.

Notes

1. Arthur R. Jensen, "How Much Can We Boost IQ and Scholastic Achievement?" *Harvard Educational Review* 39 (Winter 1969), pp. 1–123; William Shockley, "Dysgenics, Geneticity, Raceology: A Challenge to the Intellectual Responsibility of Educators," *Phi Delta Kappan* 53 (January 1972), pp. 297–307; Richard J. Herrnstein, "I.Q." *Atlantic Monthly* 228 (September 1971), pp. 43–64.

2. John Solomos et al., "The Organic Crisis of British Capitalism and Race: The Experience of the Seventies," in *The Empire Strikes Back: Race and Racism in 70s Britain* (Birmingham: Centre for Contemporary Cultural Studies, 1982).

3. Peter Steinfels, *The Neoconservatives: The Men Who Are Changing America's Politics* (New York: Simon & Schuster, 1979).

4. William J. Wilson, *The Declining Significance of Race* (Chicago: University of Chicago Press, 1978); Orlando Patterson, *Ethnic Chauvinism: The Reactionary Impulse* (New York: Stein and Day, 1977); Thomas Sowell, *Civil Rights: Rhetoric or Reality?* (New York: William Morrow, 1984).

5. William Greenbaum, "America in Search of a New Ideal: An Essay on the Rise of Pluralism," *Harvard Educational Review* 44 (August 1974), pp. 411–440.

3

Multiethnic Education: Nature, Goals, and Practices

The Emergence of Multiethnic/ Multicultural Education

In the United States, as well as in other Western nations such as the United Kingdom, Canada, Australia, France, and the Netherlands, the emergence of multiethnic and multicultural education has been a gradual and evolutionary process. This chapter describes multiethnic/multicultural education as it developed in the United States. It has also developed in a related but not identical way in the other Western nation-states. Educational developments in nations such as the United Kingdom, Canada, and Australia are often similar to developments in the United States. However, these developments often occur at different times and reflect the cultural, political, and historical context of the nation in which they occur. In both the United States and Australia in the late 1980s, for example, pluralism was strongly challenged by a call for national cohesion and identity. However, in the United States the call for nationalism occurred when a new wave of immigrants was settling in the nation. Australia, like the United Kingdom, had severely restricted new immigration.

Phase I: Monoethnic Courses

When the Black civil rights movement began in the mid-1960s in the United States, Blacks demanded that the schools and other institutions respond more adequately to their needs and aspirations. They called for more Black teachers for Black youths, community control of Black schools, and the rewriting of textbooks to make them more accurately reflect Black history and culture. They also demanded Black studies courses. During the 1970s ethnic minorities, such as Blacks and Asians in the United Kingdom and Canadian Indians, also demanded that educational institutions within their societies respond more directly and positively to their needs and goals.

In time, other ethnic groups in the United States, such as Mexican Americans and American Indians, made demands on schools and colleges similar to those made by Blacks. These institutions responded by establishing courses on specific ethnic groups, such as Black history, Black literature, Chicano history, and Chicano literature. This phase in the development of multiethnic/multicultural education may be considered Phase I. It was characterized by monoethnic courses, the assumption that only a member of an ethnic group should teach a course on that group, and a focus on White racism and how Whites have oppressed non-White minorities. A pervasive assumption made during Phase I ethnic studies courses was that Black studies were needed only by Black students and that Asian-American studies were needed only by Asian-American students.

Phase II: Multiethnic Studies Courses

As more and more ethnic groups in the United States, including White ethnic groups such as Jewish Americans and Polish Americans, began to demand separate courses and the inclusion of their histories and cultures in the curriculum, schools and colleges began to offer multiethnic studies courses, which focus on several ethnic cultures and view the experiences of ethnic groups from comparative perspectives. Courses such as "Ethnic Minority Music" and "The History and Culture of Minorities in the United States" are taught from comparative perspectives.

We may call the multiethnic studies phase of the development of multiethnic/multicultural education Phase II. Ethnic studies course became more global, conceptual, and scholarly during this period. They also became less politically oriented and began to explore diverse points of view and interpretations of the experiences of ethnic groups in the United States. The recognition emerged and grew that ethnic studies should be designed for all students, and not just for students who were members of particular ethnic groups. Basic assumptions of multiethnic studies courses are that ethnic groups have had both similar and different experiences in the United States and that a comparative study of ethnic cultures can result in useful concepts, generalizations, and theories.

Phase III: Multiethnic Education

As ethnic studies became more global and widespread, more and more educators began to recognize that even though reforming the course of study in schools and colleges was necessary it was not sufficient to result in effective educational reform. The negative attitudes of many teachers made their use of new ethnic materials and teaching strategies ineffective and in some cases harmful. Educators also began to recognize that ethnic studies courses alone could not enable students such as Afro-Americans, Chicanos, and American Indians to achieve at levels comparable with the achievement levels of most Anglo-American students.

Research emerged that indicated how minority students are often placed in low academic tracts because of middle-class and Anglo-biased IQ tests,[1] and how students who speak a first language other than standard Anglo-American English often fail to achieve in school, in part, because of their language differences.[2] Studies that documented the affects of teacher attitudes on student achievement, attitudes, and behavior were published.[3] Research also revealed the negative attitudes and interactions that teachers often have with minority and low-income students.[4]

These recognitions and studies convinced many educators involved in minority education that ethnic studies courses and materials, no matter how soundly conceptualized and taught, could not by themselves bring about the kind of substantial educational reform needed to enable students from diverse racial and ethnic groups to experience educational equality. In other words, educators began to realize that ethnic studies were necessary but not sufficient to bring about effective educational reform and equity. Educators began to call for a more broadly conceptualized kind of educational reform, with a focus on the total school environment. Multiethnic education specialists view the total school as the unit of change, and not any one variable within the educational environment, such as materials or teaching strategies. This more broadly conceptualized reform movement became known as multiethnic education, which emerged as Phase III in the development of pluralistic education.

Phase IV: Multicultural Education

Some educators became interested in an educational reform movement that would deal not only with the educational problems of ethnic minority groups but also with the educational problems of cultural groups such as women, handicapped persons, religious groups, and regional groups such as Appalachian Whites.[5] This broader reform movement is known as multicultural education, which is Stage IV of the development of pluralistic education.

Multicultural education became the preferred concept in many educational institutions, in part because the concept enabled school districts and universities to pool limited resources and thus to focus on a wide range of groups rather than limit their focus to racial and ethnic minorities. The *Standards* published by the National Council for Accreditation of Teacher Education require teacher education institutions to implement components, courses, and programs in multicultural education.[6]

Many educators support the multicultural education concept but are concerned that the focus of the movement may become so broad and global that the issues of *racism* and *racial discrimination*, important concerns of pluralistic education in the 1960s when it emerged, might become lost or deemphasized. Another problem with multicultural education is that the boundaries of the field are so broad that it is often difficult to determine which cultural groups are the primary focus or concern.

A Caveat

Because of the historical and evolutionary way in which Phases I through IV of multiethnic-multicultural education is discussed above, the reader may understandably conclude that when Phase II emerged Phase I disappeared. This is not what in fact has happened or is happening. As illustrated in Figure 3.1, when Phase II emerged, Phase I continued, although perhaps in modified form and on

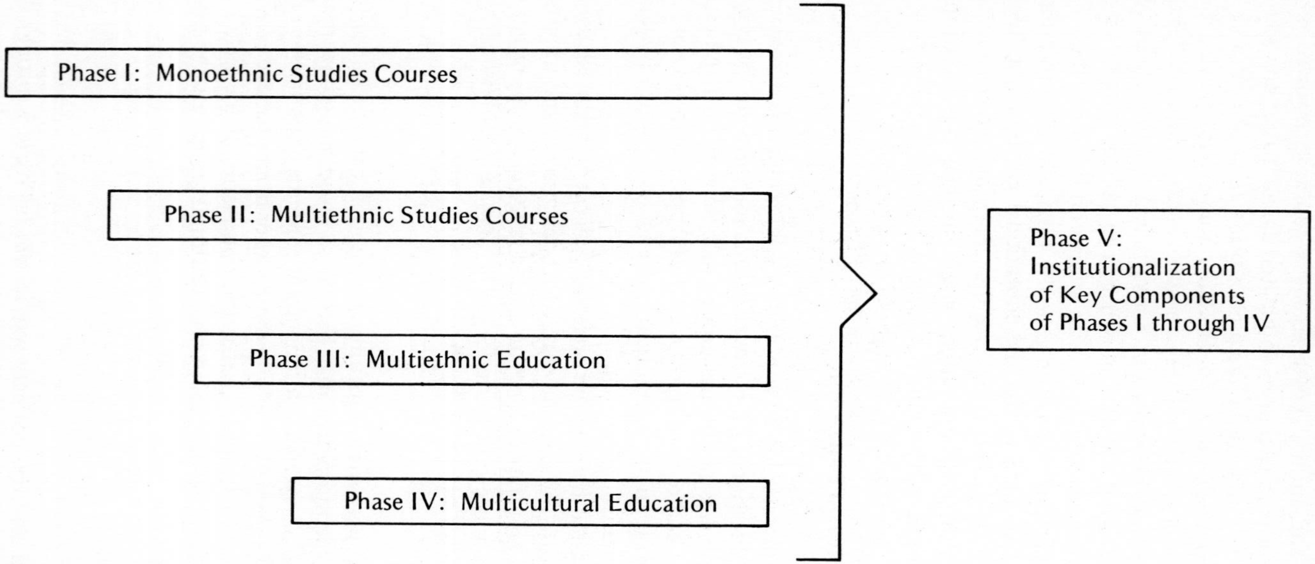

Phase V:
Institutionalization
of Key Components
of Phases I through IV

Phase I: Monoethnic Studies Courses

Phase II: Multiethnic Studies Courses

Phase III: Multiethnic Education

Phase IV: Multicultural Education

Figure 3.1. The Evolution of Multiethnic-Multicultural Education

This figure illustrates how the earlier phases of multiethnic-multicultural education continue to exist when new phases of the movement emerge. However, when the new phases emerge, the earlier phases tend to assume some of the characteristics of the newer phases and to continue on a more limited scale.

a more limited scale. The earlier phases also begin to take on some characteristics of the newly emerging phases. Phase I types of ethnic studies courses became more conceptual and scholarly when Phase II of multiethnic-multicultural education began to emerge. The assumption also grew that an academically qualified individual, regardless of his or her ethnic group membership, could effectively teach an ethnic studies course on any ethnic group.

Phase V: Institutionalization

I am conceptualizing Phase V of the development of multiethnic-multicultural education as the institutionalization of the key and most effective components of Phases I through IV. Phase V is a *process* that is slowly occurring. Elements of multiethnic-multicultural education are beginning to permeate the curriculum and the total educational environment. However, this process is much too slow and limited. Strategies need to be designed that will increase the pace and scope of the institutionalization of multiethnic-multicultural education within the schools and colleges of Western societies. Figure 3.2 summarizes the historical development of multiethnic-multicultural education as discussed in this and the previous chapters.

The Goals of Multiethnic Education

Multiethnic education is a reform movement designed to make some major changes in the education of children and youths. Advocates of multiethnic education believe that many school practices related to race and ethnicity are harmful to students and reinforce many ethnic stereotypes and discriminatory practices in Western societies.

Multiethnic education assumes that ethnicity is a salient part of the United States and other Western societies. It also assumes that ethnic diversity is a positive element in a society because it enriches a nation and increases the ways in which its citizens can perceive and solve personal and public problems. Ethnic diversity also enriches a society because it provides individuals with more opportunities to experience other cultures and thus to become more fulfilled as human beings. When individuals are able to participate in a variety of ethnic cultures, they are more able to benefit from the total human experience.

Individuals who know, participate in, and see the world from only their unique cultural and ethnic perspectives are denied important parts of the human experience and are culturally and ethnically encapsulated. Edwin Kiester, Jr., in *The Shortchanged Children of Suburbia*, tells an anecdote about an economically and culturally encapsulated child:

> The story is told about a little girl in a school near Hollywood who was asked to write a composition about a poor family. The essay began: "This family was very poor. The

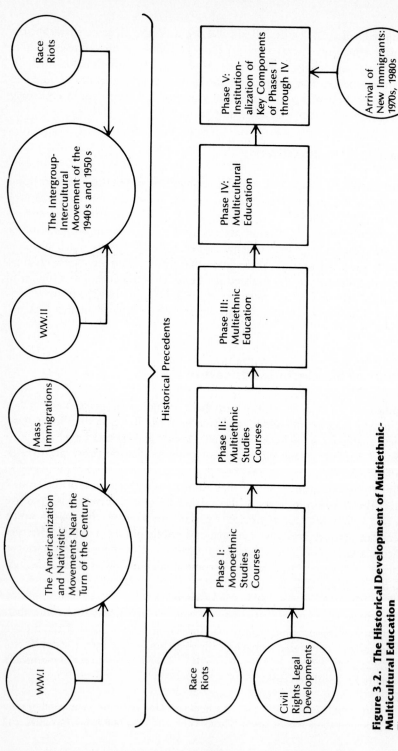

Figure 3.2. The Historical Development of Multiethnic-Multicultural Education

This figure illustrates the societal and historical forces that resulted in the development of the reforms related to multi-ethnic–multicultural education.

Mommy was poor. The Daddy was poor. The brothers and sisters were poor. The maid was poor. The nurse was poor. The butler was poor. The cook was poor. And the chauffeur was poor. . . ."[7]

Culturally and ethnically encapsulated individuals are also unable to know fully and to see their own cultures because of their cultural and ethnic blinders. We can get a full view of our own cultures and behaviors only by viewing them from the perspectives of other racial and ethnic cultures. Just as a fish is unable to appreciate the uniqueness of his aquatic environment, so are many mainstream students unable to see and fully appreciate the uniqueness of their cultural characteristics. A key goal of multiethnic education is to help individuals gain greater self-understanding by viewing themselves from the perspectives of other cultures.

Multiethnic education attempts to acquaint each ethnic group with the unique cultures of other ethnic groups. It also tries to help ethnic group members see that other ethnic cultures are just as meaningful and valid as their own. Multiethnic education assumes that with acquaintance and understanding, respect may follow.

Another major goal of multiethnic education is to provide students with cultural and ethnic alternatives. Both the Anglo-American child and the Filipino-American child should be provided with cultural and ethnic options in the school. Historically, the U.S. school curriculum has focused primarily on the culture of the Anglo-American child. The school was, and often is, primarily an extension of the Anglo-American child's home and community culture and did not present the child with cultural and ethnic alternatives.

The Anglo-Centric curriculum, which still exists to varying degrees in most U.S. schools, has harmful consequences for both Anglo-American children and ethnic minorities such as Afro-Americans and Mexican Americans. By teaching Anglo-American children only about their own culture, the school is denying them the richness of the music, literature, values, life styles, and perspectives that exist among such ethnic groups as Blacks, Puerto Ricans in the United States, and Asian Americans. Anglo-American students should know that Black literature is uniquely enriching, and that groups such as American Indians and Mexican Americans have values that they may freely embrace. Many of the behaviors and values within these ethnic groups may help Anglo-American students enrich their personal and public lives.

The Anglo-Centric curriculum negatively affects the ethnic child of color because he or she may find the school culture alien, hostile, and self-defeating. Most ethnic minority communities are characterized by some values, institutions, behavior patterns, and linguistic traits that differ in significant ways from those within the dominant society and in the schools.[8] Because of the negative ways in which ethnic students and their cultures are often viewed by educators, many of them do not attain the skills they need to function successfully within the wider society.

One major goal of multiethnic education is to provide all students with the skills, attitudes, and knowledge they need to function within their ethnic culture and the mainstream culture, as well as within and across other ethnic cultures. The Anglo-American child should be familiar with Black English; the Afro-American child should be able to speak and write standard English and to function successfully within mainstream U.S. institutions.

Another major goal of multiethnic education is to reduce the pain and discrimination members of some ethnic and racial groups experience in the schools and in the wider society because of their unique racial, physical, and cultural characteristics. Groups such as Filipino Americans, Mexican Americans, Asians in the United Kingdom, and Chinese Canadians often deny their ethnic identity, ethnic heritage, and family in order to assimilate and participate more fully in the social, economic, and political institutions of their societies. Individuals who are Polish Canadians, Jewish Americans, and Italian Australians also frequently reject parts of their ethnic cultures when trying to succeed in school and in society. As Mildred Dickeman has insightfully pointed out, schools often force members of these groups to experience "self-alienation" in order to succeed.[9] This is a high price to pay for educational, social, and economic mobility.

When individuals are forced to reject parts of their racial and ethnic cultures in order to experience success, problems are created for both individuals and society. Ethnic peoples of color, such as Afro-Americans and Chinese Canadians, experience special problems because no matter how hard they try to become like Anglos most of them cannot totally succeed because of their skin color.

Some Blacks in the United States become very Anglo-Saxon in speech, ways of viewing the world, and in their values and behavior. These individuals become so Anglicized that we might call them "Afro-Saxons." However, such individuals may still be denied jobs or the opportunities to buy homes in all-White neighborhoods because of their skin color. They may also become alienated from their own ethnic communities and families in their attempts to act and be like White Anglo-Americans. These individuals may thus become alienated from both their ethnic cultures and the mainstream Anglo culture. Social scientists call such individuals "marginal" persons.

Individuals who belong to such groups as Jewish Americans and Italian Australians may also experience marginality when they attempt to deny their ethnic heritages and to become Anglo-Americans or Anglo-Australians. Although they can usually succeed in looking and acting like Anglos, they are likely to experience a great deal of psychological stress and identity conflict when they deny and reject family and their ethnic languages, symbols, behaviors, and beliefs. Ethnicity plays a cogent role in the socialization of ethnic group members; ethnic characteristics are a part of the basic identity of many individuals. When such individuals deny their ethnic cultures, they are rejecting an important part of self.

Marginal ethnic group members are likely to be alienated citizens who feel that they do not have a stake in society. Individuals who deny and/or reject their basic group identity, for whatever reasons, are not capable of becoming fully functioning and self-actualized persons. Such individuals are more likely than other citizens to experience political and social alienation. It is in the best interest of a political democracy to protect the rights of all citizens to maintain allegiances to their ethnic groups.[10] Research has demonstrated that individuals are quite capable of maintaining allegiance to both their ethnic group and the nation-state. Social science research also indicates that individuals have a need for basic group identities, even in highly modernized societies.[11]

Another important goal of multiethnic education is to help students master essential reading, writing, and computational skills. Multiethnic education assumes that multiethnic content can help students master important skills in these areas. Multiethnic readings and data, if taught effectively, can be highly motivating and meaningful. Students are more likely to master skills when the teacher uses content that deals with significant human problems, such as ethnicity within society. Students are also more likely to master skills when they study content and problems related to the world in which they live. Students in most Western nations live in societies in which ethnic problems are real and salient. Many students live within highly ethnic communities. Content related to ethnicity in Western societies and to the ethnic communities in which many students live is significant and meaningful to students, especially to those socialized within ethnic communities. Advocates of multiethnic education believe that skill goals are extremely important.

Cross-Cultural Competency

A key goal of multiethnic-multicultural education is to help students develop cross-cultural competency.[12] However, those of us working in the areas of multiethnic/multicultural education have not clarified, in any adequate way, the minimal level of cross-cultural competency we consider appropriate and/or satisfactory for teacher-education students or for students in the common schools. Nor have we developed valid and reliable ways to assess levels of cross-cultural competency. I think we know what questions to raise about cross-cultural functioning. However, we need to devote considerable time and intellectual energy to resolving these questions.

Is the Anglo-American student, for example, who eats a weekly meal at an authentic Mexican-American restaurant, and who has no other cross-ethnic contacts during the week, functioning cross-culturally? Most of us would probably agree that the act of eating at an ethnic restaurant, in and of itself, is not an instance of meaningful cross-cultural behavior. However, if the Anglo-American student, while eating at the Mexican-American restaurant, understands and shares the ethnic symbols in the restaurant, speaks Spanish while in the restaurant, and communicates and interacts positively and comfortably with individuals within the restaurant who are culturally Mexican-American, then he or she would be functioning cross-culturally at a meaningful level.

Levels of Cross-Cultural Functioning

We need to develop a typology that conceptualizes levels of cross-cultural functioning. We also need to determine which of these levels are desirable and practical for most of our teacher education and common school students to attain. In this chapter, I present the skeletal outline of such a typology (see Figure 3.3).

Level I of cross-cultural functioning consists primarily of superficial and brief cross-cultural encounters, such as eating occasionally at a Chinese-American restaurant or speaking to the Jewish neighbor who lives across the street when you meet her in the street. Level II of cross-cultural functioning occurs when the individual begins to have more meaningful cross-cultural contacts and communications with members of other ethnic and cultural groups. He or she begins to assimilate some of the symbols, linguistic traits, communication styles, values, and attitudes that are normative within the "outside" cultural group. Level III of cross-cultural functioning occurs when the individual is thoroughly bicultural and is as comfortable within the adopted culture as he or she is within his or her primordial or first culture. Each of the two cultures is equally meaningful to the bicultural individual. The bicultural individual is bilingual and is adept at cultural-switching behavior. Level IV of cross-cultural functioning occurs when the primordial individual has been almost completely resocialized and assimilated into the "foreign" or host culture. This process occurs, for example, when the Afro-American individual becomes so highly culturally assimilated (in terms of behavior, attitudes, and perceptions) into the Anglo-American culture that he or she is for all sociological purposes an Afro-Saxon.

I think most of us working in the field of multiethnic/multicultural education do not see Level I or Level IV of cross-cultural functioning as desirable goals of multiethnic education. Most of us would probably opt for Level II or Level III or some point between these two levels. I should quickly point out that this typology of levels is an ideal-type conceptualization in the Weberian sense and that continua exist both between and within the levels.

Multiethnic Education: Nature and Promises

Multiethnic education reaches far beyond ethnic studies or the social studies. It is concerned with modifying the total educational environment so that it better reflects the ethnic diversity within a society. This includes not only studying ethnic cultures and experiences but also making institutional changes within the school so that students from diverse ethnic groups have equal educational opportunities and the school promotes and encourages the concept of ethnic diversity.

Multiethnic education is designed for all students, of all races, ethnic groups, and social classes, and not just for schools that have racially and ethnically mixed populations. A major assumption made by advocates of multiethnic education is that multiethnic education is needed as much if not more by students who

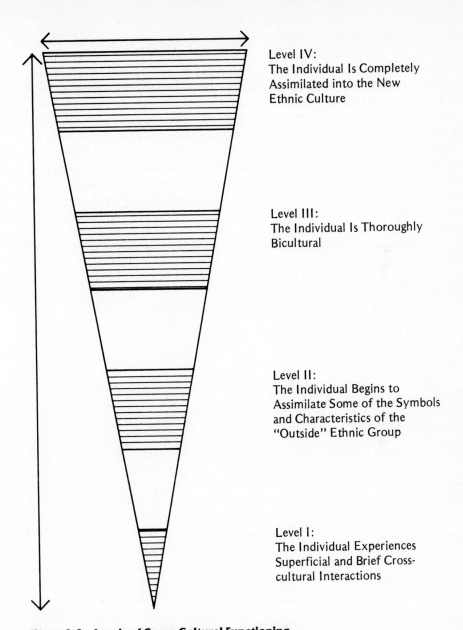

Level IV:
The Individual Is Completely
Assimilated into the New
Ethnic Culture

Level III:
The Individual Is Thoroughly
Bicultural

Level II:
The Individual Begins to
Assimilate Some of the Symbols
and Characteristics of the
"Outside" Ethnic Group

Level I:
The Individual Experiences
Superficial and Brief Cross-
cultural Interactions

Figure 3.3. Levels of Cross-Cultural Functioning
This figure presents a conceptualization of levels of cross-
cultural competency. Cross-cultural functioning can range
from Level I (brief and superficial contacts with another
ethnic culture) to Level IV (in which the individual totally
culturally assimilates into a new ethnic culture and
consequently becomes alienated from his or her own
ethnic culture).

are middle-class members of the dominant, mainstream group as it is by victimized ethnic minority students.

Since multiethnic education is a very broad concept that implies total school reform, educators who want their schools to become multiethnic must examine their total school environment to determine the extent to which it is monoethnic and promotes dominant group hegemony. They then must take appropriate steps to create and sustain a multiethnic educational environment. The ethnic and racial composition of the school staff, its attitudes, the formalized and hidden curricula, the teaching strategies and materials, the testing and counseling programs, and the school's norms are some of the factors that must reflect ethnic diversity within the multiethnic school. Figure 3.4 illustrates these and other variables of the school environment that must be reformed in order to make the school multiethnic.

The reform must be systemwide to be effective. Any one of the factors in

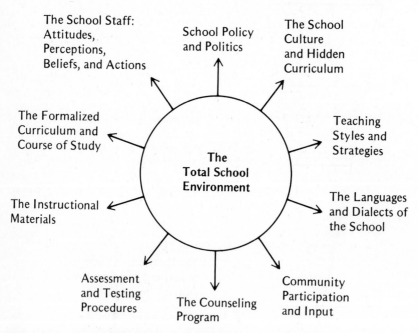

Figure 3.4. The Total School Environment
In this figure, the total school environment is conceptualized as a system that consists of a number of major identifiable variables and factors, such as the school culture, school policy and politics, and the formalized curriculum and course of study. In the idealized multiethnic school, each variable reflects ethnic pluralism. Even though any one factor may be the focus of initial school reform, changes must take place in each factor in order to create and sustain an effective multiethnic educational environment.

Figure 3.4 may be the initial focus for school reform, but changes must take place in all of the major school variables in order for multiethnic education to be successfully implemented. We learned from the ethnic studies movement of the 1960s that few substantial changes take place when you simply give teachers multiethnic materials but do not train them to use them or help them acquire new conceptual frameworks for viewing Western society and culture.

The unit of change must be the total school environment rather than any one element, such as materials, teaching strategies, the testing program, or teacher training. Teacher training is very important, but other changes must take place in the school environment in order to reform the school. Many teachers attain new insights, materials, and multiethnic teaching strategies during summer workshops. They are eager to try them in their schools. However, they become very discouraged when they return to their schools, where traditional norms toward ethnic diversity often exist and where they frequently receive no support from their administrators or peers. Without such support, teachers with new skills and insights give up and revert to their old behaviors and attitudes.

Linking Multiethnic and Global Education: Promises

The curriculum should help students develop the knowledge, attitudes, and skills needed to function within various ethnic cultures in their own society. However, because we live in a highly interdependent world society, the school should also help students develop the attitudes and competencies needed to function within cultures outside of their nation-state. Because of their interrelationships and shared goals, educators should try to relate multiethnic and global education more effectively.

A linkage would help reduce curriculum fragmentation and contribute to important student learnings in cultural studies. If students develop the ability to view events and situations from the perspectives of ethnic groups in their nation-state, they will be better able to view events within other nations from the perspectives of the major participants in these events. Students who are able to relate positively to and function within a variety of cultures within their own nation are also more likely to function successfully in foreign cultures than are individuals who view domestic ethnic cultures as exotic and strange. We can reduce nonreflective nationalism and ethnocentrism in students by helping them become more ethnically literate and competent citizens in their nation-state.

Linking Multiethnic and Global Education: Problems

We should attempt to link and relate multiethnic and global education even though each reform movement has unique characteristics that should be respected and maintained in any linkage efforts. We should not assume that multiethnic and global education are identical. This assumption would create new problems and intensify existing ones. Some teachers often confuse studies about the countries of origin of ethnic groups with the study of these groups in their nation-states. They assume, for example, that when they are teaching about Mexico they are teaching about Mexican Americans.

Other teachers ignore domestic ethnic groups and teach only about their original homelands. Some U.S. teachers are more comfortable teaching about Mexicans who live in Mexico or about Africans than they are teaching about Mexican Americans or Afro-Americans who live in their own communities. They will therefore teach about Mexico and Africa but will rarely teach content related to Mexican Americans and Afro-Americans. Teaching about distant lands is apparently less threatening to some teachers than is teaching about ethnic cultures, problems, and conflicts within their own community. Special ways to solve this problem should be discussed in any attempts to link multiethnic and global education.

Even though multiethnic and global education should be joined and related, each reform movement has unique contributions to make to the general education of students. These unique qualities should be maintained and recognized in any linkage attempts. Ethnic minority cultures within a nation should not be confused with national in other nations.

Linking Multiethnic and Global Education by Helping Students Develop Interrelated Identifications

Despite some problems that may emerge, linking multiethnic and global education can result in important learning outcomes if proper precautions are taken. Multiethnic and global education are related because of the similarity in the skills, attitudes, and behaviors that both reform movements are trying to help students develop. Both multiethnic and global education have as major goals helping students develop cross-cultural competency (the knowledge, attitudes, and skills, needed to function in diverse cultural settings) and helping students develop the ability to view events, situations, and problems from the perspectives of different ethnic and nationality groups.

Multiethnic and global education are related in still another important way: students can develop clarified and reflective global identifications only after they have developed clarified and reflective *ethnic* and *national* identifications. The rest of this chapter discusses the need for the school curriculum to help students develop three interrelated identifications: *ethnic*, *national*, and *global*.

Ethnic, National, and Global Identification

Identification is "a social-psychological process involving the assimilation and internalization of the values, standards, expectations, or social roles of another person or persons . . . into one's behavior and self-conception.[13] When an individual develops an identification with a particular group, he or she "internalizes the interests, standards, and role expectations of the group."[14] Identification is an evolving, dynamic, complex, and ongoing process and not a static or unidimensional conceptualization. All individuals belong to many different groups and consequently develop multiple group identifications. Students have a gender identification, a family identification, a racial identification, as well as identifications with many other formal and informal groups.

A *major assumption of this chapter is that all students come to school with ethnic identifications, whether the identifications are conscious or unconscious.* Many Anglo-American students are consciously aware of their national identifications as *Americans* but are not consciously aware that they have internalized the values, standards, norms, and behaviors of the Anglo-American ethnic group. Students who are Afro-Americans, Jewish Americans, Mexican Americans, and Italian Americans are usually consciously aware of both their ethnic and national identifications. However, many students from all ethnic groups come to school with confused, unexamined, and nonreflective ethnic and national identifications and with almost no global identification or consciousness.

Identity is a concept that relates to all that we are. Societal quests for single, narrow definitions of nationalism have prevented many students from getting in touch with that dimension of their identity that relates to ethnicity. Ethnic identification for many students is a very important part of their personal identity. The individual who has a confused, nonreflective, or negative ethnic identification lacks one of the essential ingredients for a healthy and positive personal identity.

The school should help students develop three kinds of highly interrelated identifications that are of special concern to multiethnic educators: an *ethnic*, a *national*, and a *global* identification. These identifications should be *clarified, reflective*, and *positive*. Individuals who have *clarified* and *reflective* ethnic, national, and global identifications understand how these identifications developed, are able to examine their ethnic group, nation, and world thoughtfully and objectively and to understand both the personal and public implications of these identifications.

Individuals who have *positive* ethnic, national, and global identifications evaluate their ethnic, national, and global communities highly and are proud of these identifications. They have both the desire and competencies needed to take actions that will support and reinforce the values and norms of their ethnic, national, and global communities. Consequently, the school should not only be concerned about helping students develop reflective ethnic, national, and global identifications, but it should also help them acquire the cross-cultural competencies (which consist of knowledge, attitudes, and skills) needed to function effectively within their ethnic, national, and world communities.

Ethnic Identification

The school within a pluralistic democratic nation should help ethnic students develop clarified, reflective, and positive ethnic identifications. This does not mean that the school should encourage or force ethnic minority students who have iden- tifications with the mainstream ethnic group or who have identifications with sev- eral ethnic groups to give up these identifications. However, it does mean that the school will help all students develop an understanding of their ethnic group iden- tifications, objectively examine their ethnic groups, better understand the rela- tionship between their ethnic groups and other ethnic groups, and learn the personal and public implications of their ethnic group identifications and at- tachments.

A positive and clarified ethnic identification is of primary importance to stu- dents beginning in their first years of life. However, rather than help students de- velop positive and reflective ethnic identifications, historically the school and other social institutions have taught ethnic minority students to be ashamed of their ethnic affiliations and characteristics. Social and public institutions have forced many individuals who are Polish Americans, Italian Australian, and Jewish Canadian to experience self-alienation and desocialization and to reject family heritages and cultures. Many members of these ethnic groups have denied impor- tant aspects of their ethnic cultures and changed their names in order to attain full participation within their society. We should not deny the fact that many ethnic individuals consciously denied their family heritages in order to attain social, eco- nomic, and educational mobility. However, within a pluralistic democratic society individuals should not have to give up all of their meaningful ethnic traits and attachments in order to attain structural inclusion into society.

National Identification

The school should also help each student acquire a clarified, reflective, and posi- tive national identification and related cross-cultural competencies. Each student should develop a commitment to national democratic ideals, such as human dig- nity, justice, and equality. The school should also help students acquire the atti- tudes, beliefs, and skills they need to become effective participants in the nation-state. Thus, the development of social participation skills and activities should be major goals of the school curriculum within a democratic pluralistic na- tion. Students should be provided opportunities for social participation activities whereby they can take action on issues and problems that are consistent with dem- ocratic values. Citizenship education and social participation activities are integral parts of a sound school curriculum.

National identification and related citizenship competencies are important for all citizens, regardless of their ethnic group membership and ethnic affilia- tions. National identification should be acknowledged and promoted in all edu- cational programs related to ethnicity and education. However, individuals can have a wide range of cultural and linguistic traits and characteristics and still be reflective and effective citizens of their nation-states.

Individuals can have ethnic allegiances and characteristics and yet endorse overarching and shared national values and ideals as long as their ethnic values and behaviors do not violate or contradict democratic values and ideals. Educational programs should recognize and reflect the multiple identifications students are developing. I believe students can develop a reflective and positive national identification only after they have attained reflective, clarified, and positive ethnic identifications. This is as true for Anglo-American students as it is for Jewish-American, Black-, or Italian-American students. Often mainstream individuals do not view themselves as an ethnic group. However, sociologically they have many of the same traits and characteristics of other ethnic groups, such as a sense of peoplehood, unique behavioral values and norms, and unique ways of perceiving the world.[15]

Mainstream students who believe that their ethnic group is superior to other ethnic groups and who have highly ethnocentric and racist attitudes do not have clarified, reflective, and positive ethnic identifications. Their ethnic identifications are based on the negative characteristics of other ethnic groups and have not been reflectively and objectively examined. Many mainstream and other ethnic individuals have ethnic identifications that are nonreflective and unclarified. It is not possible for students with unreflective and totally subjective ethnic identifications to develop positive and reflective national identifications because ethnic ethnocentrism is inconsistent with such democratic values as human dignity, freedom, equality, and justice.

Ethnic group individuals who have historically been victims of discrimination must develop positive and reflective ethnic identifications before they will be able to develop clarified national identifications. It is difficult for Polish-American, Jewish-Australian, or Métis students to support the rights of other ethnic groups or the ideals of the nation-state when they are ashamed of their own ethnicity or feel their ethnic group is denied basic civil rights and opportunities.

Global Identification

It is essential that we help students to develop clarified, reflective, and positive ethnic and national identifications. However, because we live in a global society in which the solutions to the world's problems require the cooperation of all the nations of the world, it is also important for students to develop global identifications and the knowledge, attitudes, and skills needed to become effective and influential citizens in the world community.[16] Most students have rather conscious identifications with their communities and nation-states, but they often are only vaguely aware of their status as world citizens. Most students do not have a comprehensive understanding of the full implications of their world citizenship.

There are many complex reasons why most students often have little awareness or understanding of their status as world citizens and rarely think of themselves as citizens of the world.[17] This lack of awareness results partly from the fact that most nation-states focus on helping students to develop nationalism rather than to understand their role as citizens of the world. The teaching of nationalism often results in students' learning misconceptions, stereotypes, and myths about other nations and in the acquisition of negative and confused attitudes toward them.

Students also have limited awareness of their roles as world citizens because of the nature of the world community itself. The institutions that attempt to formulate policies for the international community or for groups of nations — such as the United Nations, the Organization of African Unity, and the Organization of American States — are usually weak because of their inability to enforce their policies and recommendations, because of the strong nationalism manifested by their members, and because the international community does not have an effectively mobilized and politically efficacious constituency. Strong nationalism makes most international bodies weak and largely symbolic.

Students find it difficult to view themselves as members of an international community not only because such a community lacks effective governmental bodies, but also because very few heroes or heroines, myths, symbols, and school rituals are designed to help students develop an attachment and identification with the global community. It is difficult for students to develop identifications with a community that does not have heroes, heroines, and rituals in which they participate and benefits that can be identified, seen, and touched. We thus must identify and/or create international heroes, heroines, and school rituals to help students develop global attachments and identifications.

When educators attempt to help students develop more sophisticated international understanding and identification, they often experience complex problems. It is difficult to gain public support for programs in international education because many parents view global education as an attempt to weaken national loyalty and undercut nationalism. Many teachers are likely to view global education as an add-on to an already crowded curriculum and thus to assign it a low priority. Some teachers, like many of their students, have misconceptions about and negative attitudes toward other nations that they are likely to perpetuate in the classroom.

Goals for Global Education

When formulating goals and teaching strategies for global education, educators should be aware of the societal and instructional constraints. However, they should realize that it is vitally important for students to develop a sophisticated understanding of their roles in the world community. Students should also understand how life in their communities influences other nations and the cogent influences that international events have on their daily lives. Global education should have as major goals helping students develop an understanding of the interdependence among nations in the modern world, clarified attitudes toward other nations, and a reflective identification with the world community. This latter task is likely to be especially difficult because of the highly ambiguous nature of the international community and the tight national boundaries that exist throughout the world.

The Need for a Delicate Balance of Identifications

Professor Nagayo Homma of the University of Tokyo points out that ethnic and national identifications may prevent the development of effective global commitments and the cooperation among nations that is needed to solve the world's global problems. He writes of this paradox:

> The starting point of our quest for a global perspective should be the realization that the world today is a world of paradox. On the one hand, we live in the age of increasing interdependence among nations and growing awareness of our common destiny as occupants of the "only one earth." . . . But, at the same time, nationalism is as strong as ever, and within a nation we often witness a movement of tribalism, an assertion of ethnicity, a communitarian experiment, and, according to some critics and scholars, an ominous tendency toward narcissism. Apparently the force for integration and the force for fragmentation are working simultaneously in our world.[18]

Homma points out that nationalism and national identifications and attachments in most nations of the world are strong and tenacious. Strong nationalism that is nonreflective will prevent students from developing reflective and positive global identifications. Nonreflective and unexamined ethnic identifications and attachments may prevent the development of a cohesive nation and a unified national ideology. Thus, while we should help ethnic youths develop reflective and positive ethnic identifications, we must also help students clarify and strengthen their national identifications—which means that they will develop and internalize such democratic values as justice, human dignity, and equality.

Students need to develop a delicate balance of ethnic, national, and global identifications and attachments. In the past, however, educators have often tried to develop strong national identifications by repressing ethnicity and making ethnic students ashamed of their ethnic roots and families. Schools taught ethnic youths "shame," as William Greenbaum has compassionately written.[19] This is an unhealthy and dysfunctional approach to building national solidarity and reflective nationalism and to shaping a nation in which all of its citizens endorse its overarching values such as democracy and human dignity and yet maintain a sense of ethnic pride and identification.

I hypothesize that ethnic, national, and global identifications are developmental in nature and that an individual can attain a healthy and reflective national identification only when he or she has acquired a healthy and reflective ethnic identification; and that individuals can develop a reflective and positive global identification only after they have a realistic, reflective, and positive national identification (see Figure 3.5).

Individuals can develop a commitment to and an identification with a nation-state and the national culture only when they believe that they are a meaningful and important part of that nation and that it acknowledges, reflects, and values their culture and them as individuals. A nation that alienates and does not meaningfully and structurally include an ethnic group into the national culture runs the risk of creating alienation within that ethnic group and of fostering

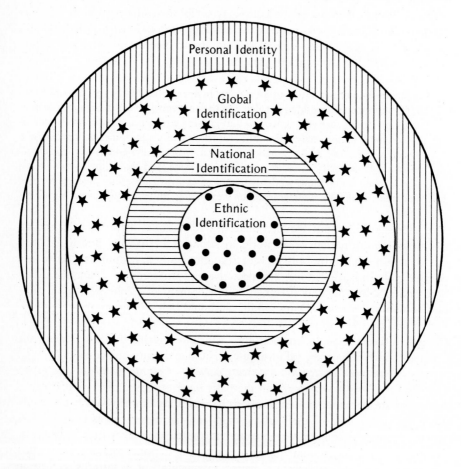

Figure 3.5. The Relationship between Personal Identity and Ethnic, National, and Global Identifications
Personal identity is the "I" that results from the lifelong binding together of the many threads of a person's life. These threads include experience, culture, and heredity, as well as identifications with significant others and many different groups, such as one's ethnic group, one's nation, and the global community.

separatism and separatist movements and ideologies.[20] Students will find it very difficult if not impossible to develop reflective global identifications with a nation-state that perpetuates a nonreflective and blind nationalism.

The Expanding Identification of Ethnic Youths: A Typology

We should first help ethnic students develop healthy and positive ethnic identifications; they can then begin to develop reflective national and global identifications. A typology of the stages of ethnicity that describes the developmental nature of ethnic, national, and global identifications and clarification is presented in Chapter 11. This typology assumes that individuals can be classified according to their ethnic identification and development. This typology, as summarized in Figure 3.6, illustrates the hypothesis that students must have clarified and positive ethnic identifications (Stage 3) before they can attain clarified and reflective national and global identifications (Stages 5 and 6). As pointed out in Chapter 11, movement among the stages may be upward or downward. Some individuals, because of their socialization, may never experience a particular stage; some individuals may never experience Stage 1 or Stage 2. However, I am hypothesizing that the Stage 2 individual must experience Stage 3 in order to reach Stage 4. See Chapter 11 for a detailed discussion of this typology.

Multiethnic Education and Educational Reform

Changing the school so that it reflects the ethnic diversity within a society provides a tremendous opportunity to implement the substantial curriculum reforms that are essential, such as conceptual teaching, interdisciplinary approaches to the study of social issues, value inquiry, and providing students with opportunities to become involved in social action and social participation activities. Thus, multiethnic education can serve as a vehicle for general and significant educational reform. This is probably its greatest promise. We can best view multiethnic education as a process as well as a reform movement that will result in a new type of schooling that will present novel views of the Western experience and will help students acquire the knowledge, skills, and commitments needed to make their societies and the world more responsive to the human condition.

Summary

Multiethnic-multicultural education has had an evolutionary development in the United States and in the other major Western nations, such as the United Kingdom, Canada, Australia, France, and Sweden.[21] The development of multiethnic-

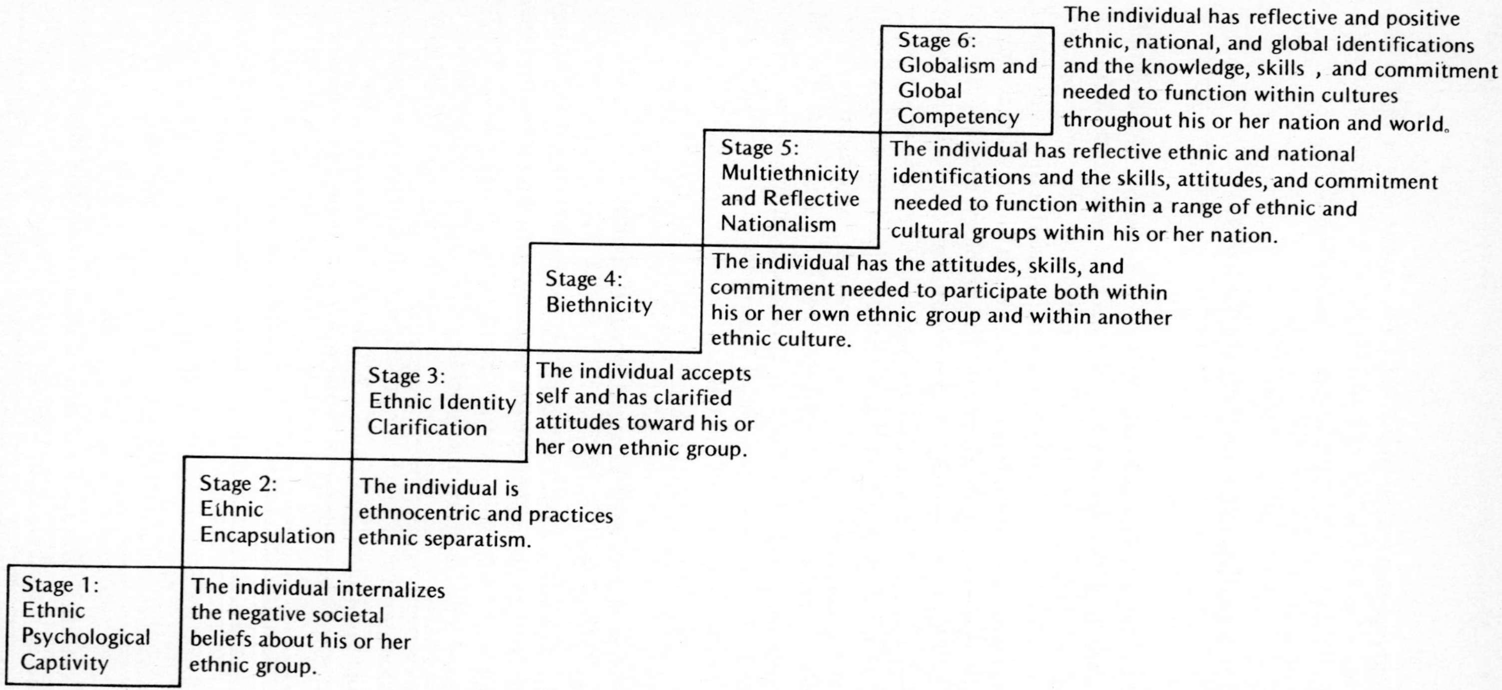

| Stage 6: Globalism and Global Competency | The individual has reflective and positive ethnic, national, and global identifications and the knowledge, skills , and commitment needed to function within cultures throughout his or her nation and world. |

| Stage 5: Multiethnicity and Reflective Nationalism | The individual has reflective ethnic and national identifications and the skills, attitudes, and commitment needed to function within a range of ethnic and cultural groups within his or her nation. |

| Stage 4: Biethnicity | The individual has the attitudes, skills, and commitment needed to participate both within his or her own ethnic group and within another ethnic culture. |

| Stage 3: Ethnic Identity Clarification | The individual accepts self and has clarified attitudes toward his or her own ethnic group. |

| Stage 2: Ethnic Encapsulation | The individual is ethnocentric and practices ethnic separatism. |

| Stage 1: Ethnic Psychological Captivity | The individual internalizes the negative societal beliefs about his or her ethnic group. |

Figure 3.6. The Expanding Identifications of Ethnic Youths: A Typology

This figure illustrates the author's hypothesis that students must have clarified and positive ethnic identifications (Stage 3) before they can attain reflective and positive national and global identifications (Stages 5 and 6).

multicultural education since the 1960s can be conceptualized in the five phases presented in this chapter. This chapter also describes major goals for multiethnic education, including: (1) helping students gain a greater self-understanding by viewing their cultures from the perspectives of other ethnic groups; (2) providing students with cultural and ethnic alternatives; (3) helping students attain cross-cultural competency; (4) helping students master essential reading, writing, and computational skills; and (5) helping students develop clarified and reflective ethnic, national, and global identifications.

Educators should attempt to link and relate multiethnic and global education because of the common goals these two educational reform movements are trying to help students attain and because of the widespread fragmentation in the school curriculum. Since both multiethnic and global education have unique contributions to make to the general education of students and because they are in many ways distinct, efforts made to link multiethnic and global education should maintain the uniqueness of each reform movement. Educators should also take special precautions to assure that domestic ethnic cultures in a nation are not confused with the cultures of nations that are the original homelands of ethnic groups.

During their socialization, students develop multiple group identifications. The school should help students develop three kinds of identifications that are of special concern to multiethnic educators: an *ethnic*, a *national*, and a *global* identification. To help students successfully develop ethnic, national, and global identifications that are clarified, reflective, and positive, the school must first recognize the importance of each of these identifications to students and to the nation-state and then acknowledge their developmental character. It is very difficult for students to develop clarified and positive national identifications and commitments until they have acquired positive and clarified ethnic identifications. Students will be able to develop clarified, reflective, and positive global identifications only after they have acquired thoughtful and clarified national identifications.

Multiethnic education includes but is much more comprehensive than ethnic studies or curriculum reform related to ethnicity. Multiethnic education is concerned with modifying the total school environment so that students from all ethnic groups will experience equal educational opportunities. Educators must reform their total educational environments in order to implement multiethnic education.

Notes

1. Jeannie Oakes, *Keeping Track: How Schools Structure Inequality* (New Haven, Conn.: Yale University Press, 1985).

2. Carlos J. Ovando and Virginia P. Collier, *Bilingual and ESL Classrooms: Teaching in Multicultural Contexts* (New York: McGraw-Hill, 1985); U.S. Commission on Civil

Rights, *A Better Chance to Learn: Bilingual-Bicultural Education* (Washington, D.C.: The Commission, 1975).

3. Ray C. Rist, "Student Social Class and Teacher Expectations: The Self-Fulfilling Prophecy in Ghetto Education," *Harvard Educational Review* 40 (August 1970), pp. 411–451; Judith Kleinfeld, "Effective Teachers of Eskimo and Indian Students," *School Review* 83 (February 1975), pp. 301–344; U.S. Commission on Civil Rights, *Teachers and Students: Differences in Teacher Interaction with Mexican American and Anglo-Students; Report V: Mexican American Study* (Washington, D.C.: The Commission, 1973).

4. Rist, "Student Social Class and Teacher Expectations"; U.S. Commission on Civil Rights, *Teachers and Students.*

5. Nancy Schniedewind and Ellen Davidson, *Open Minds to Equality: A Sourcebook of Learning Activities to Promote Race, Sex, Class, and Age Equity* (Englewood Cliffs, N.J.: Prentice-Hall, 1983); Donna M. Gollnick and Philip C. Chinn, *Multicultural Education in a Pluralistic Society*, 2nd ed. (Columbus, Ohio: Merrill, 1986); Carl A. Grant and Christine E. Sleeter, "Race, Class, and Gender in Education Research: An Argument for Integrative Analysis," *Review of Educational Research* 56 (Summer 1986), pp. 195–211.

6. *Standards for the Accreditation of Teacher Education* (Washington, D.C.: National Council for the Accreditation of Teacher Education, 1977).

7. Alice Miel with Edwin Kiester, Jr., *The Shortchanged Children of Suburbia* (New York: American Jewish Committee, 1967), p. 5.

8. Susan U. Philips, *The Invisible Culture: Communication in Classroom and Community on the Warm Spring Indian Reservation* (New York: Longman, Inc., 1983); Joseph L. White, *The Psychology of Blacks: An Afro-American Perspective* (Englewood Cliffs, N.J.: Prentice-Hall, 1984).

9. Mildred Dickeman, "Teaching Cultural Pluralism," in James A. Banks, ed., *Teaching Ethnic Studies: Concepts and Strategies* (Washington, D.C.: National Council for the Social Studies, 1973), pp. 5–25.

10. James Lynch, "Multicultural Education: Agenda for Change," in James A. Banks and James Lynch, eds., *Multicultural Education in Western Societies* (New York: Praeger, 1986), pp. 178–195.

11. Harold R. Isaacs, "Basic Group Identity: The Idols of the Tribe," in Nathan Glazer and Daniel P. Moynihan, eds., *Ethnicity: Theory and Experience* (Cambridge, Mass.: Harvard University Press, 1975), pp. 29–52.

12. For a typology of cross-cultural awareness in international settings, see Robert G. Hanvey, *An Attainable Global Perspective* (New York: Center for War/Peace Studies, undated), pp. 10–11.

13. George A. Theodorson and Achilles G. Theodorson, *A Modern Dictionary of Sociology* (New York: Barnes and Noble Books, 1969), pp. 194–195.

14. Ibid., p. 195.

15. Milton M. Gordon, *Assimilation in American Life: The Role of Race, Religion and National Origins* (New York: Oxford University Press, 1964).

16. Steven L. Lamy, ed., "Global Perspectives Education," *Educational Research Quarterly* 1 (1983), special issue; James M. Becker, ed., *Schooling for a Global Age* (New York: McGraw-Hill, 1979); John Goodlad, "The Learner at the World's Center," *Social Education* 50 (October 1986), pp. 424–436.

17. The next several paragraphs of this chapter are adapted from my National Council for the Social Studies Presidential Address, "Cultural Democracy, Citizenship Education, and the American Dream," *Social Education* 47 (March 1983), pp. 178–179, 222–232. Used with permission of the National Council for the Social Studies.

18. Nagayo Homma, "The Quest for a Global Perspective: A Japanese View," paper

presented as a keynote address at the 59th Annual Meeting of the National Council for the Social Studies, November 23, 1979, Portland, Oregon, p. 1.

19. William Greenbaum, "America in Search of a New Ideal: An Essay on the Rise of Pluralism," *Harvard Educational Review* 44 (August 1974), p. 431.

20. An example of this phenomenon is the situation of the French Canadians. See Frank G. Vallee, Mildred Schwartz, and Frank Darkness, "Ethnic Assimilation and Differentiation in Canada," in Bernard R. Blishen, Frank E. Jones, Kaspar D. Naegele, and John Porter, eds., *Canadian Society: Sociological Perspectives*, 3rd ed. abridged (Toronto: Macmillan of Canada, 1971), pp. 390–400.

21. James A. Banks and James Lynch, eds. *Multicultural Education in Western Societies*; Louis Porcher, *The Education of the Children of Migrant Workers in Europe: Interculturalism and Teacher Training* (Strasbourg: Council of Europe, 1981); Department of Education and Research Planning, *Intercultural Training of Teachers*, Report from a Conference in Kolmärden, Sweden, June 10–14, 1985 (Stockholm: National Board of Universities and Colleges, 1986); Ronald J. Samuda, John W. Berry, and Michel Laferrière, eds., *Multiculturalism in Canada: Social and Educational Perspectives* (Toronto: Allyn and Bacon, Inc., 1984).

PART II

Conceptual Issues

This second part of the text discusses and analyzes some of the major concepts and conceptual issues and problems related to education and ethnic diversity. It is necessary to formulate precise and valid concepts before sound educational programs related to ethnic and cultural diversity can be implemented.

Chapter 4 describes the major characteristics of ethnic groups in modernized Western societies and presents a typology for defining and classifying ethnic groups. The United States is used as a case study to describe the salient characteristics of ethnic groups in modernized Western societies. The major concepts related to ethnic and cultural diversity, such as culture, ethnic group, and multicultural education, are described in Chapter 5. The components of culture identified in this chapter are essential for understanding the complex aspects of race, ethnicity, and culture in modernized societies. Chapter 6 presents major paradigms related to race and ethnic diversity that have developed in various Western nation-states. The chapters in Part II are interrelated by a focus on important conceptual issues and their policy and programmatic implications.

4

The Nature of Ethnic Groups

During the 1940s and 1950s social scientists predicted that ethnic groups would fade from modernized societies as the people in these groups became culturally assimilated and acculturated. The Black civil rights movement of the 1960s in the United States and the consequent ethnic revival movements in the United States and other parts of the world contravened the predictions of social scientists and indicated that ethnic groups were important parts of modernized pluralistic societies. Ethnic group affiliations and identifications are complex social, political, and psychological processes in modernized societies. Concepts and theories formulated before the 1960s do not adequately describe them.[1]

This chapter, using ethnic groups in the United States as a case study, describes some of the major characteristics of ethnic groups in modernized societies. Even though the specifics of this chapter are not generalizable to other societies, many of the salient characteristics of ethnic groups in the United States are similar to those of ethnic groups in other Western societies, such as Australia, Canada, and the United Kingdom.[2]

The final part of this chapter describes a typology for defining and classifying ethnic groups that is consistent with their complex and dynamic characteristics in modernized societies.

Ethnicity in U.S. Society

Ethnicity is a cogent factor in U.S. history, life, and culture. The expressions and manifestations of ethnicity vary with the characteristics of the ethnic group, the nature of its societal experiences, and the sociopolitical climate. Expressions of ethnicity are also related to the ways in which the dominant group responds to various immigrant and immigrant descendant groups, to the objectives that ethnic groups wish to achieve, and to the events that serve as the catalysts for revitalization movements.[3]

Individuals and groups in the United States have often been denied cultural, political, and economic opportunities because of their ethnic group characteristics and their expressions of them. By the beginning of the 1800s, Anglo-Saxon immigrants and their descendants were the most powerful and influential ethnic group in America. English cultural traits, values, and behavioral patterns were widespread in colonial America. The English were also strongly committed to "Americanizing" (Anglicizing) all other immigrant groups, as well as to "civilizing" (according to the Anglo-Saxon definition of *civilization*) Blacks and various groups of American Indians.

Through the control of the major social, economic, and political institutions, the English denied to ethnic groups who differed from themselves opportunities to participate fully in the decision-making processes. Only peoples who were culturally and racially like Anglo-Saxons received unqualified rights to total societal participation and social acceptance. Thus, groups such as the French Huguenots, the Germans, the Irish, and the Scotch Irish were victims of much discrimination in colonial America. Southern and Eastern European immigrants, such as the Greeks, the Italians, the Slavs, and the Poles, who came to the United States in massive numbers in the late nineteenth century and the first decades of the twentieth century, were denied total societal participation.[4] Both the original English and the converted Anglo-Saxons saw these new arrivals as ethnically different from themselves and thus undeserving of social acceptance and access to the social, economic, and political systems.[5]

The Assimilation and Inclusion of White Ethnic Groups

Early in America's history assimilation, or adherence to Anglo-Saxon sociocultural traditions and values, became a prerequisite to social acceptability and access to the political structure. Although in the beginning European immigrants tried desperately to establish and maintain European life-styles and institutions on American soil,[6] their efforts were largely doomed from the beginning because the English controlled the economic and political systems. The English used their power to perpetuate Anglo-Saxon institutions and culture and to discourage the continuation of life-styles and value systems that were non-Anglo-Saxon. Non-English European immigrants were faced with the decision of either assimilation and inclusion into mainstream society or nonassimilation and exclusion from total participation in the social, economic, and political systems. They chose assimilation for a variety of reasons.[7] The immigrants from Northern and Western Europe came closest to a complete realization of the goal of total cultural assimilation because they were most like Anglo-Saxons both physically and culturally.

The first generation of Southern, Central, and Eastern European immigrants also tried desperately to conform to society's demands for assimilation and integration. However, the process was not as easy or as successful to them as it had been for their Northern and Western predecessors. Undoubtedly, the degree to which they were physically, culturally, and psychologically unlike Anglo-Saxons partially accounted for their lower level of cultural and structural assimilation.[8] These factors may also partially explain the resurgence of ethnicity among second and third generation White ethnics in the United States, such as the Poles, Czechs, Slovaks, and Greeks that occurred in the 1970s and their push for the inclusion of their cultural heritages in school ethnic studies programs. This interest became so widespread that many advocates of ethnicity used that concept al-

most exclusively to refer to White ethnic groups.[9] Novak wrote, "the new ethnicity
. . . is a movement of self-knowledge on the part of members of third and fourth
generations of Southern and Eastern European immigrants to the United States."[10]

The Assimilation and Exclusion of Non-White Ethnic Groups

Non-European, non-White ethnic groups, such as Afro-Americans, Chinese
Americans, and Mexican Americans, faced a much more serious problem than did
Southern and Eastern European immigrants. Even though society demanded that
they assimilate culturally in order to integrate socially, politically, and economically, it was very difficult for them to assimilate because of their skin color. Even
when Blacks, Mexican Americans, and American Indians succeeded in becoming
culturally assimilated, they were still structurally isolated and were denied full,
unqualified entry into the organizations and institutions sanctioned by the larger
society. They became, in effect, marginal persons, for they were not accepted totally either by their own ethnic group or by the mainstream culture. Their denial
of their ethnic cultures made them unacceptable to members of their ethnic communities, and the majority culture denied them full membership because they
were non-White. The societal goals for European immigrants, especially those
from Northern and Western Europe, were cultural assimilation and structural inclusion, but the goals for non-Whites and non-European immigrants were cultural assimilation and structural exclusion.[11]

Thus, early in America's historical development Anglo-Saxon values and
cultural norms were institutionalized as "American norms" and as "acceptable
standards of behavior." They were perpetuated and transmitted through the socialization and enculturation of subsequent generations of Anglo-Saxon European
immigrants. Anglo-Saxon customs and values were also perpetuated through the
acculturation but structural exclusion of non-White, non-European immigrant
groups.

The latter goal was achieved through institutionalizing Anglo-Saxon customs and laws that demanded conformity by non-Whites to Anglo-Saxon behavioral patterns, but denied them entry into the social, political, and economic
systems. The result, for many of these "colored peoples," such as Blacks and American Indians, was the loss of important aspects of their first cultures. The Anglo-
Saxons sought to insure their dominance and power over these groups by
stigmatizing their first cultures and institutions. Thus, when Africans arrived in
America, the dominant group ridiculed their languages and punished them for
practicing their African customs. Mexican Americans were not allowed to speak
Spanish in the schools, even though the Treaty of Guadalupe Hidalgo guaranteed
them the rights to maintain and perpetuate their language and culture.[12] Texas
even passed laws that declared Mexican Americans to be Whites. In the 1800s,

after most American Indians had been forced from their lands, subjected to federal controls, and relegated to living on reservations, U.S. policy makers began an aggressive campaign to "Americanize" the Indians.[13]

Distinctive Ethnic Traits in U.S. Society

Undoubtedly, many immigrant groups lost much of the flavor of their original ethnic heritages through the evolutionary processes of assimilation, acculturation, adaptation, and cultural borrowing. Some groups (principally Northern and Western European immigrants, and to a lesser extent Southern, Central, and Eastern European immigrants) voluntarily gave up large portions of their ethnic cultures and became Anglo-Saxonized in return for the privilege of societal participation. Other groups were forced to abandon their original cultural heritages. The structural exclusion to which non-White, non-European immigrants and American Indian groups were subjected resulted in the perpetuation of distinctive ethnic traits and the development of unique cultural institutions and traditions.[14] The cultures of these ethnic minorities differed in degrees from the dominant culture because these groups created values, languages, life-styles, and symbols they needed to survive the oppression, exclusion, and dehumanization to which they were subjected. These cultural traits were institutionalized and transmitted through the generations.

To some extent these cultural components are legacies from the original homelands of non-White ethnic groups, modified to accommodate the circumstances of living in America; to some extent they are new creations designed to meet the needs of particular ethnic groups. The cultural institutions and processes that were created clearly reflect the interactions between original cultural perspectives and the realities of U.S. society. The various ethnic groups developed somewhat different cultural values because their ancestral homes, cultural perspectives, and experiences in America were different. The new cultures that emerged undoubtedly have some remnants from the original motherlands, but not necessarily in their original forms. Rather, the need to adapt to new surroundings and the effects of cultural sharing gave rise to new cultural forms.

The Black church, Black survival strategies, Black language, and Black civil rights organizations have some African cultural components, although these institutions, without question, were created by Africans in the Americas. They represent aspects of Black cultural life that were created to meet the unique social, economic, and political needs of Blacks. Black modes of communication emerged in response to the need to find viable means of surviving in a hostile environment without jeopardizing physical safety. Words, in addition to being communication devices, became power devices and helped Afro-Americans to survive. Black music has its primordial roots in the African heritage, but it is both an expression of the hopes, fears, aspirations, and frustrations of Blacks and a reflection of their experiences in U.S. society. The forces that gave rise to much of its lyrical content and rhythmic tempo were the prototype life experiences, both physical and psycholog-ical, of Blacks as a group.

The ethnic cultures of most European immigrants were largely amalgamated in the United States. America became a culturally diffused and a socially and po-litically stratified society. Northern and Eastern European immigrants were almost totally culturally assimilated and structurally integrated into the dominant Anglo-Saxon society. Eastern, Central, and Southern European immigrants were assimi-lated to a lesser extent, and the political and economic privileges they experienced reflected their lower levels of assimilation. Non-White, non-European immigrants and American Indian groups (i.e., colored, highly visible people) were culturally diffused and largely structurally excluded.

The Nature of Ethnic Groups in Contemporary U.S. Life

Our discussion of cultural and structural assimilation leads us to more complex questions concerning the nature of ethnic groups in contemporary U.S. society, the functions they serve, and the extent to which they exist in the United States today. An ethnic group may be defined as an involuntary collectivity of people with a shared feeling of common identity, a sense of peoplehood, and a shared sense of interdependence of fate. These feelings derive, in part, from a common ancestral origin, a common set of values, and a common set of experiences.[15] Isa-jiw defines an ethnic group as "an involuntary group of people who share the same culture or descendents of such people who identify themselves and/or are identified by others as belonging to the same involuntary group."[16]

Identification with and membership in an ethnic group serves many useful functions. The ethnic group provides a network of preferred individual and insti-tutional associations through which primary group relationships are established and personalities are developed. It serves psychologically as a source of self-identi-fication for individuals. It provides a cultural screen through which national cul-tural patterns of behavior and the value system of other groups are screened, assessed, and assigned meaning.[17] Isajiw suggests that ethnicity is a matter of double boundary building; boundaries from within that are maintained by the socialization process, and boundaries from without, which are established by the process of intergroup relations. The most important question to be considered in analyzing ethnicity in contemporary U.S. society is related less to the extent to which cultural assimilation has occurred and more to how ethnic groups are per-ceived and identified by other people in the larger society, especially people who exercise political and economic power.[18]

Ethnicity or ethnic group membership becomes important in relationships with other groups of people when one group discovers it has great actual or poten-tial political and economic power. Such is the case with the Japanese Americans in Hawaii and the Poles and Blacks in Chicago. Ethnicity also becomes important when one is a member of a highly visible minority group, such as Afro-Americans, Asian Americans, and Mexican Americans. It also becomes important when one ethnic group becomes conscious of being surrounded by another ethnic group,[19] such as Anglo-Saxon Protestants in Spanish Harlem and Whites who live in predominantly Black urban areas. Individuals who find themselves in these kinds of situations tend to turn to their own ethnic group for their intimate relationships, for reaffirmation of their identity, and for psychological and emotional support. Attempts to satisfy these kinds of needs often lead to ethnic alliances formed to influence social and political institutions. The individual feels that he or she benefits through the progress of his or her primary group (i.e., a sense of interdependence of fate). Therefore, as Greeley suggests:

> Many ethnic groups have emerged in this country because members of the various immigrant groups have tried to preserve something of the intimacy and familiarity of the peasant village during the transition into urban industrial living. These groups have persisted after the immigrant experience . . . because of an apparently very powerful drive in many toward associating with those who, he believes, possess the same blood and the same beliefs he does. The inclination toward such homogeneous groupings simultaneously enriches the culture, provides for diversity within the social structure and considerably increases the potential for conflict.[20]

Greeley adds, "Visibility, sudden recognition of minority status, or being a large group in an environment where ethnic affiliation is deemed important—these three variables may considerably enhance social-psychological and social-organizational influence of ethnic groups."[21]

Toward the Development of a Typology for Classifying Ethnic Groups

The functions served by ethnic group affiliation suggests that there are several different ways of classifying ethnic groups in contemporary Western societies. Existing definitions of an ethnic group are useful, but they are inadequate for studying the complex characteristics of contemporary ethnic groups in Western societies.[22] Most of these definitions were formulated when ethnic group characteristics in Western societies were considerably different and before the rise of ethnic revitalization movements during the 1960s and 1970s. New conceptualizations of ethnicity are needed to reflect more accurately the emerging characteristics of ethnic groups in the United States and other Western nations.

It is impossible for a single definition of an ethnic group to adequately describe the multiple and complex dimensions of ethnic groups in contemporary societies. We need to develop a typology that will enable us to identify and classify different types of ethnic groups and to determine the degrees to which various racial and ethnic groups manifest these identified characteristics. We attempt to formulate the basic elements of such a typology in this chapter. It is important for the reader to realize that our typology is an ideal-type construct in the Weberian sense, and that no actual ethnic group will represent a "pure" type of any of our categories. Rather, various ethnic groups will exhibit the characteristics we identify to a greater or lesser degree. It is also unlikely that any particular ethnic group will completely lack any of the characteristics we will describe. The reader should think of each ethnic group category as a continuum.

Each type of ethnic group is an involuntary group whose members share a sense of peoplehood and an interdependence of fate. A *cultural* ethnic group is an ethnic group that shares a common set of values, experiences, behavioral characteristics, and linguistic traits that differ substantially from other ethnic groups within society. Individuals usually gain membership in such a group not by choice but through birth and early socialization. Individuals who are members of cultural ethnic groups are likely to take collective and organized actions to support public policies that will enhance the survival of the group's culture and ethnic institutions. Members of cultural ethnic groups also pass on the symbols, language, and other components of the cultural heritage to the next generation. The individual's ethnic cultural heritage is a source of pride and group identification.

An *economic* ethnic group is an ethnic group that shares a sense of group identity and sees its economic fate tied together. Individual members of the group feel that their economic fate is intimately tied to the economic future of other members of the group. The members of an economic ethnic group respond collectively to societal issues they perceive as critical to determining their economic status, and they work together to influence policies and programs that will benefit the economic status of the group. The individual within an economic ethnic group tends to feel that taking individual actions to improve his or her economic status is likely to be ineffective as long as the economic status of the ethnic group is not substantially improved.

A *political* ethnic group is an ethnic group that has a sense of shared political interests and a feeling of political interdependence. The group responds to political issues collectively and tries to promote those public policies and programs that will enhance the interests of its members as a group. Groups that are political ethnic groups are also usually economic ethnic groups since politics and economics are tightly interwoven in a society. Thus, we can refer to those ethnic groups that work to influence political and economic policies that will benefit their collectivities as *ecopolitical ethnic groups*.

A *holistic* ethnic group is an entire group that has all of the characteristics of the various types of ethnic groups that we have described in their purest forms. Thus, a holistic ethnic group is an involuntary group of individuals who share a sense of peoplehood and an interdependence of fate, a common sense of identity, and common behavioral characteristics. Its members respond collectively to economic and political issues and try to promote public programs and policies that will further the interests of the group as a whole. Afro-Americans and Mexican Americans closely approach the holistic ethnic group. American Indians, Puerto

Ricans in the United States, and Asian Americans are acquiring more characteristics of a holistic ethnic group as the political maturity and collective political action of these groups increase.

Two questions arise from our discussion: What is the structural relationship between ethnic groups and the larger U.S. society? In a pluralistic society such as the United States, is everyone a member of an ethnic group? Our analysis suggests that every American is a member of an ethnic group, that ethnicity exists on a continuum in contemporary American life, and that some individuals and groups are much more "ethnic" than others (see Chapter 5). Thus it is more useful to attempt to describe the degree to which an individual or group is "ethnic," rather than to try to determine whether a particular individual or group is "ethnic." The lower-class, Black individual who lives in an all-Black community, speaks Black English, and who is active in Black political and economic activities is clearly more "ethnic" than the highly acculturated Black who tries desperately to avoid any contact with other Blacks.

Third generation Italian-Americans who are highly assimilated into the Anglo-Saxon culture may be ethnic only in a cultural sense, that is, they share the values, life-styles, and sense of peoplehood with Anglo-Americans. They may do very little, however, to advance the political and economic interests of Anglo-Americans over the interests of non-Anglo-American ethnic groups. Afro-Americans, Puerto Ricans in the United States, and Japanese Americans are all ethnic groups. However, they are structurally different kinds of ethnic groups, and unless we keep the significant differences between these groups in mind when we are deriving generalizations, our conclusions are likely to be misleading.

Of the three groups, Afro-Americans, especially in the mid-1960s, more closely approach what we have described as a holistic ethnic group. Puerto Ricans in the United States, until the 1970s, have been primarily a cultural and economic ethnic group but have not been very politically active in a collective sense. However, Puerto Ricans have been becoming more of a political ethnic group since the 1970s. Japanese Americans are probably the least ethnic of the three groups. This is true not only because Japanese Americans are highly culturally assimilated but because they are not very politically active in an "ethnic" sense. They are also very economically successful and consequently feel little need to take collective action to influence their economic condition.[23] *The degree to which a particular cultural, nationality, or racial group is ethnic varies over time, in different regions, with social class mobility, and with the pervasive sociopolitical conditions within the society.*

Frequently, third and fourth generation descendants of immigrants who came from Northern and Western Europe (e.g., French, Germans, Irish, Dutch, etc.) are thought to have become Anglo-Saxon politically, socially, culturally, and ethnically. The contention is often made that these groups, through the processes of acculturation and assimilation, have lost all traces of their ethnic distinctiveness, internalized Anglo-Saxon values and behaviors, and consider their political and economic interests to be the same as Americans whose origins are Anglo-

Saxon. The preservation of the original ethnicity of these descendants has been determined on the basis of the presence or absence of overt behaviors attributable to the original ethnic group. When many of these behaviors are not found, conclusions are drawn to the effect that any ethnicity, aside from Anglo-Saxonism, is insignificant in defining the self-identity of descendants of Northern and Western European stock, in determining their primary group relationships, and in governing their social, political, and psychological behaviors. Their ethnic origins have been dismissed as meaningless and dysfunctional, except perhaps on rare occasions when families get together for reunions and to reminisce about "great grandma, the old country, and the old days," fix an ethnic dish, hold an ethnic marriage ceremony, or observe ethnic holidays.

However, the resurgence or rediscovery of ethnicity during the 1970s and the research on White ethnic groups during this period challenged the validity of these contentions. Research by students of the "new ethnicity" such as Novak and Greeley suggests that ethnicity among Whites is a complex variable that defies such simple explanations and/or dismissals, and that it is a persistent, salient factor in the lives of different groups of White Americans, even though they may be fourth-generation immigrants.[24] Greeley explains that White "ethnicity is not a residual social factor that is slowly and gradually disappearing; it is, rather, a dynamic flexible social mechanism and can be called into being rather quickly and transformed and transmuted to meet changing situations and circumstances."[25]

During the 1970s many White ethnic group members became as concerned as ethnic minority groups with self-identity, with reestablishing contact with their ethnic and cultural histories, with developing a sense of ethnic unity, and with preserving their cultural heritages. This search for more gratifying responses to the question of "Who am I?" rekindled an interest in ethnic heritage and an awareness of the saliency of ethnicity in their lives. Whites from all sociocultural backgrounds (e.g., Irish, Italian, Polish, German, Czech, Slovak, Greek, etc.) joined Blacks, Latinos, and American Indians in this search for identity. It is more appropriate to talk about what Greeley calls the process of "ethnicization," or "ethnogenesis," instead of acculturation and assimilation, or "Americanization," if we are to understand the cultural diversity and ethnic dynamism in the United States and other Western societies.[26] According to Greeley the so-called "new ethnicity" among White Americans during the 1970s was not new at all. Rather, it was a rebirth or revival of interest in a persistent force in the history and lives of *all* Americans. Its resurgence was symbolic of the cyclical nature of the ethnicization process.

Unquestionably, a great deal of sociocultural exchange has taken place between the various immigrant groups and the American host society. But this does not mean that either one is any less ethnic. The process of ethnicization leads to the creation of a broader "common culture," shared by both the host and immigrant groups. The immigrant groups take on certain attitudes, beliefs, values, and behaviors attributable to Anglo-Saxons, and English Americans adopt some of the immigrants' values, beliefs, customs, and symbols (see Chapter 7). Other immigrant characteristics persist and become more distinctive in response to the challenge of American life. The result for third- and fourth-generation immigrants, such as Italian Americans, Polish Americans, or Irish Americans, is a cultural system that is a combination of commonly shared "American" traits and distinctive traits preserved from their original ethnic heritages.

To understand ethnicity fully when studying America's diverse populations attention needs to be given to the interrelationships among *ethnic identification, ethnic heritage*, and *ethnic culture*. This is especially important when studying White ethnic groups since ethnic differences within and between them are often subtle and complex. If identification, heritage, and culture are viewed as discrete dimensions or components of ethnicity, each with different behavioral manifestations, then an individual can proclaim his or her ethnicity by ascribing to any one or a combination of these. *Ethnic identification* refers to where one places oneself on the ethnic chart (e.g., "I am Irish, German, French, Norwegian, Slovak, Greek, or Black"). *Ethnic heritage* is the specific study and conscious recollection of one's past history, both in America and the country of origin. *Ethnic culture* refers to the attitudes, values, personality styles, norms, and behaviors that correlate with ethnic identification.[27] Even though fourth-generation Irish Americans, Polish Americans, or Italian Americans may identify neither physically, nor psychosocially with their original ethnic groups, and have little or no consciousness of their ethnic heritage, their "Irishness," "Polishness," or "Italianness" is still very much a part of their lives. Their values, behaviors, perceptions and expectations that differ considerably from those of other Americans, are determined, to a great extent, by the cultural conditioning that persists from the original ethnic experience. These cultural traits are transmitted across generations through family structures and socialization processes and are often so deeply embedded in the subconscious fiber of individuals that they are unaware of their existence. This is why we frequently assume that White ethnic groups, especially those who emigrated from Northern and Western Europe, lose their ethnic identity after three or four generations in America.

Undoubtedly, ethnicity is even stronger and more conscious among European descendants who came from Eastern, Southern, and Central Europe than among those from Northern and Western Europe. Such groups as the Poles, Greeks, Italians, Slovaks, Czechs, and Hungarians are more recent arrivals in America. Their ties with their original heritages, customs, values, and traditions are stronger, and they share less of a common culture with English Americans than do groups like the French and Germans. Their senses of ethnic identification, heritage, and culture are much more apparent in their daily lives because of the more distinct origins. They are less assimilated culturally and structurally than other White Americans, and the ethnicization process is less developed. Therefore, their original ethnicity is more highly accentuated, and they are more likely to behave in clearly discernible ways from Anglo-Saxons than are other European immigrants. These groups are likely to support ethnic candidates for public office, live in tightly formed ethnic communities, continue to speak their native languages, marry within their own ethnic groups, conform more rigidly to ethnic values, and perpetuate their ethnic heritages through family structures and socialization. The forces of differentiation acting on them are much stronger and function on more conscious, all-inclusive levels than do the forces of homogenization.[28]

The ethnic groups in the United States that are the least assimilated culturally and structurally, and the most visible physically, such as Afro-Americans, Filipino Americans, Mexican Americans, and American Indians, as groups, have maintained even stronger senses of cultural identities. To a greater degree than Americans of either Western and Northern, or Southern and Eastern European descent, they feel that their life-styles and political interests conflict with those of the dominant society. They therefore consider themselves to be more "ethnic" than these other groups. They have created and maintained distinct cultural institutions, values, norms, and languages. Excluded ethnic groups are much more likely than structurally assimilated ethnic groups to emphasize their feelings of kinship, to promote their cultural identities, and to try to influence economic and political institutions so that public policies will be more responsive to their unique group needs. Thus, in the 1970s Blacks tried to gain control of schools located in predominantly Black communities and Chinese Americans in San Francisco united to oppose efforts to bus their children to schools outside of Chinatown. Mexican Americans are more likely to vote for a Chicano for public office than for an Anglo-American because they usually feel a Chicano will make decisions more consistent with their ethnic group interests than will an Anglo-American.[29]

Both White and minority ethnic group preoccupation with their own ethnicity is situational and periodic. It surfaces and assumes a position of prominence in group activities at different times in history and as different aspects of the psychosocial and ecopolitical identification processes demand attention. The nature of the particular identity need determines the way ethnicity is articulated and the activities ethnic groups choose to accentuate their ethnicity. Whether that need is defined as the clarification or reaffirmation of cultural identity, the recollection and reevaluation of historical experiences, the manipulation of social forces to benefit the ethnic group's membership, or gaining political and economic power to advance the social positions of particular ethnic collectives, it determines the "ethnic posture" of the group at any given time. Ethnic needs influence whether an ethnic collectivity functions as an *economic, political,* or *cultural ethnic group.* All ethnic groups assume these various identities at different stages in their developmental processes within the context of American society.

Even though our generalizations are basically valid, they are not applicable to the same degree to all members of all ethnic groups. This is why it is imperative, when studying ethnicity, to distinguish ethnic *group* behavior from the behavior of *individual* members of ethnic groups, to consider ethnicity from the perspective of functionality instead of merely as a descriptive trait, and to analyze the behavior of ethnic groups in terms of ethnic identification, heritage, and culture.

Some members of ethnic groups have little or no sense of ethnic kinship or interdependence of fate. They feel little or no sense of distinction or difference between themselves and the larger society. Some members do not identify with their ethnic group, even though they share its physical and/or cultural characteristics, and the larger society considers them to belong to it. For example, some descendants of Mexican-American parentage consider themselves White. They do not speak Spanish, have Anglicized their names, and conform to Anglo-Saxon cultural norms. Some Blacks believe that they are both culturally and structurally assimilated into the larger society. They have inculcated the values and life-styles of the dominant culture, consider themselves totally accepted by the majority society, feel a sense of alienation from Blacks as a group, and find it almost impossible to identify with the cultural and political goals of Blacks.

Summary

The rise of ethnic revival movements in Western societies during the 1960s and 1970s indicated that ethnic groups and ethnic affiliations are integral parts of contemporary societies, despite the contrary predictions social scientists made in previous decades. New concepts and theories are needed to explain adequately the complex nature of ethnic groups in modernized pluralistic societies.

In this chapter, ethnic groups in the United States are used as a case study to describe some of the major characteristics of ethnic groups in Western societies. Ethnic groups in the United States and in such nations as Australia, Canada, and the United Kingdom share many characteristics. This chapter also presents a typology for classifying ethnic groups that is consistent with their complex and changing characteristics in modernized societies. We identified several types of ethnic groups—cultural, economic, political, ecopolitical, and holistic—and concluded that even though every American is a member of an ethnic group, ethnicity manifests itself in diverse forms in modern U.S. society, and that Americans belong to many different kinds of ethnic groups. The degree to which a particular cultural, national, or racial group is "ethnic" varies with a number of social, economic, and political conditions within society.

Notes

1. See Louis Wirth, "The Problem of Minority Groups," in Ralph Linton, ed., *The Science of Man in the World Crisis* (New York: Columbia University Press, 1945), pp. 347–372; and Robert E. Park, *Race and Culture* (New York: The Free Press, 1950).

2. Brian Bullivant, *The Pluralist Dilemma in Education: Six Case Studies* (Sydney: George Allen & Unwin, 1981); Janis Wilton and Richard Bosworth, *Old Worlds and New Australia: The Post-War Migrant Experience* (Ringwood, Victoria: Penguin Books Australia Ltd., 1984); Joseph F. Krauter and Morris Davis, *Minority Canadians: Ethnic Groups* (Toronto: Methuen, 1978); James L. Watson, *Between Two Cultures: Migrants and Minorities in Britain* (Oxford: Basil Blackwell, 1977).

3. Nathan Glazer and Daniel P. Moynihan, eds., *Ethnicity: Theory and Experience* (Cambridge, Mass.: Harvard University Press, 1975); Andrew D. Smith, *The Ethnic Revival in the Modern World* (Cambridge, England: Cambridge University Press, 1981); Thomas Sowell, *Ethnic America: A History* (New York: Basic Books, 1981).

4. John Higham, *Strangers in the Land: Patterns of American Nativism 1860–1925* (New York: Atheneum, 1972); George M. Fredrickson and Dale T. Knobel, "A History of Prejudice and Discrimination," in Stephan Thernstrom, Ann Orlov, and Oscar Handlin, eds., *Harvard Encyclopedia of American Ethnic Groups* (Cambridge, Mass.: Harvard University Press, 1980), pp. 829–847.

5. Maldwyn Allen Jones, *American Immigration* (Chicago: University of Chicago Press, 1960).

6. Nathan Glazer, "Ethnic Groups in America: From National Culture to Ideology," in Morroe Berger, Theodore Abel, and Charles H. Page, eds., *Freedom and Control in Modern Society* (New York: Van Nostrand, 1954), pp. 158–173.

7. Philip Gleason, "American Identity and Americanization," in Thernstrom, Orlov, and Handlin, eds., *Harvard Encyclopedia of American Ethnic Groups*, pp. 31–58; Nathan Glazer, "Cultural Pluralism: The Social Aspect," in Melvin M. Tumin and Walter Plotch, eds., *Pluralism in A Democratic Society* (New York: Praeger Publishers, 1977), pp. 3–24.

8. Richard D. Alba, *Italian Americans: Into the Twilight of Ethnicity* (Englewood Cliffs, N.J.: Prentice-Hall, 1985); Milton M. Gordon, *Assimilation in American Life: The Role of Race, Religion and National Origins* (New York: Oxford University Press, 1964).

9. Michael Novak, *The Rise of the Unmeltable Ethnics: Politics and Culture in The Seventies* (New York: Macmillan, 1972).

10. Michael Novak, "The New Ethnicity," *Center Magazine* 3 (July/August, 1974), p. 18.

11. Gordon, *Assimilation in American Life*.

12. Wayne Moquin and Charles Van Doren, eds., *A Documentary History of Mexican Americans* (New York: Bantam Books, 1971).

13. Alvin M. Josephy, Jr., *The Indian Heritage of America* (New York: Bantam Books, 1968).

14. Melvin Herskovits, *The Myth of the Negro Past* (New York: Harper and Row, 1941).

15. Wsevolod W. Isajiw, "Definitions of Ethnicity," *Ethnicity* 1 (July 1974), pp. 111–124.

16. Ibid., p. 122.

17. Gordon, *Assimilation in American Life*.

18. Isajiw, "Definitions of Ethnicity," p. 122.

19. Andrew M. Greeley, *Why Can't They Be Like Us? America's White Ethnic Groups* (New York: E. P. Dutton and Company, 1971).

20. Ibid., p. 44.

21. Ibid., p. 46.

22. Isajiw, "Definitions of Ethnicity."

23. Harry H. L. Kitano, *Japanese Americans: The Evolution of A Subculture*, 2nd ed. (Englewood Cliffs, N.J.: Prentice-Hall, 1976).

24. See Michael Novak, *The Rise of the Unmeltable Ethnics*; "How American Are You if Your Grandparents Came from Serbia in 1888?", in Sallie TeSelle, ed., *The Rediscovery of Ethnicity* (New York: Harper and Row, 1973), pp. 1–20; "Cultural Pluralism for Individuals: A Social Vision," in Tumin and Plotch, pp. 25–57; Andrew M. Greeley, *Eth-*

nicity in the United States: A Preliminary Reconnaisance (New York: Wiley Publishing Co., 1974); and Greeley, *Why Can't They Be Like Us?*

25. Greeley, *Ethnicity in the United States*, p. 205.

26. Ibid., pp. 291–317.

27. Ibid.

28. Novak, in *The Rediscovery of Ethnicity*

29. Edgar Litt, *Ethnic Politics in America* (Glenview, Ill.: Scott, Foresman, 1970).

5

Culture, Ethnicity, and Education

A wide range of concepts has emerged since the 1960s to describe the diverse programs and practices related to ethnic and cultural diversity. These concepts reflect the many different and often conflicting goals, approaches, and strategies in multiethnic education. Concepts such as multicultural education, multiethnic education, intercultural education, ethnic studies, cultural pluralism, and antiracist education are sometimes used interchangeably and at other times to describe different but interrelated programs and practices. The study of ethnicity and cultural diversity became more legitimate in the schools and universities during the 1960s and 1970s than it had been in previous decades.[1]

During the 1980s the national emphasis in the United States and several other nations shifted from intranational diversity to nationalism and national identity. However, some aspects of the curriculum reforms related to diversity that emerged in the 1960s and 1970s had become partially institutionalized by the late 1980s. More ethnic images in textbooks, various forms of bilingual education, and multicultural education requirements for teachers were found in many educational institutions by the late 1980s. However, the pace of reform had slowed considerably.

The major concepts related to multiethnic and multicultural education, and related practices, are imprecise and ambiguous. Concept clarification within this area is needed so objectives can be more clearly delineated and strategies for attaining them more appropriately designed. Concepts are very important—they influence our questions, research methods, findings, programs, and evaluation strategies. Multicultural education and multiethnic education, for example, have different programmatic and policy implications. Multicultural education focuses on a wide range of cultural groups, such as ethnic groups, women, and the handicapped. Multiethnic education focuses on the educational needs of racial and ethnic groups.

In this chapter, I define and delineate the boundaries of some of the major concepts related to education and cultural diversity and suggest their different programmatic and policy implications. This conceptual analysis is designed to help educators at all levels better clarify, specify, and evaluate goals related to cultural and ethnic diversity in Western societies.

Multicultural Education

Of the concepts currently popular, multicultural education is one of the most frequently used, not only in the United States but also in such nations as Australia,

71

the United Kingdom, and Canada. However, intercultural education, rather than multicultural education, is frequently used on the European continent.[2] Researchers and policy makers who prefer intercultural to multicultural education contend that intercultural implies an education that promotes interaction among different cultures whereas multicultural does not imply such interaction. However, intercultural education is rarely used outside of the European continent.

The use of multicultural education varies widely in different school districts and in the educational literature.[3] Sometimes it is used synonymously with ethnic studies; at other times it is used to describe multiethnic education. It is necessary to discuss the meaning of culture in order to describe what multicultural education suggests theoretically since *culture* is the root of multicultural and thus of multicultural education.

The Meaning of Culture

There are many different definitions of *culture*, but no single definition that all social scientists would heartily accept. Some definitions, however, are fairly widely accepted. During much of this century, the famous definition of culture formulated by Sir E. B. Taylor in 1871 was very influential: "Culture . . . is that complex whole which includes knowledge, belief, art, morals, law, custom, and any other capabilities and habits acquired by man as a member of society."[4] Today, Taylor's definition is not popular among social scientists because they believe it is not a very helpful guide for research. They think the definition is too broad and lacks sufficient boundaries. As Dimen-Schein points out, we can neither observe nor explain everything.[5] Research efforts and policy analyses need to be guided by a definition of culture that is more specific and focused. In recent years, social scientists have formulated definitions of culture that are more precise and functional for modernized societies.

In a comprehensive study of the definitions of culture published in 1952, Alfred L. Kroeber and Clyde Kluckhohn report more than 160. They concluded that most social scientists agreed that "culture consists of patterns, explicit and implicit, of and for behavior acquired and transmitted by symbols, constituting the distinctive achievements of human groups, including their embodiments in artifacts; the essential core of culture consists of traditional (i.e., historically derived and selected) ideas and especially attached values."[6]

In their summary definition of culture, Kroeber and Kluckhohn, like most social scientists today, emphasize the intangible, symbolic, and ideational aspects of group life as the most important aspects of culture. Some social scientists go so far as to exclude material objects (artifacts) from their definition of culture.[7] Even social scientists who view tangible or material objects as a part of culture believe that the interpretation of these objects and the rules governing their use constitute the essence of culture and not the artifacts themselves.

Some social scientists distinguish between the terms *society* and *culture*. These social scientists "reserve the word society for the observable interactions among people, and the word culture for the intangible symbols, rules, and values that . . . people use to define themselves."[8] Symbolic anthropologists, such as Clifford Geertz and Victor Turner, "study ideology, such as the multiple meaning of words and things, and the role of symbols in ordering social life by unifying opposing meanings."[9]

Culture is sometimes defined as a strategy or program for survival. In this view of culture, it is created when human groups try to satisfy their survival needs. Bullivant, who views culture as a survival strategy, states that culture is not static, but is subject to the circumstances (environment) in which a society finds itself. He describes three kinds of environments to which human groups respond when creating culture: the geographical environment, the social environment, and the metaphysical environment. Bullivant defines culture as "an interdependent and patterned system of valued traditional and current public knowledge and conceptions, embodied in behaviors and artefacts, and transmitted to present and new members, both symbolically and non-symbolically, which a society has evolved historically and progressively modifies and augments, to give meaning to and cope with its definitions of present and future existential problems."[10]

The Characteristics of Cultures

Most contemporary social scientists view culture as consisting primarily of the symbolic, ideational, and intangible aspects of human societies. Even when they view artifacts and material objects as a part of culture, most social scientists regard culture as the way people interpret, use, and perceive such artifacts and material objects. It is the values, symbols, interpretations, and perspectives that distinguish one people from another in modernized societies and not artifacts, material objects, and other tangible aspects of human societies. Both the Japanese and the Americans use the automobile, but how they organize the making of it and how they interpret it within their societies may differ considerably and thus constitutes an essential component of their respective cultures.

Cultures are dynamic, complex, and changing. Often in the schools cultures are perceived as static, unchanging, and fragmented. Concepts such as "American-Indian culture" and "Black culture" often imply static, unchanging life-styles. American Indians are often described in misleading ways, such as living in tepees. One result of such perceptions and descriptions is the perpetuation of stereotypes about different cultural groups.

Cultures are also systems; they must be viewed as wholes, not as discrete and isolated parts. Any change in one aspect of a culture affects all of its components. For example, the large number of women who entered the work force in the 1970s and 1980s has influenced how women view themselves, how men view women, and the family socialization of children. Many more children today are in child-care facilities at a much younger age than was the case in the 1950s, when fewer women in the United States worked outside the home.

Gilligan describes caring, interconnection, and sensitivity to the needs of other people as dominant values among women and of the female microculture in the United States.[11] Most of the research she cites was done with women socialized before the women's rights movement of the 1960s and 1970s. Future research might reveal that increased women's rights during the 1960s and 1970s may have had a significant influence on the values held by women, particularly those related to caring and interconnection.

Culture, Macroculture, and Microcultures

The concept of culture as formulated by most social scientists does not deal with variations within the national culture or the smaller cultures within it. However, when dealing with multicultural education, it is necessary to discuss cultural variation within the national culture because multicultural education focuses on equal educational opportunities for different groups within the national culture. Two related concepts can help us deal with cultural variations within the national culture. We can call the national or shared culture of the nation-state or society the big or *macroculture*. The smaller cultures that constitute it can be called *microcultures*.

Every nation-state has overarching values, symbols, and ideations shared to some degree by all microcultures. Various microcultural groups within the nation, however, may mediate, interpret, reinterpret, perceive, and experience these overarching national values and ideals differently. Figure 5.1 shows the relationship between microcultures and the national macroculture.

The national, overarching ideals, symbols, and values can be described for various nation-states. Myrdal, the Swedish economist, identifies values such as justice, equality, and human dignity as overarching values in the United States. He calls these values the American Creed.[12] Myrdal also describes the "American Dilemma" as an integral part of U.S. society. This dilemma results from the fact that even though most U.S. citizens internalize American Creed values, such as justice and human dignity, they often violate them in their daily behavior. Myrdal concludes that a tremendous gap exists between American ideals and American realities. Other U.S. overarching values include the Protestant work ethic, individualism as opposed to a group orientation, distance, and materialism and material progress.[13]

The Variables and Components of Culture

As indicated in the previous section, most social scientists today emphasize the intangible components of culture, such as symbols, values, ideations, and ways of interpreting reality. I have identified six major cultural elements or components that are useful for interpreting the behavior of students and teachers and for

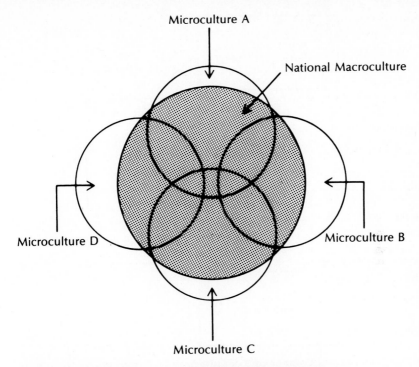

Figure 5.1. Microcultures and the National Macroculture
The shaded area represents the national macroculture. All
ethnic and cultural groups and citizens of the nation-state
share this culture. A, B, C, and D represent microcultures that
consist of unique institutions, values, and cultural elements
that are nonuniversalized and shared primarily by members of
specific ethnic and cultural groups. A major goal of the school
should be to help students acquire the knowledge, skills, and
attitudes needed to function effectively within the national
macroculture, their own microcultures, and within and across
other microcultures.

teaching about various microcultural groups in Western nation-states. Figure 5.2
shows the elements and components of cultures discussed in the following
sections.

Values and Behavioral Styles

Values are abstract, generalized principles of behavior to which members of society attach a high worth or regard. Individuals acquire their values during socialization. Values are one of the most important elements of cultures and microcultures

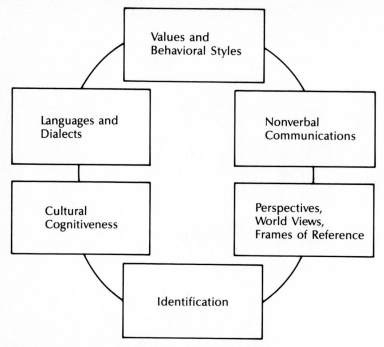

Figure 5.2. Elements and Components of Culture
These components of culture, which can be conceptualized as distinct, exist within a holistic and highly interrelated system.

that distinguish one group from another. Values influence behavior and also how people perceive their environment.

Each nation-state has national values that are to some extent shared by all of its microcultural groups; it also has other important values that distinguish one microcultural group from another. In their research on the cognitive styles of students, Ramírez and Castañeda found that Mexican-American and Anglo-American students, as groups, had some different values that are revealed in their cognitive styles or approaches to learning. They found that Mexican Americans tend to be field-sensitive whereas Anglo-Americans are more field-independent. Field-sensitive students prefer to work with other people to achieve a goal; field-independent students prefer to work independently. Field-sensitive and field-independent learners also differ in other important ways.[14]

Research on women has revealed that men and women exhibit some significant differences in value orientations. As pointed out previously, individualism is very important to men, whereas relationships, caring, and interconnection tend to be more important to women. Women also experience more problems with competitive achievement and more "fear of success" than do men.[15]

Languages and Dialects

Languages and dialects are important components of culture. How people view and interpret the world is reflected in their language. Within most nation-states, people speak the national language (or lingua franca) plus many variations of the national language as well as other languages. In the United States, Americans speak many different varieties of English, including Black English and English with Southern and Eastern regional accents. The first language for many Americans is not English but Spanish, Korean, Chinese, or Vietnamese. People in nations such as the United Kingdom, Australia, and Canada also speak many different dialects and languages in addition to the shared national language or languages. Canada has two national languages, English and French. Many other languages are also spoken in Canada. Cultural differences are both reflected and perpetuated by languages and dialects.

Nonverbal Communications

The way people communicate nonverbally is an important part of culture. How people look at each other and what the particular looks mean often vary within and across different microcultural groups within a society. Philips, in her study of the Indians on the Warm Spring Indian Reservation in Oregon, describes how the communication styles of Indian students and their Anglo teachers—both verbal and nonverbal—differ and often conflict.[16] Nonverbal communication often reveals latent but important components of a culture or microculture. Looking an older person directly in the eye is considered offensive in some U.S. microcultures.

Cultural Cognitiveness

Cultural cognitiveness occurs when individuals or a group are aware of and think about their culture or microculture as unique and distinct from other cultures or microcultures within a society. Cultural cognitiveness involves the process of knowing, including both awareness and judgment.

Cultural cognitiveness differs from cultural identification. An individual may have a strong identification with a culture but little awareness of it as a unique culture, distinct from others. Conversely, an individual may have strong cultural cognitiveness or awareness but little identification with his or her microculture. An individual with strong cultural awareness could be a staunch assimilationist who tries to escape most or all of the symbols of his or her culture.

Perspectives, World Views, and Frames of Reference

Certain perspectives, points of view, and frames of reference are normative within each culture and microcultural group. This does not mean that every individual within a particular cultural or microcultural group endorses a particular point of view or perspective. It does mean, however, that particular views and perspectives occur more frequently within some microcultural groups than do others or within the macroculture. Japanese-American perspectives on their World War II internment, Afro-American perspectives on the civil rights movement of the 1960s, and women's perspectives on caring, independence, and individuation[17] are various examples of perspectives held by microcultural groups that differ from perspectives within other microcultural groups and the macroculture.

Identification

When an individual identifies with his or her cultural or microcultural group, he or she feels a part of the group; internalizes its goals, interests, and aspirations; and also internalizes its values and standards. An individual's level of identification with his or her cultural group can vary greatly, from practically no identification to almost total identification. An individual Afro-American, Jewish American, or Jamaican in the United Kingdom may have a weak or a strong identification with his or her ethnic group.

Microcultural Groups and Individuals

Individuals are not just Black or White, male or female, or middle or working class. Even though we discuss variables such as race/ethnicity, gender, social class, and exceptionality (member of a special population, such as handicapped or gifted) as separate variables, individuals belong to these groups at the same time (see Figure 5.3). Each variable influences the behavior of individuals. The influence of these variables is rarely singular; they often interact to influence the behavior of individuals. Gilligan points out that women are less oriented toward individuation than are men. Afro-American culture tends to be more group oriented than is the mainstream U.S. culture. A reasonable hypothesis is that Afro-American women are even less oriented toward individuation than are White women.

Figure 5.4 illustrates how four major variables — race/ethnicity, gender, social class, and exceptionality — influence student behavior both singly and interactively. This figure also shows that many other variables, which are not identified, also simultaneously influence student behavior.

Multicultural Education: Nature and Limitations

Multicultural education suggests a type of education concerned with creating educational environments in which students from a variety of microcultural groups —

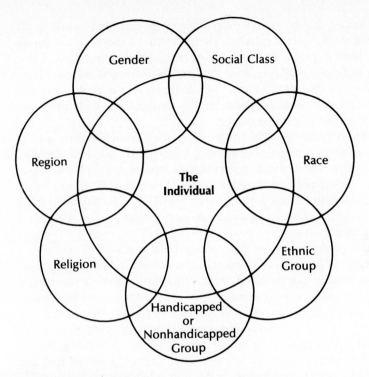

Figure 5.3. Individuals Belong to Many Different Microcultural Groups

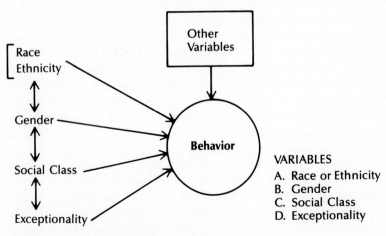

Figure 5.4. Multicultural Subvariants

such as race/ethnicity, gender, social class, regional groups, and handicapped persons—experience educational equality. The problems of these various groups are highlighted and compared. The total school environment is reformed so that it promotes respect and equity for a wide range of microcultural groups. Multicultural education, conceptualized in this way, is based on the assumption that such concepts as prejudice, discrimination, identity conflicts, and marginalization are common to diverse microcultural groups.

A generic focus within a school reform effort, such as multicultural education, can make a substantial contribution to the liberal education of students. However, school reform efforts should go beyond the level of multicultural education and focus on the unique problems that women, Blacks, handicapped people, and other victimized cultural groups experience in the United States and in other nations. Many problems these groups face are unique and require specialized analyses and strategies.

Multicultural education is a popular concept because it is often interpreted to mean combining the problems of ethnic minorities, women, and other groups. Public and school policies that are based primarily on this combining process will prove ineffective and perhaps detrimental to all of the groups concerned. Because of the unique problems of each ethnic and racial group, educational institutions should implement multiethnic education to complement and strengthen multicultural education. These concepts are complementary but not interchangeable.

Because multicultural education is a very broad and inclusive concept, and because it focuses on *cultural* differences, it is not an adequate concept to guide research and policy decisions on problems related to racial and ethnic minorities. It is not clear from the literature on multicultural education, for example, which groups constitute the target populations in multicultural educational reform. Multicultural education also does not deal adequately with the ways in which the needs of the various microcultural groups conflict, interact, and intersect.

Multicultural education theorists sometimes imply that cultural differences and cultural ethnocentrism are the major causes of intergroup tensions and conflicts. *However, racial problems are often more significant in intergroup relations than are cultural differences.* Multicultural education is a useful concept in that it enables the educational reformer to focus on a range of marginalized and victimized groups within society. This is the strength of the concept and is probably why it has so many educational advocates. However, it is not an adequate concept. We need other concepts related to multicultural education, such as race and ethnicity, to guide educational policy that will focus more directly on the unique problems and characteristics of particular groups in society.

Multicultural education provides a useful umbrella for the education of victimized groups within society. However, we need more specific concepts related to multicultural education to guide theory, research, and educational policy on specific groups such as ethnic groups and women. The concept of sexism, for example, is very important when dealing with women's issues just as the concepts of race and racism are important for the individual who is researching or designing educational policy for ethnic minorities.

The Nature of an Ethnic Group

An ethnic group is a microcultural group with several distinguishing characteristics. Social scientists do not completely agree on one definition of *ethnic group*. However, we can define an ethnic group as a group that shares a common ancestry, culture, history, tradition, and sense of peoplehood and that is a political and economic interest group. An ethnic group is primarily an involuntary group, although identification with the group may be optional.[18]

This definition suggests that Anglos in the United States and Australia, and the British and French in Canada, are ethnic groups. Pakistanis in the United Kingdom and Mexicans in the United States are *ethnic minority* groups, a specific type of ethnic group. Members of an ethnic minority group have unique physical and/or cultural characteristics that enable members of other groups to identify its members easily, often for purposes of discrimination.[19]

Ethnic Group: A Multidimensional Concept

The definition of an ethnic group just discussed suggests that all people in modernized, culturally pluralistic nation-states are members of ethnic groups. Within a modernized society, however, almost no individuals are totally "ethnic," since ethnic characteristics within a modernized society are mediated by technology, acculturation, the physical amalgamation of ethnic groups, and other aspects of modernization. Thus, the appropriate question to ask is not whether an individual is "ethnic," but to what extent he or she *is* ethnic.

Ethnic group membership is a multidimensional concept. The previous discussion and Figure 5.2 identify six major components of culture. These same major variables exist within an ethnic group, which is one type of microcultural group. These separate variables within an ethnic group, although highly interrelated, are conceptually distinct and can be identified. An individual's level of ethnic behavior and characteristics can be determined by ascertaining the extent to which he or she has behavior and characteristics that reflect these ethnic variables.

The Relationship between Physical Characteristics and Ethnic Behavior

It is very important to realize that ethnic behavior and characteristics should not be confused with an individual's biological characteristics and physical traits. It is true that a close relationship often exists between an individual's biological traits and his or her ethnic and cultural characteristics. In premodern societies, there was usually a 100 percent correlation between an individual's biological "ethnic" group and his or her cultural characteristics. This relationship exists to some extent today. Most Black Americans, for example, have some "Black" cultural characteristics.

However, some Black Americans have so few cultural traits that are "Black" and so little identification with Afro-Americans as an ethnic group that we might call them Afro-Saxons. This same situation exists for many highly assimilated and upwardly mobile members of ethnic groups such as Mexican Americans, Italian Australians, and Canadian Indians. Americans with an Italian surname may be so totally culturally assimilated in terms of their values, behaviors, and perceptions that they are culturally not Italian Americans but Anglo-Americans. An individual American who is one-eighth each German, Australian, Romanian, Algerian, Chilean, Scotch, Italian, and Korean ancestry, and whose parents did not provide any conscious ethnic influence, is not necessarily without an ethnic identification or ethnic behavior. He or she is most likely culturally an Anglo-American who has an identification with Anglo-Americans as an ethnic group. This identification with Anglo-Americans may be conscious or unconscious. Most frequently, this type of individual will have an unconscious identification with Anglo-Americans as an ethnic group and will offer a self-description as "merely an American."

The Variables of Ethnic Group Behavior

The six major variables of culture identified in Figure 5.2 can be used to conceptualize and determine the level of ethnic behavior of individuals or groups and the level of cross-cultural competency (see Table 5.1). Each of these variables can be conceptualized as existing on a continuum. Measurement techniques can be structured to determine the level of ethnic behavior and traits possessed by individual members of ethnic groups. This multidimensional conceptualization of ethnic behavior can help students understand that an individual may be highly ethnic linguistically but highly assimilated in terms of ethnic values and perspectives. This multidimensional conceptualization of ethnic group can also help students better understand the complex nature of ethnic group life in Western societies and to mitigate some of the serious and damaging misconceptions about ethnic groups pervasive within the schools and the larger society.

The last variable of ethnic group behavior identified in Table 5.1 is the individual's psychological identification with his or her ethnic group. This variable is called *ethnicity*. It is one of the most important variables of ethnic group behavior within a modernized society. In some cases, ethnicity may be the only significant variable of ethnic group behavior possessed by highly assimilated and upper-status members of ethnic groups within a modernized democratic society.

Multiethnic Education

Since an ethnic group is a unique kind of cultural group, multiethnic education is a specific form of multicultural education. Multiethnic education is concerned with modifying the total school environment so that it is more reflective of the

Table 5.1. Matrix for Conceptualizing and Assessing Cross-Cultural Behavior

Variables	*Understandings and Behavior*	*Levels of Competency*
		1 2 3 4 5 6 7
Values and Behavioral Styles	The ability to understand and interpret values and behavioral styles that are normative within the ethnic group.	◄─────────►
	The ability to express values behaviorally that are normative within the ethnic group.	
	The ability to express behavioral styles and nuances that are normative within the ethnic group.	
Languages and Dialects	The ability to understand, interpret, and speak the dialects and/or languages within the ethnic culture.	◄─────────►
Nonverbal Communications	The ability to understand and accurately interpret the nonverbal communications within the ethnic group.	◄─────────►
	The ability to communicate accurately nonverbally within the ethnic group.	
Cultural Cognitiveness	The ability to perceive and recognize the unique components of one's ethnic group that distinguishes it from other microcultural groups within the society and from the national macroculture.	◄─────────►
	The ability to take actions that indicate an awareness and knowledge of one's ethnic culture.	
Perspectives, World Views, and Frames of Reference	The ability to understand and interpret the perspectives, world views, and frames of reference normative within the ethnic group.	◄─────────►
	The ability to view events and situations from the perspectives, world views, and frames of reference normative within the ethnic group.	
Identification	The ability to have an identification with one's ethnic group that is subtle and/or unconscious.	◄─────────►
	The ability to take overt actions that show conscious identification with one's ethnic group.	

ethnic diversity within a society. This includes not only studying ethnic cultures and experiences but also making institutional changes within the school setting so that students from diverse ethnic groups receive equal educational opportunities and the school promotes and encourages the concept of ethnic diversity.

Multiethnic education is a generic concept that implies systemic school reform. Schools that wish to become multiethnic must undertake an institutional analysis to determine the degree to which they are assimilationist oriented and must take effective actions to create and sustain a pluralistic school environment. The staff's attitudes, the testing program, counseling, power relationships, and grouping practices are some of the variables that reflect ethnic diversity within multiethnic schools. (See Figure 3.4 in Chapter 3.)

Ethnic Studies

Ethnic studies can be defined as the scientific and humanistic study of the histories, cultures, and experiences of ethnic groups within a society. It includes but is not limited to a study of ethnic minority groups, such as Chinese Canadians, Australian Aborigines, British Jamaicans, and Afro-Americans. Ethnic studies refers primarily to the objectives, methods, and materials that make up the courses of study within schools and other educational institutions. It constitutes one essential component of multiethnic education. Since the 1960s, many attempts have been made in nations such as the United States, Canada, the United Kingdom, and Australia to infuse ethnic studies into school and university curricula.

The concept of ethnic studies suggests that a wide variety of ethnic groups are studied within a comparative framework. Students are helped to develop concepts, generalizations, and theories that they can use to better understand a range of human behavior. Modernized ethnic studies programs are not only comparative and conceptual but also are interdisciplinary and cut across subject matter lines. Thus, within a globally conceptualized ethnic studies program, teachers of the humanities, the communication arts, and the sciences incorporate ethnic content into the total curriculum. Ethnic content is not reserved for special days, occasions, or courses.

Even though specialized courses such as Black studies, Asian studies, and Canadian Indian studies can help attain specified curricular objectives, a major goal of curriculum reform should be to infuse ethnic content into the core or general curriculum that all students experience. Ethnic content should be for all students, not just for those who are members of ethnic minority groups.

Table 5.2 summarizes the focuses, objectives, and strategies of multicultural education, multiethnic education, and ethnic studies. Figure 5.5 illustrates how these concepts are related. Efforts to implement each of these ideas should be a major part of reform in schools, colleges, and universities in the Western nation-states.

Race as a Factor in Intergroup Problems

Multicultural education assumes that the intergroup problems in Western nation-states are primarily cultural rather than racial. Widespread cultural assimilation

Table 5.2. Programs and Practices Related to Pluralism

Program and Practice	Focus	Objectives	Strategies
Multicultural education	Cultural groups in a society	To help reduce discrimination against diverse cultural groups and provide them with equal educational opportunities To present all students with cultural alternatives	Creating a school atmosphere that has positive instititional norms toward diverse cultural groups within a nation-state
Multiethnic education	Ethnic groups within a society	To help reduce discrimination against victimized ethnic groups and to provide all students equal educational opportunities To help reduce ethnic isolation and encapsulation	Modifying the total school environment to make it more reflective of the ethnic diversity within a society
Ethnic studies	Ethnic groups within a society	To help students develop valid concepts, generalizations, and theories about ethnic groups in a society, to clarify their attitudes toward them, and to learn how to take action to eliminate racial and ethnic problems within a society To help students develop ethnic literacy	Modifying course objectives and teaching strategies, materials, and evaluation strategies so they include content and information about ethnic groups in a society

has taken place among ethnic minorities in nations such as the United States and Canada, especially among people who are upwardly mobile. Some research indicates that the values, goals, and aspirations of lower-class Afro-American youths are strikingly similar to those of middle-class Whites in the United States.[20] Thus, even though significant cultural differences exist between Anglo-Americans and most ethnic minorities in the United States, Anglo-Americans and ethnic minorities in the United States share many cultural characteristics. When cultural differences are minimized, conflict between non-White minorities and Whites frequently occurs. The cause of most of this conflict is often racial rather than cultural. Gordon seriously questions the extent of cultural pluralism in U.S. society:

> Structural pluralism . . . is the major key to the understanding of the ethnic makeup of American society, while cultural pluralism is the minor one. . . . The most salient fact . . . is the maintenance of structurally separate subsocieties of the three major religious and the racial and quasi-racial groups, and even vestiges of the nationality groups, along with a massive trend toward acculturation of all groups . . . to American culture patterns.[21]

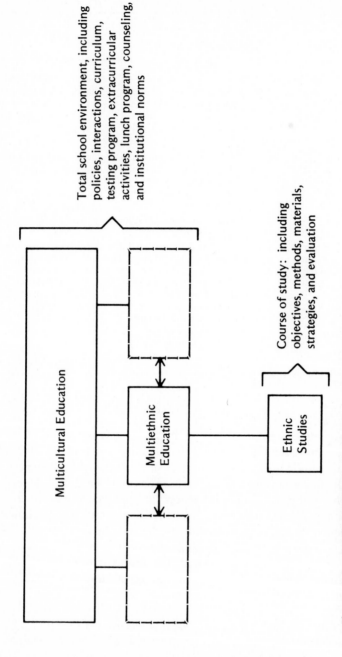

Total school environment, including policies, interactions, curriculum, testing program, extracurricular activities, lunch program, counseling, and institutional norms

Course of study: including objectives, methods, materials, strategies, and evaluation

Multicultural Education

Multiethnic Education

Ethnic Studies

Figure 5.5. The Relationships among Multicultural Education, Multiethnic Education, and Ethnic Studies

86

The cultural and ethnic differences among racial groups must be reflected in educational programs designed to reduce intergroup tension and to foster interracial understanding. Overemphasis on cultural differences and cultural pluralism, however, may divert attention from racial differences and hostility. We err seriously when we try to understand ethnic conflict in the schools by focusing exclusively on cultural differences between dominant ethnic groups and ethnic minorities. Racism and racial conflict were very evident in the late 1980s, not only in the United States, but also in other Western societies, such as the United Kingdom, Australia, and Canada.

If we develop educational programs and policies designed to make students more accepting of cultural differences but fail to deal seriously with problems caused by racial differences, we will not solve our basic intergroup problems. This is especially true because widespread cultural assimilation is taking place in Western societies, and thus cultural differences between ethnic minorities and dominant ethnic groups will probably be less significant in the future than they are today.

Education for Ethnic and Racial Diversity

Concepts and terms related to ethnicity are the most useful and appropriate for conceptualizing the problems related to the education of ethnic minorities. Most definitions of ethnicity focus on the culture and race of immigrants and immigrant descendant groups. We must concentrate on both variables when designing programs to reduce interethnic and interracial conflict. In his study of definitions of ethnicity, Isajiw found that culture was the second most frequently mentioned attribute of ethnicity, and race (and physical characteristics) was the fourth. Other frequently occurring attributes included common national or geographic origin, religion, language, sense of peoplehood, common values, separate institutions, and minority or subordinate status.[22] Gordon's definition of ethnic group highlights the importance of race: "When I use the term 'ethnic,' I shall mean by it any group which is defined or set off by race, religion, or national origin, or some combination of these categories. . . . However, all of these categories have a common social-psychological referent in that all of them serve to create, through historical circumstances, a sense of peoplehood."[23]

Both racial and cultural differences must be reflected in educational programs designed to reduce intergroup conflict and misunderstanding. Many of our efforts, however, most focus directly on reducing institutional, individual, and cultural racism,[24] since racial differences, and not more generalized cultural differences, are the causes of the most serious psychological problems that minority youths often experience in the schools,[25] and of racial conflict in Western Societies.

The relationship between racism and the rejection of the cultures of ethnic minorities by dominant groups must also be considered when formulating educational policy to reduce interethnic conflict. Racism is a major reason why many Whites perceive and evaluate the cultures of ethnic minority groups negatively. Intergroup problems frequently arise not because of the nature of the cultural differences between Whites and non-Whites, but because of the race of the individual or group who exhibits the specific cultural characteristics. The language of poor Blacks in the United States is often ridiculed, while the speech of White Bostonian Brahmins, which is as much a dialect as Black English, is frequently admired by Anglo-Americans. In the recent past, Mexican-American children were often prohibited from speaking Spanish in many schools in the Southwest.[26] However, when Spanish was spoken by Whites it was usually viewed as a useful and esteemed language. Gay has called this phenomenon "cultural racism":

> [Another] form of racism is that which involves the elevation of the White Anglo-Saxon Protestant cultural heritage to a position of superiority over the cultural experiences of ethnic minority groups. It involves elements of both institutional and individual racism. The idea that "White is right" prevails in this expression of racism. Only those values, attitudes, beliefs, traditions, customs, and mores ascribed to by Whites are considered acceptable and normal prescriptions of behavior. Anything else is labeled deviant, abnormal, degenerate, and pathological. If this belief were to remain in the realm of attitudes, it would be merely ethnocentrism. It becomes racism when Whites use power to perpetuate their cultural heritage and impose it upon others, while at the same time destroying the culture of ethnic minorities.[27]

Because we need to focus our attention on variables related to both race and culture, and the complex interactions and relationships between these two major variables, *ethnic and racial diversity* is a much better concept than is *multicultural education* to describe and guide research and policy efforts related to the education of ethnic minorities.

Reducing Racial Conflict

A number of basic issues and problems related to race, ethnicity, and education warrant immediate and decisive action. A top priority should be to implement programs and practices designed to modify the negative racial attitudes of students. Research indicates that children are aware of racial differences at an early age and often express negative racial attitudes.[28] Research further suggests that the racial attitudes of students tend to become more negative and crystallized as they grow older if deliberate efforts are not made to influence them.[29]

To modify the racial attitudes of students successfully, experiences designed to influence the racial feelings and perceptions of teachers must be implemented. The attitudes, behavior, and the perceptions of classroom teachers have a profound impact on the social atmosphere of the school and the attitudes of students. Teachers are even more important than the materials they use because the ways in which they present material highly influence how they are viewed by students.

Teachers must be strongly committed to a racially tolerant school atmosphere before such a setting can be created and maintained.

Unfortunately, research indicates that many teachers display negative attitudes and behavior toward minority students, especially those who are poor. Studies by Leacock, Rist, and Gay indicate that many teachers, in both subtle and overt ways, communicate negative feelings to their minority students and have a disproportionate number of negative verbal and nonverbal interactions with them.[30]

These types of studies suggest that teacher in-service training is essential if we are going to reduce institutional racism in the school setting. In-service training for teachers and other school personnel must have at least two major objectives: (1) to help teachers gain a new conceptualization of the history and culture of their societies and (2) to help them confront their own racial feelings, which can be a painful process, and if not handled competently, can be destructive, and unsettling. However, despite these risks, it is essential that teachers clarify their racial feelings before they can contribute positively to the reduction of racial prejudice in students and function effectively within a multiethnic setting.

The school can also help reduce cultural racism and ethnocentrism by maximizing the cultural options of mainstream youths and helping them break out of their ethnic encapsulations. These youths need to learn that there are other ways of being, of feeling, and of perceiving. Most individuals are socialized within ethnic enclaves where they learn one basic life-style. Consequently, they assume that their way is the only way, or that it is the only legitimate cultural style. Other life-styles seem strange, different, and exotic. Most ethnic minority individuals are forced to function within the dominant culture. However, many mainstream individuals are never required to function within other ethnic cultures. The school should provide all students with opportunities to become familiar with other races, life-styles, and cultures and should help young people develop *ethnic literacy* and become more sophisticated about other cultures. Most people are ignorant about ethnic cultures other than their own.

Mainstream youths should be taught that they have cultural options. We severely limit the potentiality of students when we merely teach them aspects of their own cultures. Anglo-American students should realize that using Black English is one effective way to communicate; that American Indians have values, beliefs, and life-styles that may be functional for them; and that alternative ways of behaving and of viewing the universe are practiced within the United States that they can freely embrace. By helping mainstream students view the world beyond their limited racial and ethnic perspectives, we will enrich them as human beings and enable them to live more productive and fulfilling lives.

Summary

A wide range of concepts are used to describe programs and practices related to ethnic, cultural, and racial diversity in Western societies. The proliferation of concepts in part reflects the ideological conflicts in multicultural education and the emergent status of educational reform related to ethnic and cultural diversity. Concepts related to multicultural and multiethnic education must be better clarified before pluralistic educational reforms and research can be more effectively designed and implemented.

This chapter examines the major concepts in the field, such as culture, multicultural education, multiethnic education, and ethnic studies. I have tried to clarify the meanings of these concepts and to describe their policy implications.

The issue and problems related to race and education are complex and difficult to diagnose and solve. Many variables influence the relationship between non-White ethnic minorities and Whites, such as socioeconomic status, ethnicity, values, languages, and behavioral patterns. Variables related to culture and ethnicity will remain important in explaining interactions between racial groups as long as the groups are socialized within different ethnic communities and have negative attitudes toward the cultural differences exhibited by other racial groups.

However, a focus on ethnic and cultural variables should not divert attention from the role of individual and institutional racism in Western societies. Racism is the basic cause of many of the serious psychological problems that ethnic minorities experience in the schools and also in the larger society. The interaction of race and culture also explains many interracial problems. Individuals and groups frequently respond negatively to specific cultural behaviors because they are exhibited by racially stigmatized ethnic minorities.

Effective educational policy and programs must be based on research and theory that focus on both race and culture and on the complex interactions between these two major variables, such as socioeconomic status. Programs that focus exclusively on cultural differences are not likely to lead to positive interracial interactions and understandings. An exclusively "culture" approach is also limited by the extensive degree to which cultural assimilation has taken place in Western societies. Race, however, cannot totally explain interethnic problems because significant cultural differences exist among some minority cultures and mainstream cultures in the various Western societies.

Because of the complexity of the problem, we need to examine multiple variables when trying to determine causes and to devise effective educational programs related to race and education. Further research and analyses are needed to clarify the relationship between culture and race in explaining interracial problems and conflict. Concepts related to race and ethnicity can best guide research and programmatic efforts related to the education of ethnic minority students.

Notes

1. Talcott Parsons, "Some Theoretical Considerations on the Nature and Trends of Change of Ethnicity," in Nathan Glazer and Daniel P. Moynihan, eds., *Ethnicity: Theory and Experience* (Cambridge, Mass.: Harvard University Press, 1975), pp. 53–83; Daniel

Bell, "Ethnicity and Social Change," in Glazer and Moynihan, eds., *Ethnicity*, pp. 141–174.

2. Peter Batelaan, *The Practice of Intercultural Education* (London: Commission For Racial Equality, 1983).

3. Carl A. Grant, guest ed., "Multicultural Education in the International Year of the Child: Problems and Possibilities," *Journal of Negro Education* 48 (Summer 1979); Donna M. Gollnick and Philip C. Chinn, *Multicultural Education in a Pluralistic Society*, 2nd ed. (Columbus, Ohio: Charles E. Merrill, 1986).

4. E. B. Taylor, *Primitive Culture*, vol. 1 (London: John Murray, 1871).

5. Muriel Dimen-Schein, *The Anthropological Imagination* (New York: McGraw-Hill, 1977).

6. Alfred L. Kroeber and Clyde Kluckhohn, *Culture: A Critical Review of Concepts and Definitions* (New York: Vintage Books, 1952), p. 161.

7. George A. Theodorson and Achilles G. Theodorson, *A Modern Dictionary of Sociology* (New York: Barnes and Noble, 1969), p. 95.

8. Dimen-Schein, *The Anthropological Imagination*, p. 23.

9. Ibid.

10. Brian M. Bullivant, *Pluralism: Cultural Maintenance and Evolution* (Clevedon, Avon, England: Multilingual Patterns Ltd., 1984), p. 4.

11. Carol Gilligan, *In a Different Voice: Psychological Theory and Women's Development* (Cambridge, Mass.: Harvard University Press, 1982).

12. Gunnar Myrdal, with Richard Sterner and Arnold Rose. *An American Dilemma: The Negro Problem and Modern Democracy* (New York: Harper and Row, 1944).

13. William Greenbaum, "America in Search of a New Ideal: An Essay on the Rise of Pluralism," *Harvard Educational Review* 44 (1974), pp. 411–444.

14. Manuel Ramírez III and Alfredo Castañeda, *Cultural Development, Bicognitive Development and Education* (New York: Academic Press, 1974).

15. Gilligan, *In a Different Voice*.

16. Susan U. Philips, *The Invisible Culture* (New York: Longman, 1983).

17. Gilligan, *In a Different Voice*.

18. James A. Banks, Carlos E. Cortés, Geneva Gay, Ricardo L. Garcia, and Anna S. Ochoa, *Curriculum Guidelines for Multiethnic Education* (Washington, D.C.: National Council for the Social Studies, 1976), pp. 9–10.

19. James A. Banks, *Teaching Strategies for Ethnic Studies*, 4th ed. (Boston: Allyn & Bacon, 1987), p. 19.

20. Charles A. Valentine, "Deficit, Difference, and Bicultural Models of Afro-American Behavior," *Harvard Educational Review* 41 (May 1971), pp. 137–157.

21. Milton M. Gordon, *Assimilation in American Life* (New York: Oxford University Press, 1964), p. 159.

22. Wsevolod W. Isajiw, "Definitions of Ethnicity," *Ethnicity* 1 (July 1974), p. 117.

23. Gordon, *Assimilation in American Life*, pp. 27–28.

24. Geneva Gay, "Racism in America: Imperatives for Teaching Ethnic Studies," in James A. Banks, ed., *Teaching Ethnic Studies: Concepts and Strategies* (Washington, D.C.: National Council for the Social Studies, 1973), pp. 31–34.

25. Kenneth B. Clark, *Prejudice and Your Child*, 2nd ed. (Boston: Beacon Press, 1963).

26. U.S. Commission on Civil Rights, *Toward Quality Education for Mexican Americans*. Report VI (Washington, D.C.: The Commission, 1974).

27. Gay, "Racism in America," p. 33.

28. Phyllis A. Katz, ed. *Towards the Elimination of Racism* (New York: Pergamon Press, Inc., 1976); David Milner, *Children and Race: Ten Years On* (London: Ward Lock Educational, 1983).

29. Mary Ellen Goodman, *Race Awareness in Young Children* (New York: Collier Books, 1964).

30. Eleanor B. Leacock, *Teaching and Learning in City Schools* (New York: Basic Books, 1969); Ray C. Rist, "Student Social Class and Teacher Expectations: The Self-Fulfilling Prophecy in Ghetto Education," *Harvard Educational Review* 40 (August 1970), pp. 411–451; Geneva Gay, "Differential Dyadic Interactions of Black and White Teachers with Black and White Pupils in Recently Desegregated Social Studies Classrooms: A Function of Teacher and Pupil Ethnicity" (Washington, D.C.: National Institute of Education, 1974).

6

Race, Ethnicity, and Educational Paradigms

The academic and social problems that lower-class and ethnic minority students experience in the schools have been discussed widely since the ethnic revival movements of the 1960s. The academic achievement of ethnic minority groups such as Japanese Americans and Chinese Americans exceeds that of Whites, but the academic achievement of most other minority groups in the United States is considerably below that of Whites. In 1980 the percentage of high school graduates for persons twenty-five years or older was 81.6 for Japanese Americans, 73.3 for Chinese Americans, 69.6 for Whites of non-Spanish origin, and 66.5 for all persons in the United States. However, the percentages for Mexican Americans, Puerto Ricans, and Afro-Americans were 37.6, 40.1, and 51.2, respectively.[1] Ethnic minority students in other Western nations, such as the West Indians in the United Kingdom and the Métis in Canada, also achieve below their mainstream peers.

A wide range of educational reforms designed to increase equality for students from diverse ethnic, racial, and social-class groups has been implemented since the 1960s. These various educational reforms have emanated from concepts, theories, and paradigms based on different and often conflicting assumptions, values, and goals. In this chapter I identify, describe, and critically analyze the major concepts and paradigms that have been used to explain the low academic achievement of ethnic, racial, and low-income students; the educational programs and practices that exemplify these concepts and paradigms; and their values and assumptions. I also describe how extensively single-factor paradigms are used to guide educational research and practice and what their limitations are and then briefly outline a multifactor, *holistic* theory of multicultural education that can be used to guide educational practice and research.

The Nature of Paradigms

Kuhn uses paradigm to describe the "entire constellation of beliefs, values, techniques, and so on shared by members of a given [scientific] community."[2] The laws, principles, explanations, and theories of a discipline are also part of its paradigm. Kuhn argues that during the history of a science, new paradigms arise to replace older ones. He calls this phenomenon a "scientific revolution." Kuhn refers primarily to natural science disciplines and draws most of his examples from the natural sciences. It is not clear, in the Kuhnian sense, whether social science has developed true paradigms because of the paucity of universal laws, principles, and theories in social science and because social science is characterized by many competing systems of explanations. Writes Kuhn, "It remains an open question what parts of social science have yet acquired such paradigms at all. History suggests that the road to a firm research consensus is extraordinarily arduous."[3]

Barnes, building on Kuhn's work, defines a paradigm as "an existing scientific achievement, a specific concrete *problem-solution* which has gained universal acceptance throughout a scientific field as a valid procedure, and as a model of valid procedure for pedagogic use."[4] He writes further,

> The culture of an established natural science is passed on in the form of paradigms. The central task of the teacher is to display them. The central task of the students is to assimilate them, and to acquire competence in their routine use. . . . *Scientific training . . . demands acceptance of the existing orthodoxy in a given field. Accordingly, it tends to avoid anything which might undermine or offer an alternative to that orthodoxy* [emphasis added]. The history of a field, wherein are found radically variant concepts, problems and methods of problem-solution, is either ignored, or is systematically rewritten as a kind of journey toward, and hence a legitimation of, present knowledge.[5]

Multicultural Education Paradigms

I am using *paradigm* in this chapter to describe an interrelated set of facts, concepts, generalizations, and theories that attempt to explain human behavior or social phenomena and that imply policy and action. A paradigm, which is also a set of explanations, has specific goals, assumptions, and values that can be described. Paradigms compete with one another in the arena of ideas and public policy.

The various problem-solutions or paradigms in multicultural education, like other systems of explanations, have many of the characteristics of paradigms discussed by Kuhn and Barnes, although they are *quasi* or *partial* paradigms in the Kuhnian sense. The *cultural deprivation*, *language*, and *radical* paradigms in multicultural education constitute constellations of beliefs, values, and techniques and are shared by members of a given scientific community. These conceptions are also problem-solutions that have gained acceptance as valid procedures and explanations.

Each paradigm, such as the cultural deprivation, the language, and the radical, demands acceptance of its orthodoxy and tends to avoid concepts, explanations, and theories that might offer an alternative view or explanation. Each paradigm is also a *partial* theory that provides an incomplete explanation of social reality.[6] *Each paradigm is perspectivistic and emanates from specific values, assumptions, and conceptions of the good society.* Paradigms both mirror and perpetuate specific ideologies and lead to different educational policies and practices. Some, such as the cultural deprivation and the genetic, support dominant ethnic group hegemony and inequality; others, such as the radical and racism, imply re-construction of the political and economic systems so that excluded ethnic and social class groups can experience equality.

Response Paradigms: The Schools React to Ethnic Revitalization Movements

When we examine the development of ethnic revitalization movements in West-ern democratic nations such as the United States, Canada, the United Kingdom, and Australia and the responses that educational institutions have made to them, we can identify and describe specific types and patterns of institutional responses. These patterns and prototypical responses are called *paradigms* in this chapter. These paradigmatic responses do not necessarily occur in a linear or set order in any particular nation, although some of them tend to occur earlier in the develop-ment of ethnic revitalization movements than do others. Thus, the response para-digms relate in a general way to the phases of ethnic revitalization movements described in Chapter 2. The ethnic additive and self-concept development para-digms, for example, tend to arise during the first or early phase of an ethnic revi-talization movement. Single-explanation paradigms tend to emerge before multiple explanation ones. Single-explanation paradigms usually emerge during the first phase of ethnic revitalization, but multiple-explanation paradigms usu-ally do not emerge or become popular until the later phase.

A sophisticated neoconservative paradigm tends to develop during the final phase of ethnic revitalization when the groups that are trying to institutionalize pluralism begin to experience success and those committed to assimilationism and to defending the status quo begin to fear that the pluralistic reformers might insti-tutionalize a new ideal and create new goals for the nation-state.

I will describe a number of response paradigms that develop when ethnic revitalization movements emerge (see Table 6.1). These multicultural education paradigms might develop within a nation at different times or they may co-exist at the same time. Each paradigm is likely to exist in some form in a nation that has experienced an ethnic revitalization movement. However, only one or two are likely to be dominant at any particular time. The leaders and advocates of particu-lar paradigms compete to make their paradigms the most popular in academic, government, and school settings. Proponents of paradigms that can attract the most government and private support are likely to become the prevailing voices for multicultural education within a particular time or period.

Sometimes one dominant paradigm replaces another, and something akin to what Kuhn calls a "scientific revolution" takes place.[7] However, what happens more frequently is that a new paradigm will emerge that challenges an older one but does not replace it. During the late 1960s in the United States, the cultural deprivation paradigm dominated the theory, research, and practice related to ed-ucating lower-income and minority groups.[8] This paradigm was seriously chal-

Table 6.1. Multicultural Education Paradigms

Paradigm	Major Assumptions	Major Goals	School Programs and Practices
Ethnic Additive	Ethnic content can be added to the curriculum without reconceptualizing or restructuring it.	To integrate the curriculum by adding special units, lessons, and ethnic holidays to it.	Special ethnic studies units; ethnic studies classes that focus on ethnic foods and holidays; units on ethnic heroes.
Self-Concept Development	Ethnic content can help increase the self-concept of ethnic minority students. Ethnic minority students have low self-concepts.	To increase the self-concepts and academic achievement of ethnic minority students.	Special units in ethnic studies that emphasize the contributions ethnic groups have made to the making of the nation; units on ethnic heroes.
Cultural Deprivation	Many poor and ethnic minority youths are socialized within homes and communities that prevent them from acquiring the cognitive skills and cultural characteristics needed to succeed in school.	To compensate for the cognitive deficits and dysfunctional cultural characteristics that many poor and ethnic minority youths bring to school.	Compensatory educational experiences that are behavioristic and intensive, e.g. Head Start and Follow Through programs in the United States.
Language	Ethnic and linguistic minority youths often achieve poorly in school because instruction is not conducted in their mother tongue.	To provide initial instruction in the child's mother tongue.	Teaching English as a Second Language programs; bilingual-bicultural education programs.
Racism	Racism is the major cause of the educational problems of non-White ethnic minority groups. The school can and should play a major role in eliminating institutional racism.	To reduce personal and institutional racism within the schools and the larger society.	Prejudice reduction; antiracist workshops and courses for teachers; antiracist lessons for students: an examination of the total environment to determine ways in which racism can be reduced, including curriculum materials, teacher attitudes, and school norms.
Radical	A major goal of the school is to educate students so they will willingly accept their social-class status in society. The school cannot help liberate victimized ethnic and cultural groups because it plays a key role in keeping them oppressed.	To raise the level of consciousness of students and teachers about the nature of capitalist, class-stratified societies; to help students and teachers develop a commitment to radical reform of the social and economic systems in capitalist societies.	

Table 6.1. (continued)

Paradigm	Major Assumptions	Major Goals	School Programs and Practices
	Lower-class ethnic groups cannot attain equality within a class-stratified capitalist society. Radical reform of the social structure is a prerequisite of equality for poor and minority students.		
Genetic	Lower-class and ethnic minority youths often achieve poorly in school because of their biological characteristics. Educational intervention programs cannot eliminate the achievement gap between these students and majority-group students because of their different genetic characteristics.	To create a meritocracy based on intellectual ability as measured by standardized aptitude tests.	Ability-grouped classes; use of IQ tests to determine career goals for students; different career ladders for students who score differently on standardized tests.
Cultural Pluralism	Schools should promote ethnic identifications and allegiances. Educational programs should reflect the characteristics of ethnic students.	To promote the maintenance of groups; to promote the liberation of ethnic groups; to educate ethnic students in a way that will not alienate them from their home cultures.	Ethnic studies courses that are ideologically based; ethnic schools that focus on the maintenance of ethnic cultures and traditions.
Cultural Difference	Minority youths have rich and diverse cultures that have values, languages, and behavioral styles that are functional for them and valuable for the nation-state.	To change the school so it respects and legitimizes the cultures of students from diverse ethnic groups and cultures.	Educational programs that reflect the learning styles of ethnic groups, that incorporate their cultures when developing instructional principles, and that integrate ethnic content into the mainstream curriculum.
Assimilationism	Ethnic minority youths should be freed of ethnic identifications and commitments so they can become full participants in the national culture. When schools foster ethnic commitments and identifications, this retards the academic growth of ethnic youths and contributes to the	To educate students in a way that will free them of their ethnic characteristics and enable them to acquire the values and behavior of the mainstream culture.	A number of educational programs are based on assimilationist assumptions and goals, such as cultural deprivation programs, most Teaching English as a Second Language programs, and the mainstream curriculum in most Western nations. Despite the challenges they received

Table 6.1. (continued)

Paradigm	Major Assumptions	Major Goals	School Programs and Practices
	development of ethnic tension and balkanization.		during the 1970s, the curricula in the Western nations are still dominated by assimilationist goals and ideologies.

lenged by the cultural difference paradigm in the 1970s.[9] The cultural difference paradigm did not replace the cultural deprivation paradigm; rather, the two paradigms co-existed. However, the cultural deprivation paradigm lost much of its influence and legitimacy, especially among young ethnic minority scholars.[10] The cultural deprivation paradigm experienced a renaissance in the early 1980s, when a neoconservative movement emerged in the United States.

The Ethnic Additive and Self-Concept Development Paradigms

Often the first phase of a school's response to an ethnic revitalization movement consists of the infusion of bits and pieces of content about ethnic groups into the curriculum, especially into courses in the humanities, the social studies, and the language arts. Teaching about ethnic heroes and celebrating ethnic holidays are salient characteristics of the ethnic additive paradigm.

This paradigm usually emerges as the first one for a variety of reasons. It develops in part because ethnic groups usually demand the inclusion of their heroes, holidays, and contributions into the curriculum during the first phase of ethnic revitalization. This paradigm also emerges because teachers usually have little knowledge about victimized ethnic groups during the early phase of ethnic revitalization. It is much easier for them to add isolated bits of information about ethnic groups to the curriculum and to celebrate ethnic holidays than meaningfully to integrate ethnic content into the curriculum. Thus, Black History Week, American Indian Day, and Asian and Afro-Caribbean feasts and festivals become a part of the curriculum.

The ethnic additive paradigm also arises early because educational institutions tend to respond to the first phase of ethnic revitalization with quickly conceptualized and hurriedly formulated programs that are designed primarily to silence ethnic protest rather than to contribute to equality and the structural inclusion of ethnic groups into society. In each of the major Western nations, many early programs related to ethnic groups were poorly conceptualized and implemented without careful and thoughtful planning. Such programs are usually attacked and eliminated during the later phases of ethnic revitalization, when the institutionalization of ethnic programs and reforms begins. The weaknesses of these early programs become the primary justification for their elimination. When such programs were attacked and eliminated in the United States in the 1980s, many careful and sensitive observers stated that they had been designed to fail.

Two other major goals educators express during the first phase of ethnic revitalization are to raise the self-concepts of ethnic minority youths and to increase their racial pride. These goals develop because leaders of ethnic movements try to shape new and positive ethnic identities and because educators assume that ethnic groups who have experienced discrimination and structural exclusion have negative self-concepts and negative attitudes toward their own racial and ethnic groups. Much of the social science research before the 1960s reinforced this belief;[11] some leaders of ethnic movements also express it. Many educators assume that students need healthy self-concepts in order to do well in school. They also assume that content about ethnic heroes and holidays will enhance the self-concepts and academic achievements of ethnic groups. Stone has described some of the serious limitations of the self-concept paradigm.[12]

Implications for School Practice

The ethnic additive and self-concept development paradigms often result in policies and school practices that require no fundamental changes in the views, assumptions, and institutional practices of teachers and administrators. These paradigms often lead to the trivialization of ethnic cultures by well-meaning teachers.[13] The emphasis is usually on the life-styles of ethnic groups rather than on reform of the social and political systems so that the opportunities and life-chances of poor and minority students can be substantially improved.

Policy that emanates from the ethnic additive and self-concept development paradigms often results in educators' doing little more than adding to the curriculum isolated bits of ethnic content designed to enhance the self-concepts of ethnic minority students. A fundamental rethinking of the total curriculum does not take place because the assumption is made that only ethnic minorities need to study ethnic content. Much of the ethnic studies curricula in the schools, especially during the early phase of ethnic revitalization movements, reflects the ethnic additive and self-concept development paradigms.

The Cultural Deprivation Paradigm

Cultural deprivation theories, programs, and research often develop during the first phase of an ethnic revitalization movement. Cultural deprivation theorists assume that lower-class youths do not achieve well in school because of family disorganization, poverty, and the lack of effective concept acquisition, and also because of other intellectual and cultural deficits these students experience during their first years of life. Cultural deprivation theorists assume that a major goal of school programs for the so-called "culturally deprived" children is to provide them with cultural and other experiences that will compensate for their cognitive and intellectual deficits. Cultural deprivation theorists believe that lower-class students can learn the basic skills taught by the schools but that these skills must often be taught using intensive, behaviorally oriented instruction.[14]

Program based on cultural deprivation theory, such as most of the compensatory education programs in the United States, are structured in such a way that they require students to make major changes in their behavior. Teachers and other educators are required to make few changes in their behavior or in educational institutions. Such programs also ignore the cultures that students bring to school and assume that poor and minority children are "culturally deprived" or "disadvantaged." Some of these programs in the United States have been able to help poor and minority youths experience achievement gains, but these gains are often not maintained as the students progress through the grades.

Implications for School Practice

Teachers and administrators who accept the cultural deprivations paradigm often blame the victims for their problems and academic failure.[15] These educators argue that lower-class and ethnic minority students often do poorly in school because of their cultural and social-class characteristics, not because they are ineffectively taught. They believe that the school is severely limited in what it can do to help these students to achieve because of the culture into which they are socialized.

School programs based on the cultural deprivation paradigm try to alienate students from their first cultures since these cultures are regarded as the primary reason students from specific cultural groups are not achieving well in school.[16] Students are forced to choose between commitment to their first cultures and educational success.

Educational programs and practices based on the cultural deprivation paradigm reflect and perpetuate the status quo and dominant group hegemony, ideology, and values. They do not question the extent to which dominant group values, assumptions, and societal practices keep lower-class and ethnic youths oppressed and prevent them from becoming empowered and structurally integrated into the mainstream society.

The Language Paradigm

Often during the early stage of ethnic revitalization or when a large number of immigrants settle in a nation and enroll in the schools, educators view the problems of these groups as resulting primarily from their language or dialect differences. When the West Indians and Asians first enrolled in British schools in significant numbers in the 1960s, many British educators believed that if they could solve the language problems of these youths they would experience academic success in British schools. British educators' early responses to the problems of immigrant children were thus almost exclusively related to language.[17] Special programs were set up to train teachers and to develop materials for teaching English as a second language to immigrant students. French educators also viewed the problems of the North African and Asian students in their schools in the late 1970s as primarily language-related.[18]

In the United States, the educational problems of Puerto Ricans and Mexican Americans are often assumed to be rooted in language. Proponents of bilingual education in the United States argued during the 1970s that if the language problems of these students were solved, the students would experience academic success in the schools. As bilingual programs were established in the United States, educators began to realize that many other factors, such as social class, learning styles, and motivation, were also important variables that influenced the academic achievement of Hispanic ethnic groups in the United States.

The experiences with programs based on the language paradigm in the Western nations teach us that an exclusive language approach to the educational problems of ethnic and immigrant groups is insufficient. Languages are integral parts of cultures. Consequently, any attempt to educate students effectively from diverse language and cultural groups must be comprehensive in scope and must focus on variables in the educational environment other than language. An exclusive language approach is unlikely to help language minority students attain educational parity with mainstream students.

The Racism Paradigm

Sometime early during an ethnic revitalization movement, ethnic minority groups and their liberal allies usually state that institutionalized racism is the only or most important cause of the problems of ethnic groups in school and society. This claim by ethnic minorities usually evokes a counterclaim by those who defend the status quo, and an intense debate ensues. This debate usually takes place during the first phase of ethnic revitalization, when ethnic polarization and tension are high. The debate between those who claim that racism is the cause of the problems of ethnic groups and those who deny this claim is usually not productive because each side sets forth extreme and competing claims.

A major goal of the racism advocates is not so much to convince other people that racism does, in fact, cause all of the problems of victimized ethnic groups. Rather, their goals are to legitimize racism as a valid explanation and to convince leaders and people who defend the status quo that racism is an important and tenacious part of Western societies. The debate between radical reformers and conservative defenders of the status quo remains stalemated and single-focused until the dominant group acknowledges the existence of racism and takes meaningful steps to eliminate it. Until this acknowledgment is made in official statements, policies, and actions, radical reformers will continue to state that racism is the single cause of the social, economic, and educational problems of victimized ethnic groups.

Radical reformers will not search for or find more complex paradigms that explain the problems of victimized ethnic groups until mainstream leaders acknowledge the existence of institutionalized racism. In other words, institutionalized racism must become legitimized as an explanation, and serious steps must be taken to eliminate it before an ethnic revitalization movement can reach a phase in which other paradigms will be accepted by radical reformers who articulate the interests of groups that are victims of institutionalized racism. Societies and nations are successful in making the racism paradigm less popular when official bodies and leaders validate it, acknowledge that racism exists in the society, and take visible and vigorous steps to eliminate it, such as enacting legislation that prevents discrimination and hiring minorities for influential jobs in the public and private sectors.

The Radical Paradigm

A radical paradigm tends to develop during the early or later stage of ethnic revitalization. It is usually reproductionist or neo-Marxist in orientation. The other paradigms assume that the school can successfully intervene and help ethnic minority youths attain social and political equality, but the radical paradigm assumes that the school is part of the problem and plays a key role in keeping ethnic groups oppressed. Thus, it is not possible for the school to help liberate oppressed groups because one of its central purposes is to educate students so that they will willingly accept their assigned status in society. A primary role of the school is to reproduce the social class structure.

The radical paradigm stresses the limited role that schools can play to eliminate racism and discrimination and to promote equality for low-income students. Christopher Jencks is an "ineffectiveness of school" theorist in the United States.[19] He argues that the most effective way to bring about equality for poor people is to equalize incomes directly rather than to rely on the schools to bring about equality in the adult life of students. He suggests that the schooling route is much too indirect and will most likely result in failure. Bowles and Gintis wrote a neo-Marxist critique of schools in the United States that copiously documents how schools reinforce the social class stratification within society and make students politically passive and content with their social-class status.[20]

The radical paradigm argues that multicultural education is a palliative to keep excluded and oppressed groups such as Blacks from rebelling against a system that promotes structural inequality and institutionalized racism. The radical critics contend that multicultural education does not deal with the real reasons that ethnic and racial groups are oppressed and victimized. It avoids any serious discussion of class, institutionalized racism, power, and capitalism. Multicultural education, argue the radical critics, diverts attention from the real problems and issues. They argue that we need to focus on the institutions and structures of society rather than on the characteristics of minority students and cultural differences.

Responding to the Radical Critics

Multicultural theorists need to study seriously the critics of the field, evaluate their arguments for soundness and validity, and incorporate their ideas that will contribute to the main goals of multicultural education. These goals include reforming the total school environment so that students from diverse racial, ethnic, and cultural groups will experience educational equality. Realistically, goals for multicultural education must be limited. Educators have little control over the wider society or over students when they leave the classroom. Educators can teach students the basic skills and help them to develop more democratic attitudes by creating school and classroom environments that promote cultural democracy. However, schools alone cannot eliminate racism and inequality in the wider society. They can reinforce democratic social and political movements that take place beyond the school walls and thus contribute in important ways to the elimination of institutional racism and structural inequality. The multicultural curriculum can give students keen insights into racism and inequality within their societies and thus help them develop a commitment to social change.

Multicultural theorists need to think seriously about the radical arguments that multicultural education is a palliative to contain ethnic rage and that it does not deal seriously with the structural inequalities in society and with such important concepts as racism, class, structural inequality, and capitalism. During the early stages of multicultural education in the United States, when it focused primarily on teaching the cultures and histories of non-White ethnic groups, the attention devoted to such concepts as racism and structural inequality was salient. Yet, as the ethnic studies movement expanded to include more and more ethnic groups and eventually to include feminist issues and other cultural groups, increasingly less attention was devoted to racism and to the analysis of power relationships. Gay has expressed concern about the wide boundaries of the field:

> Another potential threat to multiethnic education comes from within. Although any educational idea must grow and change if it is to stand the test of time, such growth must remain within reasonable boundaries and retain a certain degree of continuity. If many new dimensions are added to an idea too rapidly, the original idea may be distorted beyond recognition. This may be beginning to happen to multiethnic education.[21]

The radical critique of multicultural education should stimulate multicultural educators to devote more attention to such issues as racism, power relationships, and structural inequality. The radical writers are accurate when they argue that racism and structural inequality are the root cause of many problems of ethnic groups in modernized Western nations such as the United States and the United Kingdom. However, as Green perceptively points out, multicultural educators must live with the contradiction that they are trying to promote democratic and humane reforms within schools, which are institutions that often reflect and perpetuate some of the salient antidemocratic values pervasive within the wider society.[22] Green writes, "Contradiction is the essence of social change."[23]

The school itself is contradictory, since it often expounds democratic values while at the same time contradicting them. Thus, the radical scholars overstate their case when they argue that the schools merely perpetuate and reproduce the inequalities in society. The influence of the schools on individuals is neither as unidimensional nor as cogent as some radical critics claim. The school, both explicitly and implicitly, teaches both democratic and anti-egalitarian values, just as the wider society does. Thus, the schools, like the society of which they are a part, create the kind of moral dilemma for people that Gunnar Myrdal described when he studied U.S. race relations in the forties.[24] Myrdal believed that this moral dilemma made social change possible because most Americans felt a need to make the democratic ideals they inculcated and societal practices more consistent.

The Genetic Paradigm

The ideology and research developed by radical reformers do not go unchallenged. An ideological war takes place between radical reformers and conservatives who defend the status quo. While radical and liberal reformers develop ideology and research to show how the major problems of ethnic groups are caused by instititionalized racism and capitalism, anti-egalitarian advocates and researchers develop an ideology and research stating that the failure of ethnic groups in school and society is due to their own inherited or socialized characteristics.

Both radical reformers and conservative scholars tend to develop single-causal paradigms during the early phase of ethnic revitalization. The paradigms developed by radical theorists tend to focus on racism and other problems in society, and those developed by conservative researchers usually focus on the characteristics of ethnic students themselves, such as their genetic characteristics and their family socialization.

In the United States the most popular anti-egalitarian theories focus on the genetic characteristics of Black and poor students; these theories were developed by such researchers as Jensen, Shockley, and Herrnstein.[25] Jensen argues that the genetic makeup of Blacks is the most important reason that compensatory educational programs, designed to increase the IQ of Black students, have not been more successful. Shockley developed a theory about the genetic inferiority of Blacks that is less accepted by the academic community than is Jensen's. Herrnstein published his controversial article, which argued that social class reflects genetic differences, in the *Atlantic Monthly*, a widely circulated and highly respected popular magazine. Herrnstein's views evoked more controversy than did Jensen's, perhaps because he argued that social class rather than race was related to heredity. Educators not committed to educational equality for lower-class and ethnic minority students often embrace the genetic paradigm. They use it as an alibi for educational neglect.

Implications for School Practice

The assumption that IQ and other tests of mental ability can accurately measure innate mental ability is institutionalized and perpetuated within the schools. Students are assigned to academic tracks based on their performance on tests of mental ability and on other factors such as teacher recommendations and grades. A highly disproportionate number of lower-class and ethnic minority students are assigned to lower-ability tracks. Assignment to lower academic tracks actualizes the self-fulfilling prophecy.[26] Research by Oakes documents how teacher expectations of students vary in different kinds of tracks.[27] Students in higher academic tracks are expected to learn more and are consequently taught more; those in lower tracks are expected to learn less and are consequently taught less.

The tracking system, which is widespread within U.S. schools, perpetuates social class and ethnic inequality and teaches students to be content with their social class status. The genetic paradigm is used to support and justify the tracking system. It perpetuates dominant ethnic group hegemony, inequality, and class and ethnic stratification.

Competing Paradigms

Particularly during the later stage of ethnic revitalization, when aspects of ethnic diversity are being implemented within the schools, an intense clash of ideologies and paradigms is likely to occur between people committed to ethnic pluralism and people who endorse assimilationism and are committed to preserving the status quo. The language paradigm (which often includes a call for bilingual education), the racism paradigm, and the radical paradigm are especially likely to evoke strong responses from assimilationists who are committed to nationalism and to developing strong national commitments and identifications. In the United States, the call for bilingual education and the federal legislation and court decisions that promoted it stimulated one of the most acid educational debates in recent history.

A cultural pluralism paradigm tends to emerge during the first phase of ethnic revitalization. It maintains that a major goal of the schools should be to help students develop commitments and attachments to their ethnic groups so they can participate in its liberation. Cultural pluralists believe that ethnicity and ethnic cultures have a significant influence on the socialization of students and thus should strongly influence the formulation of educational policies and programs.

As the ethnic revitalization movement develops, more moderate paradigms emerge, such as the cultural difference and bicultural paradigms. The cultural difference paradigm maintains that ethnic minority youths often do not achieve well in school not because they have a deprived culture, but because their cultures are different from the culture of the school. The school should therefore modify the educational environment in order to make it more consistent with the cultures of ethnic minority youths. If this is done, the students will experience academic gains in the school.

Assmilationists often oppose such pluralist programs as bilingual education and ethnic studies because, they argue, these programs prevent students from learning the skills needed to become effective citizens of the nation-state and from developing strong national loyalties. They also argue that pluralist educational programs promote ethnic attachments and loyalties that contribute to ethnic conflict, polarization, and stratification. Assimilationists maintain that the primary goal of the school should be to socialize students so that they attain the knowledge, attitudes, and skills needed to become effective citizens of their nation-states. During the final phases of ethnic revitalization, assimilationist paradigms tend to become increasingly conservative. In the United States during the 1980s assimilationism developed into a neoconservative ideology that was strongly nationalistic and reactionary.[28]

The Need for a Multifactor Paradigm and Holism

The field of multicultural education is replete with single-factor paradigms that attempt to explain why lower-class and minority students often achieve poorly in school. Proponents of these paradigms often become ardent in their views, insisting that one major variable explains the problem of minority students and that their educational problems can be solved if major policies are implemented related to a specific explanation or paradigm. Many existing reforms in multicultural education, such as compensatory education and bilingual programs, are based on single-factor paradigms. Proponents of the ethnic additive and self-concept development paradigms believe that ethnic content and heroes can help minority students increase their academic achievement; cultural deprivation proponents view cultural enrichment as the most important variable influencing academic achievement; radical scholars often view the school as having little possibility of significantly influencing the life-chances of poor and minority students.

Experiences in the major Western nations since the late 1960s teach us that the academic achievement problems of ethnic minority students are too complex to be solved with reforms based on single-factor paradigms and explanations.[29] Education is broader than schooling, and many problems that ethnic minority students experience in the schools reflect the problems in the wider society. The radical critique of schooling is useful because it helps us see the limitations of formal schooling. However, the radical paradigm is limited because it gives us few concrete guidelines about what can be done after we have acknowledged that schools are limited in their ability to bring about equality for poor and minority students.

When designing reform strategies, we must be keenly sensitive to the limitations of formal schooling. However, we must also be tenacious in our faith that the school can play a limited but cogent role in bringing about equal educational opportunities for poor and minority students and in helping all students develop cross-cultural understandings and competencies. To design school programs that will effectively help ethnic minority youths increase their academic achievement and help all students develop ethnic literacy and cross-cultural competency, we must conceptualize the school as a system in which all major variables and components are highly interrelated. *A holistic paradigm, which conceptualizes the school as an interrelated whole, is needed to guide educational reform.* Viewing the school as a social system can help us derive an idea of school reform that can help minority students increase their academic achievement and help all students develop more democratic attitudes and values. Although our theory and research about multicultural education is limited and developing, both research and theory indicate that educators can successfully intervene to help students increase their academic achievement and develop more democratic attitudes and values.[30]

Conceptualizing the school as a social system suggests that we must formulate and initiate a change strategy that reforms the total school environment in order to implement multicultural education successfully. Reforming any one variable, such as curriculum materials and the formal curriculum, is necessary but not sufficient. Multiethnic and sensitive teaching materials are ineffective in the hands of teachers who have negative attitudes toward different ethnic and cultural groups. Such teachers are not likely to use multiethnic materials or to use them in a detrimental way when they do. Thus, helping teachers and other members of the school staff develop democratic attitudes and values is essential when implementing multicultural programs and experiences.

When formulating plans for multicultural education, educators should conceptualize the school as a microculture that has norms, values, roles, statuses, and goals like other cultural systems. The school has a dominant culture and a variety of subcultures. Almost all classrooms in Western societies are multicultural because White students, as well as Black and Brown students, are socialized within diverse cultures. Teachers in schools in Western societies also come from many different ethnic groups and cultures. Although they may be forgotten and repressed, many teachers were socialized in cultures other than the mainstream one. The school is a microculture in which the cultures of students and teachers meet. *The school should be a cultural environment in which acculturation takes place: both teachers and students should assimilate some of the views, perceptions, and ethos of each other as they interact* (see Figure 6.1). Both teachers and students will be enriched by this process, and the academic achievement of students from diverse

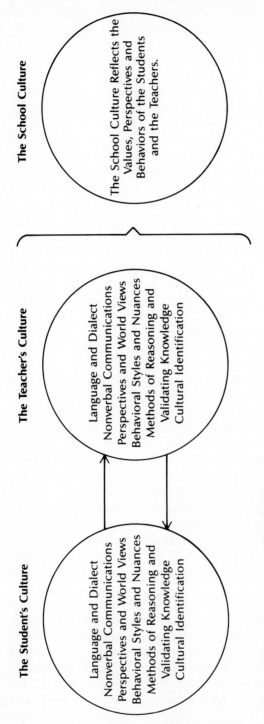

The Student's Culture

Language and Dialect
Nonverbal Communications
Perspectives and World Views
Behavioral Styles and Nuances
Methods of Reasoning and
Validating Knowledge
Cultural Identification

The Teacher's Culture

Language and Dialect
Nonverbal Communications
Perspectives and World Views
Behavioral Styles and Nuances
Methods of Reasoning and
Validating Knowledge
Cultural Identification

The School Culture

The School Culture Reflects the
Values, Perspectives and
Behaviors of the Students
and the Teachers.

Figure 6.1. Acculturation as a School Goal
When the student assimilates elements of the teacher's culture and the teacher assimilates elements of the student's
culture, the school culture becomes a synthesized cultural
system that reflects the cultures of all of its participants.

cultures will be enhanced because their cosmos and ethos will be reflected and legitimized in the school.

Historically, schools in Western societies have had assimilation rather than acculturation as their major goal. The students were expected to acquire the dominant culture of the school and society, but the school neither legitimized nor assimilated parts of the student's culture. Assimilation and acculturation are different in important ways. Assimilation involves the complete elimination of cultural differences and differentiating group identifications. When acculturation occurs, a culture is modified through contact with one or more other cultures but maintains its essence.[31]

Both acculturation and accommodation should take place in today's schools in Western democratic societies. *When accommodation occurs, groups with diverse cultures maintain their separate identities but live in peaceful interaction.* However, in order for successful accommodation to take place, various ethnic and cultural groups must have equal status and share power. It is essential that schools in Western democracies acculturate students rather than foster tight ethnic boundaries because all students, including ethnic minority students, must develop the knowledge, attitudes, and skills needed to become successful citizens of their cultural communities, their nation-states, and the global world community.

Summary

The achievement of most ethnic minority students is far below that of mainstream students in the major Western nations, such as the United States, Canada, the United Kingdom, and Australia. Groups such as Mexicans in the United States, Indians and Métis in Canada, Jamaicans in the United Kingdom, and the Australian Aborigines have academic achievement scores far below those of dominant mainstream groups in their societies. Since the ethnic revival movements emerged in the 1960s, a number of explanations have been formulated to posit why the academic achievement of these students is below that of their mainstream peers. The various explanations—called paradigms in this chapter—have been formulated at different times in the various Western nations. These paradigms are based on different assumptions and values and imply disparate policy, action, and educational programs.

This chapter describes ten major paradigms: ethnic additive, self-concept development, cultural deprivation, language, racism, radical, genetic, cultural pluralism, cultural difference, and assimilationism. Single-factor paradigms dominate the field of multicultural education. However, multifactor paradigms must be used to guide educational reform and practice if educational institutions are to promote equality and help all students develop the knowledge, attitudes, and skills needed to function effectively in a culturally diverse society and world.

Notes

1. U.S. Bureau of the Census, Census of Population, *General Social and Economic Characterics*, Part 1, *United States Summary* (Washington, D.C.: U.S. Government Printing Office, 1983), PC80-1-C1.

2. Thomas S. Kuhn, *The Structure of Scientific Revolutions*, 2nd ed. enlarged (Chicago: University of Chicago Press, 1970).

3. Ibid., p. 15.

4. Barry Barnes, *T. S. Kuhn and Social Science* (New York: Columbia University Press, 1982), p. 17.

5. Ibid., pp. 18–19.

6. Robert K. Merton, *Social Theory and Social Structure*, enlarged ed. (New York: The Free Press, 1968).

7. Kuhn, *The Structure of Scientific Revolutions*.

8. Carl Bereiter and Sigfried Engelmann, *Teaching Disadvantaged Children in the Preschool* (Englewood Cliffs, N.J.: Prentice-Hall, 1966).

9. Stephan S. Baratz and Joan C. Baratz, "Early Childhood Intervention: The Social Science Base of Institutional Racism," *Harvard Educational Review* 40 (1970), pp. 29–50.

10. James A. Banks, "Values, Ethnicity, Social Science Research, and Educational Policy," in *The Humanities in Precollegiate Education*, Benjamin Ladner, ed., *Eighty-third Yearbook of the National Society for the Study of Education*, Part II (Chicago: University of Chicago Press, 1984), pp. 91–111.

11. Kenneth B. Clark, *Prejudice and Your Child* (Boston: Beacon Press, 1963).

12. Maureen Stone, *The Education of the Black Child in Britain: The Myth of Multiracial Education* (Glasgow: Fontana, 1981).

13. Kogila A. Moodley, "Canadian Multicultural Education: Promises and Practice," in *Multicultural Education in Western Societies*, James A. Banks and James Lynch, eds., (New York: Praeger, 1986), pp. 51–75.

14. Bereiter and Engelmann, *Teaching Disadvantaged Children*.

15. William Ryan, *Blaming the Victim* (New York: Vintage Books, 1971).

16. Mildred Dickeman, "Teaching Cultural Pluralism," in *Teaching Ethnic Studies: Concepts and Strategies*, James A. Banks, ed. (Washington, D.C.: National Council for the Social Studies, 1973), pp. 5–25.

17. Schools Council Working Paper 29, *Teaching English to West Indian Children: The Research Stage of the Project* (London: Evans Brothers, 1970).

18. James A. Banks, "Multiethnic Education across Cultures: United States, Mexico, Puerto Rico, France, and Great Britain," *Social Education* 42 (1978), pp. 177–185.

19. Christopher Jencks et al., *Inequality: A Reassessment of the Effect of Family and Schooling in America* (New York: Basic Books, 1972).

20. Samuel Bowles and Herbert Gintis, *Schooling in Capitalist America* (New York: Basic Books, 1967).

21. Geneva Gay, "Multiethnic Education: Historical Developments and Future Prospects," *Phi Delta Kappan* 64 (April 1983), pp. 560–563.

22. Andy Green, "In Defense of Anti-racist Teaching: A Reply to Recent Critiques of Multicultural Education," *Multiracial Education* 20 (Spring 1982), p. 34.

23. Ibid.

24. Gunnar Myrdal, *An American Dilemma: The Negro Problem and Modern Democracy* (New York: Harper & Row, 1944).

25. Arthur R. Jensen, "How Much Can We Boost IQ and Scholastic Achievement?" *Harvard Educational Review* 39 (Winter 1969), pp. 1–123; William Shockley, "Dysgenics, Geneticity, Raceology: A Challenge to the Intellectual Responsibility of Educators," *Phi Delta Kappan* 53 (January 1972), pp. 297–307; Richard J. Herrnstein, "I.Q.," *Atlantic Monthly* 43 (September 1971), p. 64.

26. Robert Merton, *Social Theory and Social Structure.*

27. Jennie Oakes, *Keeping Track: How Schools Structure Inequality* (New Haven, Conn.: Yale University Press, 1985).

28. Peter Steinfels, *The Neoconservatives: The Men Who Are Changing America's Politics* (New York: Simon & Schuster, 1979).

29. James A. Banks and James Lynch, eds., *Multicultural Education in Western Societies* (New York: Praeger, 1986).

30. Meyer Weinberg, *Minority Students: A Research Appraisal* (Washington, D.C.: U.S. Government Printing Office, 1977); Phyllis A. Katz, ed., *Towards the Elimination of Racism* (New York: Pergamon Press, 1976).

31. George A. Theodorson and Achilles G. Theodorson, *A Modern Dictionary of Sociology* (New York: Barnes and Noble, 1969).

PART III

Philosophical Issues

The chapters in Part III describe and clarify the major philosophical issues and concepts related to education and ethnic diversity. Educators and social scientists with divergent and conflicting ideological positions are recommending a range of educational programs and practices.

Chapter 7 presents a typology for classifying ideologies related to ethnicity and schooling and proposes a multiethnic ideology to guide educational reform in schools, colleges, and universities. The multiethnic ideology is derived by analyzing the nature of ethnic group relations in a modernized democratic society—the United States—and by conceptualizing goals that will enhance cross-cultural competency and interaction. Chapter 8 describes philosophical issues related to citizenship education in pluralistic nation-states. It discusses the complex relationship between ethnic and national commitments and ways to help ethnic students become effective and reflective citizens within a modernized democratic nation-state.

Part III

Philosophical Issues

7

Pluralism, Ideology, and Educational Reform

Since the 1960s, educational institutions throughout the United States and other Western nations have implemented a variety of programs and projects related to ethnic and cultural diversity. Many of these programs and practices lack clear goals, definitions, and effective staff development components. Some problems in multiethnic education result from conceptual ambiguity and ideological polarization. A number of important questions concerning the relationship between educational institutions and ethnicity have not been satisfactorily clarified or resolved. These questions must be better clarified and resolved before we can design and implement more effective and justifiable educational programs related to ethnic diversity in Western societies.

One key question relates to the proper role of public institutions such as the common school in the area of ethnicity. Should the common schools promote, remain neutral to, or ignore the ethnic characteristics of its students and the ethnic diversity within a society? Many educational leaders believe that the school should not ignore ethnicity and should implement curricular reforms related to ethnic diversity. However, little agreement exists about what kinds of reforms should be initiated and how they can best be implemented.

Views on ethnicity and the schools range from beliefs that ethnicity should be an integral and salient part of the school curriculum to cautions that too much emphasis on ethnicity in the schools might be inimical to the shared national culture and might promote divisiveness in society.[1] Views on ethnicity and the schools reflect divergent ideologies and have conflicting policy and programmatic implications. These ideologies and their implications for educational policy merit careful examination and discussion.

I identify two major ideological positions related to race and ethnic diversity that are evident in most theoretical discussions on ethnicity and pluralism in the major Western nation-states such as the United States, the United Kingdom, Canada, Australia, and the Netherlands.[2] The major assumptions and arguments of these positions is discussed and their limitations as guides to educational reform are identified. I then describe an eclectic ideological position that reflects both major ideologies and argue that it can best guide educational policy and reform. The final part of this chapter discusses the implications of this eclectic ideology — called the *multiethnic ideology* — for educational policy and practice.

It is very important for the reader to realize that the ideological positions identified and described are ideal types in the Weberian sense. The two major positions in their ideal forms do not accurately describe the views of any particular writer or theorist. However, various views on ethnicity and pluralism can be roughly classified using a continuum that has the two ideologies, in their ideal forms, at the extreme ends.

The two major positions are the *cultural pluralist* ideology and the *assimilationist* ideology. I am not the first observer to structure a typology related to ideologies and theories of ethnic diversity in Westernized societies. Gordon classifies theories of assimilation into three major categories: Anglo-conformity, the melting pot, and cultural pluralism.[3] Higham also identifies three ideologies: integrationist, pluralist, and pluralistic integrationist.[4] These two typologies as well as the one presented here are in some ways similar, but they are different conceptualizations.

The Cultural Pluralist Ideology

The cultural pluralist ideology has been formulated in different societies and takes various forms.[5] The pluralist makes various assumptions about the nature of pluralistic democratic societies, the function of the ethnic group in socializing the individual, and the responsibility that the individual member of a presumed oppressed ethnic group has to the liberation struggle of that group. The pluralist also makes certain assumptions about research, learning, teacher training, and the proper goals of the school curriculum.

The pluralist argues that ethnicity and ethnic identities are very important in pluralistic Western societies. Western nation-states, according to the pluralist, consist of competing ethnic groups, each of which champions its own economic and political interests. It is extremely important, argues the pluralist, for individuals to develop a commitment to their ethnic group, especially if that ethnic group is oppressed by more powerful ethnic groups within society. The energies and skills of each member of an ethnic group are needed to help in that group's liberation struggle. Each individual member of an ethnic group has a moral obligation to join the liberation struggle. Thus, the pluralist stresses the rights of the ethnic group over the rights of the individual. The pluralist also assumes that an ethnic group can attain inclusion in and full participation within a society only when it can bargain from a powerful position and when it has closed ranks within.[6]

The pluralist views the ethnic group as extremely important in the socialization of the individual within a highly modernized society. It is within their own particular ethnic groups that individuals develop their languages, life-styles, and values and experience important primary group relationships and attachments. The ethnic community also serves as a supportive environment for individuals and helps to protect them from the harshness and discrimination they might experience in the wider society. The ethnic group thus provides individuals with a sense of identity and psychological support, both of which are extremely important within a highly modernized society controlled primarily by one dominant ethnic group. The pluralist views the ethnic group as important and believes that public institutions such as the school should actively promote the interests of the various ethnic groups in its policies and in the curriculum.

The pluralist makes assumptions about research that differ from those made by the assimilationist. The pluralist assumes that ethnic minority cultures in Western societies are not disadvantaged, deviant, or deficient; rather, they are well-ordered and highly structured but *different* from each other and from the mainstream, dominant culture. Thus, the pluralist uses a culture difference model when researching ethnic groups, whereas the assimilationist researcher uses a deficit model or a genetic model[7] (see Chapter 6). Because of their different research assumptions, the cultural pluralist researcher and the assimilationist researcher frequently derive different, and often conflicting, research conclusions. Several researchers have used the cultural difference model extensively in their research studies on ethnic groups and have done a great deal to legitimize it within the social science and educational communities.[8]

The cultural pluralist also assumes that ethnic minorities have unique learning styles and that the school curriculum and teaching strategies should be revised to be more consistent with the cognitive and learning life-styles of ethnic group students. Ramìrez and Castañeda have written insightfully about the unique learning styles of Mexican-American youths.[9] Research summarized by Stodolsky and Lesser also supports the notion that the cognitive styles among ethic groups sometimes differ.[10]

Pluralists, because of their assumptions about the importance of the ethnic group in the lives of students, believe the curriculum should be drastically revised to reflect the cognitive styles, cultural history, and present experiences and aspirations of ethnic groups, especially the visible minorities. The cultural pluralist believes that if the school curriculum were more consistent with the experiences of ethnic groups, the learning and adjustment problems minority students experience in the schools would be greatly reduced. Thus, the cultural pluralist argues that learning materials should be culture-specific and that the major goal of the curriculum should be to help the students function more successfully within their own ethnic culture. The curriculum should be structured to stress events from the points of view of the specific ethnic groups. The curriculum should promote ethnic attachments and allegiances and help students gain the skills and commitments that will enable them to help their ethnic group gain power and exercise it within the larger civic culture.

The Assimilationist Ideology

The assimilationist feels that the pluralist greatly exaggerates the extent of the cultural differences within Western societies. However, the assimilationist does not deny that ethnic differences exist within Western societies or that ethnicity is very important to some groups. However, the assimilationist and the pluralist interpret ethnicity in Western societies quite differently. The assimilationist tends to see ethnicity and ethnic attachments as fleeting and temporary within an increasingly modernized world. Ethnicity, argues the assimilationist, wanes or disappears under the impact of modernization and industrialization. The assimilationist believes that ethnicity is more important in developing societies than in highly modernized societies and that it crumbles under the forces of modernization and democratization. The assimilationist sees the modernized state as being universalistic rather than characterized by strong ethnic allegiances and attachments.[11]

Not only do the assimilationists view ethnicity as somewhat noncharacteristic of modernized societies, but they also believe that strong ethnic attachments are rather dysfunctional within a modernized state. Assimilationists believe that the ethnic group promotes group rights over the rights of the individual and that the individual must be freed of ethnic attachments in order to have choices within society. The assimilationist also views ethnicity as a force inimical to the goals of a democratic society. Ethnicity, argues the assimilationist, promotes divisions, exhumes ethnic conflicts, and leads to the Balkanization of society. The assimilationist sees integration as a societal goal in a modernized state and not ethnic segregation and separatism.

The assimilationist believes that the best way to promote the goals of society and to develop commitments to democratic ideals is to promote the full socialization of all individuals and groups into the shared culture. Every society, argues the assimilationist, has national values, ideologies, and norms to which each member of society must develop commitments if it is to function successfully and smoothly. In the United States, these values are embodied in the American Creed and in such documents as the United States Constitution and the Declaration of Independence. Each society also has a set of common skills and abilities that every successful member of society should master. In the United States these skills include speaking and writing the English language.

The primary goal of the common school, like other publicly supported institutions, should be to socialize individuals into the common culture and enable them to function more successfully within it. At best, the school should take a position of benign neutrality in matters related to the ethnic attachments of its students.[12] If ethnicity and ethnic attachments are to be promoted, this should be done by private institutions like the church, the community club, and the private school.

The Assimilationist Ideology and Education

Like the cultural pluralists, the assimilationists make assumptions about research related to minorities. Their conclusions reflect their assumptions. Assimilationists usually assume that microcultural groups with characteristics that cause its members to function unsuccessfully in the common culture are deficient, deprived, and pathological and lack needed functional characteristics. Researchers who embrace an assimilationist ideology usually use the genetic or the social pathology research model when studying ethnic minorities.[13]

The assimilationist learning theorist assumes that learning styles are rather universal across cultures (such as the stages of cognitive development identified by Piaget) and that certain socialization practices, such as those exemplified among middle-class Anglo-Americans, enhance learning, whereas other early socialization practices, such as those found within most lower-class ethnic groups, retard children's ability to conceptualize and to develop the verbal and cognitive abilities. Consequently, assimilationist learning theorists often recommend that ethnic minority youths from lower-class homes enter compensatory educational programs at increasingly early ages. Some theorists have suggested that these youths should be placed in a middle-class educational environment shortly after birth.[14]

The assimilationist believes that curriculum materials and teaching styles should relate primarily to the common culture. Emphasis should be on the shared culture within the nation-state because all citizens must learn to participate in a common culture that requires universal skills and competencies. Emphasis on cultural and ethnic differences might promote societal polarization and fail to facilitate socialization into the shared civic culture of the nation-state. The school's primary mission within a democratic society should be to socialize youths into the national civic culture.

The curriculum should stress the commonality of the heritage all people share in the nation-state. It should also help students develop a commitment to the common culture and the skills to participate in social action designed to make the practices in a society more consistent with its professed ideologies. The school should develop within youths a critical acceptance of the goals, assumptions, and possibilities of democratic nation-states.

Attacks on the Assimilationist Ideology

Chapter 1 discussed how the assimilationist ideology has historically dominated U.S. intellectual and social thought. In other Western societies such as Australia and Canada, social and public policy has also been most heavily influenced historically by the assimilationist ideology. Multicultural educational policies were not developed in Canada and Australia until the 1970s. The United States still does not have an official multicultural policy, although a number of legal cases and some federal legislation directly or indirectly support education related to cultural and ethnic diversity.

In the United States near the turn of the century, writers such as Horace Kallen, Randolph Bourne, and Julius Drachsler set forth the concepts of cultural pluralism and cultural democracy, thereby challenging assimilationist policies and practices.[15] When the ethnic revival movements emerged in the various Western societies in the 1960s and 1970s the assimilationist ideology experienced one of its most serious challenges in the history of Western nation-states.

Since the 1960s in the various Western nation-states, both ethnic minority and liberal White scholars and researchers have attacked the assimilationist ideology and the practices associated with it.[16] The rejection of the assimilationist ideology by ethnic minority intellectuals and leaders is historically very significant. This rejection represents a major break from tradition within ethnic groups, as Glazer observes.[17] Traditionally, most intellectuals and social activists, particularly in the United States, have supported assimilationist policies and regarded acculturation as a requisite for full societal participation. Historically, there have been a few staunch separatists among Afro-Americans and other ethnic groups in the United States. However, these leaders have represented a cry in the wilderness. Significant, too, is the fact that many White liberal writers and researchers also began to attack the assimilationist ideology and the practices associated with it in the 1960s. This criticism represented a major break from White liberal tradition in the United States.[18]

Ethnic minority writers and researchers attacked the assimilationist ideology for many reasons. They saw it as a weapon of the oppressor designed to destroy the cultures of ethnic groups and to make their members personally ineffective and politically powerless. These writers also saw it as a racist ideology that justified damaging school and societal practices that victimized minority group students. Many minorities also lost faith in the assimilationist ideology because they had become very disillusioned with what they perceived as its unfulfilled promises. The rise of ethnic awareness and ethnic pride also contributed to the rejection of the assimilationist ideology by many ethnic minorities in the 1960s. Many minority spokespersons and writers searched for an alternative ideology and endorsed some version of cultural pluralism. They viewed the pluralist ideology as much more consistent with the liberation of oppressed and stigmatized ethnic groups than was the assimilationist ideology.

A Critique of the Pluralist and Assimilationist Ideologies

Although both the pluralist and assimilationist positions make some useful assumptions and set forth arguments that curriculum specialists need to ponder seriously as they attempt to revise the school curriculum, neither ideology, in its ideal form, is sufficient to guide educational reform. The pluralist ideology is useful because it informs us about the importance of ethnicity within a society and the extent to which an individual's ethnic group determines his or her life-chances. The assumptions the pluralist makes about the nature of minority cultures, the learning styles of minority youths, and the importance of ethnic identity to many students are also useful to the educational reformer.

However the pluralist exaggerates the extent of cultural pluralism within modern societies and fails to give adequate attention to the fact that high levels of cultural (if not structural) assimilation have taken place in societies such as the

United States. Gordon, who seriously questions the extent of cultural pluralism in U.S. society, writes, "Structural pluralism . . . is the major key to the understanding of the ethnic makeup of American society, while cultural pluralism is the minor one. . . ."[19] Exaggerating the extent of cultural differences between and among ethnic groups might be as detrimental for school policy as ignoring those that are real.

The pluralist also fails to pay adequate attention to the fact that most members of ethnic groups in modern societies participate in a wider and more universalistic culture than the ones in which they have their primary group attachments. Thus the pluralist appears unwilling to prepare youths to cope adequately with the real world beyond the ethnic community. The cultural pluralist also has not clarified, in any meaningful way, the kind of relationship that should exist between antagonistic and competing ethnic groups that have different allegiances and conflicting goals and commitments. In other words, the pluralist has not adequately conceptualized how a strongly pluralistic nation will maintain an essential degree of societal cohesion.

The assimilationist argues that the school within a common culture should socialize youths so they will be effective participants within that culture and will develop commitments to its basic values, goals, and ideologies. The assimilationist also argues that the schools should help youths attain the skills that will enable them to become effective and contributing members of the nation-state in which they live. It is important for educators to realize that most societies expect the common schools to help socialize youths so they will become productive members of the nation-state and develop strong commitments to the idealized societal values. Educators should keep the broad societal goals in mind when they reform the curriculum of the common schools.

However, the assimilationist makes a number of highly questionable assumptions and promotes educational practices that often hinder the success of youths socialized within ethnic communities that have cultural characteristics quite different from those of the school. The assimilationist's assumption that learning styles are universalistic rather than to some extent culture-specific is questionable. The assumption that all students can learn equally well from teaching materials that reflect only the cultural experiences of the majority group is also questionable and possibly detrimental to minority group children with strong ethnic identities and attachments.

When assimilationists talk about the common culture, most often they mean the mainstream national culture and are ignoring the reality that most Western societies are made up of many different ethnic groups, each of which has some unique cultural characteristics that are part of the shared national culture. The curriculum builder should seriously examine the common culture concept and make sure that the view of the common national culture promoted in the school is not racist, ethnocentric, or exclusive, but is multiethnic and reflects the ethnic and cultural diversity within society. We need to redefine what the common culture actually is. Our new conceptualization should reflect the social realities within a nation-state, not a mythical, idealized view of the life and culture within a particular nation-state.

The Multiethnic Ideology

Since neither the cultural pluralist nor the assimilationist ideology can adequately guide educational reform within educational institutions, we need a different ideology that reflects both positions and yet avoids their extremes. We also need an ideology that is more consistent with the realities in Western societies. We might call this position the *multiethnic ideology* and imagine that it is found near the center of our continuum, which has the cultural pluralist and the assimilationist ideologies at the extreme ends (see Table 7.1).

The multiethnic ideology has not historically been a dominant ideology in Western societies such as the United States and Australia. However, the experiences of some ethnic groups in the United States, the Jews being the most salient example, are highly consistent with the multiethnic vision of society. Although the multiethnic ideology is less theoretically developed than the other two positions, it, like the other ideologies, makes a number of assumptions about the nature of modernized society; about what a nation's goals should be; and about research, learning, teacher training, and the school curriculum.

The multiethnic theorist feels that the cultural pluralist exaggerates the importance of the ethnic group in the socialization of the individual and that the assimilationist greatly understates the role of ethnic groups in Western societies and in the lives of individuals. Thus, the multiethnic theorist believes that both the pluralist and the assimilationist have distorted views of societal realities. He or she assumes that even though the ethnic group and the ethnic community are very important in the socialization of individuals, individuals are also strongly influenced by the common culture during their early socialization, even if they never leave the ethnic community or enclave. A nation's common culture influences every member of society through such institutions as the school, the mass media, the courts, and the technology that its citizens share. Thus, concludes the multiethnic theorist, even though ethnic groups have some unique cultural characteristics, all groups in a society share many cultural traits. As more and more members of ethnic groups become upwardly mobile, ethnic group characteristics become less important—but they do not disappear. Many ethnic group members who are highly culturally assimilated still maintain separate ethnic institutions and symbols.[20]

The multiethnic theorist sees neither separatism (as the pluralist does) nor total integration (as the assimilationist does) as ideal societal goals, but rather envisions an open society, in which individuals from diverse ethnic, cultural, and social class groups have equal opportunities to function and participate. In an open society, individuals can take full advantage of the opportunities and rewards within all social, economic, and political institutions without regard to their an-

Table 7.1. Ideologies Related to Ethnicity and Pluralism in Western Societies

The Cultural Pluralist Ideology ←	*The Multiethnic Ideology* →	*The Assimilationist Ideology*
Separatism	Open society Multiculturalism	Total integration
Primordial Particularistic	Universalized-primordialism	Universalistic
Minority emphasis	Minorities and majorities have rights	Majoritarian emphasis
Groups rights are primary	Limited rights for the group and the individual	Individual rights are primary
Common ancestry and heritage unifies	Ethnic attachments and ideology of common civic culture compete for allegiances of individuals	Ideology of the common culture unifies
Research Assumption Ethnic minority cultures are well-ordered, highly structured, but different (language, values, behavior, etc.)	*Research Assumption* Ethnic minority cultures have some unique cultural characteristics; however, minority and majority groups share many cultural traits, values, and behavior styles	*Research Assumption* Subcultural groups with characteristics that make its members function unsuccessfully in the common culture are deprived, pathological, and lack needed functional characteristics
Culture difference research model	Bicultural research model	Social pathology research model and/or genetic research model
Minorities have unique learning styles	Minorities have some unique learning styles but share many learning characteristics with other groups	Human learning styles and characteristics are universal
Curriculum Use materials and teaching styles that are culture specific. The goal of the curriculum should be to help students function more successfully within their own ethnic cultures and help liberate their ethnic groups from oppression.	*Curriculum* The curriculum should respect the ethnicity of the child and use it in positive ways; the goal of the curriculum should be to help students learn how to function effectively within the common culture, their ethnic culture, and other ethnic cultures	*Curriculum* Use materials and teaching styles related to the common culture; the curriculum should help the students develop a commitment to the common civic culture and its idealized ideologies.
Teachers Minority students need skilled teachers of their same race and ethnicity for	*Teachers* Students need skilled teachers who are very knowledgeable about and sensitive to	*Teachers* A skilled teacher who is familiar with learning theories and is able to

Table 7.1. (Continued)

The Cultural Pluralist Ideology	The Multiethnic Ideology	The Assimilationist Ideology
role models, to learn more effectively, and to develop more positive self-concepts and identities	their ethnic cultures and cognitive styles	implement those theories effectively is a good teacher for any group of students, regardless of their ethnicity, race, or social class. The goal should be to train good teachers of students.

cestry or ethnic identity. They can also participate fully in the society while preserving their distinct ethnic and cultural traits and are able to "make the maximum number of voluntary contacts with others without regard to qualifications of ancestry, sex, or class."[21]

In the multiethnic, open society envisioned by the multiethnic theorist, individuals would be free to maintain their ethnic identities. They would also be able and willing to function effectively within the common culture and within and across other ethnic cultures. Individuals would be free to act in ways consistent with the norms and values of their ethnic groups as long as they did not conflict with overarching national idealized values, such as justice, equality, and human dignity. All members of society would be required to conform to these values. *These values would be the unifying elements of the culture that would maintain and promote societal cohesion.*

Because of their perceptions of the nature of Western societies and their vision of the ideal society, multiethnic theorists believe that the primary goal of the curriculum should be to help students learn how to function more effectively within their own ethnic culture, within the mainstream national culture, and within other ethnic communities. However, multiethnic theorists feel strongly that during the process of education the school should not alienate students from their ethnic attachments but should help them clarify their ethnic identities and make them aware of other ethnic and cultural alternatives.

The multiethnic theorist believes that the curriculum should reflect the cultures of various ethnic groups *and* the shared national culture. Students need to study all of these cultures in order to become effective participants and decision makers in a democratic pluralistic nation. The school curriculum should respect the ethnicity of students and use it in positive ways. However, the students should be given options regarding their political choices and the actions they take regarding their ethnic attachments. The school should not force students to be and feel ethnic if they choose to free themselves of ethnic attachments and allegiances.

The multiethnic theorist also assumes that ethnic minorities do have some unique learning styles, although they share many learning characteristics with other students. Educators should be knowledgeable about the aspects of their learning styles that are unique so they can better help minorities attain more success within the school and in the larger society.

Even though the multiethnic ideology can best guide educational reform and school policy, difficult questions regarding the relationship between the school and the student's ethnic culture are inherent within this position. The multiethnic theorist argues, for example, that the school should reflect both the student's ethnic culture and the common societal culture. These questions emerge: How does the individual function within two cultures that sometimes have contradictory and conflicting norms, values, and expectations? What happens when the ethnic cultures of the students seriously conflict with the goals and norms of public institutions like the school? Do the institutions change their goals? If so, what goals do they embrace? The assimilationist solves this problem by arguing that the student should change to conform to the expectations and norms of public institutions.

Although I support the multiethnic ideology and have presented my proposals for curriculum reform within that ideological framework,[22] it is very difficult to resolve satisfactorily all the difficult questions inherent within this ideology. However, public institutions like the school can and should allow ethnic group members to practice their culture-specific behaviors as long as they do not conflict with the major goals of the school. One of the school's major goals is to teach students how to read, to write, to compute, and to think. The school obviously cannot encourage ethnic behavior if it prohibits students from reading. On the other hand, some students might be able to learn to read more easily from culturally sensitive readers than from Anglo-Centric reading materials.

The Multiethnic Ideology and Education

The multiethnic educational reform movement has had very limited success in most of the Western nation-states in which it has developed. Practices such as ethnic studies, bilingual-bicultural education, multicultural education, and intercultural education have not permeated mainstream educational thought and practice in Western societies. An important question that concerns multiethnic educators is how to enhance this permeation process and the process of institutionalization. A philosophy of ethnic pluralism must permeate educational institutions before multiethnic educational practices can be effectively integrated into the mainstream curriculum. It is important to focus on ways to institutionalize a philosophy of ethnic education while discussing strategies and tactics for implementing change.

We cannot assume that most educators have accepted the idea of multiethnic education and are waiting for appropriate strategies and materials to be developed before participating in educational reforms related to multiethnic education. I hypothesize that just the opposite is true: that educators are not using many available multiethnic strategies and materials because they believe that multiethnic strategies and materials will not contribute to their major educational goals and objectives.

Multiethnic education has not acquired legitimacy within mainstream educational thought and practice in the United States or in other nations where I have studied multiethnic education programs and practices, such as Australia, France, the United Kingdom, and Canada.[23] An important question is: How can we legitimize multiethnic education within a nation's educational institutions? Once the concept of multiethnic education has become legitimized and most educators have internalized a philosophy of ethnic pluralism, the implementation of multiethnic education will become a logistical and technical problem.

The Root of the Problem: Ideological Resistance

Educators set forth many reasons to explain their basic indifference and limited response to educational reforms related to ethnic pluralism. These responses include the following:

1. Our students are unaware of racial differences; we will merely create problems that don't exist if we teach ethnic content. All of our students, whether Black or White, are happy and like one another. They don't see colors or ethnic differences.

2. We don't have any racial problems in our school and consequently don't need to teach about ethnic groups.

3. We don't teach about ethnic groups because we don't have any ethnic minorities attending our schools.

4. Ethnic studies will negatively affect societal unity and the common national culture.

5. We don't have time to add more content to what we are already teaching. We can't finish the books and units we already have. Ethnic content will overload our curriculum.

6. We don't teach much about ethnic groups because we don't have the necessary materials. Our textbooks are inadequate.

7. We can't teach ethnic studies in our schools and colleges because most of our teachers are inadequately trained in this area of study. Many of them also have negative attitudes toward ethnic groups. They would probably do more harm than good if they tried to teach about ethnic and racial groups.

8. The local community will strongly object if we teach about race and ethnicity in our schools.

9. We don't teach much about ethnic groups in our schools because there is a lack of scholarship in this area. The research in ethnic studies is largely political and polemical.

Some of these explanations, *but not most of them*, have a degree of validity and partially explain why multiethnic education has not become institutionalized within most schools and colleges. Most of these explanations do not reveal the root of the problem, however. *Ideological and philosophical conflicts between pluralistic and mainstream educators (who are basically assimilationists) are the major reasons that educational reforms related to ethnic diversity have not become institutionalized within the educational systems in the Western nations.* In other words, the resistance to pluralistic education is basically ideological and political.

The Ideological Clash

Mainstream educators, who are primarily assimilationists, make most of the major decisions that are implemented and institutionalized within schools and colleges. They are the gatekeepers of the status quo. Pluralistic educators are those small group of educators who advocate reforms to make education more ethnically pluralistic. Mainstream and pluralistic educators embrace conflicting and oftentimes contradictory ideological positions about the nature of society, the nature of schooling, and the purposes of schooling in a democratic nation.

The Quest for a New Ideology

Neither the *assimilationist* nor the *cultural pluralistic ideology*, in their ideal or pure forms, can effectively guide educational reform in a democratic nation that has a universal culture that is both heavily influenced by and shared by all ethnic groups. Programs based primarily on assimilationist assumptions perpetuate misconceptions about the nature of society and violate the ethnic identities of many students. Curricular practices that reflect an extreme notion of cultural pluralism also distort societal realities and give inadequate attention to the universal culture that strongly influences the behavior of all citizens within a society.

Both the assimilationist and cultural pluralist ideologies emanate from misleading and/or incomplete analyses of the nature of ethnicity in modernized societies such as the United States. The assimilationist ideology in the United States derives primarily from two conceptionalizations of ethnicity in U.S. society: *Anglo-conformity* and the *melting pot*. The cultural pluralist ideology emanates from a conceptualization of ethnicity in American society called *cultural pluralism.* I summarize these conceptualizations of ethnicity in the United States and indicate why each is an inadequate and/or misleading conceptualization.[24] I then present my own analysis of ethnicity in U.S. society and derive a new ideology, called the *multiethnic ideology*, from my analysis. The multiethnic ideology I present is one possible way to reduce the ideological and political resistance to pluralistic education.

Anglo-conformity suggests that ethnic groups gave up their cultural attributes and acquired those of Anglo-Saxon Protestants. This concept describes a type of unidirectional assimilation. The *melting pot*, long embraced as an ideal in U.S. society and culture, suggests that the various ethnic cultures in the United States were mixed and synthesized into a new culture, different from any of the original ethnic cultures. *Cultural pluralism* suggests, at least in its extreme form, that the United States is made up of various ethnic subsocieties, each of which has a set of largely independent norms, institutions, values, and beliefs.

Each conceptualization presents major problems when one views the reality of ethnicity and race in the United States.[25] The Anglo-conformity conceptualization suggests that Anglo Saxons were changed very little in America and that other ethnic groups did all of the changing. This conceptualization is incomplete, unidirectional, and static. The melting pot conceptualization is inaccurate and misleading because human cultures are complex and dynamic and do not melt like iron. Consequently, the melting pot is a false and misleading metaphor.

The strong cultural pluralist conceptualization denies the reality that there is a universal American culture that every American, regardless of ethnic group, shares to a great extent. This culture includes American Creed values as *ideals*, American English, a highly technological and industrialized civilization, a capitalistic economy, and a veneration of materialism and consumption. Richard Hofstadter argues convincingly that anti-intellectualism is another key component in the universal American culture.[26] This is not to deny that there are important subcultural variants within the different ethnic subsocieties in the United States or that there are many nonuniversalized ethnic characteristics in U.S. ethnic communities. These nonuniversalized ethnic subvariants will be discussed later.

Gordon believes that *structural pluralism* best describes the ethnic reality in U.S. society.[27] According to Gordon, the ethnic groups in the United States have experienced high levels of cultural assimilation but the nation is characterized by structural pluralism. In other words, ethnic groups are highly assimilated culturally (into the Anglo-American culture) but have separate ethnic subsocieties, such as Black fraternities, Jewish social clubs, and Chicano theaters.

Multiple Acculturation

Even though Gordon's notion of structural pluralism is helpful and deals more adequately with the complexity of ethnic diversity in modern U.S. society than the other three concepts, I believe that multiple acculturation more accurately describes how the universal U.S. culture was and is forming than does the concept of cultural assimilation. The White Anglo-Saxon Protestant culture was changed in America as were the cultures of Africans and of Asian immigrants. African cultures and Asian cultures influenced and changed the WASP culture as the WASP culture influenced and modified African and Asian cultures. What was experienced in the United States, and what is still occurring, is multiple acculturation and not a kind of unidirectional type of cultural assimilation whereby the Black culture was influenced by the WASP culture and not the other way around.

The general or universal culture in the United States resulted from this series of multiple acculturations. This culture is still in the process of formation and change (see Figure 7.1). The universal U.S. culture is not just a WASP culture but contains important elements of the wide variety of ethnic cultures that are and/or were part of U.S. society. Those ethnic cultural elements that became universalized and part of the general U.S. culture have been reinterpreted and mediated by the unique social, economic, and political experience in the United States. *It is inaccurate and misleading to refer to the universal U.S. culture as a WASP culture.*

This notion of U.S. culture has been and is often perpetuated in the school and university curricula. It is, of course, true that the White Anglo-Saxon Protestants have had a more profound impact on the universal U.S. culture than has any other single ethnic group. However, we can easily exaggerate the WASP influence on the general U.S. culture. European cultures were greatly influenced by African and Asian cultures before the European explorers started coming to the Americas in the fifteenth century. The earliest British immigrants borrowed heavily from the American Indians on the East coast and probably would not have survived if they had not assimilated Indian cultural components and used some of their farming methods and tools.

Ethnic Subsocieties and Nonuniversalized Cultural Components

Figure 7.1 describes the development of U.S. culture by emphasizing multiple acculturation and how ethnic cultural elements became universalized. Other U.S. ethnic realities are not shown in Figure 7.1. These realities include the significant number of ethnic cultural elements that have not become universalized (that are still shared primarily by ethnic subgroups) and the separate ethnic institutions and groups that constitute ethnic subsocieties within the larger U.S. society and culture. The sociocultural environment for most Americans is consequently bicultural. Almost every American participates both within the universal American culture and society as well as within his or her ethnic subsociety. Like other U.S. ethnic groups, there is a subsociety within the WASP culture that has cultural elements not universal or shared by the rest of society. Patterson believes that this is a small subsociety in which few individuals participate and that most WASP cultural elements have become universalized. He writes, "with the exception of small pockets such as the New England Brahmin elite, the vast majority of WASPs have abandoned the ethnic specificities of their original culture in favor of the elite version of the American universal culture."[28]

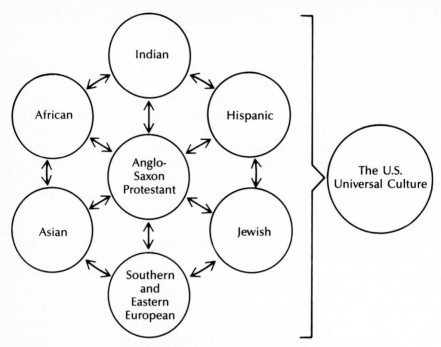

Figure 7.1. The Development of U.S. Culture
This figure illustrates how the U.S. universal culture developed through a process conceptualized as *multiple acculturation*. The Anglo-Saxon Protestant culture had the greatest influence on the development of U.S. culture, and each of the various ethnic cultures influenced the Anglo culture and was influenced by it. Each culture was also influenced by and influenced the others. These complex series of acculturations, which were mediated by the U.S. experience and the U.S. sociocultural environment, resulted in the universal U.S. culture. This process is still taking place today.

Nonuniversalized ethnic cultural characteristics and ethnic subsocieties are realities in contemporary U.S. society. These cultural elements and subsocieties play an important role in the socialization of many Americans and help individual members of ethnic groups satisfy important needs. Figure 7.2 illustrates the relationship between the universal U.S. culture and ethnic subsocieties.

The Multiethnic Ideology

My analysis of ethnicity in U.S. society leads to a philosophical position that can be called the *multiethnic ideology* since one of its key assertions is that Americans function within several cultures, including the mainstream culture and various

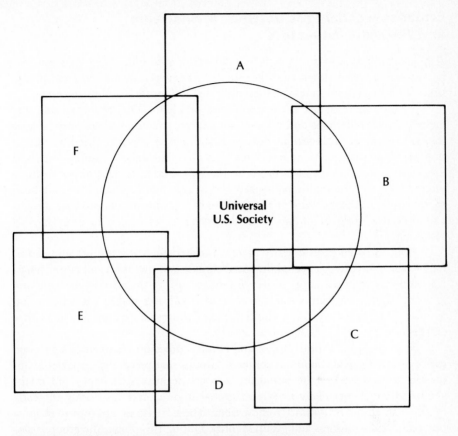

Figure 7.2. Ethnic Subsocieties and the Universal U.S. Society
In this figure, the universal U.S. society is represented by the
circle. This culture is shared by all ethnic groups within the
United States. A, B, C, D, E, and F represent ethnic subsocieties that consist of unique ethnic institutions, values,
and cultural elements that are nonuniversalized and shared
primarily by members of specific ethnic groups.

ethnic subcultures. This multiethnic ideology suggests specific goals for curriculum reform related to ethnicity. A major goal of multiethnic education derived
from my analysis of the nature of ethnicity in the United States, is to help students develop cross-cultural competency (discussed in Chapter 3). Edward T. Hall,
in his insightful book *Beyond Culture*, underscores the importance of helping
students develop the skills and understandings needed to function cross-culturally. He writes, "The future depends on man's transcending the limits of individual cultures."[29] Another important goal of multiethnic education is to help
individuals gain greater self-understanding by viewing themselves from the perspectives of other microcultures within their nation-state.

Establishing Dialogue between Mainstream and Pluralistic Educators

A major implication of my analysis for multiethnic education is that personal contact situations and dialogue must be established between mainstream and pluralistic educators so they can resolve their philosophical conflicts and disagreements.

Ideological resistance is the root of our problem. Personal contact and dialogue between pluralistic and mainstream educators is essential to derive a basic solution. However, little serious discussion and debate about multiethnic education have taken place among educators with divergent beliefs, assumptions, and ideologies about the role of ethnicity in the formal educational process.[30] This is partly because of the highly politicized and racially tense climate that gave birth to the ethnic studies movement and because of the strong emotions that scholars and educators often exemplify when discussing issues related to ethnicity and schooling.

Born in social protest, early practices related to ethnic studies and multiethnic education often reflected the social climate and the racial and ethnic polarization pervasive in the larger society. Ethnic groups, in their quests to shape new identities and to legitimize their histories and cultures within the schools and within the larger society, often glorified their cultures and emphasized how they had been oppressed by the dominant society.

Early phases of ethnic protest and ethnic studies programs must be viewed within broad social and political contexts. Groups that perceive themselves as oppressed and internalize the dominant society's negative stereotypes and myths about themselves are likely to express strong in-group feelings during the early phase of an ethnic revitalization movement. There is also an attempt to shape a new ethnic consciousness and group identity. During this phase, the group is also likely to strongly reject outside ethnic and racial groups, to romanticize its past, and to view contemporary social and political conditions from a highly subjective perspective.

An ethnic group that is experiencing the early stages of an ethnic revitalization movement is also likely to demand that the school curriculum portray a romanticized version of its history and to emphasize how the group has been oppressed and victimized by other ethnic and racial groups within the society. Extremely negative sanctions are directed against members of the ethnic group who do not endorse a strong ethnic position. Consequently, little fruitful dialogue is likely to take place among individuals who hold conflicting ideological positions regarding ethnicity and educational policy. Members of both the oppressed and the oppressive group are likely to be ardent in their positions during the early phases of an ethnic revitalization movement (see Chapter 2).

Sharing Power

Another important implication of my analysis is that powerful groups that now dominate educational policy and decisions must be willing to share power with currently excluded and powerless ethnic groups before a multiethnic ideology can be developed and educational policy can be shaped that reflects the interests and aspirations of ethnic minority groups. Historically in the United States, educational policy for powerless and structurally excluded ethnic groups, such as Blacks and Mexican Americans, has been made by powerful Anglo-American groups that controlled the educational system.[31] As pointed out in Chapter 1, an Anglo-centric education alienates minority groups from their ethnic cultures and frequently fails to help them attain the attitudes, skills, and abilities needed to function effectively within the mainstream society and within other ethnic subsocieties.

Powerless and excluded ethnic groups, such as Mexican Americans and Puerto Rican Americans, must participate in shaping educational policy in order for educational reforms related to ethnic diversity to become institutionalized within the U.S. educational system.[32] The groups that exercise power in the American educational establishment design and run the schools so that they reflect their ideology, assumptions, values, and perspectives. The assimilationists who control the schools often see pluralism as a threat to the survival of the United States as they envision it. Ways must be devised for currently excluded ethnic groups to gain power in education and to participate in major educational decisions that affect the education of their youths. Only in this way will a philosophy of ethnic pluralism become institutionalized within the educational system, and the system will become legitimate from the perspectives of ethnic minorities.[33] Curricular models that can help lead to a sharing of power by structurally included and excluded groups are conceptualized and discussed in Chapter 10.

Summary

Educational institutions in the various Western nations, stimulated by social forces and supported by private and public agencies, are implementing a wide variety of educational reforms related to pluralism and ethnic diversity in their societies. However, there is widespread disagreement about what these reforms should be designed to attain and about the proper relationship that should exist between the school and the ethnic identities and attachments of students. Educators and social scientists who embrace divergent ideologies are recommending conflicting educational policies and programs.

We can think of these varying ideologies as existing on a continuum, with the cultural pluralist position at one extreme end and the assimilationist position at the other. I argue that neither of these ideologies, in their ideal forms, can effectively guide educational policy in pluralistic democratic societies. Rather, educational policy can best be guided by an eclectic ideology that reflects both the cultural pluralist position and the assimilationist position, but avoids their extremes. I call this the *multiethnic ideology*.

The second part of this chapter discusses the multiethnic ideology and describes how it derives from an accurate analysis of ethnic and race relations in the United States. The assimilationist ideology, which most mainstream educators in the United States embrace, derives from two misleading and incomplete conceptions of the nature of ethnicity in the United States: Anglo-conformity and the melting pot. Structural pluralism and multiple acculturation accurately describe the nature of ethnic group life in the United States. The multiethnic ideology derives from these conceptions of ethnicity and race in the United States. This ideology can be used to help reduce the ideological resistance to pluralistic education and to establish a dialogue between mainstream and pluralistic educators. However, in order for a multiethnic ideology to be developed and to influence educational policy, powerful mainstream ethnic groups must share power with structurally excluded ethnic groups in the various Western nation-states.

Notes

1. John Tierney et al., *Race, Migration and Schooling* (London: Holt, Rinehart and Winston, 1982); James A. Banks, ed., *Teaching Ethnic Studies: Concepts and Strategies* (Washington, D.C.: National Council for the Social Studies, 1973); Ronald J. Samuda, John W. Berry, and Michael Laferrière, *Multiculturalism in Canada* (Toronto: Allyn & Bacon, Inc., 1984); Brian Bullivant, *The Pluralist Dilemma in Education: Six Case Studies* (Sydney: George Allen & Unwin, 1981); Orlando Patterson, *Ethnic Chauvinism: The Reactionary Impulse* (New York: Stein and Day, 1977).

2. Maurice Craft, ed., *Education and Cultural Pluralism* (London: The Falmer Press, 1984); James Lynch, *Multicultural Education: Principles and Practice* (London: Routledge and Kegan Paul, 1986); John R. Mallea and Jonathan C. Young, eds; *Cultural Diversity and Canadian Education: Issues and Innovations* (Ottawa: Carleton University Press, 1984); James A. Banks and James Lynch, eds., *Multicultural Education in Western Societies* (New York: Praeger, 1986).

3. Milton M. Gordon, *Assimilation in American Life: The Role of Race, Religion, and National Origins* (New York: Oxford University Press, 1964), p. 84.

4. John Higham, "Integration vs. Pluralism: Another American Dilemma," *The Center Magazine* 7 (July/August 1974), pp. 67–73.

5. See, for example, Len Barton and Stephen Walker, *Race, Class and Education* (London: Croom Helm, 1983); Barbara A. Sizemore, "Shattering the Melting Pot Myth," in Banks, ed., *Teaching Ethnic Studies*, pp. 73–101.

6. Stokely Carmichael and Charles V. Hamilton, *Black Power: The Politics of Liberation in America* (New York: Vintage Books, 1967); Barbara A. Sizemore, "Separatism: A Reality Approach to Inclusion?" in Robert L. Green, ed., *Racial Crisis in American Education* (Chicago: Follett Educational Corporation, 1969), pp. 249–279.

7. Stephen S. Baratz and Joan C. Baratz, "Early Childhood Intervention: The Social Science Base of Institutional Racism," *Harvard Educational Review* 40 (Winter 1970), pp. 29–50; Gary Simpkins, Robert L. Williams, and Thomas S. Gunnings, "What a Culture a Difference Makes: A Rejoinder to Valentine," *Harvard Educational Review* 41 (November 1971), pp. 535–541.

8. Baratz and Baratz, "Early Child Intervention"; Jane R. Mercer, "Latent Functions of Intelligence Testing in the Public Schools," in Lamar P. Miller, ed., *The Testing of Black Students* (Englewood Cliffs, N.J.: Prentice-Hall, 1974), pp. 77–94.

9. Manuel Ramìrez III and Alfredo Castañeda, *Cultural Democracy, Bicognitive Development and Education* (New York: Academic Press, 1974).

10. Susan S. Stodolsky and Gerald Lesser, "Learning Patterns in the Disadvantaged," *Harvard Educational Review* 37 (Fall 1967), pp. 546–593.

11. David Apter, "Political Life and Pluralism," in Melvin M. Tumin and Walter Plotch, eds., *Pluralism in a Democratic Society* (New York: Praeger, 1977), pp. 59–81; John Porter, "Ethnic Pluralism in Canadian Perspective," in Nathan Glazer and Daniel P. Moynihan, eds., *Ethnicity: Theory and Experience* (Cambridge, Mass.: Harvard University Press, 1975).

12. Nathan Glazer, "Cultural Pluralism: The Social Aspect," in Tumin and Plotch, *Pluralism in a Democratic Society*, pp. 3–24.

13. Arthur R. Jensen, "How Much Can We Boost IQ and Scholastic Achievement?" *Harvard Educational Review* 39 (Winter 1969), pp. 1–123; William Shockley, "Dysgenics, Geneticity, Raceology: Challenges to the Intellectual Responsibility of Educators," *Phi Delta Kappan* 53 (January 1972), pp. 297–307.

14. Betty Caldwell, "What Is the Optimal Learning Environment for the Young Child?" *American Journal of Orthopsychiatry* 37 (1967), pp. 9–21.

15. Horace M. Kallen, *Culture and Democracy in the United States* (New York: Boni and Liveright, 1924); Randolph S. Bourne, "Trans-National America," *The Atlantic Monthly* 118 (July 1916), p. 95; Julius Drachsler, *Democracy and Assimilation* (New York: Macmillan, 1920).

16. Tierney et al. *Race, Migration and Schooling*; Banks, ed., *Teaching Ethnic Studies: Concepts and Strategies*; Bullivant, *The Pluralist Dilemma*.

17. Glazer, "Cultural Pluralism: The Social Aspect," in Tumin and Plotch, *Pluralism in a Democratic Society*, pp. 3–24.

18. Joan C. Baratz and Roger Shuy, eds., *Teaching Black Children to Read* (Washington, D.C.: Center for Applied Linguistics, 1969); William Labov, "The Logic of Nonstandard English," in Frederick Williams, eds., *Language and Poverty: Perspectives on a Theme* (Chicago: Markham Publishing Company, 1970), pp. 153–189.

19. Gordon, *Assimilation in American Life*, p. 159.

20. Ibid.

21. Barbara A. Sizemore, "Is There a Case for Separate Schools?" *Phi Delta Kappan* 53 (January 1972), p. 281.

22. James A. Banks, *Teaching Strategies for Ethnic Studies*, 4th ed. (Boston: Allyn & Bacon, Inc., 1987).

23. Banks, "Multicultural Education: Development, Paradigms, and Goals," in Banks and Lynch, eds. *Multicultural Education in Western Societies*, pp. 2–28; James A. Banks, "Multiethnic Education across Cultures: United States, Mexico, Puerto Rico, France and Great Britain," *Social Education*, 42 (March 1978), pp. 177–185. See also: Tierney et al., *Race, Migration and Schooling*; Bullivant, *The Pluralist Dilemma in Education*.

24. These conceptualizations are discussed in considerable detail in Milton Gordon, *Assimilation in American Life* (New York: Oxford University Press, 1964).

25. I first presented the concept of multiple acculturation in James A. Banks, "Ethnicity: Implications for Curriculum Reform," *The Social Studies* 70 (January/February 1979), pp. 3–10.

26. Richard Hofstadter, *Anti-Intellectualism in American Life* (New York: Vintage, 1963). Other cultural components of the general American culture are discussed in Edward C. Stewart, *American Cultural Patterns: A Cross-Cultural Perspective* (LaGrange Park, Ill.: Intercultural Network, Inc., 1972).

27. Gordon, *Assimilation in American Life*.

28. Orlando Patterson, *Ethnic Chauvinism: The Reactionary Impulse* (New York: Stein and Day, 1977), p. 151.

29. Edward T. Hall, *Beyond Culture* (Garden City, N.Y.: Doubleday, 1977), p. 2.

30. This section is adapted from my paper, "A Response to Philip Freedman," *Phi Delta Kappan* 58 (May 1977), pp. 695–697.

31. Samuel Bowles and Herbert Gintis, *Schooling in Capitalist America: Educational Reform and the Contradictions of Economic Life* (New York: Basic Books, 1976); Michael B. Katz, *Class, Bureaucracy, and Schools: The Illusion of Educational Change in America*, expanded ed. (New York: Praeger, 1975).

32. Barbara A. Sizemore, "Separatism: A Reality Approach to Inclusion?" in Robert L. Green, ed., *Racial Crisis in American Education* (Chicago: Follett Educational Corporation, 1969), pp. 249–279.

33. Charles V. Hamilton, "Race and Education: A Search for Legitimacy," *Harvard Educational Review* 38 (Fall 1968), pp. 669–684.

8

Ethnicity and Citizenship Education

Citizenship education should help students acquire the knowledge, skills, and values needed to make reflective public decisions consistent with democratic ideals. The effective citizen in a democratic nation-state has a commitment to the overarching and shared national values and the skills, competencies, and commitment to act on them. The effective democratic citizen also takes actions to promote the shared and idealized values of the nation-state. A major goal of civic education in a pluralistic, democratic nation is to help students acquire the values and the competencies needed to engage in successful and humane social and political action.

Ethnic Groups and National Values

To develop *clarified*, *reflective*, and *positive* commitments and identifications with their nation-state and its overarching values, the diverse ethnic groups within a culturally pluralistic nation such as the United States or Canada must perceive themselves as legitimate groups that are structurally included into the fabric of the social, economic, and political institutions in society. Individuals and groups who have clarified and reflective national attachments and identifications understand how these identifications and attachments developed, are able to examine their nation thoughtfully and objectively, and understand both the personal and public implications of their national identifications. Individuals and groups who have *positive* national attachments and identifications evaluate their national identifications highly and are proud of their national attachments and affiliations.

Many members of ethnic groups within modernized Western nation-states, although deeply loyal and patriotic citizens, have conflicting attachments to their nation-states and often experience political alienation and anomie. Groups such as the Chamorros in Guam, the French and Indians in Canada, and Blacks and Puerto Ricans in the United States often feel alienated because their contributions to their national cultures have not been sufficiently recognized or legitimized and because they have not been given opportunities to participate fully in the institutions of their nation-states or to share fully in the benefits of modernization and high technology. These alienated ethnic groups often feel they do not have a stake in the dominant societies of their nations or territories. Their shared sense of alienation and deprivation helps maintain tight ethnic boundaries and ethnic communities.

Groups that are excluded from full participation in the nation-state in which they are legal citizens and from the mainstream societies in which they live are likely to focus on particularistic concerns and goals rather than on the universalistic needs and problems of the nation-state. Politically powerless and lower-status ethnic groups within a society, such as the Puerto Ricans and Indians in the United States, the North Africans in France, and the West Indians and Asians in the United Kingdom, are often so engrossed by their own problems of powerlessness, alienation, poverty, and institutionalized racism that they devote little attention to the overarching problems of the nation-state that are shared by all groups in their societies.

Ethnic groups that are structurally excluded and politically marginal and that experience institutionalized discrimination within their nation-states are likely to interpret both domestic and international events from particularistic perspectives, especially if the ethnic group has experienced a diaspora, still has attachments to its original homeland, perceives its members as marginal citizens, and has a distinctive ethnic culture and a cogent sense of peoplehood.

Jewish, Cuban, and Greek citizens of the United States often interpret world events that affect Israel, Cuba, and Greece from perspectives influenced by their ethnic affiliations and senses of kinship with their original homelands. Members of these groups often experience psychological conflicts when they believe the interests of their original homelands and those of the United States are inconsistent. Jews are citizens of many nation-states throughout the world. Consequently, Jewish Americans are likely to be concerned about the human rights of Jews in nations as far apart as Brazil and the Soviet Union.

Ethnicity and Citizenship within a Democracy

I have stated that structural exclusion of ethnic groups within a nation-state is likely to promote and support ethnic group attachments and strong ethnic boundaries and to foster particularistic and primordial concerns among ethnic group members.* What are the implications of primordial and ethnic attachments for citizenship and citizenship education within a modernized, democratic nation such as the United States? Can and should ethnic attachments coexist with modernity in a pluralistic democratic nation such as the United States? Should the school curriculum within a modernized or a modernizing democratic nation-state recognize, acknowledge, and legitimize the ethnic attachments and identifications of ethnic youths? These complex questions are raised by the coexistence of

---

*By a *primordial attachment* is meant one that stems from the "givens" — or, more precisely, as culture is inevitably involved in such matters, the assumed "givens" — of social existence: immediate contiguity and kin connection mainly, but beyond them the givenness that stems from being born into a particular religious community, speaking a particular language, or even a dialect of a language, and following particular social practices. These congruities of blood, speech, custom, and so on, are seen to have an ineffable, and at times overpowering, coerciveness in and of themselves. One is bound to one's kinsman, one's neighbor, one's fellow believer, ipso facto; as the result not merely of personal affection, practical necessity, common interest, or incurred obligation, but at least in great part by virtue of some unaccountable absolute import attributed to the very tie itself. (Clifford Geertz, *The Interpretation of Cultures.* New York: Basic Books, 1973, p. 259.)

ethnicity and modernity within Western democratic nation-states. I explore these questions in this chapter. During the 1960s and 1970s, the expressions of ethnic affiliations and primordial attachments increased significantly, thus making the question of the coexistence of ethnicity and modernity within society even more complex.[1]

The Assimilationist and Multiethnic Assumptions

The assimilationist assumes that the most effective way to reduce strong ethnic boundaries, primordial attachments, and ethnic affiliations within a nation-state is to provide excluded ethnic and racial groups opportunities to experience equality in the nation's social, economic, and political institutions.[2] As they begin to participate more fully in the universalistic or mainstream society and its institutions, argues the assimilationist, lower-status ethnic groups will focus less on particularistic concerns and more on national issues and priorities.

When ethnic groups experience equality, suggests the assimilationist, ethnicity and primordial attachments die of their own weight. Individuals who endorse a multiethnic or bicultural ideology believe that equality will not eliminate ethnicity from modernized democratic societies but that ethnicity will take new forms within an equal society and that ethnic traits will become part of the universal culture shared by all. Ethnic characteristics within an equal society would become universalized. All ethnic groups, according to the multiethnic ideologist, share power and have equal-status interactions in an equal and just society. The assimilationist views the ideal society as one that has no traces of ethnicity. All groups would share a common national culture. The multiethnic ideologist believes that the ideal society is characterized by equal status among ethnic groups and a universal culture that consists of universalized ethnic characteristics.

The Assimilationist Fallacy

Apter, while ackowledging that he is an assimilationist and a pluralist,* calls the assimilationist position the "assimilationist fallacy."[3] This position holds that as modernization occurs, ethnic groups experience social, political, and economic

---

*When he calls himself a pluralist, Apter is using *pluralism* in the political science sense and not in the anthropological sense of cultural pluralism.

"Political pluralism is the name applied to those political doctrines, ranging from extreme to modern claims on behalf of group interests in society, which assert that certain groups (e.g., family, church, union, local government) embody important social values prior to and independent of their authorization or approval by the state. The scope of pluralism is not usually interpreted as including anarchism or revolutionary syndicalism because, unlike such theories, most pluralists retain for government the functional responsibilities of compulsory citizenship and taxation, and admit the necessity for an inclusive governmental authority transcending group associations to regulate, direct, or coordinate, inter alia the domestic economy, personal liberties, national security, and foreign affairs." (Julius Gould and William L. Kolb, eds., *A Dictionary of the Social Sciences*. New York: Free Press, 1964, p. 507.)

equality, enlightenment eventuates, and commitments to ethnic and primordial attachments weaken and disappear. When modernization arises, ethnicity disappears, and vice versa. Assimilationists see ethnicity and primordial attachments as fleeting and temporary within an increasingly modernized society. They view modernity and ethnicity as contradictory concepts. Ethnicity, argues the assimilationist, promotes divisions, exhumes ethnic conflicts, and leads to the polarization of society. Assimilationists such as Patterson also argue that ethnic groups promote groups rights over individual rights and that individual rights are paramount in a democratic pluralistic nation. He writes:

> The defense of pluralism not only neglects individuality; much worse, an emphasis on group diversity and group tolerance works against a respect for individuality. This is what I call the *pluralist fallacy*, which originates in the failure to recognize a basic paradox in human interaction; the greater the diversity and cohesiveness of groups in a society, the smaller the diversity and personal autonomy of individuals in that society.[4] [Emphasis added.]

Assimilationists see the continuing expressions and existence of ethnicity within modernized democratic nation states as a "pathological condition."[5] Ethnic affiliations and cultures still exist in modernized societies, argues the assimilationist, because political and economic equality for ethnic groups such as Blacks, Indians, Mexican Americans, and Puerto Ricans have been only partially attained. Thus, the assimilationist ideal is viable and possible but has yet to be completely realized. This will happen when inequality and structural exclusion of ethnic groups, such as Blacks and Mexican Americans, ends. Include ethnic groups into the structure of society and enable them to experience political and economic mobility, and ethnicity will, for all important purposes, disappear. Some symbolic forms of ethnicity might remain within the equal society, such as St. Patrick's Day and Chinese New Year, but ethnicity will not be an important social, cultural, or political force in society. This is the assimilationist's argument.

As Apter perceptively states, the assimilationist vision and ideal is not so much wrong as it is an incomplete and inadequate explanation of ethnic realities in modernized, pluralistic, and democratic nation-states. Writes Apter:

> Clearly [modernizing] historical forces are at work. There is a widening of universalistic and pluralistic beliefs. However, primordialism is at work too. It pops up where we least expect it, in Scotland, Wales, and Quebec, and among the Basques, Catalans, and Bretons. Old primordialisms can fade away and yet revive. The reasons why are puzzling to pluralists and liberals, who have not expected it or have considered it to be of passing significance.[6]

A central fallacy of the assimilationist position is the assumption that when the "high culture" of modernization develops within a nation-state, primordial and ethnic affiliations disappear into thin air and are no longer a problem for mainstream political leaders and modernizers. States Apter, "The enlightenment myth on which the assimilationist fallacy rests is that modern history is moving in a single direction away from provincial and local attachments and toward a greater common consciousness of the world."[7] However, as the ethnic revitalization movements of the 1960s and 1970s made dramatically and sometimes poignantly clear, ethnic attachments and identifications can become cogent forces within a modernized democratic society when particular political, social, and economic events develop.

The ethnic revitalization movements of the 1960s and 1970s caught mainstream social scientists almost completely by surprise and without the conceptual frameworks either to understand or adequately interpret these movements. When they emerged, most established social scientists still accepted some form of Robert E. Park's notions about ethnic groups in society. Park believed that race and ethnic relations proceeded through four inevitable stages: *contact, conflict, accommodation*, and *assimilation*.[8] When the Black civil rights movement of the 1960s and the consequent Black power movement emerged, it was clear that Park's conceptualization inadequately explained ethnic relations in modernized democratic nation-states.

Ethnic Revitalization Movements Develop and Spread

Ethnic attachments and movements are more likely to develop among structurally and politically excluded ethnic groups than among ethnic groups who perceive themselves as included within the fabric of society and as beneficiaries of technology and modernization. Blacks led the ethnic revitalization movements in the United States because of their historic and profound discrimination and because of their rising expectations caused by social and political events in the 1950s and 1960s. However, shortly after the Black-led ethnic revitalization movement arose, ethnic groups such as Mexican Americans, American Indians, Puerto Ricans, and Asian Americans echoed concerns similar to those raised by Blacks and started their own ethnic movements.

Ethnic revitalization movements then spread like a chain reaction among White ethnic groups in the United States such as Italians, Poles, and other Slavic-American ethnic groups. The rise of White ethnic movements was signaled by the publication of Michael Novak's book, *The Rise of the Unmeltable Ethnics*.[9] This book was a sign that the time had come for ethnic expressions in modernized America. Some writers argued that the White ethnic movement was not genuine or legitimate and that it arose as a racist reaction to the civil rights movement led by Blacks. It was designed, some argued, to divert attention from the plight of non-White ethnic groups.[10] However, Judith Herman believed that the movement was both genuine and authentic.[11]

Many members of White ethnic groups who had in the past perceived themselves as full beneficiaries of modernization and high technology organized ethnic movements to fight for more political, economic, and cultural rights.[12] Ethnic expressions became strong in White ethnic communities in Boston when court-ordered desegregation of public schools took place in the 1970s. The ethnic attachments and feelings of Anglo-Americans heightened as other ethnic groups attacked their values and behaviors and blamed them for the national mentality that resulted in the Vietnam war and the destruction of the nation's environment and for perpetuating institutional and cultural racism that victimized other ethnic groups.[13] Jewish expressions of ethnicity became more cogent in the 1960s and 1970s when tensions developed between Jews and ethnic groups such as Blacks and Puerto Ricans over issues such as affirmative action and bilingual education and as Israel's position in the world seemed to many Jews increasingly precarious.

These examples of ethnic movements and behaviors indicate that both ethnicity and modernity can and do coexist within society and that various political, social, and economic events influence whether members of particular ethnic groups act universal or primordial within particular times, settings, and cultural contexts. These examples also illustrate that ethnic attachments not only exist within ethnic groups that have been historic victims of institutionalized racism such as Blacks and American Indians, but that highly acculturated ethnic groups, such as Irish Americans and Anglo Americans, often act ethnic and express ethnic attachments and affiliations. *Ethnicity and assimilationism coexist in modernized democratic nation-states*. Writes Apter, "The two tendencies, toward and against primordialism, can go on at the same time. Indeed, the more development and growth that take place, the more some primordial groupings have to gain by their parochialism."[14]

Ethnicity and the Needs of Individuals and Groups

Ethnic attachments and assimilationism coexist within modernized and modernizing societies for a number of complex reasons, some of which social scientists do not understand. They coexist in part because of what the assimilationist calls the "pathological condition"; that is, ethnic groups such as Blacks and Mexican Americans maintain strong attachments to their ethnic groups and cultures in part because they have been excluded from full participation in the social, economic, and political institutions in the United States.

However, members of these ethnic groups, as well as members of ethnic groups such as Poles, Italians, and Greeks, maintain ethnic affiliations and ethnic attachments for more fundamental psychological and sociological reasons. It helps them fulfill some basic psychological and sociological needs that the "thin" culture of modernization leaves starving. Apter comments insightfully on this point: "Primordialism is a response to the thinning out of enlightenment culture, the deterioration of which is a part of the process of democratization and pluralization. . . . Assimilationism itself then vitiates the enlightenment culture. As it does, it leaves what might be called a primordial space, a space people try to fill when they believe they have lost something fundamental and try to recreate it."[15]

Ethnic individuals also hold onto their ethnic attachments because they help them satisfy communal and personal needs. Ethnic group membership provides individuals with a bond that enables them to consider themselves a group that is distinct and unique from other groups. Ethnic group members share a culture that binds them together. This shared culture equips individuals with a sense of belonging. Within a complex and impersonal modernized society, ethnic group identification and membership provide individuals with a "familiar and reassuring anchor in a climate of turbulence and uncertainty."[16] Ethnic group membership also provides individuals with a foundation for self-definition, a sense of belonging, of shared traditions, and a sense of interdependence of fate.

Schooling, Citizenship Education, and Ethnic Minorities

I have argued that ethnic groups that are structurally excluded from society often focus on particularistic issues and concerns rather than on the universal concerns of their nation-states. One implication of this observation is that schools, in order to support effective civic education for all youths, should promote equality and should itself become a democratic institution that promotes social class, economic, and cultural democracy.

However, my analysis also suggests that structural inclusion and equity will not eliminate ethnic affiliations and attachments. Ethnicity and modernity coexist in pluralistic democratic nation-states. Apter uses the analogy of the pendulum to describe the relationship between assimilationism and ethnicity in modernized democratic nation-states. The pendulum between universalism and ethnicity continues to swing back and forth.[17]

My analysis of the nature of ethnicity within modernized democratic nation-states suggests that the school, in order to foster effective civic education for all youths, should recognize, legitimize, and respect the students' ethnic attachments and should practice cultural democracy. Ethnic affiliations and attachments help students satisfy important psychological and sociological needs caused by the thin culture of modernization. Civic education should also help students attain the commitments and skills needed to participate in reflective and humane political action designed to reform their societies so that all groups will experience justice and equality.

Anglo-Conformity and Citizenship Education

Historically, the United States, using the schools and other public institutions as its agents, has tried to shape its diverse racial and ethnic groups into one nation with shared characteristics, values, and goals by a policy of *Anglo-conformity.*[18] The goals of this policy are to eradicate the ethnic attachments and characteristics of individuals and groups and to force them to endorse Anglo-Saxon values, characteristics, and behaviors. Within Anglo-conformity, ethnic youths experience the desocialization of their ethnic characteristics and the assimilation of Anglo-cultural characteristics. This process of Anglicization became known as "Americanization," since "American" was perceived by the people in power and in control of the public schools as the same as "Anglo-American."

Anglicization was perceived as consistent with modernization, whereas the ethnicity of non-Anglo ethnic youths was viewed as inconsistent with modernization and dysfunctional within a modernized democratic nation-state. *Assimilation into Anglo-Saxon Protestant culture became viewed as a necessary and essential condition for effective civic participation in the United States.* "American" became defined as "Anglo-American." Groups with non-Anglo-Saxon languages and cultural characteristics were viewed as un-American and often as unpatriotic and disloyal. Nativistic sentiments became especially pervasive and cogent when the United States faced a real or imagined threat—such as during the turn of the century when masses of Southern, Central, and Eastern European immigrants were entering the United States, and during the two great world wars.[19] A suspicion and distrust of all foreigners became rampant and widespread near the turn of the century. Occasionally, extreme events took place. In 1891, eleven Italian Americans were lynched in New Orleans during the height of American nativism, after being accused of murdering a police superintendent. Immigrant groups were not only suspected of being disloyal and un-American, but also of being radicals and communists.

The outbreak of World War I in Europe in 1914 increased the suspicion and distrust of immigrant groups in the United States and further stimulated nativistic feelings and groups. After the United States entered the war against Germany in 1917, the loyalty of German Americans to the United States was seriously questioned. German Americans became the victims of verbal and other forms of public and private abuse.

During World War II, the Japanese citizens of the United States were victimized by nativistic sentiments after Japan attacked the United States naval forces on Pearl Harbor in 1941. Historical scholarship now reveals that most Japanese Americans were loyal and patriotic citizens during the war and that none were found guilty of engaging in fifth column activities.[20] However, the Japanese were interned because they had physical and cultural characteristics inconsistent with the image of the "One Model American" held by the nation's military and political leaders and because they were perceived as stiff competitors by agri-businessmen on the West Coast. To the powerful military and political leaders, the Japanese Americans did not "look" like Americans but like "foreign enemies." Most American citizens remained conspicuously silent as 110,000 Japanese Americans were sent off to internment camps.

The attempt by the United States and its schools to shape a unified nation with shared values and characteristics by a policy of Anglo-conformity has to a large extent succeeded in the United States. Most European Americans, who constitute the largest immigrant-descendant group in the United States, consciously see themselves *first* as Americans and not as Irish, Welsh, German, or Swedes and then as Americans. Individual members of these ethnic groups tend to have weak ethnic identifications and strong national identifications.

Because of the cogency of Anglicization in American life, most members of European heritage groups in the United States are culturally Anglo-Saxons. They are members of the Anglo-American ethnic group, even though they may have a German or Swedish biological heritage or surname. Ethnicity, in its most important forms in a modernized society, consists of behavioral characteristics and psychological identifications, and not of biological traits and physical characteristics. Groups with the same or highly similar physical traits are members of both the same and very different ethnic groups. Individuals whom most people in the United States would regard as Black, White, and racially mixed are all part of the Puerto Rican ethnic group in cities such as New York City and Chicago.[21]

However, the Anglo-conformity approach to shaping a nation with shared values and characteristics has been only partially successful. Some ethnic groups in the United States, for a variety of historical, cultural, economic, and biological reasons, have been unable and/or unwilling to become identical to Anglo-Americans in their values, behaviors, and cultural characteristics.

The experiences of some ethnic groups, such as Blacks, Indians, and Mexican Americans, have been and are characterized by societal contradictions. Anglo-Saxon cultural characteristics and values are presented to them as ideals to attain, yet they have been denied, sometimes through legal means and castelike institutions and practices, the opportunities to acquire the behaviors and characteristics needed to become culturally like Anglo-Americans.[22] The cultures of these ethnic groups have often been harshly condemned in U.S. history, yet they have been and still are frequently denied opportunities to acquire alternative cultural characteristics and values. Throughout most of the history of the United States, groups such as Blacks, Indians, and Mexican Americans have tried to acquire Anglo-Saxon cultural characteristics and to become effective citizens in ways defined by the Anglo-conformity conceptualization of U.S. citizenship.[23]

However, when the ethnic revitalization movements of the 1960s emerged, many members of structurally excluded ethnic groups such as Blacks, Indians, and Puerto Ricans lost faith in the assimilationist ideal and advocated cultural pluralism.[24] Many ethnic individuals began to perceive the Anglo-conformity idea as a racist concept that required them to strive to attain the impossible — to become totally like White Anglo-Saxon Protestants in their values, behaviors, and physical characteristics. They realized that their skin color prevented them from becoming identical to White Anglo-Saxon Protestants. They also realized that they needed to hold onto important aspects of their cultural heritages and identities in order to satisfy many of their sociological and psychological needs. These ethnic groups began quests for ethnic pride and ethnic cultural components. They highlighted the positive and substantial contributions that cultural diversity makes to a pluralistic democratic nation such as the United States.

The Need for a Broader Conceptualization of *American*

A conception of *American* is needed in the United States that is consistent with the ethnic and cultural diversity within the United States and the world. The Anglo-Saxon Protestant culture is only one of the cultures in U.S. society (albeit it is politically and economically the most powerful ethnic group in the United States). Other ethnic groups, such as Blacks and Mexican Americans, are just as American as Anglos, even though these groups have a wide range of cultures, dialects, languages, values, and behaviors. Jack Forbes argues compellingly that American Indians are in some ways the most *American* of the groups that make up the United States.[25] One can challenge Forbes's claim. However, ethnic groups such as Indians, Blacks, and Puerto Ricans are American because they are legal citizens of the United States and because they share the overarching values and ideals of the nation-state. This is true even though these ethnic groups often focus on particularistic concerns and issues and sometimes experience conflicting allegiances when they believe that their ethnic group interest and what are described as the universalistic interests of the nation-state are in conflict.

The School as a Democratic Institution: Traditional Interpretations

To help ethnic youths attain structural inclusion and to develop clarified, reflective, and positive identifications and commitments to the nation-state, the school itself should promote cultural, ethnic, and social class democracy. The school should be a microdemocratic community that is just and that promotes social change consistent with such democratic values as equality, justice, and human rights. Educational historians have traditionally described the American public school as a citadel of democracy that promotes democratic ideals, values, and social justice.[26]

Educational historians near the turn of the century, such as Cubberley and Monroe, saw the U.S. school as a democratic institution that helped mold immigrant children into responsible adults who had democratic political attitudes and the knowledge, skills, and abilities needed to experience upward social class mobility.[27] They viewed the school as the major institution within society that enabled immigrant and other poor youths to experience social class mobility and to become effective democratic citizens of the nation-state.

The Revisionists' Critiques of Schooling

Since the 1970s, a number of revisionist educational historians and economists, such as Michael B. Katz, Colin Greer, Martin Carnoy, and Samuel Bowles and

Herbert Gintis, have strongly attacked traditional interpretations of U.S. schools, such as those written by Cubberly and Monroe.[28] These revisionist writers argue that rather than promoting social class mobility and cultural and political democracy, the schools reflect the social class stratifications of society and teach students political apathy and to fit into the class structure of society. The schools, they argue, educate for political apathy and not for political and social reform.

The revisionists argue that the public school was designed primarily to reinforce the status quo, to legitimize the positions of those in power, to perpetuate and reinforce the social class stratification that exists within society, to make students politically passive, and to perpetuate myths about lower class and minority groups in order to make them content with their social and economic conditions in society. Writes Carnoy:

> Rather than building independence and self-reliance among the poor in America, schools are used to ensure, as much as possible and apparently with some success, that those in the worst economic positions do not rebel against the system which represses them and identifies with leaders who would work within the framework of action set by the dominant ruling class. . . . Schooling as a colonial institution attempts to make children fit certain molds, to shape them to perform predetermined roles and tasks based on their social class.[29]

Bowles and Gintis also argue that the schools teach political apathy and reinforce the social class stratification in society.

> Education helps defuse and depoliticize the potentially explosive class relations of the production process, and thus serves to perpetuate the social, political, and economic conditions through which a portion of the product of labor is expropriated in the form of profits. . . . Schools legitimate inequality through the ostensibly meritocratic manner by which they reward and promote students, and allocate them to distinct positions in the occupational hierarchy.[30]

Greer calls the belief that the schools promote social justice for poor and minority youths "the great school legend" that has harmful consequences for today's minority students. If the schools helped European immigrants to experience upward social class mobility and is not helping groups such as Blacks and Mexican Americans today, then groups such as Blacks and Mexican Americans must have genetic deficiencies. This is how, according to Greer, the great legend results in reasoning that harms today's ethnic minority youths.

How Valid Are the Revisionists' Critiques of Schooling?

The interpretations of schools set forth by writers such as Katz, Carnoy, Greer, and Bowles and Gintis contrast sharply with traditional educational literature about the nature and purpose of schooling and with popular conventional wisdom about the public schools. Katz, for example, argues that the schools of a century ago, and that schools today, were and are "universal, tax-supported, free, compulsory, bureaucratic, racist, and class-biased."[31] Traditional educational literature and popular beliefs about schools suggest that they are democratic institutions that help poor and minority youths experience social class mobility and equality.

The revisionist historians and economists have stimulated thoughtful and creative dialogue about traditional assumptions about schools and about the power and willingness of the school to promote social class and political democracy. However, the revisionists have not escaped criticism and rigorous analyses. Diane Ravitch has written a book-length critique of their arguments and positions.[32] She argues that the revisionists have oversimplified history, have been too purist and ideological in their interpretations, and have not acknowledged the extent to which the public schools have helped poor and minority youths experience economic mobility. She writes, "Because the demands of them are simultaneously liberal and conservative. . . . The continuing strength of the schools is due to the fact that they have at least *partially fulfilled* the expectations of their differing constituencies."[33] (Italics added.)

How accurate and valid are the revisionist critiques of schooling? Because the school is only one of the educational institutions within society, and because of the complex variables that influence student learning, occupational mobility, and political participation, it is very difficult for social scientists and historians to resolve complex questions such as the extent to which the school helps bring about social and economic equality for minority youths. Because schools are social institutions that reflect the values, attitudes, and beliefs of the culture and society of which they are a part, the arguments and analyses of the revisionist historians and economists have much validity. Public schools are usually controlled by leaders in the business and professional communities. They are also tax supported. It is logical to assume that the schools reflect the values and attitudes of the peoples and groups who control them. Thus, in a society that is capitalistic, class stratified, and racist, it is reasonable to assume that its public schools will, at least to some extent, also be capitalistic, class stratified, and racist. Schools do not exist in a vacuum. They are social institutions that reflect the values and goals of the social systems of which they are a part.

However, the important question is not whether American public schools are capitalistic, bureaucratic, class stratified, and racist, but to what extent can American public schools be so characterized. The influences on the public schools within a democratic society are complex, diverse, and conflicting. The United States consists of realities such as racism and class stratification. However, as Myrdal points out in his landmark study of race relations in the United States, the "American Creed" and the values inherent within it, such as liberty, equality, justice, and fair opportunity, is a cogent ideal that is articulated by most institutions within the United States.[34]

Because the "American Creed" is institutionalized within U.S. society, it is reasonable to assume that the ideals of the Creed are, to some extent, perpetuated in U.S. public schools. They are reflected, at the very least, to the extent that they are often taught in textbooks, with patriotic songs, legendary stories about national heroes, and with national symbols and myths. Thus, the revisionists are not wrong when they say that U.S. schools are class stratified, capitalistic, and racist. However, they are misleading when they state or imply that the schools can be totally or completely so characterized.

The schools are racist and class stratified, but they, at least to some extent, also teach students American Creed values and ideals, such as equality, justice, and human rights. Consequently, the influences on the schools are multiple and conflicting rather than singular and consistent as the revisionists sometimes imply. *The values that public schools teach or try to teach are contradictory and conflicting.* Students are often asked to read stories and sing songs that reflect American Creed values within a classroom setting that is racist and economically stratified. One could argue that the nondemocratic environment in which students are taught about American Creed values makes it impossible for them to inculcate democratic values and ideologies. However, my hunch is that some students learn both democratic and antidemocratic values in the public schools. This may sometimes result in the phenomenon Myrdal calls the "American dilemma"—with some students inculcating conflicting values related to justice and equality. Myrdal writes:

> The "American dilemma" . . . is the ever-raging conflict between, on the one hand, the valuations preserved on the general plane which we shall call the "American Creed," where the American thinks, talks, and acts under the influence of high national and Christian precepts, and, on the other hand, the valuations on specific planes of individual and group living, where personal and local interests; economic, social, and sexual jealousies; considerations of community prestige and conformity; group prejudice against particular persons or types of people; and all sorts of miscellaneous wants, impulses, and habits dominate his outlook.[35]

The Problems with the Grand Theories Used by the Revisionists

The revisionists, such as Bowles and Gintis and Carnoy and Katz, use *grand theories* to explain and interpret the U.S. public school. Grand theories are all-embracing, unified explanations of events and phenomena.[36] Bowles and Gintis use a neo-Marxist theory to interpret U.S. schools; Carnoy uses a "colonial domination" theory. He writes, "The domination of one people by another has taken place throughout history. This domination has been exercised for its own ends by a powerful group or class in a particular society."[37] One problem with social science grand theories is that researchers usually feel obligated to interpret their findings in ways that will support their theories.

The theory must remain intact. Observed phenomena and behavior must be interpreted in ways consistent with the theoretical framework used by the researcher. Grand theories are useful because they help the social scientists order the universe and explain and interpret relationships; they are also limiting because they often force researchers to depict extremes in order to make their observations and theoretical frameworks consistent.

Merton discusses the problems of social science grand theories and the advantages of middle-range theories. Middle-range "theories consist of limited sets of assumptions from which specific hypotheses are logically derived and confirmed by empirical investigation."[38] Merton believes that sociologists are not ready to develop grand theories because not enough preparatory work has been done. He states that grand theories cannot be developed until "a great mass of basic observations have been accumulated."[39]

When they are guided by grand theories, social scientists often formulate theories or use existing ones and then make their empirical observations. Consequently, their findings are described in ways that will fit the theory. This often results in descriptions of events and institutions that are extreme, and that are characterized by an inattention to details that the grand theory does not explain and by explanations that are incomplete and/or misleading.

The revisionist interpretations of public schools by historians and economists are not so much wrong as they are overdrawn and incomplete. Schools are racist, bureaucratic, social class stratified, and capitalistic. However, as Sowell, Ravitch, and Clark have pointed out, the U.S. public school can and does help many minority youths escape poverty and experience social class and economic mobility.[40] Most minority parents retain an unshaken faith in the power of the public schools to help their children attain upward social class mobility. Even though their faith in the public school may be overly optimistic, perceptions are enormously important in influencing behavior. Blacks and many other ethnic groups perceive the public school and formal education as one of the few means by which they can escape poverty and attain the benefits of a highly technological society. The important question before us is how can we reform the state school so it will become socially, culturally, and economically democratic and will help all youths experience social class mobility and consequently become more effective and productive citizens of the nation-state.

Cultural Democracy and Citizenship Education

The most effective way for the schools to help students develop the attitudes, values, and commitments needed to function effectively within a democratic nation-state is for the school to structure a total educational environment that enables students to experience democracy. Civic education involves the total school, as Mehlinger states: "Civic education is a process permeating the entire school. It exists in many planned and unplanned ways through extracurricular activities, the pattern of school governance, and the informal school culture."[41]

A public-issues curriculum and social action and participation activities can help students develop the knowledge, skills, and commitments needed to function within a democracy.[42] However, because many ethnic youths have unclarified and conflicting national commitments and allegiances, the school should also help these students develop clarified commitments to the nation-state. This can happen only when structurally and economically excluded ethnic and racial groups feel included into society and view themselves as legitimate citizens of the nation-state. The school can help this occur.

As the works by Jencks and Coleman indicate, the schools are probably limited in what they can do to help ethnic minority youths attain structural inclusion into society and upward social mobility.[43] However, the school is a very important institution from which students learn many values, attitudes, and views of their ethnic groups and their cultures. *The school can play a significant role in legitimizing the cultures, values, and life-styles of minority groups and in helping them gain a sense of inclusion into the fabric of society.* If the school accepts and legitimizes the cultures of ethnic minority youths, this will also affect the knowledge and attitudes of majority group students, many of whom will be policy makers and opinion makers in the future society. Consequently, the school's legitimization of the cultures of ethnic youths may very well have an impact on the norms and values of future institutions.

To legitimize, accept, and respect the cultures of ethnic minority youths, the school will need to practice what Julius Drachsler called "cultural democracy."[44] Cultural democracy "posits the right of ethnic groups in a democratic society to maintain their communal identity and their own subcultural values. . . . Democratic values prescribe free choice not only for groups but also for individuals."[45] However, much evidence indicates that the school usually practices Anglo-conformity and cultural imperialism rather than cultural democracy. It usually forces non-Anglo ethnic youths to become alienated from their ethnic groups and to assimilate Anglo-Saxon cultural characteristics and values.

Summary

Citizenship education should help students develop the knowledge, skills, and values needed to participate in political action that will promote the nation's democratic ideals. To develop clarified, reflective, and positive commitments and identifications with their nation-state, the ethnic groups within a nation must perceive themselves as legitimate groups that are structurally included into the national society. Ethnic groups that are excluded from full participation in their nation-state have conflicting national identifications and often focus on particularistic concerns and problems rather than on the universal goals and problems of the nation-state.

The assimilationist assumes that ethnicity and particularistic concerns of ethnic groups can be eliminated by creating a just society in which ethnic groups will gain inclusion and equality. An analysis of the assimilationist position indicates that it does not adequately explain the nature of ethnicity in complex, modernized, and democratic nation-states. Ethnicity persists in modernized nation-states not only because of the exclusion of ethnic groups but also because it helps individuals and groups satisfy important psychological and sociological needs left unfilled by the "thin" culture of modernization.

To foster effective civic education, the school should promote social class and cultural democracy and legitimize the cultures of ethnic groups. Historically, the U.S. public school has practiced cultural imperialism and fostered an Anglo-conformity conception of citizenship. Assimilation into Anglo-Saxon culture became viewed as an essential requisite for civic participation. A broader conception of "American" is needed to guide civic education. This conception should recognize that individuals who are members of diverse ethnic and cultural groups are *American* because they endorse the overarching values of the nation-state.

Traditional educational literature and conventional wisdom have fostered the idea that the school has promoted democracy and enabled ethnic and poor youths to experience social class mobility and equality. Since the 1960s, revisionist historians and economists have rejected these views and argued that the schools perpetuate and reflect the social class and racial stratifications in society. An analysis of the revisionists arguments and grand theories indicates that their positions are not so much wrong as they are incomplete, overdrawn, and sometimes misleading.

Ethnic minorities retain an unshaken faith in the school's ability to help them attain equality and social class mobility. The school remains a cogent factor in the lives of many youths who are members of excluded ethnic and social-class groups. Consequently, the total school environment should be reformed so it will help students attain clarified, positive, and reflective ethnic, national, and global identifications, and the skills and commitments needed to help close the gap between society's realities and ideals.

Notes

1. Nathan Glazer and Daniel P. Moynihan, eds., *Ethnicity: Theory and Experience* (Cambridge, Mass.: Harvard University Press, 1975); Michael Banton, *Racial and Ethnic Competition* (Cambridge: Cambridge University Press, 1983); Thomas Sowell, *Ethnic America: A History* (New York: Basic Books, 1981).

2. John Porter, "Ethnic Pluralism in Canadian Perspective," in Glazer and Moynihan, eds., *Ethnicity: Theory and Experience*, pp. 267–304; Orlando Patterson, *Ethnic Chauvinism: The Reactionary Impulse* (New York: Stein and Day, 1977).

3. David E. Apter, "Political Life and Cultural Pluralism," in Melvin M. Tumin and Walter Plotch, eds., *Pluralism in a Democratic Society* (New York: Praeger, 1977), pp. 58–91.

4. Orlando Patterson, "Ethnicity and the Pluralist Fallacy," *Change* (March 1975): 11.

5. Apter, "Political Life and Cultural Pluralism."

6. Ibid., p. 60.

7. Ibid., p. 61.

8. "Robert Ezra Park 1864–1944," in Lewis A. Coser, ed., *Masters of Sociological Thought*, 2nd ed. (New York: Harcourt, 1977), pp. 357–384.

9. Michael Novak, *The Rise of the Unmeltable Ethnics* (New York: Macmillan, 1971).

10. Patterson, *Ethnic Chauvinism*, pp. 158–159.

11. Judith Herman, ed., *The Schools and Group Identity: Educating for a New Pluralism* (New York: Institute on Pluralism and Group Identity of the American Jewish Community, 1974), p. 15.

12. Andrew M. Greeley, *Why Can't They Be Like Us? America's White Ethnic Groups* (New York: Dutton, 1975).

13. Peter Schrag, *The Decline of Wasp* (New York: Simon and Schuster, 1973).

14. Apter, "Political Life and Cultural Pluralism," p. 65.

15. Ibid., p. 75.

16. Cynthia H. Enloe, *Ethnic Conflict and Political Development* (Boston: Little, Brown, 1973), p. 15.

17. Apter, "Political Life and Cultural Pluralism," p. 89.

18. Milton M. Gordon, *Assimilation in American Life* (New York: Oxford University Press, 1964), pp. 84–114.

19. John Higham, *Strangers in the Land: Patterns of American Nativisim 1860–1925* (New York: Atheneum, 1972).

20. Roger Daniels, *Concentration Camps U.S.A.: Japanese Americans and World War II* (New York: Holt, 1971).

21. Lloyd Roger and Rosemary Santana Cooney, *Puerto Rican Families in New York: Intergenerational Processes* (Maplewood, N.J.: Waterfront Press, 1984).

22. Mary Frances Berry and John W. Blassingame, *Long Memory: The Black Experience in America* (New York: Oxford University Press, 1982); Thomas J. Archdeacon, *Becoming American: An Ethnic History* (New York: The Free Press, 1983).

23. Meyer Weinberg, *A Chance to Learn: A History of Race and Education in the United States* (New York: Cambridge University Press, 1977).

24. Stokley Carmichael and Charles V. Hamilton, *Black Power: The Politics of Liberation in America* (New York: Vintage Books, 1967).

25. Jack D. Forbes, "Teaching Native American Values and Cultures," in James A. Banks, ed. *Teaching Ethnic Studies: Concepts and Strategies* (Washington, D.C.: National Council for the Social Studies), pp. 201–225.

26. Arthur Lean, "Review of Public Education of the Future," *History of Education Journal* 6 (Fall 1954): 167.

27. Diane Ravitch, *The Revisionists Revised: A Critique of the Radical Attack on the Schools* (New York: Basic Books, 1978), pp. 22–23.

28. Michael B. Katz, *Class, Bureaucracy, and Schools: The Illusion of Educational Change in America*, expanded ed. (New York: Praeger, 1975); Colin Greer, *The Great School Legend: A Revisionist Interpretation of American Public Education* (New York: The Viking Press, 1973); Martin Carnoy, *Education as Cultural Imperialism* (New York: David McKay, 1974); Samuel Bowles and Herbert Gintis, *Schooling in Capitalist America: Educational Reform and the Contradictions of Economic Life* (New York: Basic Books, 1976).

29. Carnoy, *Education as Cultural Imperialism*, p. 18.

30. Bowles and Gintis, *Schooling in Capitalist America*, p. 11.

31. Katz, *Class, Bureaucracy, and Schools*, p. xviii.

32. Ravitch, *The Revisionists Revised.*

33. Ibid., pp. 16–17.

34. Gunnar Myrdal, *An American Dilemma: The Negro Problem and Modern Democracy*, vols. 1 and 2 (New York: Harper Torchbooks, 1963).

35. Ibid., vol. 1, p. lxxi.

36. Robert K. Merton, *Social Theory and Social Structure*, enlarged ed. (New York: The Free Press, 1968), p. 45.

37. Carnoy, *Education as Cultural Imperialism*, pp. 33–34.

38. Merton, *Social Theory and Social Structure*, p. 68.

39. Ibid., p. 46.

40. Thomas Sowell, "Patterns of Black Excellence," *The Public Interest* 45 (Spring 1976), pp. 26–58; Ravitch, *The Revisionists Revised*; Kenneth B. Clark, "Social Policy, Power, and Social Science Research," *Harvard Educational Review* 43 (February 1973), pp. 113–121.

41. Howard D. Mehlinger, "The Crisis in Civic Education," in *Education for Responsible Citizenship: The Report of the National Task Force on Citizenship Education*, edited by B. Frank Brown, Director (New York: McGraw-Hill, 1977), p. 69.

42. Donald W. Oliver and James P. Shaver, *Teaching Public Issues in the High School* (Boston: Houghton Mifflin, 1966).

43. Christopher Jencks et al., *Inequality: A Reassessment of the Effect of Family and Schooling in America* (New York: Basic Books, 1972); James S. Coleman et al., *Equality of Educational Opportunity* (Washington, D.C.: U.S. Government Printing Office, 1966).

44. Julius Drachsler, *Democracy and Assimilation* (New York: The Macmillan Company, 1920).

45. Gordon, *Assimilation in American Life*, p. 263.

PART IV

The Curriculum

A major goal of the ethnic revival movements of the 1960s and 1970s was to change the curriculum so it would more accurately reflect the ethnic and cultural diversity within Western societies. The chapters in Part IV describe the efforts made to reform the curriculum within the last two decades, the limited extent to which curriculum reform has occurred, the nature and goals of the multiethnic curriculum, factors that inhibit curriculum reform, and how the curriculum can reflect the ethnic characteristics of students.

Chapter 9 describes the extent to which curriculum reform has occurred, how diverse ethnic perspectives enrich the curriculum, and how the teacher can become a cultural mediator and change agent. The problems involved in changing the curriculum to reflect ethnic diversity, the nature of the multiethnic curriculum, and curricular models that can help create an open society are discussed in Chapter 10. The ways in which the curriculum can be designed to reflect the stages of ethnic development of students are described in Chapter 11.

9

The Curriculum, Ethnic Diversity, and Social Change

The Ethnic Revival Movements

The Black civil rights movement that emerged in the 1960s stimulated the rise of ethnic revival movements throughout the United States as well as in other parts of the world. A major goal of these ethnic movements was to change the social, economic, and political systems so that structurally excluded and powerless ethnic groups would attain social and economic mobility and educational equality. The demand for changes in the educational system was a major goal of the ethnic revival movements throughout the Western world.[1] Ethnic groups demanded changes in the educational system because they believed the school could be an important instrument in their empowerment and liberation. Most ethnic groups have a tenacious faith in the school to help them attain social mobility and structural inclusion,[2] despite the arguments by revisionists such as Jencks et al. and Bowles and Gintis that the school merely reproduces the social structure and depoliticizes powerless ethnic groups.[3]

Educational Responses to Ethnic Revival Movements

In the various Western societies in which ethnic revival movements have taken place, such as the United States, Canada, the United Kingdom, and Australia, educators have responded with a wide range of programs, projects, and curricular innovations to silence ethnic protest, increase the achievement of ethnic groups, and close the gap between their expressed democratic ideals and practices.[4] The social studies (history in particular) was one of the first curricular areas to be scrutinized and criticized by ethnic reformers.[5] Major goals of the ethnic revival movements were to shape new identities of ethnic groups and to highlight the roles that various ethnic groups had played in the development of their nations. Ethnic reformers saw history as an important part of the curriculum that perpetuated old images and stereotypes and that therefore needed radical revision and reconstruction.[6]

More than two decades have passed since the ethnic protest and revival movements first emerged in the United States. This period has been characterized by intense ethnic polarization and debate, rapid and often superficial curriculum changes and innovations, the birth and death of promising ideas, progress and retrenchment, hope and disillusionment, and a flurry of activity related to ethnic and immigrant groups. The late 1980s was characterized by conservatism and a back-to-the-basics ideology ushered in partly by the movement for academic excellence, which devoted scant attention to equality and the needs of victimized ethnic groups.[7]

In this chapter, I describe the visions and goals that ethnic reformers had for multiethnic studies when the ethnic revival movements emerged more than two decades ago and the limited extent to which these goals have been realized; I also identify the factors that have restrained significant curriculum reform. Finally, I propose a reform strategy that views the teacher as a change agent and cultural mediator. Such a teacher interprets ethnic and majority cultures for mainstream and minority students and helps them see why social change is essential if we are to close the gap between our nation's democratic ideals and its social, economic, and political realities.

Life-Style Versus Life-Chance Approaches

During the early phases of ethnic revitalization movements in the United States as well as in other Western nations, ethnic leaders demanded that ethnic heroes and cultures become a part of the school curriculum. Educators often responded to these demands quickly and without careful planning and sufficient teacher in-service training. As a result, ethnic heroes such as Crispus Attucks and Martin Luther King, Jr., were inserted into the curriculum along with bits and pieces of content about ethnic cultures and traditions.[8] This additive approach to the study of ethnic content emanates from several assumptions that preclude substantial curriculum reform, perpetuate stereotypes and misconceptions of ethnic cultures and life-styles, and prevent teachers from dealing effectively and comprehensively with such concepts as racism, class stratification, powerlessness, and the reforms needed to empower ethnic groups.

When educators add ethnic heroes and bits and pieces of ethnic content to the curriculum, the assumption is made that ethnic heroes and content are not integral parts of the mainstream U.S. experience. Consequently, it is also assumed that it is sufficient to add special units and festivals to teach about ethnic groups and their cultures. Particularly in the elementary grades, ethnic content is taught primarily with special lessons and pageants on holidays and birthdays. Blacks often dominate lessons during Black History Week or on Martin Luther King's birthday but are largely invisible in the curriculum during the rest of the year. Even though Blacks and other ethnic minority groups are now a more integral part of textbooks than they were before the 1960s, their presence is neither comprehensive nor sufficiently integrated into the total curriculum.[9]

The infusion of bits and pieces of ethnic content into the curriculum not only reinforces the idea that ethnic minority groups are not integral parts of U.S. society, it also results in the trivialization of ethnic cultures. The study of the foods eaten by Mexican Americans or of Indian tepees will not help students develop a sophisticated understanding of Mexican-American culture and of the tremendous cultural diversity among American Indians. This kind of teaching about ethnic cultures often perpetuates misconceptions and stereotypes about ethnic cultures and leads well-meaning but misinformed teachers to believe they have integrated their curricula with ethnic content and helped their students better understand ethnic groups.

Superficial teaching about ethnic groups and ethnic cultures may do more harm than good. Excluding a study of ethnic cultures in the curriculum might be preferable to the trivialization and marginalization of ethnic cultures and life-styles. The distortion of ethnic cultures that has taken place in the schools has led some critics of multicultural education to argue that teaching about ethnic groups in the schools should focus on their life-chances rather than on their life-styles.[10]

A curriculum that focuses on life-chances describes the ways structurally excluded ethnic groups are victimized by social, economic, and political variables such as institutionalized racism, class stratification, and political powerlessness. Critics of multicultural education who make this argument are concerned that a focus on cultures and life-styles not only trivializes the cultures of ethnic groups, but also diverts attention from the real causes of ethnic group victimization and poverty. They believe that a focus on life-styles might cause majority groups to blame the victims for their victimization and thus help entrench institutionalized stereotypes. Writes Moodley:

> Given the complexity of cultures, they are frequently trivialized in presentation in the elementary curriculum. Werner et al. refer to the common isolated use of artifacts and other aspects of the material culture, without a holistic interpretation, as the "museum approach." It reinforces the "us"–"them" differences and highlights a "hierarchy of cultures" based on the way the outsider perceives the minority.[11]

Teachers do not need to decide whether they will approach the teaching of ethnic content from a life-style or life-chance perspective. Both cultural knowledge and knowledge about why many ethnic groups are victimized by institutionalized racism and class stratification are needed in a sound curriculum that accurately and sensitively reflects the experience of ethnic groups. Both perspectives are needed to help students gain a comprehensive and sophisticated understanding of the experiences of ethnic groups in the United States and in other nations. However, teaching accurately about the cultures of ethnic groups is a complex and difficult task.

To teach about ethnic cultures accurately, teachers must help students understand that ethnic cultures, especially within a modernized society such as the United States, are dynamic, holistic, and changing processes.[12] Students also need to understand that a culture consists of many aspects or variables, such as symbols, language, and behavior, and that an individual member of a culture may exemplify the characteristics of a group completely or hardly at all. Consequently, knowing what have been called Afro-American cultural characteristics[13] may give an individual few clues about the behavior of a particular Black individual and reinforce stereotypes and misconceptions.

The Search for New Perspectives

Major goals of the ethnic revival movements of the 1960s and 1970s were not only to include more information about the cultures and history of ethnic groups in the curriculum, but also to infuse the curriculum with new perspectives, frames of reference, and values. However, in textbooks and in teaching, even though ethnic events and heroes are often added to the curriculum, the interpretations and perspectives on these events and heroes remain those of mainstream historians and scholars.[14] When concepts, events, and situations in the curriculum are viewed only or primarily from the perspectives of mainstream scholars and historians, students obtain a limited view of social reality and an incomplete understanding of the human experience. As James Baldwin perceptively points out in several trenchant essays, White Americans cannot fully understand their history unless they study Black history from myriad perspectives because the history of Blacks and Whites is intricately interwoven.[15]

In an important essay on the sociology of knowledge published in the midst of the civil rights movement, Merton[16] discusses insiders and outsiders and their competing knowledge claims. Both insiders and outsiders claim that only they can obtain valid knowledge about group life. Insiders claims that only a member of their group can formulate accurate and valid knowledge about the group because of the special insights that result from being socialized within the group. Outsiders claim that valid knowledge results only when they study groups because of the dispassionate objectivity they bring to the study of group life. Merton concludes that both insiders and outsiders can make important contributions to understanding group life, and that insiders and outsiders should unite in their quests for knowledge.

Social and historical knowledge reflects the values, experiences, times, and social structure in which scholars are socialized and work. In an ethnically and racially stratified society such as the United States, ethnic and racial microcultures also influence the formulation of knowledge. Social scientists and historians who are insiders in the Black community and those who are outsiders are likely to agree on many observations about Black life and behavior; they also are likely to formulate some findings and interpretations that differ in significant ways. Many mainstream social scientists conducted studies of Blacks before the civil rights movements of the 1960s that were strongly attacked by Black social scientists in the 1970s.[17] Much of this controversy focused on historical interpretations of such topics as slavery and the Civil War, sociological interpretations of the Black family, and descriptions and interpretations of Black English and Black culture. Mainstream social scientists frequently described Black culture and life as disorganized, pathological, and deviant.[18] Black students were often labeled "culturally deprived."[19] Traditional research assumptions, methods, and conclusions of mainstream social scientists often differed sharply from those of the new Black social scientists during this period.[20]

Even though ethnicity and race often influence the knowledge claims, research, and perspectives of social scientists and historians, these influences are complex and difficult to describe precisely. Individual White, Mexican-American, or Black scholars may be influenced more by their own class interests, commitment to scholarly objectivity, or other values than they are by race or ethnicity. The revisionist and sensitive studies of Blacks by White social scientists such as Baratz, Gutman, and Genovese during the 1970s are cases in point,[21] as are the more conservative analyses of the Black experience written by Black scholars such as Wilson and Sowell.[22]

Even though the influences of race, ethnicity, and class on social knowledge are complex and difficult to describe precisely, they are nonetheless significant and far-reaching. Insider perspectives on such important social and historical events as the Holocaust, the internment of Japanese Americans, and the civil rights movements of the 1960s provide students with insights, perspectives, and feelings about these events that cannot be gained from reading source materials or accounts by individuals who have experienced these events only from a distance.[23] Scholars who are socialized within ethnic cultures in which these events are important parts of the social and cultural history are also likely to have perspectives on them that differ from those of mainstream scholars.[24]

It is important for students to experience a curriculum that not only presents the experience of ethnic and cultural groups in accurate and sensitive ways, but that also enables them to see the experiences of both mainstream and minority groups from the perspectives of different cultural, racial, and ethnic groups. A curriculum that includes the experiences of different ethnic groups *and* presents these experiences from diverse perspectives and points of view is needed to help students understand the complexity of the human experience and how a nation's various groups have strongly influenced each other culturally and interacted within the social structure. Table 9.1 summarizes the dominant and desirable characteristics of multiethnic studies described above.

The Ideological Resistance to a Pluralistic Curriculum

After more than two decades of debates and attempts to reform the school and the curriculum to reflect ethnic and cultural diversity in the United States, multiethnic reforms remain on the periphery of the mainstream curriculum in most U.S. schools. Most examples of blatant racism and stereotypes of ethnic groups have been deleted from textbooks and teaching materials, but content about racial and ethnic groups is not yet thoroughly integrated into mainstream textbooks

Table 9.1. Dominant and Desirable Characteristics of Multiethnic Studies

Dominant Characteristics	*Desirable Characteristics*
Focuses on isolated aspects of the histories and cultures of ethnic groups.	Describes the history and cultures of ethnic groups holistically.
Trivializes the histories and cultures of ethnic groups.	Describes the cultures of ethnic groups as dynamic wholes and processes of change.
Presents events, issues, and concepts primarily from Anglo-centric and mainstream perspectives and points of view.	Presents events, issues, and concepts from the perspectives and points of view of diverse racial and ethnic groups.
Is Euro-centric—shows the development of America primarily as an extension of Europe into the Americas.	Is multidimensional and geocultural—shows how peoples and cultures came to America from many different parts of the world, including Asia and Africa, and the important roles they played in the development of U.S. society.
Content about ethnic groups is an *appendage* to the regular or core curriculum.	Content about ethnic groups is an *integral part* of the regular or core curriculum.
Ethnic minority cultures are described as deprived or pathological.	Ethnic minority cultures are described as *different* from mainstream Anglo culture but as normal and functional.
Concepts such as institutional racism, class stratification, powerlessness, and the victimization of ethnic and racial groups are given scant attention.	An important focus is on such concepts as institutional racism, class stratification, powerlessness, and the victimization of ethnic and racial groups.
The curriculum is dominted by the assimilationist ideology. Pluralist and radical ideologies are either ignored or depicted as undesirable.	The curriculum reflects a pluralistic ideology, with some attention given to radical ideas and conceptions.
Focuses on lower-level knowledge, ethnic heroes, holidays, and the recall of factual information	Focus on higher-level knowledge, such as concepts, generalizations, and theories.
Emphasizes the mastery of knowledge and cognitive outcomes.	Emphasizes decision making and citizen action. Knowledge formulation, value analysis, and citizen action are important components of the curriculum. Knowledge is synthesized with clarified values in order to make reflective decisions that guide action.
Encourages acceptance of existing ethnic, class, and racial stratification.	Focuses on social criticism and social change.

and teaching materials.[25] Intead, materials about racial and ethnic groups are usually relegated to special units and holidays and are appendages to the main story about the development of U.S. society.

Most content about Afro-Americans is studied when topics such as slavery,

Reconstruction, and the civil rights movement of the 1960s are covered.[26] A uni-linear, Euro-centric approach is used most frequently to teach about the development of U.S. history and society. The story of the development of America is often told by describing the sojourn of the Europeans across the Atlantic to the Americas and then from the Atlantic to the Pacific oceans. The focus of the story is on European settlers, on the way they shaped America in their image, created a nation that promised freedom for all people, and made the United States a world power. Ethnic minorities such as Blacks, Mexican Americans, and Indians are discussed primarily at points at which they interacted with the Europeans in North America.

A number of reasons have been set forth to explain why the school curriculum remains primarily Anglo-centric and Euro-centric after more than two decades of attempted reform. Many teachers and principals state they have not reformed the curriculum to reflect ethnic diversity in their schools because they do not have ethnic minorities in their school populations and consequently have no racial or ethnic problems. These educators believe that ethnic content is needed only by ethnic minority students or to help reduce ethnic conflict and tension within schools that have racial problems. This assumption is widespread within the schools and has existed at least since the early 1950s, when Hilda Taba and her colleagues did their pioneering work in intergroup education.[27]

Other reasons often given for the lack of progress in substantially reforming the curriculum to reflect ethnic and cultural diversity since the 1960s include the lack of effective teaching materials, ambivalent teacher attitudes toward ethnic diversity, lack of effective in-service training, and the lack of administrative support. Each of these reasons explains in part why multicultural content has not permeated the school curriculum in the last two decades, but as a group they do not reveal the basic reason that multicultural content has not permeated, in any meaningful way, the U.S. school curriculum. I believe the resistance to multicultural content is basically ideological.

An ideology is a system of ideas, beliefs, traditions, principles, and myths held by a social group or society that reflects, rationalizes, and defends its particular social, political, and economic interests.[28] Dominant ethnic and cultural groups develop ideologies to defend and rationalize their attitudes, goals, and social structure. Writes Bullivant, "In an analysis of ethnoculturally pluralistic societies the term *ideology* can be used to refer to the system of beliefs and values employed by a dominant ethnocultural group to legitimize its control over the life chances of subordinate ethnocultural groups."[29] Bullivant calls this situation a form of *ethnic hegemony*.

The dominant ideology related to ethnic and racial pluralism within the United States has been described with several different concepts, including the melting pot, Anglo-conformity, and cultural assimilation.[30] This ideology states that the diverse ethnic and racial groups within the United States not only should but will eventually surrender their unique cultural and ethnic characteristics and acquire those of Anglo or mainstream Americans. Robert E. Park, the eminent

U.S. sociologist who played a key role in the development of the Chicago School, believed that race and ethnic relations were characterized by four inevitable phases: *contact, conflict, accommodation, and assimilation.*[31]

Park's notion about inevitable cultural assimilation dominated U.S. social science until the ethnic revival movements emerged in the 1960s.[32] The assimilationist envisions a society and nation-state in which ethnic characteristics die of their own weight. Group affiliations within a modernized society, argues the assimilationist, are related to social class, occupation, education, and to other voluntary and achieved statuses. The assimilationist believes that ethnic affiliations and attachments are antithetical to a modernized democratic society because they promote primordial affiliations, groups rights over the rights of the individual, and particularistic concerns rather than the overarching goals of the nation-state.[33]

The assimilationist conception is not so much wrong as it is flawed and incomplete.[34] Ethnic minorities such as Afro-Americans, Mexican Americans, and Indians realized by the late 1960s that no matter how culturally assimilated they became, they were often unable to attain structural assimilation and full participation in U.S. society. During most of their histories in the United States these groups had worked diligently to become culturally assimilated and full participants in U.S. society.[35] In the late 1960s most non-White ethnic groups had become disillusioned with assimilation as a societal goal and with the assimilationist ideology. They began seriously to question not only its desirability but its latent function. Many ethnic minority leaders and scholars began to view it as a tool of dominant ethnic groups used to rationalize and maintain their power and to keep victimized ethnic groups content with the status quo and yet striving to attain implausible goals.[36]

During the ethnic revival movements of the 1960s and 1970s, ethnic minority scholars and leaders stridently attacked the assimilationist ideology and began to exhume, fashion, and shape a pluralist ideology that they saw as more consistent with their social, economic, political, and educational aspirations.[37] This ideology maintains that the assimilationist claims about individual opportunity in the United States are a myth and that U.S. citizens are judged first as members of groups and only secondarily as individuals. The pluralists argue that individuals are rarely able to experience social and economic mobility that is beyond that of their ethnic or cultural group.[38] Pluralists envision a curriculum that will strengthen family and ethnic attachments and help students develop a commitment to the liberation of their ethnic group.

Assimilationists contend that they oppose a pluralist curriculum because it is un-American, will undercut American patriotism, will create ethnic Balkanization, and will prevent ethnic minority students from attaining the knowledge, attitudes, and skills they need to become effective participants in mainstream U.S. society and culture.[39] Pluralists maintain that mainstream Americans are strongly opposed to a pluralistic curriculum that reinterprets the U.S. experience and represents diverse ethnic perspectives on the development of American society. They fear it will undercut their dominant position in society and legitimize the quest of excluded ethnic groups for empowerment and significant social change.[40]

Teaching for Social Change

A major goal of education has traditionally been to socialize students so they would unquestionably accept the existing ideologies, institutions, and practices within their society and nation-state.[41] Political education within the United States has traditionally fostered political passivity rather than political action. Although several experimental political studies courses designed to foster political action were developed for students during the flurry of social studies curricular activity during the 1970s,[42] these projects have not substantially changed the nature of political education in the nation's schools. Students are taught to vote and to participate in the political systems in ways that will not significantly reform U.S. society. Writes Newmann:

> By teaching that the constitutional system of the U.S. guarantees a benevolent government serving the needs of all, the schools have fostered massive public apathy. Whereas the protestant ethic calls for engagement (to survive economically one must *earn* a living), the political creed breeds passivity. One need not struggle for political rights, but only maintain a vague level of vigilance, obey the laws, make careful choices in elections, perform a few duties (taxes, military service), and his political welfare is assured.[43]

Even though the schools teach students the expressed ideals about justice and equality that are dominant within U.S. society, rarely do we *deliberately* educate students for social change and help them acquire the knowledge, attitudes, and skills needed to help close the gap between our democratic ideals and societal realities. A major goal of the curriculum should be to help students acquire the knowledge, values, and skills they need to participate in social change so that victimized and excluded ethnic and racial groups can become full participants in their societies. To participate effectively in social change, students must be taught social criticism and must be helped to understand the inconsistency between our ideals and social realities, the work that must be done to close this gap, and how they can, as individuals and groups, become empowered to influence the social and political systems of their societies.

When conceptualizing a curriculum designed to promote civic action and social change, we need to ponder seriously the arguments by the revisionists and neo-Marxist scholars.[44] They contend that the schools are incapable of teaching students to be change agents because two of their major roles are to reproduce the social structure and to socialize students so they will passively accept their position in our class- and ethnically stratified society. The radical critics of the schools, especially those in the United Kingdom, have been keenly critical of multiethnic studies as a strategy to promote social change.[45] They argue that multiethnic studies is a palliative to keep excluded and oppressed groups from rebelling against a system that promotes structural inequality and institutionalized racism.[46] The radical scholars also claim that multiethnic studies avoids any serious analysis of class, racism, power, capitalism, and other systems that keep excluded ethnic groups powerless. Multiethnic studies, they argue, divert attention from the real problems and issues. Instead, it focuses on the victim as the problem.

It is difficult to reject completely the argument that one of the school's major roles is to socialize students so they will fit into the existing social order. However, the revisionists and other radical scholars overstate the case when they argue that the schools *merely* socialize students into the existing social order. The school itself is contradictory, since it often expounds democratic values while at the same time contradicting them. The school does socialize students into the existing social structure; it also enables some students to acquire the knowledge, attitudes, and skills needed to participate effectively in social action and social change.

The Teacher as Cultural Mediator and Change Agent

Whether they are deliberate goals of the school or not, many students learn compassion and democratic ideals and develop a commitment to participate in social change from powerful and influential classroom teachers. These teachers are also cultural mediators who interpret the mainstream and ethnic cultures to students from diverse cultural groups and help students understand the desirability of and possibility for social change. Many such teachers participated in social action in the 1960s and 1970s to promote social justice and human rights. Today, many teachers are deeply concerned about apartheid in South Africa and about the possibility of a nuclear holocaust.

The school—primarily through the influence of teachers who have clarified and reflective commitments to democratic values, knowledge, and pedagogical skills and who have the charisma to inspire other people—can play a significant role in teaching social criticism and in motivating students to become involved in social change (see Figure 9.1). Some teachers have a significant influence on the values, hopes, and dreams of their students. The classroom should be a forum of open inquiry, where diverse points of view and perspectives are shared and analyzed reflectively. Teachers who are committed to human freedom should feel free to express their views in the classroom, provided that students have first had an opportunity to express freely and to defend their own beliefs and that teachers defend their beliefs reflectively and in ways consistent with democratic values.[47] In the democratic classroom, both students and teachers should have the freedom to express their values and beliefs but should be required to defend them and to point out ways in which their moral choices are related to overarching democratic ideals, such as human dignity, justice, and equality.

In a democratic society, students and teachers should freely express morally and intellectually defensible values and beliefs about human freedom.[48] Teaching, like social science inquiry, is not a value-neutral activity. This is especially the case in ethnic studies, where teachers and students must deal with human problems, conflicts, and dilemmas toward which it is impossible to remain neutral. Both

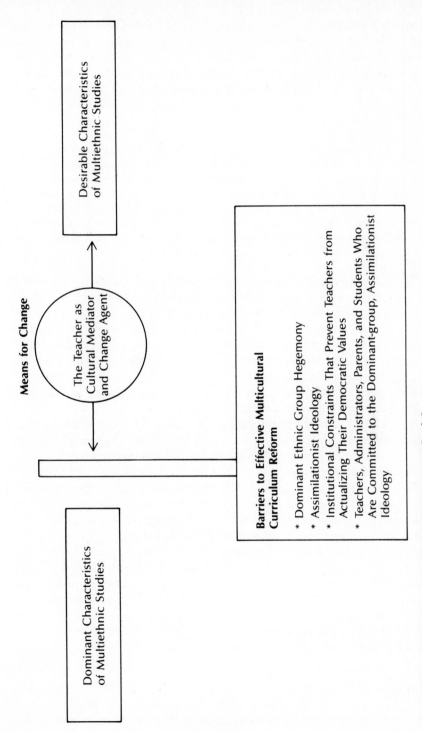

Figure 9.1. The Teacher as Cultural Mediator and Social Change Agent

teachers and social scientists have often been admonished to strive for objectivity in their work. Teachers should not use the classroom as a forum to promote partisan political beliefs, but they should, like caring social scientists, become "involved observers," to borrow Kenneth B. Clark's apt phrase.[49] They should support and defend moral and ethical positions that are consistent with democratic values and ideals. Clark eloquently states his creed as a social scientist. It is an appropriate one for teachers:

> An important part of my creed as a social scientist is that on the grounds of absolute objectivity or on a posture of scientific detachment and indifference, a truly and serious social science cannot ask to be taken seriously by a society desperately in need of moral and empirical guidance in human affairs. . . . I believe that to be taken seriously, to be viable, and to be relevant social science must dare to study the real problems of men and society, must use the real community, the market place, the arena of politics and power as its laboratories, and must confront and seek to understand the dynamics of social action and social change.[50]

Teachers who support human freedom, justice, and equality can motivate students to engage in social action to improve the human condition. It is individual teachers—and not schools per se—who can and do help students develop the ideals, knowledge, and skills needed to reform society. They do this by exemplifying a commitment to democratic values in the content they select, in their interpretations of social and historical events, and in their words and deeds. Teachers, while respecting the beliefs and diversity of their students and helping them develop social science inquiry skills, can support democracy, equality, and the empowerment of victimized racial and ethnic groups.[51]

If teachers are to be the primary agents for change in schools, when we select and train individuals for teaching we must keep democratic values, teaching, and commitments foremost in mind. A major goal of our selection and training process must be to place in the classroom teachers who have strong and clarified democratic values and the knowledge and skills to implement a curriculum that will enable students to acquire the content, commitment, and competencies needed to participate in democratic social change. Training programs that are designed to help teachers become effective cultural mediators and change agents must help them to acquire (a) social science knowledge, derived using a process in which the goals, assumptions, and values of knowledge are learned; (b) clarified cultural identifications; (c) positive intergroup and racial attitudes; and (d) pedagogical skills (see Figure 9.2). To select and train teachers successfully is probably the most challenging and difficult task that lies ahead for those of us who would like to see the schools—and the multiethnic curriculum in particular—become a vehicle for social change and human betterment.

Summary

A series of ethnic revival movements emerged in Western societies, such as the United States, Canada, the United Kingdom, and Australia, during the 1960s

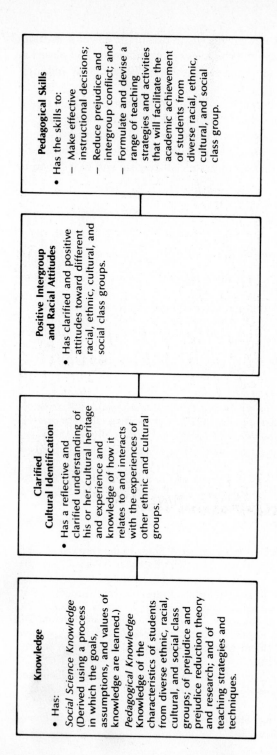

Knowledge

• Has:

Social Science Knowledge (Derived using a process in which the goals, assumptions, and values of knowledge are learned.)

Pedagogical Knowledge Knowledge of the characteristics of students from diverse ethnic, racial, cultural, and social class groups; of prejudice and prejudice reduction theory and research; and of teaching strategies and techniques.

Clarified Cultural Identification

• Has a reflective and clarified understanding of his or her cultural heritage and experience and knowledge of how it relates to and interacts with the experiences of other ethnic and cultural groups.

Positive Intergroup and Racial Attitudes

• Has clarified and positive attitudes toward different racial, ethnic, cultural, and social class groups.

Pedagogical Skills

• Has the skills to:
  – Make effective instructional decisions;
  – Reduce prejudice and intergroup conflict; and
  – Formulate and devise a range of teaching strategies and activities that will facilitate the academic achievement of students from diverse racial, ethnic, cultural, and social class group.

The Effective Multicultural Teacher

Figure 9.2. Characteristics of the Effective Teacher in a Multicultural Society

and 1970s. A major goal of these movements was to reform the school curriculum so that the images of ethnic groups and the roles ethnic minorities had played in the development of their nation-states and societies would be accurately and comprehensively depicted.

This chapter describes the curricular visions and goals of the ethnic revival movements, the limited extent to which these goals have been realized, and the factors that have prevented significant curriculum reform. This chapter also proposes a reform strategy that conceptualizes the teacher as a cultural mediator and change agent and a curriculum that promotes social criticism and civic action to improve the human condition.

Notes

1. James A. Banks and James Lynch, *Multicultural Education in Western Societies* (New York: Praeger, 1986).

2. Kenneth B. Clark, "Social Policy, Power and Social Science Research," *Harvard Educational Review* 43 (1973), pp. 113–121; Ronald R. Edmonds et al., "A Black Response to Christopher Jenck's Inequality and Certain Other Issues," *Harvard Educational Review* 43 (1973), pp. 76–91.

3. Samuel Bowles and Herbert Gintis, *Schooling in Capitalist America* (New York: Basic Books, 1976).

4. Banks and Lynch, *Multicultural Education*.

5. James A. Banks, *Teaching Ethnic Studies: Concepts and Strategies* (Washington, D.C.: National Council for the Social Studies, 1973); Frances Fitzgerald, *America Revisited: History Textbooks in the Twentieth Century* (New York: Vintage Books, 1979).

6. John W. Blassingame, *New Perspectives on Black Studies* (Urbana: University of Illinois Press, 1971).

7. William J. Johnston, ed., *Education on Trial* (San Francisco: Institute for Contemporary Studies, 1985); National Commission on Excellence in Education, *A Nation at Risk* (Washington, D.C.: U.S. Department of Education, 1983).

8. Larry Cuban, "Black History, Negro History, and White Folk," *Saturday Review*, (1968), pp. 64–65 (September 21).

9. Jesus Garcia and Julie Goebel, "A Comparative Study of the Portrayal of Black Americans in Selected U.S. History Textbooks," *The Negro Educational Review* 36 (1985), pp. 118–127.

10. Brian Bullivant, "Towards Radical Multiculturalism: Resolving Tensions in Curriculum and Educational Planning," in Sohan Modgil, Gajendra K. Verma, Kanka Malick, and Celia Modgil, eds., *Multicultural Education: The Interminable Debate* (London: The Falmer Press, 1986); Chris Mullard, *Racism in Society and Schools: History, Policy, and Practice*, Occasional Paper No. 1 (London: Centre for Multicultural Education, University of London Institute of Education, 1980).

11. Kogila A. Moodley, "Canadian Multicultural Education," in James A. Banks and James Lynch, eds., *Multicultural Education in Western Societies* (New York: Praeger, 1986), p. 62.

12. Allan R. Beals, with George Spindler and Louise Spindler, *Culture in Process* (New York: Holt, Rinehart and Winston, 1967).

13. Joseph L. White, *The Psychology of Blacks* (Englewood Cliffs, N.J.: Prentice-Hall).

14. Garcia and Goebel, "A Comparative Study."

15. James Baldwin, *The Price of the Ticket: Collected Nonfiction 1984–1985* (New York: St. Martin's/Marek, 1985).

16. Robert K. Merton, "Insiders and Outsiders: A Chapter in the Sociology of Knowledge," *The American Journal of Sociology* 78 (1972), pp. 9–47.

17. Joyce Ladner, ed., *The Death of White Sociology* (New York: Vintage, 1973).

18. Ibid.

19. Frank Reisman, *The Culturally Deprived Child* (New York: Harper and Row, 1962).

20. James A. Banks, "Values, Ethnicity, Social Science Research, and Educational Policy," in Benjamin Ladner, ed., *The Humanities in Precollegiate Education*, 83rd Yearbook of the National Society for the Study of Education (Chicago: University of Chicago Press, 1984); Ladner, *The Death of White Sociology*.

21. Joan Baratz, "Teaching Reading in an Urban Negro School System," in Frederick Williams, ed., *Language and Poverty: Perspectives on a Theme* (Chicago: Markham Publishing Co., 1970); Herbert G. Gutman, *The Black Family in Slavery and Freedom, 1750–1925* (New York: Oxford University Press, 1964); Eugene D. Genovese, *Roll, Jordan Roll: The World the Slaves Made* (New York: Pantheon, 1974).

22. William J. Wilson, *The Declining Significance of Race: Blacks and Changing American Institutions* (Chicago: University of Chicago Press, 1978); Thomas Sowell, *Civil Rights: Rhetoric or Reality?* (New York: William Morrow, 1984).

23. James Farmer, *Lay Bare the Heart: An Autobiography of the Civil Rights Movement* (New York: Arbor House, 1985); Takeo U. Nakano and Leatrice Nakano, *Within the Barbed Wire Fence: A Japanese Man's Account of His Internment* (Seattle: University of Washington Press, 1980); Howell Raines, *My Soul Is Rested: Movement Days in the Deep South Remembered* (New York: Putnam's, 1977).

24. Blassingame, *New Perspectives on Black Studies*; Ladner, *The Death of White Sociology*.

25. Garcia and Goebel, "A Comparative Study."

26. Ibid.

27. Hilda Taba, Elizabeth H. Brady, and John T. Robinson, *Intergroup Education in Public Schools* (Washington, D.C.: American Council on Education, 1952).

28. George A. Theodorson and Achilles G. Theodorson, *A Modern Dictionary of Sociology* (New York: Barnes and Noble, 1969).

29. Brian Bullivant, "Multicultural Education in Australia: An Unresolved Debate," in James A. Banks and James Lynch, eds., *Multicultural Education in Western Societies* (New York: Praeger, 1986), p. 103.

30. Milton M. Gordon, *Assimilation in American Life* (New York: Oxford University Press, 1964).

31. Louis A. Coser, *Masters of Sociological Thought: Ideas in Historical and Social Context*, 2nd ed. (New York: Harcourt, 1977).

32. Nathan Glazer and Daniel P. Moynihan, eds., *Ethnicity: Theory and Experience* (Cambridge, Mass.: Harvard University Press, 1975).

33. Orlando Patterson, *Ethnic Chauvinism: The Reactionary Impulse* (New York: Stein and Day, 1977).

34. Daniel E. Apter, "Political Life and Cultural Pluralism," in Melvin M. Tumin and Walter Plotch, eds., *Pluralism in a Democratic Society* (New York: Praeger, 1977).

35. Nathan Glazer, "Cultural Pluralism: The Social Aspect," in Melvin M. Tumin and Walter Plotch, eds., *Pluralism in a Democratic Society* (New York: Praeger, 1977).

36. Barbara A. Sizemore, "Shattering the Melting Pot Myth," in James A. Banks, ed., *Teaching Ethnic Studies: Concepts and Strategies* (Washington, D.C.: National Council for the Social Studies, 1973).

37. Ladner, *The Death of White Sociology*; Sizemore, "Shattering the Melting Pot Myth."

38. Mildred Dickeman, "Teaching Cultural Pluralism," in James A. Banks, *Teaching Ethnic Studies: Concepts and Strategies*, 43rd Yearbook (Washington, D.C.: National Council for the Social Studies, 1973).

39. Theodorson and Theodorson, *A Modern Dictionary*.

40. Dickeman, "Teaching Cultural Pluralism."

41. Fred M. Newmann, "Discussion: Political Socialization in the Schools," *Harvard Educational Review* 38 (1968), pp. 536–545.

42. Judy A. Gillespie and John J. Patrick, *Comparing Political Experiences* (Washington, D.C.: The American Political Science Association, 1974).

43. Fred M. Newmann, "Discussion: Political Socialization in the Schools," *Harvard Educational Review* 38 (1968) p. 536.

44. Michael B. Katz, *Class, Bureaucracy, and Schools: The Illusion of Educational Change in America*, expanded ed. (New York: Praeger, 1975); Bowles and Gintis, *Schooling in Capitalist America*.

45. Sohan Modgil, Gajendra K. Verma, Kanka Mallick, and Celia Modgil, *Multicultural Education: The Interminable Debate* (London: The Falmer Press, 1986).

46. Hazel V. Carby, *Multicultural Fictions*, Stenciled Occasional Paper, Race Series, SP No. 58, The University of Birmingham (England), 1980.

47. Donald W. Oliver and James P. Shaver, *Teaching Public Issues in the High School* (Boston: Houghton Mifflin, 1966).

48. James P. Shaver and William Strong, *Facing Value Decisions: Rationale-Building for Teachers*, 2nd ed. (New York: Teachers College Press, 1982).

49. Kenneth B. Clark, *Dark Ghetto: Dilemmas of Social Power* (New York: Harper Torchbooks, 1965).

50. Ibid., p. xxi.

51. Jim Cummins, "Empowering Minority Students: A Framework for Intervention," *Harvard Educational Review* 56 (1986), pp. 18–36.

10

The Multiethnic Curriculum: Issues and Models

Several widespread assumptions about teaching ethnic content have adversely affected the development of the multiethnic curriculum in educational institutions. We need to examine and to challenge these assumptions and related practices and to formulate new assumptions and goals for the multiethnic curriculum if integrating the curriculum with ethnic content is to become a vehicle for general curriculum reform. If we merely add ethnic content to the traditional curriculum, which has many problems, our efforts to modify the curriculum with ethnic content are likely to lead to a dead end. We need to reform the total school curriculum.

Assumptions about Ethnic Content

Ethnic Content as Ethnic Minority Studies

One pervasive assumption many educators embrace is that ethnic content deals exclusively or primarily with non-White minority groups, such as the Jamaicans in Britain, the Indians in Canada, and Blacks in the United States. This assumption is widespread within the schools of Western societies, such as the United Kingdom, Canada, and the United States. The multiethnic curriculum is often based on and reflect it. The multiethnic curriculum of many schools in the United States, for example, devotes little or no attention to the experiences of European-American ethnic groups, such as Jewish Americans, Polish Americans, and Italian Americans. This narrow conceptualization of ethnic content emerged out of the social forces that gave rise to the ethnic studies movement in the 1960s and 1970s.[1]

As pointed out in Chapter 1, during the 1960s Black Americans staged a struggle for their civil rights that was unprecedented in their history. They demanded control of various social, economic, and political institutions within the Black community. They also demanded that the school curriculum be reformed so it would more accurately reflect their historical and cultural experiences in the United States. Other ethnic minority groups, both in the United States and other Western societies, such as the Asians in the United Kingdom, Mexicans in the United States, and the Métis in Canada, became acutely aware of their own ethnic identity and struggles, in part, because of the Black civil rights movement.[2] These groups also called for new versions of school and college history that would more accurately reflect their experiences.

173

The types of ethnic studies courses, curricula, and experiences formulated during the 1960s and 1970s often reflected the political and social demands made within local communities. Responding largely to crises and public pressures, curriculum specialists often developed ethnic studies units and courses without giving serious thought to the basic issues that should be considered when curriculum changes are made. The nature of learning, the social and psychological needs of students, and social science theory and research are the types of problems and issues that received little if any attention in many of the hurriedly formulated ethnic studies units and courses created during the 1960s and 1970s. Rather, the overriding consideration was to create some kinds of curricula and courses so that ethnic demands would be met and militant ethnic students and faculty would be silenced. Consequently, during the 1960s and 1970s ethnic studies often became defined as the study of ethnic minority groups. Many curricula and courses formulated were parochial in scope and fragmented and were structured without careful planning and clear rationales. Even though ethnic studies courses and curricula today are often more global in scope, scholarly, and educationally sound than they were in the 1960s and 1970s, they are frequently haunted by their early history and problems.[3] The problems ethnic studies experienced increased in the 1980s because of the push for conservatism and nationalism in Western nations such as the United States, the United Kingdom, and Australia.

Ethnic Studies as an Addition to the Curriculum

Many educators assume that ethnic studies is essentially additive in nature and that we can create a valid multiethnic curriculum by leaving the present curriculum essentially intact; we can simply add a list of ethnic minority people and events to the list of mainstream people and events already studied in schools and colleges. These educators believe we should teach about the heroic deeds of Booker T. Washington and Geronimo just as we teach about the heroic deeds of Betsy Ross and Abraham Lincoln and that pictures of Black and American Indian heroes should be added to those of eminent mainstream Americans already in the textbooks and hanging in the school corridors and classrooms. In additive types of ethnic studies curricula, students are required to memorize isolated facts about mainstream history and ethnic minority history.

Conceptualizing ethnic content as essentially additive in nature is problematic for several reasons. A large body of educational literature has documented the traditional and nonstimulating nature of many school courses and has stated why reform in classroom teaching is sorely needed.[4] Even though much curriculum reform took place in the teaching of school subjects in the United States during the 1970s, especially in textbooks, in many classrooms teachers continue to emphasize the mastery of low-level facts and do not help students master high-level concepts, generalizations, and theories.

Modifying the curriculum to include ethnic content provides a tremendous opportunity to reexamine the assumptions, purposes, and nature of the curriculum and to formulate a curriculum with new assumptions and goals. Merely adding low-level facts about ethnic content to a curriculum already bulging with discrete and isolated facts about mainstream history will result in an overkill. Isolated facts about Crispus Attucks do not stimulate the intellect any more than isolated facts about Betsy Ross and Abraham Lincoln. To integrate content about ethnic groups meaningfully into the total curriculum we must undertake more substantial and innovative curriculum reform.

Ethnic Studies as the Study of Strange Customs

Other assumptions are made about ethnic studies, and many school practices reflect them. Some teachers, especially in the primary grades, believe ethnic studies should deal primarily with the tangible elements of minority cultures that seem strange and different to themselves and their students. Consequently, experiences in the primary grades often focus on the foods and unique customs and artifacts of minority cultures, such as soul food, tepees, igloos, and chow mein. Focusing on the customs within ethnic minority groups that seem strange to teachers and their students is likely to reinforce stereotypes and misconceptions rather than help students develop cultural sensitivity and knowledge of other cultures, which is usually the goal teachers state when they plan these types of learning experiences.

Since many primary grade teachers are unlikely to approach the study of cultural differences from an anthropological and sensitive perspective, their students are likely to conclude that cultural characteristics that are different from their own are indeed strange and unusual and therefore that many minority peoples share few characteristics with them. The multiethnic curriculum should emphasize the intangible aspects of culture discussed in Chapter 5 (such as values, cultural cognitiveness, perspectives, and world views), and not strange customs or tangible cultural elements like matzo and sombreros. Ethnic content should be used to help students learn that all human beings have common needs and characteristics, although the ways in which these traits are manifested frequently differ cross-culturally.

Ethnic Studies as the Celebration of Ethnic Holidays

Some teachers, again usually in the primary and elementary grades, see ethnic studies as the celebration of ethnic holidays, such as Martin Luther King's birthday and Cinco de Mayo. In many schools, lessons about ethnic groups are limited primarily to these types of special days and holidays. Some schools set aside particular days or weeks of the year for Black history and culture, Afro-Caribbean feasts and celebrations, and Asian history and culture. The long-range effects of these kinds of special ethnic days might be detrimental and serve to reinforce the notion that ethnic groups, such as Blacks in the United States, Jamaicans in the United Kingdom, and the Aborigines in Australia, are not integral parts of their national society and culture. This is especially likely to happen if ethnic groups are studied only on special days or in special units and lessons. The students are likely to conclude that U.S. history and Black history, for example, are separate and mutually exclusive entities.

The notion that Asians in Britain, Mexicans in the United States, and Aborigines in Australia are integral parts of their national societies should be reflected in how the multiethnic curriculum is organized and in all activities and teaching strategies. Special units and days might prevent the students from developing the notion that these groups are integral parts of their national societies. However, if ethnic minority groups are integral parts of the school curriculum, highlighting the experiences of a particular ethnic group is less likely to result in negative learnings by students. The danger of negative learnings occurring is greatly increased when these types of experiences are isolated and are not integral parts of the total school curriculum.

Expanding the Definition of Ethnic Studies

Each of the major assumptions discussed and criticized here, although widespread and in some cases understandable, is intellectually indefensible and continues to have adverse effects on the teaching of ethnic content. The assumption that ethnic studies is equivalent to ethnic minority studies is one of the most widespread beliefs held by educators.

It is both inaccurate and educationally unsound to assume that ethnic studies should be limited to a study of ethnic minority groups. Ethnic studies should be, in part, the scientific and humanistic examination of the variables related to ethnicity that influence human behavior. Any individual or group whose behavior can be totally or partially explained by variables related to ethnicity is an appropriate subject in the multiethnic curriculum.

A definition of ethnic group can help us determine the parameters of ethnic studies and the curricular implications of the concept. In Chapter 5, I defined an *ethnic group* as a group that shares a common ancestry, culture, history, tradition, and sense of peoplehood and that is a political and economic interest group. These characteristics of an ethnic group suggest that all individuals in Western pluralistic societies can be considered members of ethnic groups. However, individual members of an ethnic group vary widely in their levels of ethnic identification and ethnic behavior (see Chapter 5).

Our definition of ethnic groups indicates that Anglo-Australians, Italian Australians, German Americans, Jewish Americans, as well as Afro-Americans and the Australian Aborigines, should be studied within a comparative multiethnic curriculum. Members of each group exhibit behavioral characteristics that can be partially explained by variables related to ethnicity.

The multiethnic curriculum should include but not be limited to a study of ethnic minority groups. An ethnic minority group is a particular type of ethnic group with the distinguishing characteristics described in Chapter 5 (see page 81). Jewish Americans are an ethnic minority group with unique cultural characteristics; Afro-Americans have unique physical and cultural characteristics. Ethnic minorities are frequently a numerical minority and are often politically and economically powerless within a society. However, this is not always the case. In the Republic of South Africa, the Blacks are politically and economically powerless but are a numerical majority. However, they are considered a sociological minority.

To conceptualize ethnic studies as the study of ethnic minorities is inconsistent with how sociologists define ethnicity and prevents the development of a broadly conceptualized multiethnic curriculum that compares and contrasts the experiences of all of the diverse groups within a society and that helps students fully understand the complex role of ethnicity in modern Western societies such as the United States, the United Kingdom, Canada, and Australia. Conceptualizing ethnic studies exclusively as the study of ethnic minority groups also promotes a kind of "we-they" attitudes among mainstream students and teachers. Many students believe that ethnic studies is the study of "them," whereas other historical and cultural studies in the school is the study of "us." Some teachers assume that because ethnic studies is the study of "them," it should be taught only when there are ethnic minority students within the school.

Ethnic Studies: A Process of Curriculum Reform

Ethnic studies should not be limited to the study of ethnic minority groups although it should definitely include them. It should not be an addition or an appendage to the regular curriculum. Rather, ethnic studies should be viewed as a process of curriculum reform that will result in the creation of a new curriculum based on new assumptions and new perspectives. This new curriculum will help students gain novel views of the experiences of Western societies and new conceptions of what it means to be American, British, Australian, or Canadian. Since the English immigrants gained control over most economic, social, and political institutions early in the national histories of nations such as the United States and Australia, to become American or Australian has meant to become Anglicized. Especially during the height of nativism in the United States in the late 1800s and early 1900s, the English Americans defined Americanization as Anglicization. This notion of Americanization is still widespread within U.S. society and schools today. When many Americans think of American history and American literature they tend to think of Anglo-American history and Anglo-American literature.

Reconceptualizing Western Societies

Since the assumption that only what is Anglo-Australian is Australian and what is Anglo-American is American is so deeply ingrained in curriculum materials and in the hearts and minds of many students and teachers, we cannot significantly change the curriculum by merely adding a unit or a lesson here and there about Aborigine, Italian-Australian, or Afro-American history. Rather, we need to examine seriously the conception of Australian or American perpetuated in the curriculum and its basic purposes and assumptions.

We need to reconceptualize how we view Western societies and cultures in the school curriculum. We should teach the history of the Western nation-states from diverse ethnic perspectives rather than primarily or exclusively from the point of view of mainstream historians, writers, and artists. Most courses in the school curriculum in the major Western nations are taught from mainstream perspectives. These types of courses and experiences are based on what I call the Mainstream Centric Model or Model A (see Figure 10.1). Ethnic studies, as a process of curriculum reform, can and often does proceed from Model A to Model B, the ethnic additive model. In courses and experiences based on Model B, ethnic content is an additive to the major curriculum thrust, which remains mainstream centric. Many schools and other educational institutions have implemented Model B types of curricular changes. Black studies courses, Asian studies courses, and special units on ethnic groups in the elementary grades are examples of Model B types of curricular experiences.

However, I am suggesting that curriculum reform proceed directly from Model A to Model C, the multiethnic model. In courses and experiences based on Model C, the students study concepts, themes, issues, and events from several ethnic perspectives and points of view. Mainstream perspectives are only one group of several and are neither superior nor inferior to other ethnic perspectives. I view Model D, the Ethnonational Model, types of courses and curricula as the ultimate goal of curriculum reform. In this curriculum model, students study historical and social events from the perspectives of different ethnic groups within other nations. Since we live in a global society, students need to learn how to become effective citizens of the world community. This is unlikely to happen if they study historical and contemporary social events primarily from the perspectives of the ethnic and cultural groups within their own nation.

Teaching Multiethnic Perspectives

When studying a period in U.S. history, such as the colonial period, in a course organized on the Multiethnic Model (Model C), the inquiry does not end when students view the period from the perspectives of mainstream historians and writers. Rather, they ponder these kinds of questions: Why did Anglo-American historians name the English immigrants *colonists* and the other nationality groups *immigrants?* How do American-Indian historians view the colonial period? Do

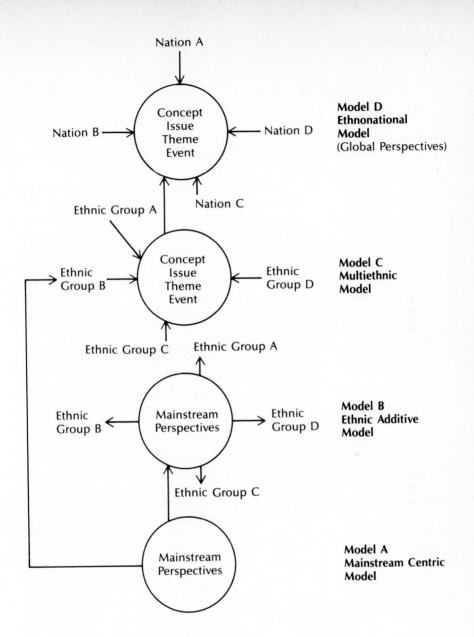

Figure 10.1. Ethnic Studies as a Process of Curriculum Reform
Ethnic studies is conceptualized as a process of curriculum reform that can lead from a total mainstream perspective on a society's history and culture (Model A), to multiethnic perspectives as additives to the major curriculum thrust (Model B), to a completely multiethnic curriculum in which every event, concept, and issue is viewed from the perspectives of different ethnic groups (Model C). In Model D, the ultimate goal of curriculum reform, students view events, concepts, and issues from the perspectives and points of view of various groups within different nations.

their views of this period differ in any substantial ways from the views of Anglo-American historians? Why or why not? What was life like for the Jews, Blacks, and other ethnic groups in America during the seventeenth and eighteenth centuries? How do we know? In other words, in courses and curricula organized on Model C, students view historical and contemporary events from the perspectives of different ethnic and cultural groups.

I am not suggesting that we eliminate or denigrate mainstream history or mainstream perspectives on historical events. I am suggesting that mainstream perspectives should be among many different ethnic and cultural perspectives taught in the school. Only by approaching the study of society in this way will students get a global rather than an ethnocentric view of the history and culture of their nation and other societies.

A historian's experience and culture, including his or her own ethnic culture, cogently influences his or her views of the past and present. However, it would be simplistic to argue that there is one mainstream view of history and contemporary events or one Black and Mexican-American view. Wide differences in experiences and perceptions exist both within and across ethnic groups. However, people who have experienced a historical event or social phenomenon, such as racial bigotry or internment, often view the event differently than do those who have watched it from a distance. There is no one mainstream American perspective on the internment of Japanese Americans during World War II and no one Japanese-American view of it. However, accounts written by people who were interned, such as Takashima's powerful *A Child in Prison Camp*, often provide insights and perspectives on the internment that cannot be provided by people who were not interned.[5] Individuals who viewed the internment from the outside can also provide us with unique and important perspectives and points of view. Both perspectives should be studied in a sound multiethnic curriculum.

Only by looking at events, such as the internment, from many different perspectives can we fully understand the history and culture of a society. Various ethnic groups within a society are often influenced by events differently and perceive and respond to them differently. One goal of the multiethnic curriculum should be to present students with new ways of viewing the history and culture of their society. Any goals that are less ambitious, although important, will not result in the substantial curricular reform I consider imperative.

Curricular Models for an Open Society

The multiethnic curriculum should do more than help students view concepts, events, and situations from diverse cultural and ethnic perspectives. It should also help students acquire the knowledge, skills, and attitudes needed to promote and participate in an open society. We can define an *open society* as one in which individuals from diverse ethnic, cultural, and social class groups have equal opportunities to participate. Individuals can take full advantage of the opportunities and rewards within all social, economic, and political institutions without regard to their ancestry or ethnic identity. They can also participate in the society while preserving their distinct ethnic and cultural traits and can "make the maximum number of voluntary contacts with others without regard to qualifications of ancestry, sex, or class."[6] This kind of society has never existed in the human experience, but it is an ideal toward which we should strive.

Powerful and Excluded Ethnic Groups

In every past and present society, individuals have had and still have widely unequal opportunities to share fully in the reward systems and benefits of their society. The basis for the unequal distribution of rewards is determined by elitist groups in which power is centered. Powerful groups decide which traits and characteristics are necessary for full societal participation. They determine traits on the basis of the similarity of such traits to their own values, physical characteristics, life-styles, and behavior. At various times in history, powerful groups have used celibacy, sex, ethnicity, race, religion, as well as many other variables, as determinants of which individuals and groups would be given or denied opportunities for social mobility and full societal participation. In colonial America, for example, White Angle-Saxon male protestants with property controlled most social, political, economic, and military institutions. They excluded from full participation in decision making peoples, such as American Indians and Blacks, who were different from themselves. They both invented and perpetuated stereotypes and myths about groups that were politically, economically, and socially excluded to justify their exclusion.[7]

Creating an Open Society

To create the kind of open society I have defined, we will either have to redistribute power so that groups with different ethnic and cultural characteristics will control entry to various social, economic, and political institutions, or we will have to modify the attitudes and actions of individuals who will control future institutions so they will become less ethnocentric and permit people who differ from themselves culturally and physically to share in society's reward system on the basis of the real contributions they can make to the functioning of society. We can conceptualize these two means to an open society as models.

Curricular Models

Model I can be called a Shared Power Model. The goal of this model would be to create a society in which currently excluded ethnic groups would share power with dominant ethnic groups. They would control a number of social, economic, and political institutions. The methods used to attain the major ends of this model would be an attempt to build group pride, cohesion, and identity among excluded ethnic groups and to help them develop the ability to make reflective political decisions, to gain and exercise political power effectively, and to develop a belief in the humanness of their own groups.

The alternative means to an open society can be called Model II, Enlightening Powerful Groups Model. The major goal of this model would be to modify the attitudes and perceptions of dominant ethnic groups so that they would be willing, as adults, to share power with excluded ethnic groups. They would also be willing to regard victimized ethnic groups as human beings, unwilling to participate in efforts to continue their oppression, willing to accept and understand the actions by victimized ethnic groups to liberate themselves, and willing to take action to change the social system so it would treat powerless ethnic groups more justly. The major goals within this model focus on helping dominant ethnic groups expand their conception of who is human, develop more positive attitudes toward ethnic minorities, and be willing to share power with excluded ethnic groups. Figures 10.2 and 10.3 summarize these two models.

Characteristics of Model I: Shared Power Model

Most individuals who are aware of the extent to which victimized ethnic groups are powerless in Western societies will probably view the shared power model as more realistic than Model II. The shared power model, if successfully implemented, would result in the redistribution of power so that excluded ethnic groups in Western societies would control such institutions as schools, courts, industries, health facilities, and the mass media. They would not necessarily control all institutions within their society, but would control those in which they participated and that are needed to fulfill their individual and group needs. These groups would be able to distribute jobs and other rewards to persons who, like themselves, are denied such opportunities by present powerful ethnic groups. Elements within this model have been used by such groups as Jews and Catholics to enable them to participate more fully in shaping public policy in the United States.[8]

In a society in which different ethnic groups share power, victimized ethnic groups would control and determine the traits and characteristics necessary for sharing societal rewards and opportunities. IQ test scores may cease to be an important criterion, but the ability to relate to ethnic minorities may become an essential one.[9] A major assumption of this model is that presently excluded ethnic groups, if they attained power, would, like present powerful groups, provide opportunities for those persons who are most like themselves physically and culturally. This assumption may or may not be valid since ethnic group individuals sometime have ambivalent attitudes toward their own ethnic group.[10]

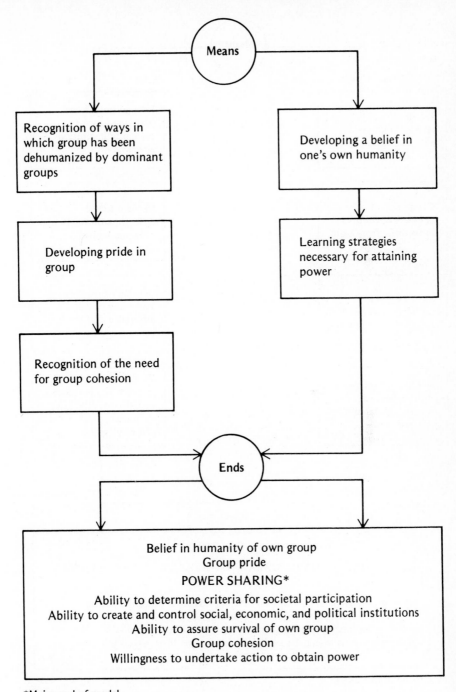

*Major end of model.

Figure 10.2. Model I—Shared Power Model

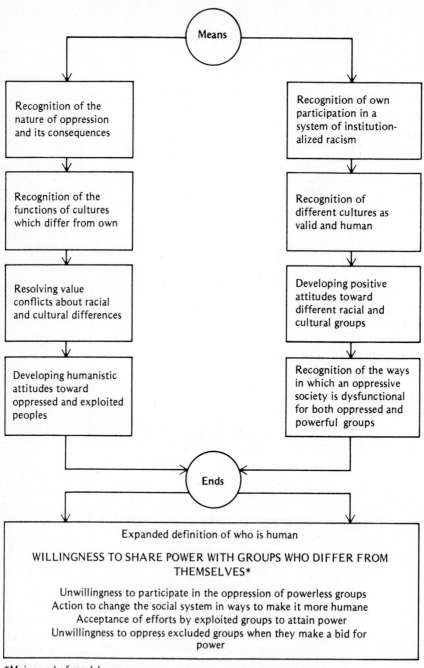

Means

Recognition of the nature of oppression and its consequences

Recognition of own participation in a system of institutionalized racism

Recognition of the functions of cultures which differ from own

Recognition of different cultures as valid and human

Resolving value conflicts about racial and cultural differences

Developing positive attitudes toward different racial and cultural groups

Developing humanistic attitudes toward oppressed and exploited peoples

Recognition of the ways in which an oppressive society is dysfunctional for both oppressed and powerful groups

Ends

Expanded definition of who is human

WILLINGNESS TO SHARE POWER WITH GROUPS WHO DIFFER FROM THEMSELVES*

Unwillingness to participate in the oppression of powerless groups
Action to change the social system in ways to make it more humane
Acceptance of efforts by exploited groups to attain power
Unwillingness to oppress excluded groups when they make a bid for power

*Major end of model.

Figure 10.3. Model II—Enlightening Powerful Groups Model

If this model is used to achieve an open society, we will have to think of how a shared power model can be implemented without violence directed against ethnic minority groups, and how essential societal cohesion can be maintained without conflict between competing powerful groups that would totally disrupt a nation's social system. There are valid reasons to believe that educators and policy makers should seriously consider both concerns if we intend to create societies in which a number of competing ethnic groups share power. Writes Clark, "No human being can easily and graciously give up power and privilege. Such change can come only with conflict and anguish and the ever present threat of retrogression."[11]

Translating the shared power model into curriculum goals and strategies, our attention would focus primarily on the victims of structural and political exclusion, such as Australian Aborigines, Canadian Indians, British Asians, and Afro-Americans. We would try to help these students attain the skills, attitudes, abilities, and strategies needed to attain power while maintaining an essential degree of societal cohesion. We would help these students see, through valid content samples, how previously excluded and politically powerless ethnic groups in history have attained power and how certain nonreflective actions and inactions can result in further exclusion and victimization.

The Assumptions of Model II: Enlightening Powerful Groups Model

Model II, whose primary goal is to help mainstream students develop more positive attitudes toward marginalized ethnic groups, rests on several assumptions. We have little evidence to support the validity of these assumptions. If anything, current data give us little hope in this model as an effective way to achieve an open society.[12] This model assumes that most members of the mainstream experience a moral dilemma that results from the inconsistency between the ideals about equality they hold and the discrimination that ethnic minorities experience in society. Myrdal, in his classic study of race relations in the United States, stated that most White Americans in the United States experienced such a dilemma.[13] It is possible that such a dilemma does not exist for many mainstream individuals in Western nation-states, including the United States.

It may be unrealistic to assume that teaching mainstream students about the harsh experiences ethnic minorities have experienced will cause them to become more willing to regard ethnic minorities as fellow human beings with certain entitlements in order to resolve their moral dilemmas related to democracy and inequality. Revisionist historians argue that discriminatory policies toward ethnic minorities are deliberate.[14] If their arguments are valid, then teaching mainstream students about the brutalities of slavery or the denial of land rights to the Australian Aborigines cannot be expected to significantly influence how mainstream students perceive or treat marginalized ethnic minorities.

Purposes of Models I and II

Even though these two models represent what I feel are the basic ways by which we can create an open society, they are ideal-types concepts. Like any ideal-type concepts or models, they are best used for conceptualizing and thinking about issues and problems. The laws in Western nation-states, the current organization of schools, and the types of student populations in many schools make it difficult, in many cases, to implement either Model I or Model II in pure form. However, these models can help the curriculum specialist determine the kinds of emphases necessary for the curricula for different student populations. The curricula for excluded and dominant ethnic groups should have many elements in common, but I also believe that the central messages these groups receive in the curriculum should in some cases differ.

Using the two models as departure points, I discuss the kinds of emphases I believe should constitute the curriculum for excluded and powerful ethnic groups in order to create and sustain an open society. I consider the limitations of each model in my recommendations and suggest how they can be reduced. In situations in which teachers have students from both powerful and excluded ethnic groups, it will be necessary for them to combine elements from both models in order to structure an effective curriculum.

The Curriculum for Excluded Groups: Curriculum Implications of Model I

The curriculum I recommend for victimized ethnic groups will include most of the elements of Model I. However, it will also include elements from Model II because a pure, shared power model curriculum may result in a totally fragmented and dehumanized society.

The curriculum for marginalized ethnic groups should recognize their feelings toward self, help them clarify their racial attitudes, liberate them from psychological captivity, and convince them of their humanness, since the dominant society often makes them believe they are less than human. Ethnic minorities will be able to liberate themselves from psychological and physical oppression only when they know how and why the myths about them emerged and were institutionalized and validated by the scholarly community and the mass media. A curriculum that has as one major goal the liberation of excluded ethnic groups must teach these groups how social, political, and economic institutions in the mainstream society, including the schools, the academic community, and the mass media, have contributed to their feelings of inferiority and powerlessness.

They should be taught how social science knowledge often reflects the norms, values, and goals of the powerful ethnic and cultural groups in society, and how it often validates those belief systems that serve the needs of powerful groups and are detrimental to ethnic minorities.[15] When teaching students about how social knowledge has served to validate the stereotypes and beliefs about them, the teacher can use as examples historical and current textbook descriptions of ethnic minority groups.

Studying about how they have been psychologically and physically dehumanized is necessary to help victimized ethnic groups liberate themselves, but it is not sufficient. They must also be helped to develop the ability to make reflective public decisions so they can gain power and shape public policies that affect their lives. They must develop a sense of political efficacy and be given practices in social action strategies that teach them how to get power without violence and further exclusion. In other words, excluded ethnic groups must be taught the most effective ways to gain power. The school should help them become both effective and reflective political activists.

I define *reflective decision-making* and *social action* as the kinds of decisions and social action that will enable ethnic minorities to attain power but will at the same time ensure their existence as a group and their essential societal cohesion. A curriculum designed to help liberate victimized ethnic groups should emphasize opportunities for social action, in which students have experience obtaining and exercising power.[16]

The curriculum for victimized ethnic groups should not only help release them from psychological captivity and focus on social action, it should also help them develop humanistic attitudes toward their own ethnic group, other victimized ethnic groups, and members of the mainstream society. The school should make an effort, when teaching victimized ethnic groups how to attain power and clarify their ethnic identity, to prevent them from becoming chauvinistic and ethnocentric. Marginalized ethnic groups should learn to value their own cultures, try to attain power, and develop group solidarity and identity in order to participate fully in society. However, they should also become effective citizens of their nation-states and acquire the knowledge, attitudes, and skills required to participate fully and effectively within it. The multiethnic curriculum should acknowledge and respect the national culture and the need for national identity. The humanistic emphasis, which is a Model II component, must be incorporated into a curriculum for victimized ethnic groups to prevent them from developing ethnocentric attitudes, perceptions, and behaviors.

The Curriculum for Dominant Ethnic Groups: Curriculum Implications of Model II

Since we have no reliable ways of knowing that a Model I type curriculum would lead to an open society as I have defined it, the curriculum builder should also implement elements of Model II in appropriate settings, that is, in settings that contain both dominant and mainstream ethnic groups. What I suggest is that since both models have serious limitations, and since we know little about how to create an open society because we have never made a serious effort to create one, we should take a multiple approach to the problem. Also, the two models are complementary and not contradictory. If we succeed in enlightening or changing the attitudes of mainstream and dominant ethnic groups so that they become more willing to share power with excluded ethnic groups, then the struggle for power among victimized ethnic groups would consequently be less intense and thus less likely to lead to violence and societal chaos.

The elements that constitute Model II have been among the most widespread methods used by educators and policy makers to create a more just society. This approach is suggested by such terms as *intergroup education*, *human relations*, *race relations*, and *intercultural education*. In the 1940s in the United States, Hilda Taba and her colleagues did pioneering work in intergroup education.[17] A major assumption of intergroup education is that since negative intergroup attitudes are learned, they can be unlearned if students experience a curriculum specifically designed for that purpose. A seminal study by Trager and Yarrow supports the assumption that democratic attitudes can be taught to children if a deliberate program of instruction is designed for that purpose.[18]

The primary goal of intergroup education (Model II elements) is to enlighten dominant ethnic groups by changing their attitudes and perceptions of victimized ethnic minorities. Intergroup education attempts to enlighten dominant ethnic group members by creating experiences for them in which they read or hear about prejudice, discrimination, and institutionalized racism. The participants are frequently encouraged to examine their own racial and ethnic attitudes, perceptions, and behaviors.[19]

It is difficult to determine how much potential Model II approaches have for changing the racial attitudes, beliefs, and behaviors of individuals. These methods have never been extensively implemented. Individuals are often not exposed to Model II type experiences until they are adults. Such adults usually attend a two- or three-week workshop, or a course in race relations for a quarter or a semester. Evidence suggests that these experiences usually have little permanent impact on adults' racial attitudes, although other kinds of experiences (used in conjunction with lectures and readings) seem to have some lasting influence on the racial attitudes of adults.[20] It is predictable that a short workshop would have limited affect on adults' racial attitudes since an experience of twenty hours or less cannot be expected to change attitudes and perceptions an individual has acquired over a twenty-year period, especially when the basic institutions in which they live reinforce their preexperimental attitudes.

Because of the meager results obtained from Model II approaches, some educators feel that this model should be abandoned and that a shared power model is the only realistic way in which to achieve an open society. As an individual who has conducted many race relations workshops, I greatly respect individuals who endorse this point of view. However, I feel that Model II approaches should be continued, but that how they are implemented should be greatly modified. They should be continued and expanded because (1) We have no assurance that a shared power model will succeed in this period of history (however, we also have no assurance that it will not); (2) Model II strategies have never been extensively implemented; rather, they are usually used in experiments with students or with teachers when a racial crisis develops in a school; (3) research suggests that children's racial attitudes can be modified by curriculum intervention, especially in the earliest years; the younger children are, the greater the impact that curriculum intervention is likely to have on their racial feelings;[21] and (4) racism is a serious, dehumanizing pathology in Western societies that the school has a moral and professional responsibility to help eradicate.

Earlier I discussed the severe limitations of Model II and the questionable assumptions on which it is based. I then argued that elements of this model should be implemented in appropriate settings. I do not see these two positions as contradictory; rather, I feel that when curriculum builders are aware of the limitations of their strategies, they can better use, evaluate, and modify them. A knowledge of the limitations of a curriculum strategy will also prevent the curriculum builder from expecting unrealistic outcomes. For example, a knowledge of the limitations of Model II will help teachers realize that a unit on race relations during "Black Heritage Month" will most likely have little influence on the racial attitudes of their students. They will know that only a modification of their total curriculum is likely to have any significant impact on their students' racial attitudes and beliefs, and that even with this kind of substantial curriculum modification, the chances for modification of racial attitudes will not be extremely high, especially if they are working with older students or adults. Curricular experiences are more likely to change students' racial *beliefs* than their racial *attitudes*.[22]

Increasing the Effectiveness of Model II Approaches

Despite the severe limitations of Model II as it is currently used in the schools and in teacher education, I believe that substantial modifications in the implementation of Model II components can significantly increase this model's impact on the racial attitudes and perceptions of dominant ethnic group individuals. The ultimate result of an effective implementation of the model may be that children of dominant ethnic groups, as adults, will be more likely to perceive excluded ethnic groups as human beings and thus more likely to share power with them and allow them to participate more fully in society. These statements are, at best, promising hypotheses, but I base them on experience, gleanings from research, and faith. Below, I suggest ways in which the implementation of a Model II type curriculum can have maximum opportunity to enlighten or modify the racial attitudes, beliefs, and perceptions of students.

By the time children enter school, they have already absorbed the negative attitudes toward ethnic minorities pervasive within the larger society. Although this fact has been documented since Lasker's pioneering research in 1929,[23] teachers are often surprised to learn in workshops that even kindergarten pupils are aware of racial differences and assign different values to Blacks and Whites. This fact alone gives us little hope for effective intervention. However, a related one does. The racial attitudes of kindergartners are not as negative or as crystallized as those of fifth graders.[24] As children grow older and no systematic efforts are made to modify their racial feelings, they become more bigoted. The curriculum implications of this research are clear. To modify children's racial attitudes, a deliberate program of instruction must be structured for that purpose in the earliest grades. The longer we wait, the less our chances are for success. By the time the individual reaches adulthood, the chances for successful intervention become almost—but not quite—nil.

Effective intervention programs must not only begin in the earliest grades; but the efforts must also be sustained over a long period of time, and material related to cultural differences must permeate the entire curriculum. Also, a variety of media and materials enhances chances for successful intervention. A unit on American Indians in the second grade and a book on Mexican Americans in the third grade will do little to help students understand or accept cultures different from their own. A hit-and-miss approach to the study of cultural differences may do more harm than good. There may be times when a separate in-depth unit on an ethnic minority culture is educationally justified in order to teach a concept, such as acculturation or separatism. Most often, however, when ethnic groups are studied in this way the students are likely to get the impression that ethnic minorities have not played an integral and significant role in shaping the history and culture of their society.

Summary

Several widespread assumptions about the nature of ethnic studies and the multiethnic curriculum are adversely affecting the teaching of ethnic studies in educational institutions. This chapter examines and challenges these assumptions. It also describes the characteristics of an effective multiethnic curriculum. The multiethnic curriculum should be based on a broad definition of ethnic group and should include the study of both ethnic groups and ethnic minorities. Ethnic studies should also be viewed as a process of curriculum reform. By restructuring their curriculum when integrating it with ethnic content, educators can create a new curriculum based on fresh assumptions and perspectives. This new curriculum will enable students to gain novel views of the human experience and new conceptions of Western societies.

The multiethnic curriculum should also help create and sustain an open society. To create an open society, it is necessary to define such a social system clearly and to design a curriculum specifically to achieve and perpetuate it. An open society is a social system in which individuals from diverse ethnic, cultural, and social class groups can freely participate and have equal opportunities to gain the skills and knowledge the society needs in order to function. Rewards within an open society are based on the contributions each person, regardless of his or her ancestry or social class, makes to the fulfillment of the society's functional requirements.

Two models by which we can achieve an open society are presented in this chapter. Model I, the Shared Power Model, focuses on helping victimized ethnic groups attain power so they can control a number of social, economic, and political institutions and can determine who may participate in them. These groups would also determine how rewards would be distributed. A second model, the Enlightening Powerful Groups Model, focuses on changing the attitudes, beliefs, perceptions, and behaviors of members of powerful ethnic groups so they will share power with victimized ethnic groups, regard them as groups that deserve human rights, and take actions to eliminate institutionalized racism and discrimination.

The complexity of modern Western societies makes it impossible for either model to be implemented in pure form. Also, both models are ideal-type concepts based on a number of unverified assumptions. However, these models can help the curriculum builder determine the kinds of emphases that would constitute an open-society curriculum for excluded, powerful, and mixed groups, for planning programs, and for ascertaining the effectiveness of various curriculum strategies.

Notes

1. John W. Blassingame, ed., *New Perspectives on Black Studies* (Urbana: University of Illinois Press, 1971); Livie I. Duran and H. Russell Bernard, eds., *Introduction to Chicano Studies*, 2nd ed. (New York: Macmillan, 1982).

2. James A. Banks and James Lynch, eds. *Multicultural Education in Western Societies* (New York: Praeger, 1986); Lotty V. D. Berg-Eldering, Ferry J. M. De Rijcke, and Louis V. Zuck, eds., *Multicultural Education: A Challenge for Teachers* (Dordrecht, Holland: Foris Publications, 1983).

3. "Multicultural Education," *Theory into Practice*, 23 (Spring 1984), special issue.

4. John I. Goodlad, *A Place Called School: Prospects for the Future* (New York: McGraw-Hill, 1984).

5. See Shizuye Takashima, *A Child in Prison Camp* (Montreal: Tundra Books, 1971).

6. Barbara A. Sizemore, "Is There a Case for Separate Schools?" *Phi Delta Kappan*, 53 (January 1972), p. 281.

7. John Hope Franklin, *Racial Equality in America* (Chicago: University of Chicago Press, 1976).

8. Andrew M. Greeley, *Why Can't They Be Like Us? America's White Ethnic Groups* (New York: Dutton, 1975); Leonard Dinnerstein, Roger L. Nichols, and David M. Reimers, *Natives and Strangers: Ethnic Groups and the Building of America* (New York: Oxford University Press, 1979).

9. Samuel Bowles and Herbert Gintis, *Schooling in Capitalist America: Educational Reform and the Contradictions of Economic Life* (New York: Basic Books, 1976).

10. David Milner, *Children and Race: Ten Years On* (London: Ward Lock Educational, 1983).

11. Kenneth B. Clark, "Introduction: The Dilemma of Power," in Talcott Parsons and Kenneth B. Clark, eds., *The Negro American* (Boston: Houghton Mifflin, 1965), p. xv.

12. Gordon W. Allport, *The Nature of Prejudice*, 25th anniv. ed. (Reading, Mass.: Addison-Wesley, 1979), pp. 479–500.

13. Gunnar Myrdal, *An American Dilemma: The Negro Problem and Modern Democracy*, vols. 1 & 2 (New York: Harper and Row, 1962).

14. Martin Carnoy, *Education as Cultural Imperialism* (New York: David McKay, 1974); Michael B. Katz, *Class, Bureaucracy, and Schools: The Illusion of Educational Change in America*, expanded ed. (New York: Praeger, 1975).

15. Barbara A. Sizemore, "Social Science and Education for a Black Identity," in James A. Banks and Jean D. Grambs, eds., *Black Self-Concept: Implications for Education and Social Science* (New York: McGraw-Hill, 1972), pp. 141–170.

16. For a discussion of decision-making and social-action programs, see James A. Banks with Ambrose A. Clegg, Jr., *Teaching Strategies for the Social Studies: Inquiry, Valuing and Decision-Making*, 3rd ed. (New York: Longman, 1985); and Fred M. Newmann, *Education for Citizen Action: Challenge for Secondary Curriculum* (Berkeley, Calif.: McCutchan, 1975).

17. Hilda Taba, Elizabeth H. Brady, and John T. Robinson, *Intergroup Education in Public Schools* (Washington, D.C.: American Council on Education, 1952).

18. Helen G. Trager and Marian Radke Yarrow, *They Learn What They Live: Prejudice in Young Children* (New York: Harper and Brothers, 1952), p. 362.

19. Charlotte Epstein, *Intergroup Relations for the Classroom Teacher* (New York: Houghton Mifflin, 1968).

20. For a summary of this research, see James A. Banks, "Racial Prejudice and the Black Self-Concept" in Banks and Grambs, *Black Self-Concept*, pp. 5–35.

21. Phyllis A. Katz and Sue Rosenberg, "Modification of Children's Racial Attitudes," *Developmental Psychology* 14 (1978), pp. 447–461.

22. Allport, *The Nature of Prejudice*.

23. Bruno Lasker, *Race Attitudes in Children* (New York: Henry Holt, 1929).

24. Charles Y. Glock et al., *Adolescent Prejudice* (New York: Harper and Row, 1975).

11

The Stages of Ethnicity: Implications for Curriculum Reform

Assumptions about Ethnic Students

When planning multiethnic experiences for students, we tend to assume that ethnic groups are monolithic and have rather homogeneous needs and characteristics. We often assume, for example, that individual members of ethnic minority groups, such as Jewish Americans and Afro-Americans, have intense feelings of ethnic identity and a strong interest in learning about the experiences and histories of their ethnic cultures. Educators also frequently assume that the self-images and academic achievement of ethnic minority youths will be enhanced if they are exposed to a curriculum that focuses on the heroic accomplishments and deeds of their ethnic groups and highlight the ways in which ethnic groups have been victimized by the mainstream society.

Ethnic Groups Are Complex and Dynamic

These kinds of assumptions are highly questionable and have led to some disappointments and serious problems in programs and practices related to ethnic diversity. In designing multiethnic experiences for students, we need to consider seriously the psychological needs and characteristics of ethnic group members and their emerging and changing ethnic identities. Ethnic groups, such as Afro-Americans, Italian Australians, and Anglo-Canadians, are not monolithic but are dynamic and complex groups.

Many of our curriculum development and teacher education efforts are based on the assumption that ethnic groups are static and unchanging. However, ethnic groups are highly diverse, complex, and changing entities. Ethnic identity, like other ethnic characteristics, is also complex and changing among ethnic group members. Thus there is no one ethnic identity among Blacks that we can delineate, as social scientists have sometimes suggested, but many complex and changing identities among them.[1]

Effective educational programs should help students explore and clarify their own ethnic identities. To do this, such programs must recognize and reflect the complex ethnic identities and characteristics of the individual students in the classroom. Teachers should learn how to facilitate the identity quests among ethnic youths and help them become effective and able participants in the common civic and national culture.

193

The Stages of Ethnicity: A Typology

To reflect the myriad and emerging ethnic identities among teachers and ethnic youths, we must attempt to identify them and to describe their curricular and teaching implications. The description of a typology that attempts to outline the basic stages of the development of ethnicity among individual members of ethnic groups follows. The typology is a preliminary ideal-type construct in the Weberian sense and constitutes a set of hypotheses based on the existing and emerging theory and research and on the author's study of ethnic behavior.

This typology is presented to stimulate research and the development of concepts and theory related to ethnicity and ethnic groups. Another purpose of the typology is to suggest preliminary guidelines for teaching about ethnicity in the schools and colleges and for helping students and teachers to function effectively at increasingly higher stages of ethnicity. Ford developed an instrument to measure the first five of these six stages of ethnicity and administered it to a sample of classroom teachers. She concluded that her study demonstrated that teachers are spread into the five stages that I had hypothesized.[2] The sixth stage of the typology was developed after the Ford study was completed.

Stage 1: Ethnic Psychological Captivity

During this stage the individual absorbs the negative ideologies and beliefs about his or her ethnic group that are institutionalized within the society. Consequently, he or she exemplifies ethnic self-rejection and low self-esteem. The individual is ashamed of his/her ethnic group and identity during this stage and may respond in a number of ways, including avoiding situations that bring contact with other ethnic groups or striving aggressively to become highly culturally assimilated. Conflict develops when the highly culturally assimilated psychologically captive ethnic is denied structural assimilation or total societal participation.

Individuals who are members of ethnic groups that have historically been victimized by cultural assaults, such as Polish Americans and Australian Aborigines, as well as members of highly visible and stigmatized ethnic groups, such as Afro-Americans and Chinese Canadians, are likely to experience some form of ethnic psychological captivity. The more that an ethnic group is stigmatized and rejected by the mainstream society, the more likely are its members to experience some form of ethnic psychological captivity. Thus, individuals who are members of the mainstream ethnic group within a society are the least likely individuals to experience ethnic psychological captivity.

Stage 2: Ethnic Encapsulation

Stage 2 is characterized by ethnic encapsulation and ethnic exclusiveness, including voluntary separatism. The individual participates primarily within his or her own ethnic community and believes that his or her ethnic group is superior to other groups. Many individuals within Stage 2, such as many Anglo-Americans, have internalized the dominant societal myths about the superiority of their ethnic or racial group and the innate inferiority of other ethnic groups and races. Many individuals who are socialized within all-White suburban communities in the United States and who live highly ethnocentric and encapsulated lives can be described as Stage 2 individuals. Alice Miel describes these kinds of individuals in *The Shortchanged Children of Suburbia.*[3]

The characteristics of Stage 2 are most extreme among individuals who suddenly begin to feel that their ethnic group and its way of life, especially its privileged and ascribed status, are being threatened by other racial and ethnic groups. This frequently happens when Afro-Americans begin to move into all-White ethnic communities. Extreme forms of this stage are also manifested among individuals who have experienced ethnic psychological captivity (Stage 1) and who have recently discovered their ethnicity. This new ethnic consciousness is usually caused by an ethnic revitalization movement. This type of individual, like the individual who feels that the survival of his or her ethnic group is threatened, is likely to express intensely negative feelings toward outside ethnic and racial groups.

However, individuals who have experienced ethnic psychological captivity and who have newly discovered their ethnic consiousness tend to have highly ambivalent feelings toward their own ethnic group and try to confirm, for themselves, that they are proud of their ethnic heritage and culture. Consequently, strong and verbal rejection of outgroups usually takes place. Outgroups are regarded as enemies, racists, and, in extreme manifestations of this stage, are viewed as planning genocidal efforts to destroy their ethnic group. The individual's sense of ethnic peoplehood is escalated and highly exaggerated. The ethnic individual within this stage of ethnicity tends to reject strongly members of his or her ethnic group who are regarded as assimilationist oriented and liberal, who do not endorse the rhetoric of separatism, or who openly socialize with members of outside ethnic groups, especially with members of a different racial group.

The Stage 2 individual expects members of the ethnic group to show strong overt commitments to the liberation struggle of the group or to the protection of the group from outside and "foreign" groups. The individual often endorses a separatist ideology. Members of outside ethnic groups are likely to regard Stage 2 individuals as racists, bigots, or extremists. As this type of individual begins to question some of the basic assumptions of his or her culture and to experience less ambivalence and conflict about ethnic identity, and especially, as the rewards within the society become more fairly distributed among ethnic groups, he or she is likely to become less ethnocentric and ethnically encapsulated.

Stage 3: Ethnic Identity Clarification

At this stage the individual is able to clarify personal attitudes and ethnic identity, to reduce intrapsychic conflict, and to develop clarified positive attitudes toward his or her ethnic group. The individual learns self-acceptance, thus developing the characteristics needed to accept and respond more positively to outside ethnic groups. Self-acceptance is a requisite to accepting and responding positively to other people. During this stage, the individual is able to accept and understand both the positive and negative attributes of his or her ethnic group. The individual's pride in his or her ethnic group is not based on the hate or fear of outside groups. Ethnic pride is genuine rather than contrived. Individuals are more likely to experience this stage when they have attained a certain level of economic and psychological security and have been able to have positive experiences with members of other ethnic groups.

Stage 4: Biethnicity

The individual within this stage has a healthy sense of ethnic identity and the psychological characteristics and skills needed to participate successfully in his or her own ethnic culture as well as in another ethnic culture. The individual also has a strong desire to function effectively in two ethnic cultures. We can describe such an individual as *biethnic*. Levels of biethnicity vary greatly. Many Afro-Americans, in order to attain social and economic mobility, learn to function effectively in Anglo-American culture during the formal working day. The private lives of these individuals, however, may be highly Black and monocultural.

Non-White minorities in the United States are forced to become biethnic to some extent in order to experience social and economic mobility. However, members of mainstream groups, such as Anglo-Americans, can and often do live almost exclusive monocultural and highly ethnocentric lives.

Stage 5: Multiethnicity and Reflective Nationalism

The Stage 5 individual has clarified, reflective, and positive personal, ethnic, and national identifications; positive attitudes toward other ethnic and racial groups; and is self-actualized. The individual is able to function, at least beyond superficial levels, within several ethnic cultures within his or her nation and to understand, appreciate, and share the values, symbols and institutions of several ethnic cultures within the nation. Such multiethnic perspectives and feelings, I hypothesize, help the individual live a more enriched and fulfilling life and formulate creative and novel solutions to personal and public problems.

Individuals within this stage have a commitment to their ethnic group, an empathy and concern for other ethnic groups, and a strong but *reflective* commitment and allegiance to the nation state and its idealized values, such as human dignity and justice. Thus, such individuals have reflective and clarified ethnic and national identifications and are effective citizens in a democratic pluralistic nation. Stage 5 individuals realistically view the United States as the multiethnic nation that it is. They have cross-cultural competency within their own nation and commitment to the national ideals, creeds, and values of the nation-state.

The socialization that most individuals experience does not help them attain the attitudes, skills, and perspectives needed to function effectively within a variety of ethnic cultures and communities. Although many people participate in several ethnic cultures at superficial levels, such as eating ethnic foods and listening to ethnic music (called Level I in Chapter 3), few probably participate at more meaningful levels and learn to understand the values, symbols, and traditions of several ethnic cultures and are able to function within other ethnic cultures at meaningful levels (Level II through III, see Chapter 3).

Stage 6: Globalism and Global Competency

The individual within Stage 6 has clarified, reflective, and positive ethnic, national, and global identifications and the knowledge, skills, attitudes, and abilities needed to function within ethnic cultures within his or her own nation as well as within cultures outside his or her nation in other parts of the world. The Stage 6 individual has the ideal delicate balance of ethnic, national, and global identifications, commitments, literacy, and behaviors. This individual has internalized the universalistic ethical values and principles of humankind and has the skills, competencies, and commitment needed to take action within the world to actualize personal values and commitments.

Characteristics of the Stages of Ethnicity Typology

This typology is an ideal-type construct (see Figure 11.1) and should be viewed as dynamic and multidimensional rather than as static and linear. The characteristics within the stages exist on a continuum. Thus, within Stage 1, individuals are more or less ethnically psychologically captive; some individuals are more ethnically psychologically captive than are others.

The division between the stages is blurred rather than sharp. Thus, a continuum also exists between as well as within the stages. The ethnically encapsulated individual (Stage 2) does not suddenly attain clarification and acceptance of his or her ethnic identity (Stage 3). This is a gradual and developmental process. Also, the stages should not be viewed as strictly sequential and linear. I am hypothesizing that some individuals may never experience a particular stage. However, I hypothesize that once an individual experiences a particular stage, he or she is likely to experience the stages above it sequentially and developmentally. I hypothesize, however, that individuals may experience the stages upward, downward, or in a zigzag pattern. Under certain conditions, for example, the biethnic (Stage 4) individual may become multiethnic (Stage 5); under new conditions the same individual may become again biethnic (Stage 4), ethnically identified (Stage 3), and ethnically encapsulated (Stage 2). Note, for example, the extent to which Jewish Americans, who tend to express more positive attitudes toward non-Whites than do other White ethnic groups in the United States, became increasingly in-group oriented as Israel become more threatened and as the expressions of anti-Semitism escalated in the 1970s.[4] Northern White ethnic groups became increasingly more ethnically encapsulated as busing for school desegregation gained momentum in northern cities in the 1970s.[5]

Figure 11.1 illustrates the dynamic and multidimensional characteristics of the development of ethnicity among individuals. Note especially the arrowed lines that indicate that continua exist both horizontally and vertically.

Preliminary Curricular Implications of the Stages of Ethnicity Typology

The discussion that follows on the curricular implications of the stages of ethnicity typology should be viewed as a set of tentative hypotheses that merit testing by educators and researchers interested in ethnicity and education. The reader should keep foremost in mind the tentative and exploratory nature of the following discussion.

Curricular Implications of Ethnicity: Stage 1

The student within this stage of ethnicity can best benefit from monoethnic content and experiences that will help him or her to develop ethnic awareness and a heightened sense of ethnic consciousness (see Chapter 10). Such monoethnic experiences should be designed to help the individual come to grips with personal ethnic identity and to learn how his or her ethnic group has been victimized by the larger society and by institutions, such as the media and the schools, which reinforce and perpetuate dominant societal myths and ideologies. Black studies, Chinese-Canadian studies, and Australian-Aboriginal studies courses conceptualized in *interdisciplinary* and *humanistic* ways, and other monoethnic experiences can help the individual within this stage to raise his or her level of ethnic consciousness. Strategies that facilitate moral development and decision-making skills should be an integral part of the curriculum for the ethnically psychologically captive individual.[6]

Curricular Implications of Ethnicity: Stage 2

Individuals within this stage can best benefit from curricular experiences that accept and empathize with their ethnic identities and hostile feelings toward outside groups. The teacher should accept the individual's hostile feelings and help him

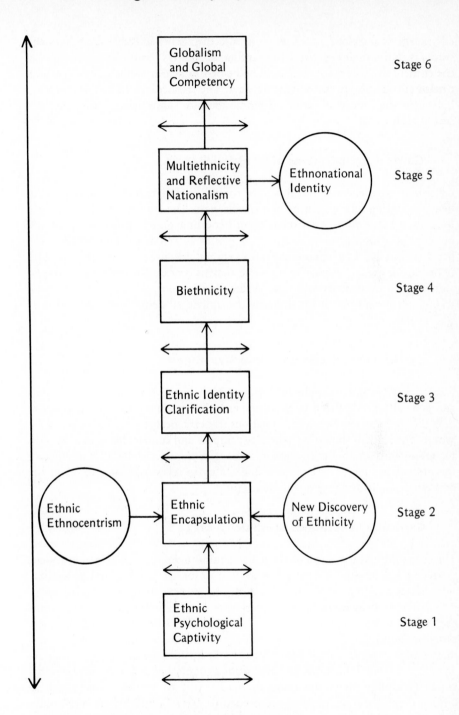

Figure 11.1. The Stages of Ethnicity: A Typology

or her express and clarify them. A strong affective curricular component that helps students clarify their negative ethnic and racial feelings should be a major part of the curriculum. The students should be helped to deal with their hostile feelings toward outside groups in constructive ways. The teacher should help the individual begin the process of attaining ethnic identity clarification during the later phases of this stage.

Curricular Implications of Ethnicity: Stage 3

Curricular experiences within this stage should be designed to reinforce the student's emerging ethnic identity and clarification. The student should be helped to attain a balanced perspective on his or her ethnic group. A true acceptance of one's ethnic group involves accepting its glories as well as its shortcomings. The individual in this stage of ethnicity can accept an objective view and analysis of his or her ethnic group, whereas an objective analysis is often very difficult for Stage 1 and Stage 2 individuals to accept. Value clarification and moral development techniques should be used to enhance the individual's emerging ethnic identity clarification.

Curricular Implications of Ethnicity: Stage 4

Curricular experiences should be designed to help the student master concepts and generalizations related to an ethnic group other than his or her own and to help the student view events and situations from the perspective of another ethnic group. The student should be helped to compare and contrast his or her own ethnic group with another ethnic group. Strategies should also be used to enhance the individual's moral development and ability to relate positively to his or her own ethnic group and to another ethnic group.

Curricular Implications of Ethnicity: Stage 5

The curriculum at this stage of ethnicity should be designed to help the student develop a global sense of ethnic literacy and to master concepts and generalizations about a wide range of ethnic groups. The student should also be helped to view events and situations from the perspectives of different ethnic groups within the United States as well as within other nations. The student should explore the problems and promises of living within a multiethnic cultural environment and discuss ways in which a multiethnic society may be nurtured and improved. Strategies such as moral dilemmas and case studies should be used to enable the individual to explore moral and value alternatives and to embrace values, such as human dignity and justice, that are needed to live in a multiethnic community and global world society.

Curricular Implications of Ethnicity: Stage 6

At this stage, the student has acquired three levels of identifications that are balanced: an ethnic, national and global identification and related cross-cultural competencies. Since the typology presented in this chapter constitutes a continuum, the process of acquiring an effective balance of ethnic, national, and global identifications and related cross-cultural competencies is a continuous and ongoing *process*. Thus, the individual never totally attains the ideal ethnic, national, and global identifications and related cross-cultural skills for functioning within his or her ethnic group, nation, and world. Consequently, a major goal of the curriculum for the Stage 6 individual is to help the student function at Stage 6 more effectively.

Knowledge, skills, attitudes, and abilities that students need to function more effectively within their ethnic group, nation, and world should be emphasized when teaching students at Stage 6. This includes knowledge about the individual's own ethnic group, other ethnic groups, the national culture, and knowledge about other nations in the world. Valuing strategies, such as moral dilemmas and case studies that relate to the individual's ethnic group, nation, and world, should also be effectively used at this stage to enhance the student's developing sense of ethnic, national, and global identifications. A major goal of teaching students within this stage is to help them understand how to determine which particular allegiance—whether ethnic, national, or global—is most appropriate within a particular situation. Ethnic, national, and global attachments should be given different priorities within different situations and events. The student within Stage 6 should learn how to determine which identification is most appropriate for particular situations, settings, and events.

Summary

When planning multiethnic experiences for students and teachers, we need to consider the ethnic characteristics of individuals. In designing curricula related to ethnicity, we often assume that ethnic groups are monolithic and have rather homogeneous needs and characteristics. However, students differ greatly in their ethnic identities and characteristics just as they differ in their general cognitive and affective development.[7] Consequently, some attempt should be made to individualize experiences for students within the multiethnic curriculum.

The description of a typology that attempts to outline the basic stages of the development of ethnicity among individual members of ethnic groups is presented in this chapter. This typology is a preliminary ideal-type construct in the Weberian sense and constitutes a set of hypotheses based on the existing and emerging theory and research and the author's study of ethnic behavior. The six stages within the typology are: Stage 1: *Ethnic Psychological Captivity*; Stage 2:

Ethnic Encapsulation; Stage 3: *Ethnic Identity Clarification*; Stage 4: *Biethnicity*; Stage 5: *Multiethnicity and Reflective Nationalism*; and Stage 6: *Globalism and Competency*. It is hypothesized that individuals within these different stages should be exposed to curricular experiences consistent with their levels of ethnic development. The curricular implications of each of the stages of ethnicity are discussed.

Notes

1. During the 1960s and 1970s social scientists frequently suggested, for example, that Afro-Americans had confused racial identities and ambivalent attitudes toward their ethnic group. The typology I present, however, suggests that only a segment of Blacks can be so characterized and that those Blacks are functioning at Ethnicity Stage 1. For the classical social pathology interpretation of the Afro-American personality see Abram Kardiner and Lionel Ovesey, *The Mark of Oppression: A Psychosocial Study of the American Negro* (New York: Norton, 1951). For a discussion of diversity among Afro-Americans see Thomas Sowell, "Three Black Histories," in Thomas Sowell, ed., *American Ethnic Groups* (Washington, D.C.: The Urban Institute, 1978), pp. 7–64.

2. Margaret Ford, "The Development of an Instrument for Assessing Levels of Ethnicity In Public School Teachers," Ed.D. diss., University of Houston, 1979.

3. Alice Miel with Edwin Kiester, Jr., *The Shortchanged Children of Suburbia* (New York: Institute of Human Relations Press, The American Jewish Committee, 1967).

4. See especially Arnold Forster and Benjamin R. Epstein, *The New Anti-Semitism* (New York: McGraw-Hill, 1974).

5. See Nathan Glazer, *Ethnic Dilemmas 1964–1982* (Cambridge, Mass.: Harvard University Press, 1983).

6. James A. Banks with Ambrose A. Clegg, Jr., *Teaching Strategies for the Social Studies*, 3rd ed. (New York: Longman, Inc., 1985).

7. Jean Piaget, *Six Psychological Studies* (New York: Random House, 1968); Lawrence Kohlberg and Rochelle Mayer, "Development as the Aim of Education," *Harvard Educational Review* 42 (November 1972), pp. 449–496.

PART V

Teaching and Instruction

The teacher is the most important variable in the successful implementation of multiethnic education. The chapters in Part V of this book are designed to help teachers attain the knowledge and skills needed to implement multiethnic education successfully in the classroom. Chapter 12 illustrates how teachers can plan and implement units on social issues that have decision-making and social action components. A key goal of multiethnic education is to help students attain more democratic attitudes and values. The research, theory, and strategies related to reducing student prejudice are described in Chapter 13. The characteristics of the effective multiethnic teacher are also described in this chapter.

Many students in the multiethnic classroom speak languages and dialects that differ from those fostered by the school and the mainstream society. Chapter 14 presents information and insights about language diversity that teachers will find useful when working with students from diverse language groups. The final chapter, Chapter 15, describes guidelines that teachers and other practicing educators can use to create multiethnic curricula and learning environments. This last chapter also summarizes some of the major issues, problems, and recommendations discussed in this book.

12

Teaching Decision-Making and Social Action Skills

The multiethnic curriculum should help students develop the ability to make reflective decisions so they can resolve personal problems, and through social action, influence public policy and develop a sense of political efficacy.[1] In many ethnic studies units and lessons, emphasis is on the memorization and testing of isolated historical facts about shadowy ethnic heroes of questionable historical significance. In these types of curricula ethnic content is merely an extension of the traditional curriculum.

The multiethnic curriculum should have goals that are more consistent with the needs of a global society. We live in a world society that is beset with momentous social and human problems. Effective solutions to these tremendous problems can be found only by an active and informed citizenry capable of making sound public decisions that will benefit the world community. It is imperative that the school play a decisive role in educating citizens capable of making reflective decisions on social issues and taking effective actions to help solve them.

Elements of Reflective Decision Making

Decision making consists of several components, including the derivation of knowledge, prediction, value analysis and clarification, the synthesis of knowledge and values, and the affirmation of a course of action (see Figure 12.1). All decisions consist of knowledge, valuing, and prediction components, but reflective decisions must also satisfy other requirements. To make a reflective decision, the decision maker must use the scientific method to attain knowledge. The knowledge must not only be scientific, but it must also be interdisciplinary and cut across disciplinary lines. Knowledge from any one discipline is insufficient to help us make reflective decisions. To make reflective decisions about social issues, such as busing to achieve school desegregation and reducing interethnic conflict, the individual must view these problems from the perspectives of such disciplines as sociology, economics, political science, and anthropology. The perspectives of any one discipline are too limited to guide intelligent decision-making and reflective social action.

This chapter consists of a teaching unit based on the decision-making model described in Figure 12.1. The key question in this sample unit is: **Should racial integration be a societal goal in a pluralistic democratic nation?**

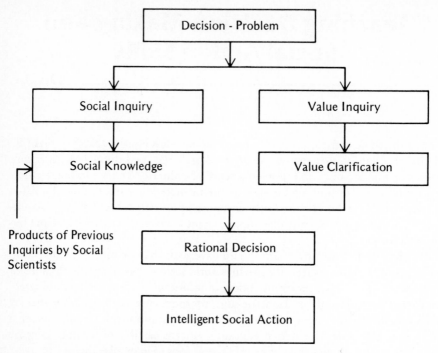

Figure 12.1. The Decision-Making Process
(*Source:* Adapted from *Teaching Strategies for Social Studies*
by J. A. Banks with A. A. Clegg. Copyright © 1985 by Longman
Inc. All rights reserved.)

Some Subissues Related to the Major Problem

There is a wide range of questions related to racial integration in a pluralistic society that students can state and research. Open housing, ethnic separatism, interracial marriage, and affirmative action are some of the key issues and problems the class can explore when studying about ethnicity and race. Specific problems related to the major question in this unit include:

- Should minorities be judged by different criteria than Whites when applying for employment and admission to colleges and universities?
- Should institutions establish quotas for hiring and admitting ethnic minorities?
- Should minorities be permitted to establish separate facilities and organizations in publicly supported institutions?
- Should busing be used to desegregate public schools?
- Should interracial and interethnic marriage be encouraged and socially accepted?

Stages in Considering This Issue

Gathering Scientific Data

To make an intelligent decision on a social issue such as "Should racial integration be a societal goal in a pluralistic nation?" the students need to acquire knowledge. However, decisions can be no better than the knowledge on which they are based. To make reflective decisions, students must study high-level concepts and master key generalizations. Generalizations can be taught in a variety of ways. However, it is necessary for students to use the *scientific method* to derive generalizations needed for decision making. When planning lessons to help students gain knowledge, the teacher should identify social science and related generalizations that will help them make intelligent decisions. Concepts should be selected from several disciplines, such as sociology, anthropology, history, and geography. *Discrimination*, *assimilation*, *ethnic group*, *culture*, *powerlessness*, and *separatism* are key concepts related to racial integration. After key concepts are identified, organizing (or key) generalizations related to the concepts are identified, and subideas related to the organizing generalizations and to the content chosen for study are stated. A detailed example of this type of curriculum planning is not presented here since I have discussed it at considerable length in other publications.[2]

Value Inquiry

After the students have had an opportunity to derive social science generalizations related to a social issue, they should undertake lessons that will enable them to *identify*, *analyze*, and *clarify* their values related to them. Value lessons should be conducted in an open classroom atmosphere so the students will be willing to express their beliefs freely and to examine them openly. If the teacher is authoritarian, the students will not express their actual feelings and attitudes. Beliefs that are unexpressed cannot be examined. Because of how teachers are viewed by most students, it is a good idea for teachers to withhold their views on controversial issues until the students have had an opportunity to express their beliefs. When teachers reveal their position on a social issue, many students then make statements they believe teachers want them to make rather than say things they actually believe. The teacher who opens a discussion on interracial marriage or open housing by saying that everybody should have the right to marry whomever they please or that open housing laws violate a seller's constitutional rights, cannot expect the students to state opposing beliefs. Some students will openly disagree with the teacher, but most will not. I am not suggesting that teachers should not state their positions on issues. However, experience suggests that when teachers openly express their views early in class discussions the dialogue usually becomes stifled or slanted in one direction.

Decision Making and Social Action

After the students have derived social science generalizations and clarified their values regarding the social issue, the teacher should ask them to list all the possible actions they could take regarding racial integration in their school and community, and to predict the possible consequences of each alternative. It is imperative that the alternatives and consequences the students identify and state are realistic and based on the knowledge they have mastered during the scientific phase of the unit. Alternatives and consequences should be intelligent predictive statements and not ignorant guesses or wishful thinking. After the students have discussed and weighed all alternative courses of action, they should decide on courses of action most consistent with their own values and implement them within their school or community. For example, the students, or some of them, may decide that racial integration should be a major goal in a pluralistic society but that it does not exist within their school. They might design a voluntary transfer plan with a local Black (or White, etc.) school and present it to the Board of Education for action. Figure 12.2 summarizes the major steps I have discussed for studying a social issue.

The Origin of the Issue

The teacher can begin a study of the key issues discussed in this chapter by asking the students to cut out newspaper items that deal with such issues as busing, open housing, affirmative action programs, and discrimination in employment.

The Definition of Key Concepts

When studying problems related to cultural pluralism and racial integration, the class should clarify the definitions of key terms and reach general agreement about what they mean. Terms such as *integration*, *race*, *desegregation*, *separatism*, *racism*, *discrimination*, and *cultural pluralism* are some of the key concepts that should be defined when racial integration is studied. Several of these terms are discussed below.

Some writers make a distinction between *integration* and *desegregation*. They define *desegregation* as the mere physical mixing of different racial and ethnic groups. *Integration*, for these writers, means much more. It occurs only when mutual respect and acceptance develop between different racial and ethnic groups who are members of the same institutions.

Separatism is sometimes said to exist when ethnic groups who are excluded from the mainstream society establish ethnic organizations and institutions to meet their exclusive needs. Students can explore other definitions of separatism and identify instances of it within their communities. When discussing separatism, the class should try to distinguish *separatism* and *segregation*. These terms are highly related and are often confused. Separatist institutions are designed to help an ethnic group attain self-determination and political power and to enhance its ethnic culture. Segregated institutions in *minority communities* are usually created by the dominant society in order to keep minorities subjugated. These

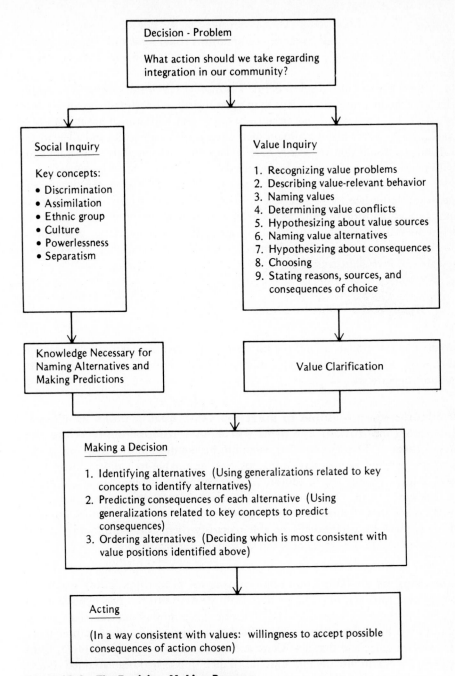

Figure 12.2. The Decision-Making Process
(*Source:* Adapted from *Teaching Strategies for Social Studies*
by J. A. Banks with A. A. Clegg. Copyright © 1985 by Longman
Inc. All rights reserved.)

types of institutions are designed and controlled by the powerful groups in a society and not by the ethnic minority community. Thus, *separatist* and *segregated* institutions in minority communities are fundamentally different in structure and function.

Students will also need to define a *culturally pluralistic society*. We *can* define a culturally pluralistic society as an open society in which individuals are able to take full advantage of the social, economic, and educational advantages of a society, and yet are able to maintain their unique ethnic identities and allegiances. Individuals would not necessarily have to become assimilated into the dominant culture in order to satisfy their survival needs.

The examples above merely suggest the kinds of working definitions students can formulate for some of the key concepts in this chapter. Many other examples and definitions could be given. It is extremely important for students to know how the concepts they are using are defined by themselves and others. Without a clear understanding of the key terms they are using, their most diligent research efforts will be frustrated.

Hypotheses

Students can formulate an infinite number of hypotheses related to racial integration and cultural pluralism when studying race relations. What follows is a list of *possible* hypotheses.

If minorities are required to meet the same qualifications as Whites, then most institutions and firms will remain predominantly White and segregated.   This hypothesis is based on the assumption that most ethnic minorities, perhaps for a variety of reasons, will be unable to compete successfully with Whites for jobs and in educational institutions if present criteria and methods are used to screen and select employees and students. An opposing hypothesis might state that if minorities are required to have the same qualifications as Whites, they would eventually be able to satisfy them because minorities could and would obtain the experiences and knowledge needed to do so.

If institutions and firms establish quotas for minorities, some qualified minorities and Whites will be discriminated against.   This hypothesis assumes that there are more qualified minorities for positions and slots than quotas would provide for, that some nonqualified minorities may be hired in preference to qualified ones, and that if a White and a minority are equally qualified, firms with quotas would hire the minorities until their quotas had been attained. It also assumes that qualified minorities would not be hired once such quotas were reached. A different hypothesis might suggest that firms and schools will recruit and hire minorities only if they are required to fulfill quotas.

If open housing laws are enacted and enforced, then Whites will be forced to sell their homes at a tremendous loss. This hypothesis assumes that property values are greatly reduced when ethnic minorities move into predominantly White neighborhoods. A related hypothesis might state that if open housing laws are not enacted and enforced, housing segregation will increase.

If busing is not used to desegregate the public schools, most Blacks and Whites will continue to attend racially segregated schools. This hypothesis assumes that because of the housing patterns of Blacks and Whites, busing is necessary to desegregate the public schools. Another hypothesis might state that if open housing laws were enacted and enforced, neighborhood schools would become voluntarily integrated.

Testing the Hypotheses

The students will need to gather data to test the hypotheses they have formulated. Because of the nature of the hypotheses formulated above and the short history of most civil rights programs and legislation, limited historical data are available about the effects of laws that prohibit segregation and discrimination. Also, like any other problems related to human behavior, problems in race relations are exceedingly complex. It is difficult to establish causal relationships with a high degree of certainty, such as if A then B, or if there is forced school integration (A), conflict (B) will develop between Blacks and Whites. There are too many other variables that may influence either A or B and thus affect the outcome of busing in a particular community. How forced integration affects the relationships between Blacks and Whites in a particular community may depend on who made the legal decision, whether a local or federal court, the extent of racial hostility within the community before the court order, the percentage of Blacks and Whites in the community involved in the busing program, the types of Black and White leaders in the community, and many other variables.

When students are gathering data to test hypotheses related to racial integration, they should be helped to see how difficult it is to establish relationships with a high degree of reliability. Another caveat is in order. Much information and data related to ethnic and racial problems are highly emotional and biased. It is often presented to support or invalidate a particular position or point of view. Examples of these types of studies abound in the literature on race relations. Rivlin has perceptively called this kind of research "forensic" social science.[3] Studies written in the forensic tradition include Jensen and Shockley's work on Black-White intelligence, Jencks et al.'s book on equality of educational opportunity, Banfield's *The Unheavenly City*, and Moynihan's *The Negro Family*.[4] Pro-Black positions on issues are presented in most of the articles in the *Black Scholar*.[5] One partial way to solve this problem is to present the students with readings that support several positions of an issue and then present data that support specific viewpoints.

Some Tentative Conclusions

The students *might* reach these four tentative conclusions after they have studied about racial integration and examined their values regarding racial mixing.

1. Ethnic minorities should be required to have the same qualifications for jobs and to enter college as any other persons. However, the ways in which these qualifications are determined should be modified so they reflect ethnic diversity and so minorities will not be victimized by discriminatory tests and other selective devices based exclusively on the dominant culture. Institutions and firms should aggressively recruit minorities to increase the pool from which they can select. This type of policy will, in the long run, result in the hiring of minorities who are as qualified as their White counterparts. In the short run, however, it might mean that industries and universities will not be able to increase the numbers of minorities in their populations at a very rapid rate.

2. Institutions should not establish quotas for minorities, but should implement affirmative action programs that will enable them to recruit minorities aggressively and give preference to them if minorities and Whites are equally qualified. The goal should be to have an integrated staff or student body that includes people who represent diverse ethnic and racial groups, and not to get a specific number from each ethnic group. This policy will result in the employment of minorities but will not restrict their number or encourage the hiring of minorities who are less qualified than White employees, or the admission of minority students who cannot succeed in college.

3. Open housing laws should be enacted in all communities to assure that every person has the opportunity to buy the house he or she wants and can afford regardless of race or ethnic group. If effectively enforced, open housing laws are not likely to result in many interracial communities since Whites usually move out of neighborhoods when minorities move into them. No legal actions should be taken to prevent freedom of movement by Whites. However, planned interracial communities should be established because people who grow up in interracial communities have more positive racial attitudes and are more likely to live in interracial neighborhoods and to send their children to interracial schools.

4. The establishment of interracial schools should be a major societal goal. Any reasonable plans, including those requiring busing, should be implemented if they are needed to establish and maintain desegregated schools. Parents opposed to interracial schools and/or busing should have the right to take their children out of the public schools. However, they should not be allowed to dictate or unduly influence school policy. Major societal goals and democratic values (such as equality and justice) should take precedence over the whims of special interest and pressure groups. If a school district takes a strong position vis-à-vis interracial schools and busing, hostile pressure groups, which are usually small but vocal minorities, will eventually accept the school's policy and lose both community support and wide public forums for their views.

Suggested Methods for Teaching about Integration and Public Controversy

Initiating the Unit

The teacher can begin a study of racial integration and public controversy by reading the class a current *case study* taken from the newspaper or a news magazine that deals with a controversial policy and/or issue related to integration. An example of such a case study taken from a newspaper and questions the class can discuss follow.

NEA Constitution, By-laws Are Racist, Illegal, Anti-Defamation League Says

Palm Beach, Fla. The Anti-Defamation League of B'nai B'rith has condemned as "unlawful, undemocratic and racist" the new constitution and bylaws of the National Educational Association. . . .

According to Peirez, the NEA Constitution specifically designates as ethnic minorities, blacks, Mexican-Americans, other Spanish-speaking groups, Asian-Americans and Indians. The NEA authorizes those minorities alone to nominate minority candidates for its board of directors and executive committees.

It further requires that there be a minimum of 20 percent ethnic minority representation on the NEA board, executive committee and all other committees and that delegates to its national representative assembly from state and local affiliates be allocated on the basis of the ethnic minority percentage of the population or be denied credentials.

The NEA Constitution also provides that nominations for NEA president be restricted to certain ethnic minority groups if, after 11 years, no member of such a group has been elected.[6]

Questions

1. Do the quotas established by the NEA Constitution constitute reverse discrimination? Why or why not?

2. Should institutions and organizations practice reverse discrimination when trying to compensate for past injustices? Why or why not?

3. Does the NEA Constitution violate the civil rights of Whites? Why or why not?

4. What effects do you think the NEA Constitution and bylaws will have on minorities in the organization? On Whites in the organization? Why?

Social Science Inquiry

When the teacher has launched the study of racial integration with a case study such as the one above, the students should study historical information that will enable them to understand the forces that have shaped public policy regarding racial integration. Attention should be given to the legalization of segregation that took place in the decades after the Civil War in the United States. Ask individual students to prepare and present reports on the following topics:

- the Black codes
- the poll tax
- the grandfather clause
- the Dred Scott Decision
- *Plessy* v. *Ferguson*

When these reports are presented to the class, the students should discuss these questions: Why did segregation become widespread in the post–Civil War period? Why was it legalized? How did these laws affect Black Americans? White Americans? Other Americans?

1. Ask the students to pretend they are the Supreme Court in 1896 and are hearing the case of Homer Plessy, a mulatto who complains that he has to sit in separate cars on trains passing through his native state of Louisiana. Plessy argues that this type of segregation violates protection guaranteed to him by the Fourteenth Amendment to the Constitution. Ask individual students to role play the roles of the Supreme Court justices, Homer Plessy, and the prosecuting and defense attorneys. After the arguments on both sides have been presented to the Court, the judges should deliberate and then rule on the case. After the role-play situation, the class should discuss:

a. ways in which their simulated court was similar to and different from the actual Supreme Court in 1896
b. whether the role-players were successfully able to assume the attitudes and viewpoints of people who lived in 1896
c. what the "separate but equal" doctrine meant in 1896 and what it means today

2. At the turn of the century, two major civil rights organizations were formed to fight for the rights of Afro-Americans: the National Association for the Advancement of Colored People and the National Urban League. Also during this period two major civil rights leaders became nationally eminent, Booker T. Washington and W. E. B. DuBois. Washington and DuBois became staunch opponents because they held opposing views about racial equality and the ways in which the Afro-American should be educated. Ask the class to read Washington's biography, *Up from Slavery*, and selections from W. E. B. DuBois's *The Souls of Black Folks*. The class should discuss the views of these two men and determine which of their ideas were valid and which were not. After the class has discussed the views of

DuBois and Washington, ask two students to role-play a debate between the two men regarding steps the Afro-American should take to achieve racial equality.

3. Most national civil rights organizations in the early 1900s were interracial. Ask the students to do required readings on the history and development of the NAACP and the National Urban League. When they have completed the readings, they should compare and contrast these two organizations with the Niagara Movement and earlier Black protest movements, such as the Negro Convention Movement and the African Civilization Society. Particular attention should be paid to: (1) reasons the organizations emerged, (2) who made policy and held key positions within them, (3) types of problems that arose within the organizations, (4) the major goals of the organizations, and (5) ways in which the organizations succeeded or failed and why.

4. Black separatist movements developed early in U.S. history. Some of the earliest were led by such Blacks as Martin R. Delaney and Paul Cuffee. Ask the students to research the lives of these men and to present dramatizations that show ways in which they were advocates of Black nationalism. Marcus Garvey, another Black separatist, attained eminence in the 1930s. Ask the class to read his biography, *Black Moses*, by E. D. Cronon, and to list ways in which Garvey was similar to and different from earlier Black nationalist leaders.

5. In the 1930s, 1940s, 1950s, and 1960s racial segregation received a number of severe blows that culminated in the *Brown* decision of 1954 and the Civil Rights Act of 1964. Ask the students to develop a chronology that lists the major civil rights legislation enacted between 1930 and 1964. After the chronology is developed, the students should discuss these two questions:

a. What were the major social and political factors that led to the passage of each of these bills?
b. Why has racial segregation actually increased in U.S. society since the 1960s even though so many civil rights bills have been enacted?

6. The major goal of the civil rights movement in the 1950s was to desegregate public accommodation facilities and other institutions. Action tactics and court battles achieved much desegregation. However, by 1965, many Afro-Americans, especially young Black activists, were disillusioned with the attainments of the movement and realized that integration alone would not eliminate the Afro-Americans' major social, economic, and political problems. These young activists felt that both the goals and tactics of the movement should be changed. They issued a call for "Black Power!" The students can gain an understanding of the concept of Black power by reading *Black Power: The Politics of Liberation in America* by Stokely Carmichael and Charles V. Hamilton. Many Black integrationists rejected the views of Black power advocates. Ask the class to research the views of the men and women listed below and to simulate a national convention of

Black civil rights leaders in which they discuss the problem, "What should be the future course of Black Americans: Integration or Separatism?"

(a) Martin Luther King, Jr.	(i) Shirley Chisholm
(b) Roy Wilkins	(j) Bobby Seale
(c) Roy Innis	(k) Huey Newton
(d) Angela Davis	(l) Imamu Amiri Baraka
(e) Stokely Carmichael	(m) Richard G. Hatcher
(f) H. Rap Brown	(n) Julian Bond
(g) Vernon Jordan	(o) Ronald V. Dellums
(h) Rev. Jesse Jackson	(p) Barbara Jordan

Individual students should be asked to research and play the roles of each leader in the convention. After the major question has been discussed, the convention participants should then develop an action agenda for Black Americans in the 1990s that they all can endorse.

Value Inquiry

After the students have had an opportunity to gather factual data related to racial integration, they should examine their values, attitudes, and beliefs regarding racial mixing. A wide variety of strategies and materials can be used to help students to examine and clarify their values. Some valuing exercises appropriate for studying about integration are given below. These strategies are adapted from techniques developed by Simon, Howe, and Kirschenbaum.[7]

Spread of opinion. The teacher should divide the class into several small groups and give each group a piece of paper with one of these issues written on it:

- forced busing
- interracial marriage
- open housing laws
- reverse discrimination
- separatism
- quotas
- interracial adoptions
- interracial dating
- segregated fraternities and sororities

Each group should identify a number of positions that can be taken on its issue. Each group member should write a statement defending one position, whether in agreement or not. When the statements have been completed, the students should discuss each issue and state their own positions on it.

Unfinished sentences. The teacher should duplicate the following list of statements and give a copy to each of the students. The students should be asked to complete the statements with the words and phrases they first think of when they read each statement. After the students have completed the statements, the teacher should divide the class into small groups and ask the students to discuss, "What I learned about myself from this exercise."

1. If I were Black (or White, Mexican American, etc.) I would . . .
2. Most Blacks are . . .
3. If a Black (or a Mexican American, etc.) family moved into my neighborhood, I would . . .
4. If I were forced to ride a bus to an integrated school each day, I would . . .
5. If my sister married a Black (or a White, etc.), I would . . .
6. People of other races make me feel . . .
7. A *racist* is a person who . . .
8. If I were called a *racist*, I would . . .
9. Most Whites are . . .
10. Special programs created for minorities are . . .
11. Minorities who participate in special programs are . . .
12. People who are opposed to interracial marriage are . . .
13. Minorities who score poorly on IQ tests are . . .

Strongly agree/Strongly disagree. The teacher should duplicate the following list of statements and give a copy to each of the students. Ask the students to indicate the extent to which they agree or disagree with the statements by writing one of the following letter combinations in front of each statement:

- SA = Strongly agree
- AS = Agree somewhat
- DS = Disagree somewhat
- SD = Strongly disagree

After the students have responded to each statement, divide the class into small groups and ask the students to discuss their responses in their groups.

_____ 1. I am prejudiced toward some racial and ethnic groups.

_____ 2. I would not live in a predominantly Black (or White, etc.) neighborhood.

_____ 3. Most Mexican Americans are poor because they are lazy.

_____ 4. Most Whites are racists.

     5. I would encourage my sister to marry a Black (or a White, etc.) if she wanted to.

     6. Minorities should meet the same college admission requirements as Whites.

     7. IQ tests are unfair to minorites and should be abandoned.

     8. Students should not be required to be bused to desegregated schools.

     9. Only Blacks should teach Black Studies.

     10. Universities and firms should establish quotas for minorities.

     11. White fraternities and sororities should be required to admit Blacks, Mexican Americans, Asian Americans, and other ethnic minorities.

Values grid. An effective summary valuing activity for this unit is the valuing grid. Place Table 12.1 on a ditto stencil and make copies for each student.*

Table 12.1.

Issue	1	2	3	4	5	6	7
1. Forced busing							
2. Interracial housing							
3. Interracial marriage							
4. Interracial dating							
5. Racial quotas							
6. Segregated schools							
7. Black separatism							
8. White racism							
9. Affirmative-action programs							
10. Black English							

*Copyright © 1988 by Allyn and Bacon, Inc. Reproduction of this material is restricted to use with *Multiethnic Education: Theory and Practice*, 2nd ed., by James A. Banks.

Ask the students to make brief notes about how they feel about each of the eleven issues listed in the table. Each issue will have been discussed during earlier parts of the unit. The following seven questions are taken from the valuing strategy developed by Simon et al.[8] List the following questions on the board and explain each one to the students.

1. Are you *proud* of (do you prize or cherish) your position?
2. Have you *publicly affirmed* your position?
3. Have you chosen your position from *alternatives?*
4. Have you chosen your position after *thoughtful consideration* of the pros and cons and consequences?
5. Have you chosen your position *freely?*
6. Have you *acted* on or done anything about your beliefs?
7. Have you acted with *repetition*, pattern, or consistency on this issue?

Ask the students to write "Yes" or "No" in each square in the chart to indicate their responses to each of the seven questions for each issue. When the students have individually completed the grid, they should break up into groups of threes and discuss as many of their responses as they would like to discuss.

Decision Making and Social Action

When the students have gathered scientific data and clarified their values, they should identify *alternative courses of actions* they can take regarding integration in a pluralistic society, and the *possible consequences* of each course of action. Individual and/or groups should then formulate plans to implement courses of action that are most consistent with their values. Below are possible action projects that some students may decide to implement.

Action projects.

1. If the school is segregated: Developing and implementing a volunteer transfer plan with a local school whose population is predominantly of another race.

2. Conducting a survey to determine the kinds of jobs most minorities have in local hotels, restaurants, and firms, and, if necessary, urging local businesses to hire more minorities in top level positions. Conducting boycotts of local businesses that refuse to hire minorities in top level positions.

3. Conducting a survey to determine the treatment of ethnic groups in all courses and textbooks in the school and recommending ways in which the school curriculum can become more integrated; suggesting that a permanent review board be established to examine all teaching materials and determine how they

present ethnic groups. Presenting these recommendations to appropriate school officials and pressuring them to act on the recommendations.

4. Conducting a survey to determine what local ethnic organizations and leaders are within the community. Inviting some of them to participate in school programs and projects, such as assemblies and classes.

5. Conducting a survey to determine whether the school and public libraries have adequate collections of books and materials about ethnic groups. If necessary, recommending books and materials to be purchased and pressuring the libraries to buy them.

6. Conducting a survey to determine what local laws exist (and how they are enforced) regarding open housing, discrimination in public accommodations, and, if necessary, developing recommendations regarding changes to be made in the laws or in how they should be implemented. Presenting these recommendations to appropriate public officials and pressuring them to act on the recommendations.

7. If the school is racially segregated: Developing plans for exchange activities and programs with a school whose population is predominantly of another race.

8. Conducting a survey to determine the racial and ethnic composition of the school staff (including secretaries, teachers, janitors, etc.) and if necessary, recommending appropriate action to take to make the school more integrated. Presenting these recommendations to appropriate school officials and pressuring them to act on the recommendations.

9. Conducting a survey to determine whether the posters, bulletin boards, photographs, and school holidays reflect the ethnic diversity within society and, if necessary, implementing a plan to make the total school environment more integrated and multiethnic.

10. If the school is interracial: Conducting a survey to determine if there are examples of racial conflict and tension within the school. If there are, formulating and implementing plans to alleviate these problems.

Summary

This chapter illustrates how the teacher can help students develop decision-making and social action skills by studying a public controversy related to racial and ethnic pluralism in the United States. The decision-making model illustrated in this chapter consists of social science inquiry, value inquiry, the synthesis of knowledge and values, and reflective decision making and social action. The sample unit on integration illustrates how each component of the decision-making model can be implemented in the classroom. Possible actions the students might take related to racial integration are also suggested.

Notes

1. James A. Banks with Ambrose A. Clegg, Jr., *Teaching Strategies for the Social Studies: Inquiry, Valuing, and Decision-Making*, 3rd ed. (White Plains, N.Y.: Longman, 1985).

2. Ibid; James A. Banks, *Teaching Strategies for Ethnic Studies*, 4th ed. (Boston: Allyn and Bacon, 1987).

3. Alice M. Rivlin, "Forensic Social Science," *Harvard Educational Review*, 43 (February 1973), pp. 61–75; see also Joyce A. Ladner, ed., *The Death of White Sociology* (New York: Vintage, 1973).

4. Arthur R. Jensen, "How Much Can We Boost IQ and Scholastic Achievement?" *Harvard Educational Review*, 39 (Spring 1969), pp. 273–356; William Shockley, "Dysgenics, Geneticity, Raceology: Challenges to the Intellectual Responsibility of Educators," *Phi Delta Kappan*, 53 (January 1972), pp. 297–307; Christopher Jencks et al., *Inequality: A Reassessment of the Effect of Family and Schooling in America* (New York: Basic Books, 1972); Edward C. Banfield, *The Unheavenly City* (Boston: Little, Brown, 1970); Daniel P. Moynihan, *The Negro Family: A Case for National Action* (Washington, D.C.: U.S. Government Printing Office, 1965).

5. A collection of articles reprinted from the *Black Scholar* are in Robert Chrisman and Nathan Hare, eds., *Contemporary Black Thought* (New York: The Bobbs-Merrill Co., 1973).

6. "NEA Constitution, By-laws Are Racist, Illegal, Anti-Defamation League says," *New York Teacher* (February 3, 1974).

7. Reprinted by permission of A & W Publishers, Inc. from *Values Clarification: A Handbook of Practical Strategies for Teachers and Students*, by Sidney B. Simon, Leland W. Howe, and Howard Kirschenbaum. Copyright © 1972; copyright © 1978 by Hart Publishing Co., Inc., pp. 35–37, 241–257, 252–254.

8. Ibid, p. 36. Reprinted by permission of A & W Publishers, Inc. from *Values Clarification: A Handbook of Practical Strategies for Teachers and Students*, by Sidney B. Simon, Leland W. Howe, and Howard Kirschenbaum. Copyright © 1972; copyright © 1978 by Hart Publishing Co., Inc.

13

Reducing Prejudice in Students: Theory, Research, and Strategies

The Causes of Prejudice

We cannot reduce racial prejudice unless we acquire an understanding of its causes. First, however, we need to define *prejudice*. The literature on race relations is replete with efforts to define *prejudice*. Even though the definitions differ to some extent, most suggest that prejudice is a set of rigid and unfavorable attitudes toward a particular group or groups that is formed in disregard of facts. Prejudiced individuals respond to perceived members of these groups on the basis of preconceptions, tending to disregard behavior or personal characteristics that are inconsistent with their biases. Simpson and Yinger have provided a lucid and useful definition of *prejudice:*

> Prejudice is an emotional, rigid attitude (a predisposition to respond to a certain stimulus in a certain way) toward a group of people. They may be a group only in the mind of the prejudiced person; that is, he categorizes them together, although they may have little similarity or interaction. Prejudices are thus attitudes, but not all attitudes are prejudices.[1]

Although social scientists have attempted for years to derive a comprehensive and coherent theory of prejudice, their efforts have not been totally successful. A number of theories explain various components of prejudice, but none sufficiently describes its many dimensions. Social scientists have rejected some of the older, more simplistic theories of prejudice; other theories are too limited in scope to be functional. Still others are extremely useful in explaining certain forms of prejudice directed toward specific groups but fail to account for its other facets. A serious study of the theories of prejudice reveals the complexity of this configuration of attitudes and predispositions; thus, simplistic explanations of prejudice only hinder our understanding of it.

Theories of Prejudice

Arnold M. Rose has critically reviewed both the older, simpler theories of prejudice and the more complex modern psychological explanations.[2] A summary of his analysis is presented below in order to illuminate the strengths and weaknesses of the various theories.

The *racial and cultural difference theory* maintains that people have an instinctive fear and dislike of individuals who are physically and culturally different from themselves. Rose dismisses this theory as untenable, since research indicates that children are tolerant of other races and groups until they acquire the dominant cultural attitudes toward ethnic minorities. Children must be *taught* to dislike different races and ethnic groups. Writes Rose, "[This theory] should be thought of as a rationalization of prejudice rather than as an explanation of it."[3]

The *economic competition theory* holds that prejudice emanates from antagonism caused by competition among various groups for jobs and other economic rewards. Although this theory sheds light on many historical examples of racial prejudice and discrimination, it has some serious limitations. It fails to explain why a group continues to practice discrimination when it no longer profits economically from doing so. A number of studies document the severe financial losses attributable to discrimination against ethnic groups.

The *social control theory* maintains that prejudice exists because individuals are forced to conform to society's traditions and norms; thus, they dislike certain groups because they are taught to do so by their culture. This theory helps explain why prejudice may be perpetuated when it is no longer functional, but it does not consider how it originates.

The *traumatic experience theory* states that racial prejudice emerges in an individual following a traumatic experience involving a member of a minority group during early childhood. This theory is inadequate because young children do not associate an unpleasant experience with a particular racial group unless they have already been exposed to the concept of racial differences. In noting another limitation of this theory, Harley writes:

> This idea can be discounted because persons can hold extreme prejudice with no contact with persons of the discriminated class, and the traumatic experiences reported by persons as reason for their prejudice are very often found to be either imagined by them or elaborated and embellished beyond recognition.[4]

The *frustration-aggression theory* is a modern psychological explanation of prejudice. It suggests that prejudice results when individuals become frustrated because they are unable to satisfy real or perceived needs. Frustration leads to aggression, which may then be directed toward minority groups because they are highly visible targets and unable to retaliate. Displacing aggression on stigmatized groups is much safer than attacking the real source of the frustration. Rose illuminates two basic weaknesses in this theory: (1) it fails to explain why certain groups are selected as targets rather than others, and (2) it assumes that all frustration must be expressed. However, a number of writers and researchers have relied heavily on this theory to help explain the emergence and perpetutation of prejudice.

The *projection theory* states that "people attribute to others motives that they sense in themselves but that they would not wish to acknowledge openly."[5]

This theory is severely limited because it fails to explain motives for prejudice or why certain characteristics are attributed to specific groups.

In attempting to derive a comprehensive theory of prejudice, Rose suggests that the modern psychological theories are the most useful explanations. He writes:

> The central theories today which seriously attempt to explain prejudice are based on the concepts of frustration-aggression, projection, and symbolic substitution. These theories have a good deal in common despite the differing kinds of evidence which lead to their formation. All of them postulate (1) a need to express antagonism (2) toward something which is not the real object of antagonism. Not only is there an essential similarity among the three theories, but they complement each other at their weakest points. The symbolic theory does most to explain which group is selected for prejudice and why. The frustration-aggression theory does most to explain the strength behind prejudice. The projection theory offers a plausible explanation of the psychological function of prejudice as a cleansing agent to dissolve inner guilt or hurt.[6]

A Comprehensive Theory of Prejudice

Simpson and Yinger have formulated a comprehensive theory of prejudice "around three highly interactive but analytically distinct factors, each the convergence of several lines of theory and evidence."[7] The first factor is the personality requirements of the individual. As a result of both constitutional and learned needs, some people develop personalities that thrive on prejudices and irrational responses. This theory has been offered by a number of other writers and researchers. We later review some research on which it is based.

An individual may also develop prejudices based not on personality needs but on the way society is structured. The power structure of society is especially important to this concept, which is similar to the economic competition theory Rose discusses. Simpson and Yinger write, "It is impossible to interpret individual behavior adequately without careful attention to the social dimension."[8]

The third basic cause of prejudice suggested by Simpson and Yinger is society itself.

> In almost every society . . . each new generation is taught appropriate beliefs and practices regarding other groups. Prejudices are, in part, simply a portion of the cultural heritage; they are among the folkways.[9]

This explanation is identical to the social control theory summarized by Rose.

Simpson and Yinger stress that all three of these factors interact: "Any specific individual, in his pattern of prejudice, almost certainly reflects all of the causes."[10] Both they and Rose emphasize that multiple explanations are needed to account for the complexity of racial prejudice.

Personality Theories of Prejudice

In his review of the theories of prejudice, Rose discusses personality explanations. As we have seen, Simpson and Yinger cite the individual's personality needs as one basic cause of prejudice; earlier researchers considered personality *the* most important variable in the formation of bigotry. The latter attributed different types of personalities to differences in child-rearing practices, some of which were thought to produce personalities intolerant of different races and groups, whereas others helped develop racial tolerance and acceptance in the child. Else Frenkel-Brunswik and her associates conducted the pioneering research on the role of personality in the formation of prejudice.[11]

In one of a series of studies, Frenkel-Brunswik compared the racial attitudes and personality characteristics of 1,500 children.[12] Interviews were conducted with the subjects and their parents; both personality and attitude tests were administered. Frenkel-Brunswik concluded that there were significant differences in the personalities of prejudiced and unprejudiced children. She found that prejudiced children evidenced more rejection of out-groups, a blind acceptance of the in-group, a greater degree of aggression, and a strong rejection of persons perceived as weak. The more prejudiced children also displayed a greater resentment of the opposite sex and an admiration for strong figures. They were more willing to submit to authority, more compulsive about cleanliness, and more moralistic. The unprejudiced children were "more oriented toward love and less toward power than the ethnocentric child . . . and more capable of giving affection."[13] In summarizing her study Frenkel-Brunswik notes, "It was found that some children tend to reveal a stereotyped and rigid glorification of their own group and an aggressive rejection of outgroups and foreign countries."[14]

Frenkel-Brunswik and her associates also studied the relationship between personality and prejudice in adults.[15] They concluded that certain individuals, because of their early childhood experiences, have insecure personalities and a need to dominate and to feel superior to other individuals. These individuals possess an *authoritarian personality*, which is manifested not only in racial prejudice but also in their sexual behavior and religious and political views. The authors write:

> The most crucial result of the present study, as it seems to the authors, is the demonstration of close correspondence in the type of approach and outlook a subject is likely to have in a great variety of areas, ranging from the most intimate features of family and sex adjustments through relationships to other people in general, to religion and to social and political philosophy. Thus a basically hierarchical, authoritarian, exploitive parent-child relationship is apt to carry over into a power-oriented, exploitively dependent attitude toward one's sex partner and one's God and may well culminate in a political philosophy and social outlook which has [*sic*] no room for anything but a desperate clinging to what appears to be a strong and disdainful rejection of whatever is relegated to the bottom.[16]

Flaws in Personality Research

Even though the research by Frenkel-Brunswik and her associates contributed greatly to the literature on the origins of prejudice, other researchers have severely criticized it because of its methodological flaws and weak theoretical base. We defer a discussion of the theory on which the research is based and review a number of its methodological weaknesses.

Simpson and Yinger have written one of the most perceptive critiques.[17] They point out that the inadequate attention given to sampling techniques limits the generalizability of the findings. The research is also weakened by heavy reliance on the subjects' memories of childhood; the inadequate control of variables, such as education and group membership; and the low reliability of the measuring instruments. The F Scale used by the researchers measured many variables simultaneously, failing to measure well any one variable. However, Simpson and Yinger conclude that the flaws in the research do not substantially diminish its import. "Despite the seriousness of such methodological problems, they do not refute, in the judgment of most observers, the significance of personality research for the student of prejudice."[18]

Other Personality Studies

Other researchers have also attempted to explain the emergence of racial prejudice as a personality variable. Lindzey studied the personalities of twenty-two individuals judged "high in prejudice" and twenty-two judged "low in prejudice."[19] The subjects were divided into experimental and control groups. After exposing members of the experimental groups to a frustration experience, Lindzey concluded that the individuals high in prejudice evidenced more "frustration susceptibility" and "more overt disturbance in response to frustration than those low in minority group prejudice."[20] The subjects high in prejudice also received higher scores on an instrument that measured "conservative nationalistic statements." Writes Lindzey:

> We have pointed to certain evidence in our data suggesting that the high in prejudice are more "frustratable," somewhat more aggressive, and more conforming to authority norms than the low in prejudice. Further, we have proposed that early exposure to strict norms is one means by which we might account for the behavior patterns that appear to characterize the high in prejudice in this study.[21]

Allport and Kramer found that the more prejudiced persons in a sample of college students maintained closer ties with their families, whereas the least prejudiced students "reacted against" their parents' attitudes.[22] The former also had more negative memories of childhood, were better able to identify racial and ethnic groups, were more religious, and expressed more hostility and aggression. "From all these results," Allport and Kramer write, "we conclude that *prejudice is woven into the very fabric of personality* [emphasis added]. A style of life is adopted. It proceeds by rule of thumb."[23] The subjects who reported that they had studied "scientific facts about race" in school were more often classified as "less prejudiced." However, only 8 percent of the subjects could recall studying racial facts in school.

Like Frenkel-Brunswik, Allport and Kramer believe that prejudice can be explained largely as a product of personality. However, both research teams compared extreme bigots with individuals who manifested few negative racial attitudes, whereas most people exhibit only an average amount of racial prejudice and do not have seriously disorganized personalities. Thus, there are severe limitations implicit in an exclusive *personality* approach to the study of prejudice.

Social Structure Theories of Prejudice

Herbert Blumer seriously questions attempts to attribute prejudice and discrimination to personality variables.[24] He almost completely dismisses the role of attitudes in influencing behavior. Blumer asserts that the social setting rather than racial attitudes is the prime determinant of behavior. In trying to understand discrimination against minority groups, he contends that we should analyze social settings and norms instead of the personal attitudes of the individual. Blumer reviews a number of studies indicating the frequently occurring discrepancy between an individual's verbalized attitudes and actual behavior.

Saenger and Gilbert found that prejudiced individuals will patronize a racially mixed store when their desire to shop exceeds their antipathy toward Blacks.[25] Research by Blalock suggests that discrimination is not always a correlate of racial prejudice.[26] In certain situations, prejudiced individuals may not discriminate, since the prevailing norms may affect their behavior more than will their personal attitudes. Merton presents a useful typology for illustrating the relationship between prejudice and discrimination.[27] He identifies four ideal-types:

1. The unprejudiced nondiscriminator.
2. The unprejudiced discriminator.
3. The prejudiced nondiscriminator.
4. The prejudiced discriminator.

Blumer summarizes an important study by Lohman and Reitzes:[28]

> In a study of race relations in a large city . . . the same set of whites behaved entirely differently toward Negroes in three situations—working establishment, residential neighborhood and shopping center; no prejudice or discrimination was shown in the working establishment where the whites and [Blacks] belonged to the same labor

union, whereas prejudice and discrimination toward [Blacks] by the same whites was pronounced in the case of residential neighborhood.[29]

Blumer seriously underestimates the role of attitudes and personality as determinants of racial discrimination and prejudice. An adequate theory of prejudice must take into account both personality variables and the social structure. Explaining prejudice and discrimination as totally a product of a disorganized personality ignores the facts that human beings are social beings and that their reactions in a social setting reflect not only their individual idiosyncrasies and biases but also the prevailing norms and expectations. Thus, bigoted teachers will be less inclined to manifest their true attitudes toward Black children when Black parents are visiting the room than those teachers would be inclined to do when they and the children are alone.

However, social setting alone cannot completely explain racial discrimination; neither can it, as Blumer implies, totally diminish the importance of racial attitudes. If the same bigoted teachers were transferred to an all-Black school in which there was little tolerance for racial discrimination, their behavior would probably become more consistent with the dominant norms of the new setting, but their attitudes would most likely be revealed to their students in subtle ways and perhaps affect them just as profoundly. *The most equalitarian social setting cannot cause an intense bigot to exhibit behavior identical to that of a person free of racial prejudice.*

Much of the research Blumer relies on to support his hypothesis is subject to serious criticism, particularly the study by Lohman and Reitzes.[30] These authors found that their White subjects behaved *"entirely differently toward [Blacks] in different social settings"* [emphasis added] and showed "no prejudice toward them at work."[31] However, I seriously question whether the Black factory workers would have endorsed these conclusions, believing instead that they most likely could have cited examples of discrimination directed against them by their White co-workers. It is highly unlikely that persons who are so bigoted that they would exclude Blacks from their neighborhoods could treat them with full equality at work or indeed in any other setting.

The *social setting* explanation of prejudice and discrimination presents other difficulties. In trying to explain an individual's reactions in a given situation, we must consider not only the group norms but also the importance the individual attaches to the group and setting. Research suggests that a group or situation must be important to an individual before he or she accepts its norms and values. Pearlin classified a random sample of 383 college students into "acceptors" and "rejectors" on the basis of their attitudes toward Blacks.[32] A majority of the subjects who accepted Blacks in different situations had broken their own close family ties and developed identifications with campus groups. The more prejudiced individuals indicated that they had maintained close ties with their families and developed few associations with campus groups. Students who became more racially liberal as a result of their college experience considered college group norms more important than their parents' attitudes, whereas the more prejudiced subjects deemed family norms more important. Thus, simply placing individuals in new settings with different norms and values does not necessarily change their behavior and attitudes. Pearlin writes:

> These findings indicate that when a person holds membership in groups having conflicting views on an issue, his own attitudes will be influenced by the relative importance of the groups to him. Generally, in such a situation the attitudes of the individual will approximate most nearly the norms of the groups to which he most closely refers himself; . . . attitude change cannot be reckoned solely in terms of exposure to new ideas. Whether or not an individual will undergo modification of his attitude depends in large part on the nature of his relationship to groups holding the opposing sentiments and opinions.[33]

The social setting hypothesis also fails to consider that individuals collectively determine the group norm. Whether a group sanctions racial discrimination or racial tolerance thus depends on the attitudes of its members. Clearly, then, we must consider both individual attitudes and social norms when attempting to explain the genesis and perpetuation of racial discrimination and prejudice. The most important variables that affect the formation of racial prejudice are summarized in Figure 13.1.

Micro Approaches to Prejudice Reduction

Both personality characteristics and the social structure of institutions influence the degree to which individuals are prejudiced and the extent to which they act on

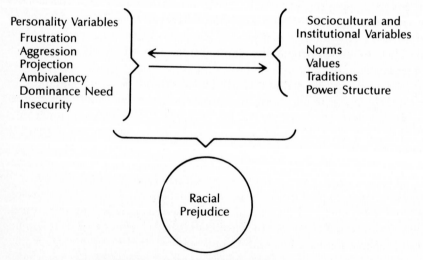

Figure 13.1. Variables That Cause Racial Prejudice

their prejudices, that is, *discriminate*. However, few researchers have studied the effects of changes in social structure on the racial attitudes of students. Most researchers have examined the effects of particular components of the school, such as materials, films, interracial contact, and special units on the racial attitudes of students. It is very difficult to identify and manipulate all of the major variables within an institution, such as a school, in an experimental situation.

Studies that have been conducted using materials, interracial contact, and special units on minority groups indicate that children's racial attitudes can be modified by school experiences specifically designed for that purpose. One of the most frequently cited studies on the effects of teaching materials on children's racial attitudes is the study reported by Trager and Yarrow.[34] Their curricula had significant effects on children's racial feelings. All changes were in the expected directions. Children exposed to a democratic curriculum expressed more positive racial attitudes; those exposed to an ethnocentric curriculum developed more negative racial feelings. Trager and Yarrow summarize their study:

> The changes achieved in the experiment demonstrate that democratic attitudes and prejudiced attitudes can be taught to young children. The experiment contributes to an understanding of some of the important conditions which are conducive to learning attitudes. Furthermore, it is apparent that children learn prejudices not only from the larger environment but from the content of the curriculum and its value. If democratic attitudes are to be learned they must be specifically taught and experienced.[35]

Research by Johnson[36] and by Litcher and Johnson[37] confirms the Trager and Yarrow findings. Both studies support the postulate that teaching materials affect children's racial attitudes toward ethnic groups and themselves. Johnson studied the effects of a special program in Black history on the racial attitudes and self-concepts of a group of Black children.[38] The course had a significant effect on the boys' attitudes. However, the effect on the girls' attitudes and self-perceptions was not significant.

> The Freedom School . . . seemed to have some effect on the boys in the areas of self-attitudes, equality of Negroes and whites, attitudes toward Negroes, and attitudes toward civil rights. That is, they became more confident in themselves, more convinced that Negroes and whites are equal, more positive toward Negroes, and more militant toward civil rights.[39]

Litcher and Johnson investigated the effects of multiethnic readers on the racial attitudes of White elementary students.[40] On all posttest measures, the children who had studied multiethnic as opposed to all-White readers expressed significantly more positive racial feelings toward Blacks. The authors write convincingly, "The evidence is quite clear. Through the use of a multiethnic reader, white children developed markedly more favorable attitudes toward Negroes."[41]

Katz and Zalk studied the effects of four short-term intervention techniques for modifying the racial attitudes of White elementary school children.[42] The techniques were (1) increased positive racial contact, (2) vicarious interracial contact, (3) reinforcement of the color black, and (4) perpetual differentiation of minority group faces. The children were posttested after two weeks and again four to six months later. The authors conclude:

> Results revealed a significant short-term reduction in prejudice for all experimental groups on combined measures. Vicarious contact and perceptual approaches were more effective than the other two. Some interaction effects with grade and race of examiner were found. Long-term treatment effects were less pronounced, although some gains were maintained in the vicarious contact and perceptual differentiation groups.[43]

In a comprehensive review of the literature on changing intergroup attitudes and behaviors, Stephan concluded that several techniques and approaches are effective in reducing racial prejudice.[44] A number of the studies he reviewed indicate that cooperation in multiethnic groups is one of the most effective ways to help students attain more positive racial attitudes. Workshops — especially when they help Whites understand the discrepancies between the reality and the ideals related to race in America — can help adults attain more positive racial attitudes. The use of multiethnic school curricula has resulted in the reduction of prejudice in seven studies reported by Stephan, including those by Leslie, Leslie, and Penfield,[45] and those by Yawkey and Blackwell.[46] Several studies discussed by Stephan reported that students developed more positive racial attitudes when they took the role of people from other racial groups. Stephan derived the following thirteen tentative principles about ways to reduce prejudice:

1. Cooperation within groups should be maximized and competition between groups should be minimized.
2. Members of the in-group and the out-group should be of equal status both within and outside the contact situation.
3. Similarity of groups members on nonstatus dimensions (beliefs, values, etc.) appears to be desirable.
4. Differences in competence should be avoided.
5. The outcomes should be positive.
6. Strong normative and institutional support for the contact should be provided.
7. The intergroup contact should have the potential to extend beyond the immediate situation.
8. Individuation of group members should be promoted.
9. Nonsuperficial contact (e.g., mutual disclosure of information) should be encouraged.

10. The contact should be voluntary.
11. Positive effects are likely to correlate with the duration of the contact.
12. The contact should occur in a variety of contexts with a variety of in-group and out-group members.
13. Equal numbers of in-group and out-group members should be used.[47]

In their important study of adolescent prejudice, Glock et al.[48] found that youths who are cognitively sophisticated exemplify less prejudice and discrimination than do students who lack cognitive sophistication. By *cognitive sophistication* Glock et al. mean the ability to think clearly about prejudice, to reason logically about it, and to ask probing questions. They write:

> The findings suggest that the best way for the schools to combat prejudice is simply for them to do their fundamental job of education more effectively. This at least appears to be the message of the consistent finding that the most effective armor against prejudice is cognitive sophistication. Presumably, if the general level of cognitive sophistication were raised, without necessarily any specific instruction about prejudice, the incidence of prejudice would be reduced.[49]

Although subject to the limitations of the research, a number of guidelines can be derived from the research on changing children's racial attitudes, some of which is reviewed above. The research suggests that children's racial attitudes can be modified if the school designs specific objectives and strategies for that purpose and if it increases students' cognitive sophistication. Most research studies indicate that specific instructional objectives must be clearly formulated; incidental teaching of race relations is not usually effective. Also, clearly defined teaching strategies must be structured to attain the objectives. Attitude changes induced by experimental intervention will persist through time, although there is a tendency for modified attitudes to revert to the pre-experimental ones.

However, the effects of the experimental treatment do not completely diminish. This finding suggests that intergroup education programs should not consist of one-shot treatments. Systematic experiences must be structured to reinforce and perpetuate the desired attitudes. Cooperative rather than competitive cross-ethnic situations should be fostered. A multiethnic curriculum will enhance the possibility for students to develop more positive attitudes toward different racial and ethnic groups, as will equal-status contact situations.

Visual materials such as pictures and films greatly enhance the effectiveness of attempts to change racial attitudes.[50] Contact with minority groups does not *in itself* significantly affect children's racial attitudes. The prevalent attitude toward different races and groups in the social situation is the significant determinant of children's racial feelings. The attitudes and predispositions of the classroom teacher are important variables in a program designed to foster positive racial feelings.[51] Students who are able to reason at a high level and to think critically tend to show less prejudice than do students who reason at lower levels and think less critically.

Macro Approaches to Prejudice Reduction

Most approaches to the reduction of prejudice in the schools have focused on limited factors in the school environment, such as instructional materials and cooperative learning,[52] and on aspects of the formalized curriculum, such as courses and increasing levels of cognitive sophistication.[53] Although it is necessary to focus on these aspects of the school environment, this approach is clearly insufficient because the school is an interrelated social system, each part of which shapes and influences the racial attitudes and behavior of students. The social structure of institutions has a cogent impact on the racial attitudes, perceptions, and behavior of individuals. Thus, intervention designed to reduce prejudice among students should be institutional and comprehensive in nature. It is necessary to use multiethnic instructional materials to increase the cognitive sophistication of students, but to focus exclusively on instructional materials and increasing the cognitive sophistication of students is too narrow and will not substantially reduce instititional prejudice and discrimination.

To reduce prejudice, we should attempt institutional or systemic reform of the total school and try to reform all of its major aspects, including institutional norms, power relationships, the verbal interactions between teachers and students, the culture of the school, the curriculum, extracurricular activities, attitudes toward minority languages, and the counseling and testing programs. The latent or hidden values within an institution like a school often have a more cogent impact on students' attitudes and perceptions than does the formalized course of study. Educators who have worked for years in curriculum reform know that helping teachers attain new skills and then placing these teachers in an institutional environment whose norms contradict and do not support the teachers' use of those newly acquired skills frequently leads to frustration and failure. Thus, any approach to school reform that is likely to succeed must focus on all major elements of the school environment identified earlier in Figure 3.4.

Prejudice among students is reinforced by many aspects of the student's environment, including the school. Cortés (1981) uses the concept of the "societal curriculum" to describe the societal factors that influence and shape students' attitudes toward different ethnic and racial groups, such as television, newspapers, and popular books.[54]

Often the negative images of ethnic groups that children learn in the larger society are reinforced and perpetuated in the school. Rather than reinforcing children's negative feelings toward ethnic groups, the school should counteract children's negative societal experiences and help them develop more positive attitudes toward a range of ethnic and racial groups. It is not possible for the school to avoid playing a role in the ethnic education of students. This is so because many children come to school with stereotypes of different racial and ethnic groups and negative attitudes toward these groups. Either the school can do nothing deliberate to intervene in the formation of children's racial attitudes (which means that the school would unwittingly participate in the perpetuation of racial bias), or it can attempt to intervene and influence the development of children's racial attitudes in a positive direction.

To take this latter course, it is imperative that the school do more than merely devise a few units or teaching strategies to reduce prejudice and focus on the histories and cultures of ethnic groups on particular days or weeks of the school year. Specialized units and teaching strategies are clearly insufficient. Teaching about ethnic groups only at particular times may do more harm than good because these kinds of activities and rituals may reinforce the idea that ethnic groups, such as Asians and Indians, are not integral parts of their societies.

The school environment consists of both a manifest and a hidden curriculum. The manifest curriculum consists of such discernable environmental factors as curriculum guides, textbooks, bulletin boards, and lesson plans. These aspects of the school environment are important and must be reformed in order to create a school environment that promotes positive attitudes toward diverse ethnic and racial groups. However, the school's latent or hidden curriculum is often a more cogent factor than is its manifest or overt curriculum. The latent curriculum has been defined as the curriculum that no teacher explictly teaches but that all students learn. It is the powerful part of the school experience that communicates to students the school's attitudes toward a range of issues and problems, including how the school views them as human beings and its attitudes toward diverse racial and ethnic groups.

How does the school communicate its cogent, latent messages to students? These messages are communicated to students in a number of subtle but powerful ways, including these:

1. By the kind of verbal and nonverbal interactions teachers have with children from different racial and ethnic groups; by the kinds of statements teachers make about different ethnic groups; and by teachers' nonverbal reactions when issues related to ethnic groups are discussed in class. Research by Gay, Rist, and the U.S. Commission on Civil Rights indicates that teachers often have more positive verbal and nonverbal interactions with middle-class, Anglo students than with ethnic minority and lower-class students.[55]

2. How teachers respond to the languages and dialects of children from different ethnic and racial groups. Some research suggests that teachers are often biased against the languages and dialects of children who are members of particular ethnic and racial groups.[56]

3. Grouping practices used in the school. Research by Mercer and Samuda indicates that members of some ethnic groups in the United States are disproportionately placed in lower ability groups because of their performance on IQ and other standardized aptitude tests that discriminate against these groups because they are normed on middle-class Anglo-Americans.[57]

4. Power relationships in the schools. Often in schools, most of the individuals who exercise the most power belong to dominant ethnic groups. Students

acquire important learning by observing which ethnic groups are represented among the administrators, teachers, secretaries, cooks, and bus drivers in the school.

5. The formalized curriculum also makes statements about the values the school has toward ethnic diversity. The ethnic groups that appear in textbooks and in other instructional material teach students which groups the school considers important and unimportant.

6. The learning styles, motivational systems, and cultures promoted by the school express many of the school's important values toward cultural differences. The educational environments of most schools are more consistent with the learning patterns and styles of mainstream students than with those of ethnic minority students, such as Blacks, Indians, and Puerto Ricans. Ramírez and Castañeda (1974) have found that Mexican-American youths tend to be more field-sensitive than field-independent in their cognitive styles.[58] Anglo-American students tend to be more field-independent. Field-sensitive and field-independent students differ in a number of characteristics and behavior. Field-sensitive students tend to work with others to achieve a common goal and are more sensitive to the feelings and opinions of other people than are field-independent students. Field-independent students prefer to work independently and to compete and gain individual recognition. Students who are field-independent are more often preferred by teachers and tend to get higher grades, although learning style is not related to IQ.

An Interdisciplinary Conceptual Curriculum

It is essential that educators take an institutional approach to school reform when intervening to reduce prejudice in students; the formalized curriculum is a vital element of the school. Hence, curriculum reform is imperative. The curriculum within a school designed to help reduce prejudice in students should be interdisciplinary, focus on higher levels of knowledge, and help students view events and situations from diverse ethnic and national perspectives.

Many ethnic studies units, activities, and programs emphasize factual learning and the deeds of ethnic heroes. These types of experiences use ethnic content but traditional teaching methods. Isolated facts about Martin Luther King do not stimulate the intellect or help students increase their levels of cognitive sophistication any more than do discrete facts about George Washington or Thomas Jefferson. The emphases in sound multiethnic programs must be on *concept attainment, value analysis, decision making*, and *social action*.[59] Facts should be used only to help students attain higher level concepts and skills. Students need to master higher level concepts and generalizations in order to increase their levels of cognitive sophistication.

Concepts taught in the multiethnic curriculum should be selected from several disciplines and, when appropriate, be viewed from the perspectives of such disciplines and areas as the various social sciences, art, music, literature, physical education, communication, the sciences, and mathematics. It is necessary for students to view ethnic events and situations from the perspectives of several disciplines because any one discipline gives them only a partial understanding of problems related to ethnicity. When students study the concept of *culture*, they can attain a global perspective of ethnic cultures by viewing them from the perspective of the various social sciences and by examining how they are expressed in literature, music, dance, art, communication, and foods. The other curriculum areas, such as science and mathematics, can also be included in an interdisciplinary study of ethnic cultures.

Concepts such as *culture* can be used to organize interdisciplinary units and activities related to ethnicity. Other concepts, such as *communication* and *interdependence*, can also be analyzed and studied from an interdisciplinary perspective (see Figure 13.2). However, it is neither possible nor desirable to teach each concept in the curriculum from the perspectives of several disciplines and curricular areas. Such an attempt would result in artificial relationships and superficial learnings by students. However, the many excellent opportunities that exist within the curriculum for teaching concepts from an interdisciplinary perspective should be fully explored and used.

Interdisciplinary teaching requires the strong cooperation of teachers in the various content areas. Team teaching will often be necessary, especially at the high school level, to organize and implement interdisciplinary units and lessons.

The Role of the Teacher in Prejudice Reduction

Teachers are human beings who bring their own cultural perspectives, values, hopes, and dreams to the classroom. They also bring their own prejudices, stereotypes, and misconceptions.[60] The teacher's values and perspectives mediate and interact with what they teach and influence how messages are communicated to and perceived by their students. Because the teacher mediates the messages and symbols communicated to the students through the curriculum, it is important for teachers to understand their own personal and cultural values and identities in order for them to help students from diverse racial, ethnic, and cultural groups develop clarified identities and relate positively to each other. Research by Rubin indicates that increases in self-acceptance are associated with a reduction in prejudice.[61]

Effective teachers in a multicultural society must have (1) democratic attitudes and values, (2) a multiethnic philosophy, (3) the ability to view events and situations from diverse ethnic perspectives and points of view, (4) an understanding of the complex and multidimensional nature of ethnicity in Western societies, (5) knowledge of the stages of ethnicity and their curricular and teaching implications, and (6) the ability to function increasingly at higher stages of ethnicity. Figure 13.3 summarizes these characteristics.

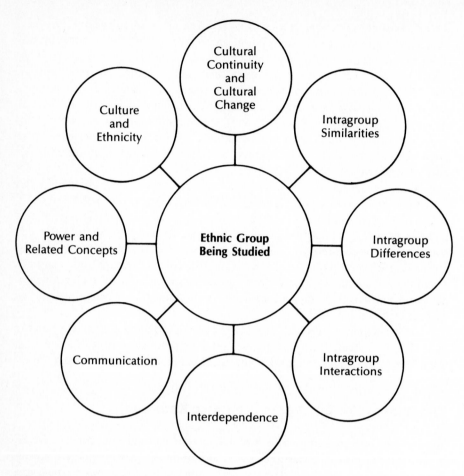

Figure 13.2. Interdisciplinary Concepts for Studying Ethnic Groups

Changing Teacher Attitudes and Behaviors

What can teachers do to change their racial attitudes, perceptions, and behaviors? Even though researchers have amply documented the nondemocratic attitudes and interactions teachers frequently have with minority and low-income students, little work has been done on effective techniques that can be used to change teachers' racial attitudes and behavior. Smith concluded that the racial attitudes of adults can be significantly modified in a positive direction by contact and involvement in minority group cultures.[62] Bogardus found that a five-week intergroup education workshop, which consisted of lectures on racial problems, research projects, and visits to community agencies, had a significantly positive effect on the participants' racial attitudes.[63]

An extensive review of the research suggests that changing the racial atti-

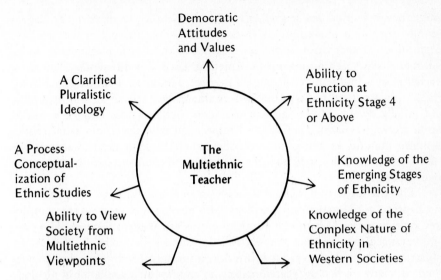

Figure 13.3. Characteristics of the Multiethnic Teacher
To function effectively in ethnically pluralistic environments,
the teacher must have democratic attitudes and values, a
clarified pluralistic ideology, a process conceptualization of
ethnic studies, the ability to view society from diverse ethnic
perspectives and points of view, knowledge of the emerging
stages of ethnicity, knowledge of the complex nature of ethnicity in Western societies, and the ability to function at Ethnicity Stage 4 or above. Reformed teacher-education
programs should be designed to help teachers acquire these
attitudes, conceptual frameworks, knowledge, and skills.

tudes of adults is a difficult task.[64] To maximize the chances for successful intervention programs, experiences must be designed specifically to change attitudes.
Courses with general or global objectives are not likely to be successful. Courses
that consist primarily or exclusively of lecture presentations have little import. Diverse experiences, such as seminars, visitations, community involvement, committee work, guest speakers, films, multimedia materials, and workshops, combined
with factual lectures, are more effective than is any single approach. Community
involvement and cross-cultural interactions (with the appropriate norms in the social setting) are the most cogent techniques. Psychotherapy is also promising. Individuals who express moderate rather than extreme attitudes are the most likely
to change. This is encouraging since few individuals exemplify extreme prejudice.

A Multiethnic Philosophy

Teachers need to clarify their own philosophical positions regarding the education
of ethnic minorities and to endorse an ideology consistent with the multiple acculturation and structural pluralism that characterize Western societies. Teachers

should be aware of the major ideologies related to ethnic pluralism and be able to examine their own philosophical positions and explore the policy and teaching implications of alternative ideologies. Teachers with an assimilationist ideology will most likely teach a unit on the American Civil War differently than will a teacher with a multiethnic ideology. Effective multiethnic teachers should embrace a philosophical position that will facilitate their effectiveness in culturally and racially diverse educational environments. Teachers who endorse a multiethnic ideology as defined in Chapter 7 respect and value the ethnic characteristics of ethnic minority students but also believe these students need to acquire the values, skills, attitudes, and abilities needed to function successfully within the mainstream culture.

Effective teachers in the multiethnic classroom must endorse what I describe in Chapter 7 as the multiethnic ideology. This ideology derives from the complex and multidimensional nature of ethnicity in modern Western societies. However, since most classroom teachers were socialized within a society, schools, and teacher education institutions that had mainstream-centric norms and were assimilationist oriented, many teachers are therefore likely to embrace an assimilationist ideology and to view pluralistic ideologies (whether weak or strong) as radical and unpatriotic. It is very difficult for individuals to change their philosophical orientations or even to question their currently held ideological beliefs. They have a great deal of affective and intellectual commitment to their ideological orientations and values. These ideologies are deeply held and result from years of informal and formal socialization.

Teachers should first examine their currently held ideological positions related to race and ethnicity. If they feel they need to change their ideological orientations in order to become effective multiethnic teachers (the teacher who is a strong pluralist is probably as ineffective in a multiethnic classroom as is the teacher who is a strong assimilationist), they should enroll in courses and seek other educational experiences related to race and ethnicity. Vicarious as well as direct experiences with other cultures, if they are open to these experiences, will help teachers examine their philosophical beliefs. The caveats about cross-cultural functioning discussed later in this chapter should be studied by teachers who seek cross-cultural experiences as a way to help them examine their philosophical beliefs. With these kinds of cross-cultural experiences, teachers will have opportunities to interact with individuals with widely differing ideologies and value positions about pluralism and race.

Teachers should also examine the *possible consequences* of embracing various philosophical beliefs. They should discuss how different philosophical orientations toward race and ethnic group life may influence their behavior in the classroom and the academic achievement and emotional growth of ethnic students. A number of researchers have observed that Black students tend to be more action-oriented and expressive in their learning styles than are Anglo-American students.[65] Mexican-American and Anglo youths tend to differ in their learning styles.[66] Mexican-American students also tend to be less individually competitive than are Anglo students.[67] The ideological positions and commitments of teachers, whether conscious or unconscious, influence how they respond to the different cultural learning styles and characteristics of Black and Mexican-American students. Teachers who are staunch assimilationists are likely to regard these different behaviors of Black and Mexican-American students as negative and pathological characteristics that should be eradicated. Teachers who are more multiethnic in their philosophical orientations are more likely to perceive these behaviors of Black and Mexican-American students as legitimate and functional cultural behaviors that they should build on and use when planning and teaching.

Assimilationism and Mainstream-Centricism: Problems for Teachers

I am often asked in workshops what is the greatest single problem teachers face when they try to plan and implement a multiethnic curriculum and school environment. Is it lack of sensitive and effective multiethnic teaching materials, lack of administrative support, student resistance, lack of adequate planning time, parental resistance, or some other problem? I have given this question much serious thought in the years that I have been training teachers in multiethnic education. Even though the factors mentioned are problems for many teachers who want to implement multiethnic education, I do not believe they are the most difficult problems faced in multiethnic teaching. The two most serious problems faced when planning and implementing multiethnic education are the strong *assimilationist ideology* many teachers have (discussed above) and their inability to view society from diverse ethnic perspectives and points of view. These problems are no doubt related to other societal problems. Many teachers, for example, might hold tenaciously to an assimilationist ideology or be unable to view their society from the perspectives of ethnic minority writers and social scientists because of racist attitudes or the fear that new ideologies and new conceptualizations of society will lead to a sharing of power by dominant and victimized ethnic groups (see Chapter 10).

Whatever the root causes of these problems, and many reasonable hyphotheses can be stated, the strong assimilationist ideology many teachers embrace and their inability to view their society from diverse ethnic perspectives are, in my view, the most difficult problems that must be overcome when the multiethnic curriculum is designed and implemented.

Viewing Society from Diverse Ethnic Perspectives

Teachers need to acquire a conceptualization of their society that is based on novel assumptions and on accurate knowledge about its role and place in the world today. Textbooks, the mass media, and other parts of a nation's culture perpetuate many myths about it that are culturally encapsulating and ethnocentric. Teachers need to acquire new perspectives about the nature and development of the society and develop the ability to view it from the perspectives of ethnic groups that have historically been victimized.

I do not mean to suggest that mainstream perspectives and views on history and contemporary society should be excluded from the school curriculum. However, students can gain a sophisicated understanding of the complex nature of a society only by viewing events, situations, and concepts from the perspectives of the diverse ethnic groups that have shaped and are shaping it.

Teachers should not only be able to view society and culture from diverse ethnic perspectives and points of view, but they should also be able to teach history, science, literature, and other disciplines from the perspectives of different ethnic groups. The school and the teacher education curriculum should be organized on what I call Models C and D (see Chapter 10). In these models, students are helped to view events, concepts, and situations from the perspectives of different ethnic groups within their society as well as within other nations.

The Complex Nature of Ethnicity

Classroom teachers need a better understanding of the complex nature of ethnicity within Western societies. Misconceptions about the nature of ethnicity within Western societies are widespread among the general population, teachers, and their students. When many teachers think of an ethnic group, they think of non-White groups such as Black Americans and Japanese Canadians. They therefore confuse an *ethnic* group with a *racial* group. Teachers can better understand the complex nature of ethnicity if they learn to distinguish several concepts that are often confused, such as ethnic group, ethnicity, ethnic minority group, race, and culture. These concepts are defined in Chapter 5.

The Teacher and the Stages of Ethnicity

To work successfully with students from diverse ethnic backgrounds, teachers should be knowledgeable about the ethnic characteristics of their students. Students differ in their ethnic identities and characteristics just as they differ in their cognitive and affective development.[68] Consequently, the teacher should make some attempt to individualize multiethnic experiences for students.

These three hypothetical students might need somewhat different curricular experiences related to race and ethnicity. Juan was socialized within a rather conservative Mexican-American community in the Southwest. Jessie Mae, who is Black, spent Saturday afternoons during her early years in a Black awareness school. John is an Anglo-American student who has never had any firsthand experiences with non-White ethnics. These students are now in the same eighth-grade social studies class. The teacher is beginning a unit on race relations in the United States. Each student will need some unique experiences tailored to his or her complex and emerging ethnic identities. Chapter 11 presents a typology that outlines the basic stages of the development of ethnicity among individual members of ethnic groups that teachers can use as a guide when trying to identify the ethnic characteristics of students.

To become more effective multiethnic educators, teachers should try to determine their own stage of ethnicity and become sensitive to their ethnic behaviors and characteristics. Teachers should not only try to help students function at higher stages of ethnicity but should also try to function at higher stages of ethnicity themselves. Teachers who are functioning primarily at Stages 1 and 2 cannot realistically be expected to help students develop positive racial attitudes toward different ethnic and racial groups or to help students to function at higher stages of ethnicity. Once teachers are aware of their own ethnic attitudes, behaviors, and perceptions, they can begin an action program designed to change their behavior if necessary. Such a program may consist of individual readings, taking courses at the local college or university, or participating in cross-cultural experiences either in their own or other nations.

Cross-Cultural Experiences: Problems and Promises

Teachers who plan to have cross-cultural experiences should be aware of both the problems and promises of functioning in a different culture. Functioning cross-culturally, in the final analysis, is usually rewarding and personally revealing. Since enculturation into our own cultures is primarily a subconscious process, we can learn a great deal about our norms, values, behaviors, and perceptions by functioning in other cultural environments.

To acquire the maximum benefits from cross-cultural functioning, individuals must be able to interpret their experiences accurately and develop a sophisticated level of *cross-cultural awareness.* Despite its positive long-range outcomes, individuals functioning within another culture frequently experience cultural shock and confusion and make embarrassing cultural mistakes. All individuals are likely to experience cultural shock during their first experiences in another culture. The greater the differences between the new culture and their own ethnic and/or national culture, the greater the cultural shock individuals are likely to experience.

Americans can experience cultural shock within ethnic cultures in their nation as well as in other nations. Anglo-Americans who have had few experiences with Black American culture and have not traveled outside the United States are likely to experience cultural shock when they first visit a traditional Black Baptist Church as well as when they first visit a nation such as Mexico.

Some preparation before experiencing another culture may help reduce cultural shock and enable the individual to function more successfully within it. Such preparation may consist of readings, (especially literary works because literature often conveys the nuances and subtleties of a culture), viewing films, and interacting with individuals socialized within the culture. However, no amount of preparation will totally eliminate cultural shock and cultural mistakes during an individual's first experience with a culture. If teachers are knowledgeable about the rewarding as well as the problems of cross-cultural functioning, they will be better able to interpret their cross-cultural experiences accurately and will therefore benefit more from them in the long run.

Hypotheses Regarding Cross-Cultural Behavior

I have developed some hypotheses regarding cross-cultural behavior based on my own functioning in other cultures (such as Guam, Mexico, Japan, and the United Kingdom, and different ethnic cultures within the United States), on my observations of and conversations with other individuals who have functioned cross-culturally, and on my reading of the literature related to cross-cultural functioning.[69] These hypotheses should be helpful to individuals who are planning cross-cultural experiences and to those who are trying to interpret their cross-cultural interactions and behavior or the cross-cultural behaviors of others.

- The weaker the ethnic boundaries are between ethnic cultures, the more likely cross-cultural functioning will occur between these cultures.
- The weaker the ethnic boundaries between ethnic cultures, the easier cross-cultural functioning will be for individuals in those cultures. Individuals who have weak ethnic cultural characteristics and ethnic identities are more likely to participate in cross-cultural behavior than are individuals with strong ethnic characteristics and ethnic identities.
- Psychological discomforts and confusion are so potentially high in cross-cultural functioning that cross-cultural behavior will occur only when motivation is high for functioning cross-culturally and the potential rewards are substantial.
- Subethnic boundaries (within an ethnic group) are often distinct and tight. Consequently, individuals who are socialized within one subethnic culture may experience problems and conflicts when functioning within another subethnic culture within his or her ethnic group.
- As an individual becomes more competent in functioning within an outside ethnic culture, his or her personal ethnicity and ethnic behavior changes and/or reduces in intensity.
- The response to the individual who is functioning cross-culturally by the outside ethnic group influences the depth and nature of his or her cross-

cultural behavior and his or her psychological interpretation of his or her cross-cultural behavior.

Summary

Major goals of the multiethnic curriculum should be to reduce prejudice and to help students acquire more democratic racial attitudes and values. Racial incidents in which negative racial attitudes were blatantly and sometimes violently expressed were increasing in the major Western nations such as the United Kingdom, the United States, and Canada in the late 1980s. Racial incidents on college and university campuses in the United States attracted national attention. The schools in Western societies need to act decisively to help students acquire more democratic attitudes and values.

This chapter critically discusses theories that explain the causes of prejudice. Various theories focus on the personality of the individual, group norms, and the social structure as the primary cause of prejudice. A comprehensive theory that incorporates each variable is needed to explain the complex nature of prejudice in contemporary societies.

Research reviewed in this chapter suggests that the school can help students become less prejudiced and acquire more democratic attitudes and values. However, instruction must be designed specifically for this purpose and must take place in a social environment that has a number of identifiable characteristics, including the promotion of cooperation rather than competition, a multiethnic curriculum, and situations in which students experience equal status. The teacher is an important variable in a curriculum that fosters democratic attitudes and values. The final part of this chapter describes the characteristics of the effective teacher in a multicultural society.

Notes

1. George E. Simpson and Milton Yinger, *Racial and Cultural Minorities* (New York: Harper and Row, 1965), p. 10.

2. Arnold Rose, "The Causes of Prejudice," in Milton L. Barron, ed., *American Cultural Minorities: A Textbook of Readings in Intergroup Relations* (New York: Alfred A. Knopf, 1962).

3. Ibid., p. 78.

4. David Harley, "Prejudice in Whites" (Unpublished paper, Michigan State University, 1968).

5. Rose, p. 83.

6. Ibid., pp. 92–93.

7. Simpson and Yinger, *Racial and Cultural Minorities*, p. 49.

8. Ibid., p. 50.

9. Ibid.

10. Ibid.

11. Else Frenkel-Brunswik, "A Study of Prejudice in Children," *Human Relations* 1 (1948), pp. 295–306.

12. Ibid.

13. Ibid., p. 305.

14. Ibid., p. 296.

15. T. W. Adorno, Else Frenkel-Brunswik, Danile J. Levinson, and R. Nevitt Sanford, *The Authoritarian Personality* (New York: Harper and Row, 1950).

16. Ibid., p. 971.

17. Simpson and Yinger, *Racial and Cultural Minorities*.

18. Ibid., p. 66.

19. Gardner Lindzey, "Differences Between High and Low in Prejudice and their Implications for the Theory of Prejudice," *Personality* 19 (1950), pp. 16–40.

20. Ibid., p. 39.

21. Ibid., p. 33.

22. Gordon Allport and Bernard Kramer, "Some Roots of Prejudice," *The Journal of Psychology* 22 (1946), 9–39.

23. Ibid., p. 35.

24. Herbert Blumer, "United States of America," in *Research on Racial Relations* (New York: UNESCO, 1966), pp. 87–133.

25. Gerhart Saenger and E. Gilbert, "Customer Reactions to Integration of Negro Sales Personnel," *International Journal of Opinion and Attitude Research* 4 (1950), pp. 57–76.

26. Hubert Blalock, "Economic Discrimination and Negro Increase," *American Sociological Review* 21 (1956), pp. 584–588.

27. Robert K. Merton, "Discrimination and the American Creed," in R. M. MacIver, ed., *Discrimination and the National Welfare* (New York: Harper and Row, 1949).

28. John Lohman and Dietrich C. Reitzes, "Note on Race Relations in Mass Society," *American Journal of Sociology* 58 (1952), pp. 241–246.

29. Blumer, "United States of America," pp. 112–113.

30. Lohman and Reitzes, "Note on Race Relations in Mass Society."

31. Blumer, "United States of America," p. 112.

32. Leonard I. Pearlin, "Shifting Group Attachments and Attitudes toward Negroes," *Social Forces* 33 (1954), pp. 41–47.

33. Ibid., p. 50.

34. Helen G. Trager and Marian R. Yarrow, *They Learn What They Live* (New York: Harper, 1952).

35. Ibid., p. 341.

36. David W. Johnson, "Freedom School Effectiveness: Changes in Attitudes of Negro Children," *The Journal of Applied Behavioral Science* 2 (1966), pp. 325–330.

37. John Litcher and David W. Johnson, "Changes in Attitudes toward Negroes of White Elementary School Students after Use of Multiethnic Readers," *Journal of Educational Psychology* 60 (1969), pp. 148–152.

38. Johnson, "Freedom School Effectiveness."

39. Ibid., p. 129.

40. Litcher and Johnson, "Changes in Attitudes. . . ."

41. Ibid., p. 151.

42. Phyllis Katz and S. R. Zalk, "Modification of Children's Racial Attitudes," *Developmental Psychology* 14 (1978), pp. 447–461.

43. Ibid., p. 447.

44. Walter G. Stephan, "Intergroup Relations," in Gardner Lindzey and Elliot Aronson, eds., *The Handbook of Social Psychology*, vol. 2, 3rd ed. (Hillsdale, N.J.: Lawrence Erlbaum Associates, 1985), pp. 599–658.

45. L. L. Leslie, J. W. Leslie, and D. A. Penfield, "The Effects of a Student Centered Special Curriculum upon the Racial Attitudes of Sixth Graders," *Journal of Experimental Education* 41 (1972), pp. 63–67.

46. T. D. Yawkey and J. Blackwell, "Attitudes of 4-year-old Urban Black Children toward Themselves and Whites Based upon Multiethnic Social Studies Materials and Experiences," *Journal of Educational Research* 67 (1974), pp. 373–377.

47. Stephan, p. 643. Reprinted with permission of Random House, Inc., from Gardner Lindzey and Elliot Aronson, *Handbook of Social Psychology*, 3rd ed., © 1985, p. 643.

48. Charles Glock, Robert Wuthnow, Jane A. Piliavin, and Metta Spencer, *Adolescent Prejudice* (New York: Harper and Row, 1975).

49. Ibid., p. 174.

50. Eunice Cooper and Helen Dinerman, "Analysis of the Film 'Don't Be a Sucker': A Study of Communication," *Public Opinion Quarterly* 15 (1951), pp. 243–264.

51. James A. Banks, "Racial Prejudice and the Black Self-Concept," in James A. Banks and Jean D. Grambs, eds., *Black Self-Concept: Implications for Education and Social Science* (New York: McGraw-Hill, 1972).

52. Robert Slavin, "How Student Learning Teams Can Integrate the Desegregated Classroom," *Integrated Education* 15 (1977), pp. 56–58.

53. Nina Gabelko and John U. Michaelis, *Reducing Adolescent Prejudice: A Handbook* (New York: Teachers College Press, 1981).

54. Carlos E. Cortés, "The Societal Curriculum: Implications for Multiethnic Education," in James A. Banks, ed., *Education in the 80s: Multiethnic Education* (Washington, D.C.: National Education Association, 1981).

55. Geneva Gay, *Differential Dyadic Interactions of Black and White Teachers with Black and White Pupils in Recently Desegregated Social Studies Classrooms: A Function of Teacher and Pupil Ethnicity* (Washington, D.C.: National Institute of Education, 1974); Ray C. Rist, "Student Social Class and Teacher Expectations: The Self-fulfilling Prophecy in Ghetto Education," *Harvard Educational Review* 40 (1970), pp. 411–451; U.S. Commission on Civil Rights, *Teachers and Students: Differences in Teacher Interaction with Mexican American and Anglo Students* (Washington, D.C.: U.S. Government Printing Office, 1973).

56. Muriel Saville-Troike, "Language Diversity in Multiethnic Education," in Banks, ed., *Education in the 80s*.

57. Jane R. Mercer, "Testing and Assessment Practices in Multiethnic Education," in Banks, ed., *Education in the 80's*, pp. 93–104; Ronald J. Samuda, *Psychological Testing of American Minorities* (New York: Dodd, Mead, 1975).

58. Manuel Ramírez III and Alfredo Castañeda, *Cultural Democracy, Bicognitive Development and Education* (New York: Academic Press, 1974).

59. James A. Banks, *Teaching Strategies for Ethnic Studies*, 4th ed. (Boston: Allyn and Bacon, 1987).

60. Rist, "Student Social Class and Teacher Expectations."

61. I. Rubin, "The Reduction of Prejudice through Laboratory Training," *Journal of Applied Behavioral Science*, 3 (1967), pp. 29–50.

62. F. T. Smith, "An Experiment in Modifying Attitudes toward the Negro," summarized in Arnold M. Rose, *Studies in the Reduction of Prejudice* (Chicago: American Council on Race Relations, 1947), p. 9.

63. Emory S. Bogardus, "The Intercultural Workshop and Racial Distance," *Sociology and Social Research* 32 (1948), pp. 798–802.

64. Research on changing the racial attitudes of adults is reviewed in James A. Banks, "Racial Prejudice and the Black Self-Concept," in James A. Banks and Jean D. Grambs, eds., *Black Self-Concept: Implications for Education and Social Science* (New York: McGraw-Hill, 1972), pp. 5–35; and in Stephan, "Intergroup Relations."

65. Geneva Gay, "Viewing the Pluralistic Classroom as a Cultural Microcosm," *Educational Research Quarterly* 2 (Winter 1978), pp. 45–59; Roger D. Abrahams and Geneva Gay, "Black Culture in the Classroom," in Roger D. Abrahams and Rudolph C. Troike, eds., *Language and Cultural Diversity in American Education* (Englewood Cliffs, N.J.: Prentice-Hall, 1972), pp. 67–84.

66. Ramírez and Castañeda, *Cultural Democracy, Bicognitive Development, and Education*.

67. James A. Vasquez, "Bilingual Education's Needed Third Dimension," *Educational Leadership* 38 (November 1979), pp. 166–168.

68. Jean Piaget, *Six Psychological Studies* (New York: Random House, 1968); Lawrence Kohlberg and Rochelle Mayer, "Development as the Aim of Education," *Harvard Educational Review* 42 (November 1972), pp. 449–496.

69. See especially Edward C. Stewart, *American Cultural Patterns: A Cross-Cultural Perspective* (LaGrange Park, Ill.: Intercultural Network, Inc., 1972).

14

Language, Ethnicity, and Education

If all students spoke school-English, there would be little need for much of this chapter. The reality, however, is that we live in a multilingual society. Many students enter school speaking a non-English language or a dialect of American English. These students are described as linguistically different, linguistic minorities, bilingual or bidialectal. Being linguistically different involves more than merely speaking a foreign language or a different English dialect. Speaking a certain language or dialect ties one to particular ethnic and cultural groups that hold values and attitudes that may conflict with the teachers' values and attitudes.

Some linguistic differences are innocuous. Whether students prefer "ain't" over "isn't" is inconsequential. No one is too concerned if a student speaks with a Hoosier twang. Or, if a student from Boston says "Cuba" as though it were pronounced "Cuber," no one seems to worry about the mispronunciation. But, if a Black student prefers to say "I be sick" rather than "I am sick," or if a Hispanic student pronounces "sit" as though it were "seat," then concern about the student's purported language deficiencies emerge.

Some differences are not innocuous, especially if they cause communication breakdowns between teachers and students. Problems for both teachers and students arise when the classroom communication system—couched in the culture reflected by speakers of school-English—conflicts with the student's communication system. Subtle but potent instances of miscommunication can lead to larger problems of student alienation, discontent, and academic failure. In effect, students who experience communicative conflict may retreat or withdraw from the school's society.

Teaching in a multilingual society poses difficult questions. Isn't it enough to teach students to communicate in the nation's main language? Doesn't every country need a national language for cohesion and international survival? Can I be expected to know every non-English language that my students speak? This chapter attempts to answer such troublesome questions by describing the myriad relationships among culture, ethnicity, and language, and the relationships between national educational policy and language instruction. Benchmarks are provided to help with the implementation of linguistic pluralism within the classroom.

This chapter is contributed by Ricardo L. Garcia, Associate Professor, School of Education, Eastern Montana College, Billings, Montana.

The Relationship between Language and National Policy

Our discussion of ethnicity, language, and education leads to broader, more complex questions regarding the role of language in United States society. Does linguistic diversity impede national cohesion? Is it possible to have a nation when everyone speaks a different language, as in the *Old Testament*'s Tower of Babel? What is the experience of other linguistically diverse nations? How do these nations build cohesion and yet allow linguistic diversity? How are a nation's goals linked with language and ethnicity? Most of these questions will be answered explicitly. Some will be answered implicitly. What is important is that we approach these questions broadly, viewing them on an international scale. Once viewing them internationally, we can better analyze them nationally.

Nationalism and ethnicity are similar group phenomena. Both involve group identity, a sense of peoplehood, and an interdependence of fates, requiring allegiance to some group. At times, the two phenomena conflict. Countries throughout the world have had to deal with the issue of how to build national unity while allowing ethnic group diversity. If ethnic groups are given too much autonomy, national unity is threatened; if ethnic groups are suppressed too much, then ethnic group dissent emerges, again threatening national cohesion. Some countries have dealt with ethnic group diversity by allowing minority groups to maintain their languages and cultures (pluralism). In India, for example, one can pledge allegiance to the national government, and without penalty or legal recrimination, identify with his or her ethnic group. Ethnic and national loyalty require bilingualism, that is, a speaking knowledge of the national language, Hindustani, and one's ethnic group language.[1] Peru, Ecuador, and Paraguay are other nations that accommodate indigenous linguistic groups.

Other nations (such as Chile, Brazil, Australia, Argentina) have dealt with ethnic group diversity by absorbing minority groups into their majority culture, imposing both their language and culture on the minority groups (assimilation). Some countries neither assimilate nor allow free pluralism. Rather, they impose forced separation of races (apartheid), such as the Republic of South Africa. In heterogeneous societies, ethnic group identity and national group identity are not mutually exclusive, if the national group has at least one language in common. (See Chapter 3 for a discussion of ethnic and national group identifications.)

Central to a nation's development of nationalism is the designation of an official language. An official language serves the functions of political and psychological integration on a national scope. A nation's official language(s) embodies, carries, and conveys the nation's symbols. National anthems, slogans, and oaths of allegiance in the national language(s) meld a nation's spirit. The national language(s) act as the political unification agent and communication medium among the nation's citizens. For national communications and political unification, the requirements for establishing an official language are simple:

1. A national language should be capable of serving as a medium of social, economic, legal, and political interchange throughout the nation.
2. It should be the speech of the majority of the nation's citizens.
3. It should have a standardized writing system throughout the nation.

Not so simple are the politics of language standardization. For example, requirement one presumes that within any nation, whose boundaries many times cut across ethnic and tribal group lines, one language can be singled out as the language comprehensible to all the language groups in the nation. Requirement two presumes that the majority of the nation's citizens have the power to implement their language as the national language. In colonized nations, for example, the language of the colonizer (usually a numerical minority) was imposed on the colonized (the numerical majority group). In multilingual nations, the difficulties of language planning depend on the number of language groups vying for their language as the national standard. The language competition and conflict emerge from the political ambitions of the various groups.

National Goals and Language Education Policy

Most nations have one or more languages stipulated as their official language(s). Some nations, such as France, have an official language regulated by a language academy. Other nations have an official bilingual policy, such as Canada, allowing for English and French to coexist as official languages. Some nations, India and Russia for example, have one official language that is used nationally and allow regional languages and dialects to be used and taught within their respective regions. Due to the centrality of language to nationalism, the selection as to which language or languages to use in a nation's school as the medium(s) of instruction is a critical national decision. The language(s) taught to the nation's future citizens become the embodiment of the national spirit and agent for national unification.

Eighteenth-century powers, such as France, Spain, and England, recognized the importance of languages for political domination and control. Consequently, they always imposed their languages on the people they wanted to colonize. In the United States during the late nineteenth and early twentieth centuries, feelings about American English ran so high that most states enacted laws that prohibited the use of any non-English languages in the public schools. During this time the United States government was trying to form a strong national identity.

Educational language policies are inextricably bound with a nation's internal and external political goals. When a nation's national goal is to assimilate all citizens so they speak a single language, its language education programs will foster monolingualism in the nation's single, standard language. When a nation's internal goal is to maintain its ethnic and linguistic plurality, then its language education programs will foster knowledge in a national language standard while concurrently fostering literacy in the differing languages or dialects spoken by its citizens and residents. When a nation's external political goal is to develop communication ties with other countries, its language programs will foster literacy in the national standard as well as literacy in other languages generally not spoken by its citizens and residents. When a nation's internal goal is to revive a lost national identity—lost as a consequence of conquest or colonialism—its language programs will foster restoration of the nation's preferred language. (See also Chapters 7 and 8.)

On a global scale at least four distinctively different forms of educational policy goals pertain to language:

1. Assimilation
2. Pluralization
3. Internationalization
4. Vernacularization

What follows is a description of the policy goals and their consequent language programs.

Assimilation

This type of language policy promotes cultural assimilation. The intent is to assimilate foreign language speakers into the dominant linguistic and cultural group of the nation. Some bilingual programs in the United States are examples. They are called transitional programs; their intent is to assimilate some linguistic minority group. The linguistic majority group perceives the nation as a monolingual melting pot that has one standard language; other languages, or dialects of the standard, are perceived as substandard languages or dialects. The student's substandard language or dialect is used as the medium of instruction to compensate for their limited English-speaking abilities. Use of the substandard language-dialect is transitional. As soon as the student learns English well enough to receive instruction, then use of the student's language is discontinued and instruction is in English only. The national standard is held up as the only acceptable standard; divergent dialects or foreign languages are perceived as separate and unequal to the national standard.

Pluralization

This language policy promotes cultural pluralism. The intents are to allow different language/cultural groups to coexist within a nation and to equalize schooling by using the student's home language and culture for instruction. Some bilingual programs in the United States are examples. In these bilingual maintenance programs, the non-English-language group is encouraged to maintain its bilingual-bicultural status. Under pluralization a nation's language standard is egalitarian, that is, each language has its respective standard; the nonnational languages and dialects are perceived as having separate and equal standards.

Internationalization

This type of language program is multilingual. Schools teach multiple languages. The intent is to create a multilingual nation. Switzerland is an example. In Switzerland, four languages are taught to students; the nation is landlocked and surrounded by European countries. To communicate with these countries successfully, the citizens need to speak the languages of neighboring countries. Under internationalization, a nation desires to communicate with other nations. It has a multiple language standard; the language standard of other languages is adopted by the country as is its national standard.

Vernacularization

This type of language restores the nation's indigenous language and establishes it as the national standard. The Republic of the Philippines is an example. The country was colonized by the Spanish and United States governments. Each government imposed its language on the nation and prohibited the use of the indigenous languages, such as Ilocano and Tagalog, in all public institutions. Now the Philippine nation is free of colonial rule; it has declared the vernacular language, Tagalog, as its standard language. Under vernacularization, the desired national goal is pride in the nation's indigenous language(s) and culture. The new vernacular is established as the nation's language standard. Yet, because its citizens speak the language(s) of their former colonizers, bilingual programs are developed, using both the restored language and the colonizer's language(s).

Language Policy in the United States

The United States has no official de jure language policy; it has an informal de facto national standard, American English. Social customs and usages, rather than governmental agencies, tend to regulate languages in the United States. Non-English languages are allowed in public documents and institutions; their use is limited by varying state laws. To a great extent the United States is still an English-centric language nation. Non-English languages are considered foreign languages. Even the languages indigenous to the United States, the languages of American Indians, are viewed as foreign by some citizens of the United States.

Within the United States, some ethnic groups developed dual or multiple dialects of English. Almost everyone in United States society is somewhat bidialectal in the sense that everyone speaks their individual idiolects as well as a group dialect. However, here *bidialectalism* is used to mean the ability to speak two distinctively different American English regional or cultural group dialects. For example, as a group, Blacks speak the Black English dialect as well as standard English. Not all Blacks speak Black English; rather, as an ethnic group, Blacks have developed skills in using two different dialects of English.

Some groups developed bilingual abilities. *Bilingualism* is used here to mean the ability to speak with two distinctively different language systems, such as Spanish and English, or German and English. At one time, German Americans were the most literate bilinguals in the United States. Bilingual German newspapers, periodicals, radio programs, and books attested to a high level of German-English bilingualism.[2] However, the anti-Germanic feelings sparked by World War I and inflamed by World War II with Germany substantially doused German-American bilingualism. Currently, Puerto Ricans, as a group, speak Spanish and English. In Puerto Rico, Spanish is considered the native language, but a speaking knowledge of American English is required for high school graduation.

Again, as with bidialectalism, not all members of a group need to be bilingual for the group to be considered bilingual. In the above illustration, Puerto Ricans as a group are Spanish-English bilingual, but not all Puerto Ricans are bilingual. The level of bilingualism varies within different bilingual groups. Some groups are attempting to restore their native language, such as many American Indian tribes. Other groups (e.g., Greek Americans) are working diligently to teach their youth the native language. Other groups use two languages for daily transactions (e.g., Chinese Americans and Cuban Americans).

More than twenty-five European languages are spoken in the United States. Some of these languages are Spanish, Italian, German, Polish, French, Yiddish, Russian, Swedish, Hungarian, and Norwegian. Add these languages to the Asian and Middle Eastern languages now spoken as well as the historically spoken American Indian languages, and it is obvious that the United States is multilingual. The most recent additions are the languages of the Hmong, Vietnamese, Laotian, Cambodian, and ethnic Chinese people. Referred to as *Indochinese*, these people come from an area of the world that is culturally diverse. In Laos, Cambodia, and Vietnam at least twenty languages are spoken.

It is important that Indochinese peoples be recognized as culturally diverse. They should not be lumped together as a single group. What they have in common is that they are refugees in an industrialized Western nation and have relocated from the Asian to the Western hemisphere. More than these few words are necessary to describe these new groups. Curriculum materials describing their language and cultural characteristics have been developed.[3]

The languages cited here are evidence of linguistic pluralism, a legacy that permeates the development of language policy in the United States.[4] Through social, economic, and political forces, American English was established as the nation's common language. Yet, the Constitution provided religious freedom, which fostered religious pluralism and the notion that the United States was a diversified nation. As immigrants settled in urban and rural parts of the United States they often clung to their native religions, cultures, and languages. Neighborhoods in cities thus became ethnic enclaves providing the individual a buffer zone that eased assimilation into the new culture. Often small settlements evolved into villages and towns peopled by one or several ethnic groups. In the urban enclaves and rural settlements, native, non-English languages were used in business affairs, schools, and religious institutions.

A lack of government interference in language planning prevailed during the nation's beginning stages. Thomas Jefferson believed the mark of an educated person was bilingualism. He taught himself Spanish and spoke French. Benjamin Franklin, however, decried the use of German by so many Pennsylvania residents. He feared German might supplant English as the nation's language. Yet, he assisted the development of Pennsylvania's German language schools. John Adams proposed the establishment of English as the nation's official language with a national academy to regulate and standardize English. The proposal was rejected by Congress as antidemocratic.[5] Noah Webster's dictionaries and spellers attempted to regulate and standardize American English; his efforts, along with the efforts of other lexicographers, did much to standardize American English spelling, but the efforts did not result in making English the nation's official language.[6]

By the middle 1800s a bilingual tradition existed in schools. As the public school movement spread, so did the idea that local communities could conduct school in their native languages, especially since the antecedent schools—the religious schools—had taught native religions, cultures, and languages. Also, to encourage immigrant parents to place their children in school rather than the workplace, some public schools insured that the home language and culture would be taught in the public schools. School districts in Milwaukee, New York, St. Louis, and Cleveland provided native language, and sometimes, bilingual instruction in elementary grades as recruitment inducements.[7] Through the Civil War era the noninterference attitude prevailed, accommodating linguistic pluralism and often encouraging public school attendance. After the Civil War era and into the industrial revolution, the need for a common language emerged to conduct business and governmental affairs. An English language ethnocentrism began to prevail.

English language ethnocentrism started as a matter of practicality. Participation in civic affairs necessitated English literacy. Most state laws, government documents, and government affairs were conducted in English. This fact required a speaking and reading knowledge of English. Also, in business and industry, non-English speakers were seriously in danger at the workplace. Unable to read the safety procedures written in English, or unable to understand warnings shouted in English, the non-English-speaking workers were often injured on the job. Consequently, knowing how to speak, read, and write in English became necessary for civic participation, upward mobility, and economic success. Events between 1890 and 1920 added a new dimension to the importance of English literacy. Knowledge of English evolved into a national imperative: it became proof that one was a loyal American.[8]

The national origins of European immigrants to the United States had changed substantially by 1896. Before 1812 most European immigrants to the United States came from Northern and Western Europe, primarily from Britain, Germany, France, Sweden, Norway, the Netherlands, and Switzerland. Between 1890 and 1920 the overwhelming majority came from Southern and Eastern Europe, primarily from the Balkan countries, Italy, Russia, and Poland.[9] These immigrants were viewed with distrust by many old immigrant citizens. The new immigrants were predominantly Jewish or Catholic; they represented diverse political traditions—monarchies, dictatorships, and democracies. The reaction to the demographic shift was xenophobia.[10] The fear arose that these new immigrants would not melt into the melting pot and would not be loyal to the traditional ways of the old immigrants.

The xenophobia was founded on the labor unrest during this time when the United States was industrializing. Labor leaders were often portrayed as agitators or anarchists bent on the overthrow of democratic traditions and the free enterprise system. The xenophobia was exacerbated by racist perceptions about the new immigrants. Europeans from Southern and Eastern Europe were considered genetically and culturally inferior to the older immigrants. The xenophobic flame was later fueled as war with Germany seemed imminent and relations with Japan and China worsened. Xenophobia reached its peak immediately following World War I, when German-American language and cultural activities (including parochial schools, magazines, and lodge meetings) and Chinese and Japanese immigration were legally curtailed.

Attempts to quell the xenophobia culminated in bills requiring immigrants to learn English as a condition for citizenship.[11] At this time, American English became the country's unofficial national language. The Nationality Act of 1906 required immigrants to speak English as a prerequisite for naturalization. The English requirement remained in force in the Nationality Act of 1940. In the Internal Security Act of 1950 the law was extended to include English reading and writing.

The public schools of the middle 1800s tolerated, at times even nurtured, the immigrant student's native language and culture. In states such as Wisconsin, many communities conducted all instruction in students' native languages, especially in private schools. As xenophobia increased the desire to forge a national identity based on the English language and Anglo-Saxon culture, the public schools shifted toward the Americanization and assimilation of non-English-speaking immigrants. The transformation started with state laws stipulating that certain school subjects be taught in English. The Bennett Law, passed in 1889 in Wisconsin, stipulated an English-only requirement in certain subjects.[12] The law's major intents were to control child labor and to provide compulsory school attendance. But the law's English-only requirement meant that the German parochial schools would have to change their medium of instruction from German to English. Also, the local public school officials resented the loss of local control—they would be under greater scrutiny by the state. The Bennett Act was summarily repealed in 1891 due to the strong reactions against it. Nonetheless, the stage was set for the English-only laws.

The intent of the English-only laws was to ensure English literacy for the multilingual, immigrant populations as part of the Americanization process. Often the laws were applied to the private and parochial schools. The English-only laws were directed toward the German-American schools, which consisted of a wide network of bilingual (elementary) and second language (secondary) programs in parochial, private, and public schools. For example, in 1914, at least one-third of the elementary students in the Milwaukee, Cincinnati, Cleveland, and Dayton public school districts were in bilingual (German/English) classrooms.[13] Between 1917 and 1919, however, when the United States was at war with Germany, the German/English bilingual programs, along with many of the secondary level German programs, were drastically reduced; practically speaking, the bilingual programs were eliminated. The English-only laws also stopped bilingual instruction in other languages: Swedish, Norwegian, Danish, Dutch, Polish, French, Czech, and Spanish.[14]

The laws often prohibited the teaching of a foreign language.[15] The anti-foreign-language part of Nebraska's English-only law was challenged at the state level—where the law was left intact—and then at the U.S. Supreme Court in *Meyer* v. *Nebraska*. The Meyer decision ruled that the Nebraska statutory prohibition against teaching a foreign language in grades lower than ninth grade limited the student's right to learn and the parents' right to control what their children would study. The intent of the statute was "to promote civic development by inhibiting training of the immature in foreign tongues and ideas before they could learn English and acquire American ideals."[16] The Nebraska law's intent was to use the schools as an agent for Americanization and assimilation. The *Meyer* decision left intact former court rulings that the state could require English-only instruction.

The English-only laws remained in effect until the Civil Rights movement of the 1960s. Before the Civil Rights movment, the English-only laws were enforced to promote the assimilation of linguistic minorities in the southwestern states[17] where large populations of linguistic minorities resided as well as in Indian boarding schools operated by the Bureau of Indian Affairs.[18]

Although the anti-foreign-language laws of the 1920s were deemed unconstitutional, the laws precipitated a tradition of excluding foreign languages from the elementary public school curriculum. During the middle 1950s foreign language programs were included in the elementary grades. By the 1959–1960 school year approximately 8,000 elementary schools offered FLES (Foreign Languages for Elementary Students) programs.[19] The FLES programs relied heavily on federal funds provided by the National Defense Education Act (NDEA). When federal funding ended, the public schools tried to continue the FLES programs. Primarily for financial reasons the programs did not maintain their initial thrusts, and by slow degrees they were discontinued. Few, if any, existed in the 1970s.

During the middle 1980s, in response to the geopolitical climate and the recognized need to teach students the languages and cultures of other countries, foreign-language education programs emerged in some elementary schools. At least sixteen cities in the United States offered elementary foreign-language programs during the 1984–1985 school year. Cities included Culver City, Calif.; San Diego; Fort Worth; Baton Rouge; Tulsa; Milwaukee; Holliston, Mass.; Washington, D.C.; and Eugene, Oregon.[20] During this same time, between 1983 and 1987, seven states made English their official language: California, Georgia, Illinois, Indiana, Kentucky, Nebraska, and Virginia. In the U.S. Congress attempts to make English the nation's official language appeared in the form of a joint resolution, SJ Resolution #20, proposing that the U.S. Constitution be amended to read:

1. The English language shall be the official language of the United States;
2. The Congress shall have the power to enforce this article by appropriate legislation.[21]

Proponents of the resolution believed that bilingualism is inimical to national solidarity. Using Canada as an example, the proponents argued that bilingualism fosters English illiteracy among immigrants and native non-English speakers, thereby making assimilation difficult for the non-English speakers.[22]

Opponents of the resolution argued that bilingualism, especially when used in educational programs, emergency services, and ballots, greatly helps non-English speakers as they make the transition from their native language to English. Further, opponents argued, bilingualism is necessary in educational and other social service agencies to help with assimilation; otherwise, non-English-speaking citizens and residents would be alienated from participation in public affairs, thereby posing a threat to national solidarity.[23] The status of the resolution was unclear in early 1987. Clearly, the legacy of linguistic pluralism again confronted English language ethnocentrism.

Equal Educational Opportunity and Language Programs

The federal government of the United States has formulated equal educational opportunity policies that focus on language education programs. Particularly the *Bilingual Education Act* and the U.S. District Court decisions, *Lau* v. *Nichols* and *School Children* v. *Ann Arbor School Board*, explicitly established policies that impact public school language instruction.

In 1968, Public Law 90–247, *The Bilingual Education Act*, was enacted. *The Bilingual Education Act*, the seventh amendment to the Elementary and Secondary Education Act of 1965 (Title VII) declared that it was "to be the policy of the United States to provide financial assistance to local education agencies to develop and carry out new and imaginative elementary and secondary school programs designed to meet the special education needs . . . [of] children who come from environments where the dominant language is other than English."[24] The act stipulated it would be the policy of the U.S. government to assist financially in the development and implementation of bilingual education programs in U.S. public schools and trust territories.

In 1973, the act was changed to the *Comprehensive Bilingual Education Amendment Act of 1973.* The act was extended for training bilingual teachers and bilingual teacher trainers. The Act's policy recognized that (1) large numbers of children have limited English-speaking ability, (2) many of these children have a cultural heritage that differs from that of English-speaking people, and (3) a primary means by which a child learns is through using his or her language and cultural heritage. The Act provided financial assistance for extending and improving existing bilingual-bicultural programs in public schools, for improving resource and dissemination centers, and for developing and publishing bilingual-bicultural curriculum materials. Assistance was also provided for stipends and fellowships so that teachers and teacher-educators could be trained in bilingual-bicultural methodology.

A major catalyst for bilingual instruction was the United States Supreme Court ruling of *Lau* v. *Nichols* that provisions for the same teachers, programs, and textbooks in the same language for all students in the San Francisco school district did not provide equal educational opportunity when the native language of a sizable number of the student body was not English. In part the ruling held:

> There is no equality of treatment merely by providing students with the same facilities, textbooks, teachers, and curriculum; for students who do not understand English are effectively foreclosed from any meaningful education. . . . Where inability to speak and understand the English language excludes national origin-minority group children from effective participation in the education program offered by a school district, the district must take affirmative steps to rectify the language deficiency in order to open its instructional program to these students.[25]

The ruling did not mandate bilingual instruction for non-English-speaking students, but it did stipulate that special educational programs were necessary if schools were to provide equal educational opportunity for such students.

Equal educational opportunity policy regarding speakers of Black English has been formulated. The policy was precipitated by the United States District Court ruling in *Martin Luther King Jr. Elementary School Children* v. *Ann Arbor School District* in 1979. A case was made for students who speak Black English, Black vernacular, or Black dialect as a home and community language. The plaintiffs argued that language differences impeded the Black students' equal participation in the school's instructional program because the instructional program was conducted entirely in the standard school English dialect. Using linguistic and educational research evidence, the lawyers for the students established

. . . that unless those instructing in reading recognize (1) the existence of a home language used by the children in their own community for much of their non-school communications, and (2) that this home language may be a cause of the superficial difficulties in speaking standard English, great harm will be done. The child may withdraw or may act out frustrations and may not learn to read. A language barrier develops when teachers, in helping the child to switch from the home ("Black English") language to standard English, refuse to admit the existence of a language that is the acceptable way of talking in his local community.[26]

Therefore, the Court ruled to require the defendant Board to take steps to help its teachers recognize the home language of the students and use that knowledge in their attempts to teach reading skills in standard English.

Bilingual Instructional Methods in the United States

Within the United States, bilingual education programs have taken the forms of either assimilation or pluralization, with assimilation being the dominant form. The goal of these bilingual education programs focuses on teaching English to students for whom English is a second language.

The purpose of bilingual instruction is to increase academic achievement by using the student's home language as the main communication medium. Bilingual instruction involves the use of two languages for instruction for part or all of the activities within the classroom. One language is English; the other language is the student's home language, that is, the language spoken in the home. English is taught as a second language. Many times the student's first significant introduction to English is when he or she enters school. In other instances, the student may begin school with minimum English language skills.

Two methods of teaching the non-English-speaking students are (1) the native language (NL), and (2) English as a second language (ESL) methods. The native language method uses the student's home language in all subject areas. After mastery in listening, speaking, reading, and writing, the student is introduced to English. The method's supposition is that native language literacy should be achieved before the student is introduced to the English language arts. Having achieved native language literacy, the student should have no difficulty transferring to English. Rarely is reading of English taught until the student masters native language listening and speaking skills.

The second method, English as a second language (ESL), is sometimes called the direct method. ESL is a method that teaches the student immediate English language skills. The ESL pull-out system takes the student out of the classroom daily for instruction in the English language arts. The student returns to the class for instruction in other subjects. The ESL intensive system immerses the student in the English language arts for extensive time periods. When the student learns to speak the language, then reading in English is introduced. When the student reads English, he or she is returned to the monolingual English classroom.

The bilingual education debate of the 1980s centered on this question: Which method (NL or ESL) best teaches English to the non-English speaker? The NL supporters cited an array of experimental, longitudinal, and ethnographic studies to back the position that the NL method best teaches English to non-English speakers.[27] The NL camp reasoned the method is effective because it builds a solid linguistic foundation in the student's native language before it attempts to teach the second language. A solid foundation in the first language provides a solid base from which the second language can be learned. However, the NL method takes longer than does the ESL method. The NL method requires the student to develop almost full literacy in the first language before attempting the second language.

The ESL supporters identified the time factor as the critical flaw with the NL method. Given the highly mobile nature of U.S. society, and given the possibility that linguistic minority students change school quite often, the ESL camp argued that the NL method was not a practical method of teaching English to highly mobile populations. Rather, the more direct ESL method is preferable, because it provided the student an immediate introduction to English, thereby ensuring the student an opportunity to learn English.

The ESL supporters also had research evidence to back their position. An especially supportive experiment conducted by the Philippine Center for Language Study and the Bureau of Public Schools, the Rizal experiment,[28] consisted of 30 teachers and 1,490 students in 30 schools for 6 years. The investigators reported that students taught in an English-only program in grades 1 through 6 achieved the highest reading and mathematic scores on standardized measures; the students taught in their home language in grades 1 through 4, and then in English in grades 5 and 6, achieved below the English-only students. The students who fared the poorest were those taught in their home language in grades 1 and 2 and in English in grades 3 through 6.

Because both groups provided equally valid research to support their claims for the efficacy of their methodological positions, the question about which method best teaches English to non-English speakers was answered as "both."[29] As with many debates about which method is superior to achieve an instructional goal, the missing element was the critical variable of the teachers—their attendant attitudes toward the academic abilities of their students as well as the quality of the teachers' training for bilingual education.

The Relationship between Language and Culture

Language and culture are two sides on the same coin. In Chapter 5 culture is defined as a cluster of attributes, such as values, beliefs, behavior patterns and symbols unique to a particular human group. Language establishes the bond between individuals and between individuals and groups, that makes group life possible. Without language, group life (as we currently know it) is inconceivable. Language, an organized social institution, serves at least three functions: (1) intergroup communications; (2) transmission of the group's ethnicity and culture; and (3) the systemic recording of the group's ethnicity, culture, and history, which serve to give a group identity.

A group's language provides the group with an organized medium of communication. Group members can tune into the group with little difficulty because they speak the same language, and in general, share the same meaning. Second, a group's language provides a medium for transmitting group values, beliefs, and attitudes. The language helps set parameters for group living. Third, the language provides a medium to record a group's ethnicity, culture, and history. Thus, language serves as a time-binding agent, tying the past with the present. Part of group existence is knowing how the past percolates into the present. A group's folklore and myths are recorded in its language; thus, the group sustains itself by way of the oral tradition (i.e., teaching its youth orally about the past), or by way of the literacy tradition (i.e., teaching its youth about the past by having its youth read the written word).

Acquisition of Speech, Dialect, and Ethnicity

A primary parental function is to prepare youth to live in society. Parents use their dialect to describe, proscribe, and otherwise delineate the rules for group and social living. Social norms and mores are taught the youth *via* parental dialect. In this respect, speech acquisition is a socialization agent parents use to prepare youth for social living. Children acquire ethnicity and speech through their parents and immediate family. Initially, children learn these attributes verbally and nonverbally (i.e., infants initially acquire ethnicity and speech by the ways parents and siblings speak, hold, and touch them). By six months of age, for example, an infant's sexual identity has been conveyed to it by parental and sibling contact.

The onset of ethnicity precedes speech acquisition. The onset of ethnicity begins at birth, when children are first introduced to their immediate social environment, their parents and family. Children are also introduced to their parents' dialect; the parental dialect organizes and categorizes the children's social environment. The primary vehicle for transmission of parental ethnicity is their dialect. Consequently, even though the onset of ethnicity precedes speech acquisition, soon after birth ethnicity and speech acquisition become concurrent.[30]

Dialect and speech acquisition are natural human phenomena. All human beings, irrespective of culture, nationality, race, social class, or caste, acquire speech. Speech acquisition is universal for all human beings. With minor exceptions (e.g., the severely handicapped or mentally retarded), speech is naturally acquired by human beings. Speech serves as a tool for living within speech communities as well as a tool for categorizing and interpreting experiences.[31]

People acquire and develop speech along a format of progressive social development. At first, a person's speech is egocentric. As an infant learns to use words to satisfy biological needs, the infant's vocabulary revolves around words that satisfy these needs, e.g., "I hungy" (hungry). As the infant develops into more of a social being, a vocabulary and grammatical system to satisfy social needs is necessitated. By six months children begin babbling, uttering streams of sounds that resemble the inflections of natural sentences, and that communicate telegraphic messages. By age four, children exhibit control over the basic sentence patterns and most sounds of their parent's dialect. Thus, meaningful speech communication begins.

Linguistically speaking, children usually acquire a unique speech system termed an *idiolect*. An idiolect is a person's unique manner of speaking that begins in early childhood and to a large extent, remains throughout life. Everyone develops unique ways of speaking, that is, everyone develops a personal dialect, by virtue of unique physical and emotional characteristics. For example, a person may develop a preference for certain consonants and thereby prefer to use words that contain these sounds; or, a person may develop a preference for certain idioms, inflections, or expressions. The ubiquitous satires of movie actors like James Cagney, "You dirty rats!" or John Wayne, "Ya gotta put muscle inta it!" exemplify exaggerated idiolects.

Language and Dialect

As children grow they develop a dialect spoken by their parents and immediate family. A dialect is a variation of an idealized language model, that is, a dialect is a valid communication medium that contains its own rules of logic and grammar.[32] In the United States, most people speak a dialect of standard American English, which is the idealized version of the English language within the United States. (Of course, for some people in the United States, English is not the first dialect.) Standard American English is perceived to be the language's grammatical rules taught in the public schools of the United States and the usage used by journalists, television newscasters, and the educated populace. However, even though teachers and journalists write in standard American English, they nonetheless speak in a dialect of English. This point is made clear by comparing the speaking and writing styles of former United States presidents. Presidents Kennedy, Johnson, and Nixon all wrote their speeches in standard American English. Yet when reading their speeches, their speech dialects became apparent. Kennedy with his Bostonian pronunciations, Johnson with his Texas drawl, and Nixon with his middle-western idioms, such as poppycock!, all spoke a different dialect of Standard English.

The point is that language and dialect are not the same. A language is an idealized model for communication; dialect is a real speech and grammatical system a group uses for communication. The Swiss linguist, Ferdinand Saussure, called the former *langue* (language) and the latter *parole* (dialect). Sometimes I may use *language* and *dialect* interchangeably. However, the distinction between language as an idealized model and dialect as an actual, real spoken communication medium is important to keep in mind.

American English

The *langue* of United States society is the so-called standard English; its *parole* consists of at least four distinctively different dialects: Black English, eastern English, general American, and southern English. The dialects are mutually intelligible but they do differ in intonations and vocabulary. The latter three dialects are diverse; eastern English is divided into three subdialects as is the southern dialect; the general American dialect is a conglomeration of all remaining United States English dialects spoken in the Midwest, Southwest, Far West, and Northwest. The three dialects differ primarily in vocabulary, intonation, and idioms; they are mutually intelligible, and their grammatical systems do not differ significantly.[33]

Black English dialect, when compared to other United States dialects, does differ grammatically. One theory about the origin of Black English is that it is a Creole or pidgin English dialect that evolved during slavery in the South.[34] With emancipation and the gradual emigration of Blacks, the dialect spread to other parts of the country, in particular to large industrial cities in the Northeast and the Ohio Valley. Currently, it is still used in Black communities. Some of the dialect's characteristics, which distinguish it from other dialects, are:

1. The use of the third person singular verbs without adding the "s" or "z" sound; e.g., "The man walk" instead of "The man walks."
2. Nonuse of "s" to indicate possessives; e.g., "The girl hat" instead of "The girl's hat."
3. The use of the "f" sound for the "th" sound at the end or middle of a word; e.g., "nuf'n" instead of "nothing."
4. Elimination of "l" or "r" sounds in words; e.g., "Tomorrow I bring the book" instead of "Tomorrow I'll bring the book;" and, "It is you book" instead of "It is your book."
5. The use of the verb "be" to indicate future time; e.g., "He be here in a few hours."
6. The use of "it" instead of "there"; e.g., "It's a boy in my room named Bill" instead of "There's a boy in my room named Bill."[35]

An interesting aside is that some southern Whites (even those with enough status to escape the label of being nonstandard speakers) show characteristics that place their dialect close to Black English. Also, not all Blacks speak Black English, but often some Whites assume that all Blacks do speak the dialect.

Linking Ethnicity and Language

The fundamental role played by a language or a dialect is group communication. Even though people are not restricted to language for communication, language is of overarching importance because it is the fundamental medium through which ethnicity is transmitted and shared. A language system in general, and a dialect in particular, serve as tools to categorize, interpret, and share experiences. Ethnicity and language thus intertwine, language being the medium and ethnicity the message.

Youngsters learn the content of their ethnic cultures through their parent's dialect. The dialect is used to convey ethnic meaning to the youngsters; later, as the youngsters master the dialect, they use it to convey ethnic content. The dialect serves the youngsters in the formation of their perceptions, attitudes, and values about their physical and social environments. Anthropologists Sapir and Whorf reported in their studies of language and perceptions that a person's dialect influences and informs his or her view and perception of reality.[36] For example, in American English there exist only several conceptions of snow (e.g., powder snow or wet snow.) Within the Eskimo language, however, there exist many conceptions of snow. The reason for the difference is that snow is of greater economic and social importance to the Eskimo than it is to most English-speaking peoples. The vocabulary of a group's language will reflect distinctions and categories important to the group. Conversely, relatively unimportant categories will be reflected minimally, or, the category may be nonexistent within the group's vocabulary.

The grammatical system of a group's language reflects the group's attitude toward its physical environment. For example, the Navajo language emphasizes the reporting of events in motion. For example, when describing a large mountain, a Navajo may say in Navajo, "the mountain is busy being big and blue." In this case, the Navajo describes the physical environment as fluid. In American English, the mountain's description, "the mountain is big and blue" perforces the description of a static physical environment. Thus, the Navajo and English descriptions reflect differing ethnic interpretations of the natural environment.[37]

These comments should not be interpreted to mean that language determines ethnicity. Rather, language serves as a mirror to ethnicity, reflecting a person's values, beliefs, and attitudes. Note what is being said regarding property in the following scenarios (based on personal observations):

Scenario I:

Ruth: Mom, where's my Barbie doll?
Mother: I lent it to Sue.
Ruth: Why'd you do that?
Mother: She wanted to play with it.
Ruth: But, it's my doll and . . .
Mother: Okay! Okay! Go tell her I said she's to give it to you.

Scenario II:

> *Rita:* Mom, where's my Barbie doll?
> *Mother:* I let your sister use it.
> *Rita:* But I want to use it.
> *Mother:* You can use one of your other dolls.
> *Rita:* But Mom!
> *Mother:* Maybe your sister would trade it for one of the other dolls.
> *Rita:* Well, okay.

In scenario I there is an implicit assumption that the doll is Ruth's exclusive property. The mother violated Ruth's property rights by lending the doll without talking to Ruth. The mother acted outside the bounds of her role. In this scenario, the mother's role is to enforce property rights. In scenario II there is an implicit assumption that the dolls are the family's collective property. The mother acted within the bounds of her role as property rights coordinator. The language used in both scenarios serves as a microscopic reflection of the attitudes toward property ownership and the mother's role governing ownership.

At one time, language was feared. The belief existed that language acted as some kind of extraterrestrial force subconsciously to tyrannize people to think and feel in certain ways.[38] Of course, people can be influenced to behave in certain ways with propagandistic linguistic manipulation. However, people give meaning to language, and meaning is derived from within the context of a language community. My hunch is that ethnicity impacts language, in particular its vocabulary items, in significant ways. Consequently, ethnicity—as a broadly based emotion and sense of group identity—is reflected in an ethnic group's dialect and lexicon. Because an ethnic group uses a dialect to embody and transmit its ethnic content, knowledge about the ethnic group presupposes knowledge of its dialect. To know an ethnic group one must know its dialect.

Toward a Policy for Multiethnic Linguistic Pluralism

A policy of linguistic pluralism is essential for multiethnic education. The policy should provide parameters so that teachers can accommodate linguistic differences as well as teach about linguistic diversity in the United States. The policy should contain two dimensions (see Figure 14.1). The two dimensions could be tied to a broader policy of ethnic pluralism (i.e., a policy setting parameters for accommodating ethnic differences and teaching about ethnic diversity in the United States) (see Figure 14.2). To form and implement a pluralistic policy the following four benchmarks are suggested.

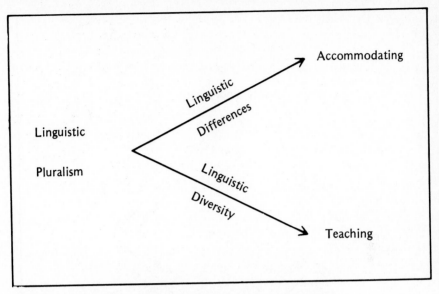

Figure 14.1. Educational Dimensions for Linguistic Pluralism
Linguistic pluralism operates within the dimensions of linguistic differences and linguistic diversity. Teachers are encouraged to accommodate their student's linguistic differences and also to teach about linguistic diversity in the United States.

Benchmark 1: A Concise Statement Supportive of Linguistic Pluralism Should Be Made

School English ethnocentrism—the attitude that school English is superior to other dialects and languages—is the nexus of the problem. The policy statement would stand for linguistic pluralism and against school English ethnocentrism. The statement would have two major dimensions: (1) accommodating linguistic differences, and (2) teaching about linguistic diversity, both fostering a climate of respect for linguistic differences.

Benchmark 2: Teachers Should Be Cognizant of Their Linguistic Biases against the Dialects or Languages of Linguistically Different Students

Again, linguistic ethnocentrism lies at the nexus of the problem. Primarily, respect for the student's home dialect should be fostered. Rather than viewing the home dialect as defective, teachers should view the dialect as a source of strength.

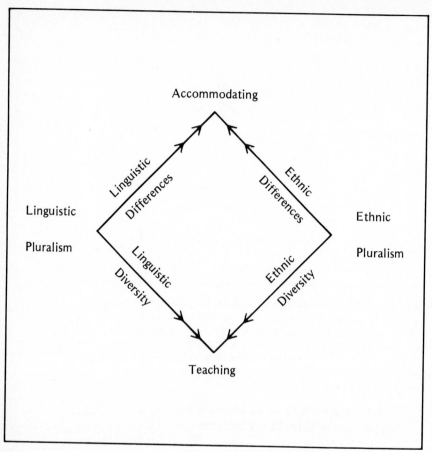

Figure 14.2. Dimensions of Linguistic and Ethnic Pluralism
Linguistic pluralism should be linked to ethnic pluralism,
which operates within the dimensions of ethnic differences
and ethnic diversity. Teachers are encouraged to accommodate their students' ethnic differences and also to teach about
ethnic diversity in the United States.

Students do not enter school speaking a substandard dialect; they may enter
school speaking non-school-standard English or a different language. The position
that youngsters speak a substandard version of English is an imposition of school
English as the only English dialect capable of use for learning.

Benchmark 3: Instructional Strategies
Should Accommodate Linguistically
Different Students

Linguistically different students should not be placed in special language programs that segregate them from the regular classroom. In fact, positive intercul-

tural experiences can be fostered in linguistically diverse classrooms. When there are a large number of non-English speakers of the same language, a bilingual teacher is feasible. However, if possible, monolingual English-speaking students should be incorporated into this otherwise linguistically segregated arrangement. With students who speak Black English, or other nonschool English dialects, standard school-English should be taught as an alternate dialect necessary for broader social interactions. All students need to learn to understand, read, and write in standard English. Therefore, the linguistic resources of linguistically different students should be maximized to teach basic English literacy.

Benchmark 4: Curriculum Materials Should Reflect the Linguistic Diversity in the United States

This benchmark requires multilingual permeation of curriculum materials. Teachers should use every opportunity to incorporate nonschool English dialects and languages into all their curriculum materials. Examples I've seen work in the classroom are:

1. Learning to count in Spanish, French, German, or some other language
2. Learning that people call their neighborhoods by differing names, *ghetto* (Italian origin), *barrio* (Spanish for neighborhood)
3. Learning to read the Chinese calendar.

The list is endless and the approach feasible. Incorporating linguistic diversity into curriculum materials does not require much language-learning for the teacher. The new language or dialect adds variety to otherwise routine learning activities.

Summary

Language and culture interweave. For students, language and culture are the heads and tails of the same coin. Rejection of the students' language is tantamount to cultural rejection.

Language provides a bond between individuals and between individuals and groups. It serves these important group functions: (1) intergroup communication, (2) transmission of a group's culture, and (3) group identity. In the United States, individuals speak some dialect of American English. Some also speak a non-English language in addition to an English dialect (bilingualism); some speak two dialects of American English, such as some Blacks (bidialectalism). All of these individuals reflect their ethnicity and cultural preferences through the language(s) or dialect(s) they speak.

All countries have a formal or informal language policy that fosters a national language standard. However, the world's nations treat the nonnational languages of their societies differently. Some have a policy of assimilation that prohibits the use of any language in public institutions except the national standard. Some have a policy of pluralism that allows the use of nonofficial languages in public institutions. Others have a policy of vernacularization that attempts to restore an indigenous language as the national standard; and, some nations have a policy of internationalization, which attempts to transform their citizens into a multilingual society.

The policy of the United States is assimilation. English as spoken and written in the United States is well established as the nation's language. Even though English is not designated as the nation's official language, it has a much more powerful designation which ensures its status as the nation's unofficial official language — the designation granted by more than two hundred years of tradition and domination. U.S. English usage is a folkway; when compared to a law, a folkway is always more powerful, resilient, and tenacious. Supporting this point are the equal educational opportunity policies, such as the *Lau* v. *Nichols* and the *Ann Arbor* decisions, which permitted linguistic pluralism but intended English language assimilation. Because the nation requires literate citizens, English literacy must be taught in schools. Yet, the legacy of linguistic pluralism should be sustained rather than discouraged as it was in the xenophobic 1920s, when the nation became isolated from the global community.

A workable policy of linguistic pluralism involves teaching within two dimensions: (1) linguistic differences and (2) linguistic diversity. The first dimension requires teachers to accommodate in both curriculum materials and teaching strategies their students' linguistic differences. The second dimension, linguistic diversity, requires teachers to teach about linguistic diversity in the United States to all their students, irrespective of their students' daily language usage. The first dimension provides linguistic minority and bidialectal students an equal opportunity to learn school subjects. The second dimension provides all students a broad, nonethnocentric understanding of the multilingual diversity of U.S. society.

Notes

1. Mohandas K. Gandhi, *Evil Wrought by the English Language* (Ahmedabad, India: Navajivan Publishing House, 1958), p. 25.

2. Joshua Fishman, *Language Loyalty in the United States* (London: Mouton Press, 1966), pp. 206–252.

3. *The Peoples and Cultures of Cambodia, Laos, and Vietnam* (Washington, D.C.: Center for Applied Linguistics, 1981). The Center has other excellent manuals that explain in detail cultural and linguistic characteristics; see also, J. K. Whitmore, *An Introduction to Indochinese History, Culture, Language, and Life* (Ann Arbor: Center for South and Southeast Asian Studies, University of Michigan, 1979).

4. Fishman, *Language Loyalty*. see also Charles Ferguson and Shirley Heath, *Language in the USA* (Cambridge, England: Cambridge University Press, 1981); Charlton Laird, *Language in America* (New York: The World Publishing Co., 1970).

5. Shirley Heath, "English in Our Language Heritage," in Ferguson and Heath, *Language in the USA*, pp. 6–20.

6. Laird, *Language in America*, pp. 263–309.

7. Edwin Zeydel, *Reports of Surveys and Studies in the Teaching of Modern Foreign Languages* (New York: Modern Language Association, 1964).

8. Ellwood Cubberly, *Changing Conceptions of Education*, (Boston: Houghton Mifflin Co., 1909), pp. 15–16.

9. Oscar Handlin, *Immigration as a Factor in American History* (Englewood Cliffs, N.J.: Prentice-Hall, 1959) p. 16.

10. Ibid., pp. 167–192. The analysis on xenophobia was culled from this work by Handlin.

11. Arnold H. Liebowitz, "Language and the Law: The Exercise of Power through Official Designation of Language," in U. M. O'Barr and J. F. O'Barr, eds., *Language and Politics* (The Hague: Mouton, 1976).

12. Lloyd Jorgenson, *The Founding of Public Education in Wisconsin* (Madison: Wisconsin Historical Society, 1956). The Wisconsin experience is used to exemplify the bilingual tradition in U.S. schools.

13. Zeydel, *Reports of Surveys*, pp. 297–299.

14. Carlos Ovando and Virginia P. Collier, *Bilingual and ESL Classrooms* (New York: McGraw-Hill, 1985) p. 24.

15. Hannah Geffert, Robert Harper, Salvador Sarmiento, and Daniel Schember, *Current Status of U.S. Bilingual Legislation* (Arlington, Va.: Center for Applied Linguistics, 1975), pp. 2–119.

16. Edmund E. Reutter and Robert R. Hamilton, *The Law of Public Education* (Mineola, N.Y.: The Foundation Press, 1970), p. 110.

17. U.S. Commission on Civil Rights, *Mexican American Education Study* (Washington, D.C.: U.S. Government Printing Office, 1970), pp. 11–40.

18. Francis Prucha, *Documents of United States Indian Policy* (Lincoln: University of Nebraska Press, 1975), pp. 253–256.

19. Zeydel, pp. 1–14.

20. "Foreign Language in the Elementary School," *Education Letter*, (Cambridge, Mass.: Harvard University Press, November, 1985), p. 4; see also N. C. Rhodes and A. R. Schreibstein, *Foreign Languages in the Elementary School* (Center for Applied Linguistics, Washington, D.C., 1983) ERIC ED 209 940.

21. *Congressional Record–Senate* (Washington, D.C.: U.S. Government Printing Office, January 22, 1985), p. S468.

22. Norman Shumway, "Should English Be Made Official? Yes," as recorded in the *Congressional Record* (June 11, 1986), p. E2046–E2047.

23. Arnoldo Torres, "Should English Be Made Official? No" as recorded in the *Congressional Record* (June 11, 1986), p. E2046–E2047.

24. Geffert et al., pp. 121–123.

25. *Lau* vs. *Nichols*, 414 U.S. 563, 39 L. Ed 2nd, 94 S. Ct 786, 1974.

26. *Martin Luther King Jr. Elementary School Children, et al.* v. *Ann Arbor School District Board*, U.S. District Court, East District, Michigan, Civil Action No. 7–71861, 1979.

27. Merrial Swain and S. Lapkin, *Bilingual Education in Ontario: A Decade of Research* (Toronto: Ontario Institute for Studies in Education, 1981); see also L. C. Moll, "The Microethnographic Study of Bilingual Schooling," *Ethnoperspectives in Bilingual Education Research* (Ypsilanti: Eastern Michigan University Press, 1981), pp. 430–446.

28. Fredrick Davis, *Philippine Language Teaching Experiments* (Quezon City: Phoenix Press, 1967).

29. Ovando and Collier, *Bilingual and ESL Classrooms*, pp. 37–46. This text provides a thorough analysis of the variations that evolved from the NL and ESL camps.

30. Robbins Burling, *Man's Many Voices: Language in Its Cultural Context* (New York: Holt, Rinehart, 1978), pp. 117–119; see also George Miller, *Language and Communication* (New York: McGraw-Hill, 1951), see especially Chapter 7, "Verbal Behavior of Children."

31. Dell Hymes, "Functions of Speech," in F. Gruber, ed., *Anthropology and Education* (Philadelphia: University of Pennsylvania Press, 1961), pp. 55–83; see also Dan Slobin, *A Field Manual for Cross-Cultural Study of the Acquisition of Communicative Competence* (Berkeley: University of California Press, 1967).

32. William Labov, "The Logic of Nonstandard English," in F. Williams, ed., *Language and Poverty* (Chicago: Markham, 1970), pp. 153–189.

33. Albert H. Marckwardt, "Regional and Social Variations," in Robert B. Glenn, ed., *Language and Culture* (Marquette: Northern Michigan Press, 1974), pp. 181–193; see also A. D. Edwards, *Language in Culture and Class* (London: Heinemann Educational Books, 1976), p. 46.

34. Paul Stoller, *Black American English* (New York: Dell Publishing Company, 1975), pp. 17–48.

35. The list was culled from Joan Baratz and Roger W. Shuy, *Teaching Black Children to Read* (Washington, D.C.: Center for Applied Linguistics, 1969); Ralph W. Fasold and Roger Shuy, *Teaching Standard English in the Inner City* (Washington, D.C.: Center for Applied Linguistics, 1970); William Labov, *Language in the Inner City* (Philadelphia: University of Pennsylvania Press, 1972); Walter Wolfram, *A Sociolinguistic Description of Negro Speech* (Washington, D.C.: Center for Applied Linguistics, 1969). The list here is meant to highlight Black dialect differences. An in-depth study of the dialect is encouraged to prevent stereotypes about it.

36. Edward Sapir, *Culture, Language, and Personality* (Berkeley: University of California Press, 1958); see also B. L. Whorf, *Language, Thought and Reality* (New York: Wiley, 1956), pp. 65–86.

37. Harry Hoijer, "Cultural Implications of Some Navajo Linguistic Categories," *Language* 27 (1951), pp. 111–120.

38. S. I. Hayakawa, *Language in Thought and Action* (New York: Harcourt Brace, World, 1949), pp. 100–117; see also Stuart Chase, *The Tyranny of Words* (New York: Harcourt, Brace, 1938).

15

Curriculum Guidelines
for Multiethnic Education

1. Ethnic Pluralism Should Permeate the Total School Environment

Effective teaching about ethnic groups can best take place within an educational setting that accepts, encourages, and respects the expression of ethnic and racial diversity. To attain this kind of educational atmosphere, the total school environment must be reformed, not merely courses and programs. The school's informal or "hidden" curriculum is just as important as, and perhaps in some ways more important than, the formalized course of study.

Teaching about different ethnic groups in a few specialized courses is obviously not enough. Ethnic content about a variety of ethnic groups should be incorporated into all subject areas, preschool through grade twelve and beyond. Concern with ethnicity is as appropriate for the fine arts, the domestic arts, the natural sciences, mathematics, vocational education, and the consumer arts as it is for the language arts and the social studies. Ethnic diversity should also be a part of all other school activities and projects.

To permeate the total school environment with ethnic pluralism, it is necessary that students have resource materials readily available that provide accurate information on the diverse aspects of the histories and cultures of different ethnic groups. Learning centers, libraries, and resource centers should include a multitude of resources on the history, literature, music, folklore, views of life, and the arts of different ethnic groups.

Ethnic diversity in the school's informal programs should be reflected in assembly programs, classroom, hallway and entrance decorations, cafeteria menus, counseling interactions, and extracurricular programs. School-sponsored dances, for example, that consistently provide only one kind of ethnic music and/or performers are as contrary to the spirit and the principles of ethnic pluralism as are curricula that teach only about mainstream ideals, values, and contributions.

Participation in activities—such as cheerleading, booster clubs, honor societies, and athletic teams—should be open to all students; in fact, the participation of students from different ethnic backgrounds should be solicited. Such activities can provide invaluable opportunities not only for the development of self-esteem, but also for students from different ethnic backgrounds to learn to work and play together and to recognize that all individuals, whatever their ethnic identities, have worth and are capable of achieving.

2. School Policies and Procedures Should Foster Positive Multiethnic Interactions and Understandings among Students, Teachers, and the Supportive Staff

School governance should protect the individual's right to (1) retain esteem for his or her home environment, (2) develop a positive self-concept, (3) develop empathy and insight into and respect for the ethnicity of others, and (4) receive an equal educational opportunity.

Each institution needs rules and regulations to guide behavior so as to attain institutional goals and objectives. School rules and regulations should enhance multiethnic harmony and understanding among students, as well as among staff and teachers. In the past, school harmony was often sought through efforts to treat everyone the same; however, experience in multiethnic settings indicates that the same treatment for everyone is unfair to many students. Instead of insisting on one ideal model of behavior that is unfair to many students, school policies should recognize and accommodate individual and ethnic group differences. This does not mean that some students should obey school rules while others should not; it means that different ethnic groups may have different behaviors that should be honored so long as they are not inconsistent with major school goals. It also means that school policies may have to make allowances for different ethnic traditions. For example, Jewish customs that affect Jewish students' eating habits and school attendance on certain religious days should be respected.

Equal educational opportunity should be increased by rules that protect linguistically and culturally different students from procedures and practices that relegate them to low ability or special education classes simply because of their low scores on standardized English reading and achievement tests.

Guidance and other student services personnel should not respond to students in stereotyped ways regarding their academic abilities and occupational aspirations, and students must be protected from such responses. Counselors should be cautioned to counsel students on the basis of their individual potentials and interests as well as on the basis of their ethnic needs and concerns. Counselors will need to be particularly aware of their biases in counseling students whose ethnicity differs from theirs.

Schools should recognize the holidays and festivities of major importance to different ethnic groups in the school. Provisions should be made to see that traditional holidays and festivities reflect multiethnic modes of celebration. For example, the ways in which some Indian tribes celebrate Thanksgiving, Orthodox Greeks celebrate Easter, and Jews celebrate Chanukah can be appropriately included in school programs.

3. The School Staff Should Reflect the Ethnic Pluralism within Society

Members of different ethnic groups must be part of the school's instructional, administrative, and supportive staffs if the school is truly multiethnic. School personnel — teachers, principals, cooks, custodians, secretaries, students, and counselors — make as important contributions to multiethnic environments as do courses of study and instructional materials. Students learn important lessons about ethnicity and ethnic diversity by observing interactions among different racial and ethnic groups in their school, observing and experiencing the verbal behavior of the professional and supportive staffs, and observing the extent to which the staff is ethnically and racially mixed. Therefore, school policies should be established and aggressively implemented to recruit and maintain a multiethnic total school staff, sensitive to the needs of multiethnicity.

Students also can benefit greatly from positive interactions with students from various racial and ethnic groups. When plans are made to mix students from diverse groups — whether through school desegregation or exchange programs and visits — extreme care must be taken to make sure that the environment in which the students interact is a positive and enhancing one. When students from different ethnic and racial groups interact within a hostile environment, their racial antipathies are more likely to increase than decrease.

4. Schools Should Have Systematic, Comprehensive, Mandatory, and Continuing Staff Development Programs

The teacher is the most important variable in the student's formal learning environment. Major attention should be devoted to the training and retraining of teachers and other members of the professional and supportive school staff in order to create the kind of multiethnic school environment recommended in these Guidelines. Sound materials and other components of the instructional program are ineffective in the hands of teachers who lack the skills, attitudes, perceptions, and content background essential for a positive multiethnic school environment. An effective staff development program must involve administrators, librarians, counselors, and members of the supportive school staff, such as cooks, secretaries, and bus drivers. This is necessary because any well-trained and sensitive teacher must work within a supportive institutional environment in order to succeed. Key administrators, such as principals, must set by example the school norms of ethnic and cultural differences. The need to involve administrators, especially building principals, in comprehensive and systematic staff development programs cannot be overemphasized.

Effective professional staff development should begin at the preservice level and continue as inservice when educators are employed by schools. The focus should be on helping the staff members (a) clarify and analyze their feelings, attitudes, and perceptions toward their own and other ethnic groups, (b) acquire content about and understanding of the historical experiences and sociological characteristics of ethnic groups, (c) increase their instructional skills within multiethnic school environments, (d) improve their skill in curriculum development as it relates to ethnic pluralism, and (e) increase their skill in creating, selecting, evaluating, and revising instructional materials.

Staff development for effective multiethnic schools must be undertaken jointly by school districts, local colleges and universities, and local community agencies. Each bears a responsibility for training school personnel, at both the preservice and inservice levels, to function successfully within multiethnic instructional settings.

Effective staff development programs must be carefully conceptualized and implemented. Short workshops, selected courses, and other short-term experiences may be essential components of such programs, but these alone cannot be characterized as total staff development programs. Sound staff development programs should consist of a wide variety of program components, such as need assessments, curriculum development, laboratory teaching, and materials selection and evalaution. Lectures alone are insufficient. Ongoing changes should be made to make staff development programs more responsive to the needs of practicing professionals.

5. The Curriculum Should Reflect the Ethnic Learning Styles of the Students within the School Community

All students in a multiethnic school cannot be treated identically and still be afforded equal educational opportunities. Some students have unique ethnic characteristics to which the school should respond deliberately and sensitively.

Research and observations indicate that students who are members of minority groups, especially those who are poor, often have values, behavioral patterns, cognitive styles, expectations, and other cultural components that differ from those of the school's culture.[1] These often lead to conflicts between students and teachers. By comparison, most mainstream youths find the school culture to be consistent with their home culture, and they are much more comfortable in school. However, many students, regardless of their ethnic or racial identity, find the school culture alien, hostile, and self-defeating.

The school's culture and its instructional programs should be modified, where necessary, to reflect the cultures and learning styles of children from diverse ethnic and social class groups. Some research indicates that the instructional strategies and learning styles that are most often favored in U.S. schools are inconsistent with the cognitive styles and cultural characteristics of some groups of minority students.[2] Other research indicates that ethnicity influences students' cognitive patterns of processing information, and that such patterns have instructional implications.[3] It is not feasible to base major educational policy on this research, because it is sparse and inconclusive. However, such findings should alert educators to the need to become more sensitive to student differences based on ethnicity, and to the implications of these findings for planning and organizing the school environment. Educators should not be blind to racial and ethnic differences when planning instruction; nor should they dismiss the question of racial and ethnic differences with the all-too-easy cliché, "I don't see racial differences in students and I treat them all alike." Research on ethnicity and cognitive styles suggests that if all students are treated alike, they are probably being denied access to equal educational opportunities.[4]

Although differences among students are accepted in an effective multiethnic school, major goals must also be to teach the students how to function effectively in social settings different from the ones in which they were socialized, and to help them to master new cognitive styles and learning patterns. The successful multiethnic school helps students be aware of and able to acquire cultural and cognitive alternatives, thus enabling them to function successfully within other cultural environments as well as their own.

6. The Multiethnic Curriculum Should Provide Students with Continuous Opportunities to Develop a Better Sense of Self

The multiethnic curriculum should help students develop a better sense of self. The development should be an ongoing process, beginning when the child first enters school and continuing throughout the child's school career. This development should include at least three areas:

1. Students should be helped to develop accurate self-identities. Who am I? What am I? These are questions with which students must deal in order to come to grips with their own identities.

2. The multiethnic curriculum should help students develop improved self-concepts. Beyond coming to grips with who they are and what they are, students should learn to feel positively about their identities, particularly their ethnic identities. Positive self-concepts may be expressed in several ways. The multiethnic curriculum, for example, should recognize the varying talents of students and capitalize on them in the academic curriculum. Students need to feel that academic success is possible. The multiethnic curriculum should also help students develop a high regard for their home languages and cultures.

3. The multiethnic curriculum should help students develop greater self-understanding. Students should develop more sophisticated understandings of why they are as they are, why their ethnic groups are as they are, and what ethnicity may mean in their daily lives. Such self-understanding will help students deal more effectively with future situations in which ethnicity may have an impact.

Students cannot fully understand why they are as they are and why certain things may occur in their future until they have a solid knowledge of the groups to which they belong and the effect of group membership on their lives. Multiethnic education should enable students to come to grips with these individual/group relationships in general and the effect of ethnicity on their own lives in particular.

Looking at group membership ought not undermine a student's individuality. Rather, it should add a dimension to the understanding of one's own unique individuality by learning how belonging to groups affects it.

Neither are students to be assigned and locked into one group. Instead, students should be aware of the many groups to which they belong in voluntary or involuntary memberships and should recognize that at various moments one or more of these groups may have significant effects on their lives.

The multiethnic curriculum should also help students understand and appreciate their personal backgrounds and family heritages. Family studies in the school can contribute to increased self-understanding and a personal sense of heritage, as contrasted with the generalized experiences presented in books. They can also contribute to family and personal pride. If parents and other relatives come to school to share their stories and life experiences, students will become increasingly aware that ethnic groups are a meaningful part of our nation's heritage, meriting study and recording.

7. The Curriculum Should Help Students Understand the Totality of the Experiences of Ethnic Groups

The social problems that ethnic group members experience are often regarded as part of their cultural characteristics. Alcohol, crime, and illiteracy, for example, are considered by many people to be cultural characteristics of particular ethnic groups. Ethnicity is often assumed to mean something negative and divisive, and the study of ethnic groups and ethnicity becomes only the examination of problems such as prejudice, racism, discrimination, and exploitation. To concentrate exclusively on these problems when studying ethnicity creates serious distortions in perceptions of ethnic groups. Among other things, it stereotypes ethnic groups as essentially passive recipients of dominant society discriminations and exploitation. These are legitimate issues to be included in a comprehensive, effective multiethnic curriculum, but they should not constitute the entire curriculum.

Many ethnic group members face staggering sociopolitical problems, but these do not comprise the whole of their lives. Nor are all ethnic groups affected to the same degree or in the same ways by these problems. Moreover, many ethnic groups have developed and maintained viable life-styles and have made notable contributions to Western culture. Moreover, the experiences of each ethnic group are part of a composite of human activities. Although it is true that each ethnic group has significant unifying historical experiences and cultural traits, no ethnic group has a single, homogeneous, historical-cultural pattern. Members of an ethnic group do not conform to a single cultural norm or mode of behavior, nor are ethnic cultures uniform and static.

Consequently, the many dimensions of ethnic experiences and cultures should be studied. The curriculum should help students understand the essential historical experiences and basic cultural patterns of ethnic groups, and the critical contemporary issues and social problems confronting each of them, as well as the dynamic diversity of the experiences, cultures, and individuals within each ethnic group.

A consistently multifaceted approach to teaching should benefit students in several major ways. It should help them become aware of the commonalities within and among ethnic groups. It should help counteract stereotyping by making students aware of the rich diversity within each ethnic group. It should also help students develop more comprehensive and more realistic understandings of the broad range of ethnic group heritages and experiences.

8. The Multiethnic Curriculum Should Help Students Understand That There Is Always a Conflict between Ideals and Realities in Human Societies

Traditionally, students in U.S. common schools have been taught a great deal about the ideals of U.S. society. Conflicts between ideals are often glossed over. Often values, such as freedom and equality, are treated as ideals that can be attained, and the realities of U.S. society have been distorted to make it appear that they have indeed been achieved. Courses in U.S. history and citizenship especially have been characterized by this kind of unquestioning approach to the socialization of youth. Many writers have described this approach to citizenship education in terms such as "passing down the myths and legends of our national heritage." This approach to citizenship education tends to inculcate parochial national attitudes, promote serious misconceptions about the nature of U.S. society and culture, and develop cynicism in youth who are aware of the gaps between the ideal and the real.

When ethnic studies emerged from the civil rights movement of the 1960s, there was a strong reaction to the traditional approach to citizenship education. A widely expressed goal of many curriculum reformers was to "tell it like it is and was" in the classroom. In many of the reformed courses, however, U.S. history and society were taught and viewed primarily from the viewpoints of specific ethnic groups. Little attention was given to basic American values, except to highlight gross discrepancies between ideals and the harsh realities of U.S. society. Emphasis was often on how minority groups had been oppressed by mainstream Americans.

The unquestioning approach and the "tell it like it is" approach both result in distortions. In a sound multiethnic curriculum, emphasis should be neither on the ways in which the United States has "fulfilled its noble ideals" nor on the "sins committed by the Anglo-Americans" or by any other groups of Americans. Rather, students should be encouraged to examine the democratic values that emerged in the United States, why they emerged, how they were defined in various periods, and to whom they referred in different eras. Students should also examine the extent to which these values as ideals have or have not been fulfilled, and the continuing conflict between values such as freedom and equality, as well as between ideals in other human societies.

Students should also be encouraged to examine various interpretations of the discrepancies between ideals and realities in U.S. life and history. From the perspectives of some individuals and groups, there has been a continuing expansion of human rights in the United States. Others see a continuing process of weighing rights against rights as the optimum mix of values, none of which can be fully realized as ideals. Many people argue that basic human rights are still too much limited to Americans with certain class, racial, ethnic, and cultural characteristics. Students should consider why these various interpretations arose and why different Americans view differently the conflicts between the ideals and realities of U.S. society.

9. The Multiethnic Curriculum Should Explore and Clarify Ethnic Alternatives and Options within Society

Educational questions regarding students' ethnic alternatives and options are complex and difficult. Some individuals, for a variety of complex reasons, are uncomfortable with their ethnic identities and wish to deny them. Some individuals are uncomfortable when their own ethnic groups are discussed in the classroom. This discomfort means that the teacher must be careful about assuming, without adequate evidence, that students want to discuss and study their own ethnic heritages.

The degree of resistance when the class is studying their ethnic groups is influenced by the teacher's approach to the study of ethnicity. Students can sense when both the teacher and other students in the class are intolerant of their ethnic group or some of its characteristics. Students often receive such messages from nonverbal responses. The teacher can minimize student resistance to studying their ethnic heritage by creating a classroom atmosphere that reflects acceptance and respect for ethnic differences.

Moreover, teachers should help students understand the options related to their own ethnicity as well as the nature of ethnic alternatives and options in Western societies. Students should be helped to understand that, ideally, all individuals should have the right to select the manner and degree of identifying or not identifying with their ethnic groups. However, they should also learn that some individuals, such as members of many White ethnic groups, have the privilege;

whereas others, such as most Afro-Americans, have more limited options. Most persons of White ethnic ancestry in the United States can become assimilated into the mainstream society. When they become highly assimilated, they can usually participate completely in most American economic, social, and political institutions. However, no matter how culturally assimilated members of some ethnic groups become — Black Americans, for example — they are still perceived and stigmatized by the larger society on the basis of their ethnicity.

Students should also be helped to understand that even though individualism is strong in U.S. society, in reality many Americans, such as Native Americans and Chinese Americans, are often judged not as individuals but on the basis of the racial and/or ethnic group to which they belong. Teachers may give Native-American or Chinese-American students the option of examining or not examining their ethnic heritage and identity; such students also need to be helped to understand how they are perceived and identified by the larger society. Educators must respect the individual rights of students, but at the same time they have a professional responsibility to help students learn basic facts and generalizations about the nature of race and ethnicity in Western democratic societies.

10. The Multiethnic Curriculum Should Promote Values, Attitudes, and Behaviors That Support Ethnic Pluralism

Ethnicity is a salient factor in the lives of many people. It helps individuals answer the question, "Who am I?" by providing them with a sense of peoplehood, identity, and cultural and spiritual roots. It provides a filter through which events, lifestyles, norms, and values are processed and screened. It provides a means through which identity is affirmed, heritages are validated, and some preferred associates are selected. Therefore, ethnicity serves necessary functions in many persons' lives. Ethnicity is neither always positive and reinforcing, nor always negative and debilitating, although it has the potential for both. The effective multiethnic curriculum should examine all of these dimensions of ethnicity.

The curriculum should help students understand that diversity is an integral part of most Western societies. Because ethnic diversity permeates most societies, schools should teach about ethnic diversity to help students acquire more accurate assessments of history and culture. Major goals of ethnic pluralism include improving respect for human dignity, maximizing cultural options, understanding what makes people alike and different, and accepting diversity as valuable to human life.

Students should learn that to be different does not necessarily mean to be inferior or superior, and that the study of ethnic group differences need not lead to ethnic polarization. They should also learn that even though some conflict is unavoidable in ethnically and racially pluralistic societies, it does not necessarily have to be destructive or divisive. Conflict is an intrinsic part of the human condition, especially so in a pluralistic society, in which values rub against each other. Conflict is often a catalyst for social progress. Multiethnic curricula that explore ethnic pluralism in positive, realistic ways will present ethnic conflict in proper perspective. They will help students understand that there is strength in diversity, and that social cooperation among ethnic groups is not necessarily predicated on their having identical beliefs, behaviors, and values.

The multiethnic curriculum should help students understand and respect ethnic diversity and broaden their cultural options. Too many people now learn only the values, behavioral patterns, and beliefs of their own ethnic groups, cultural groups, and/or communities. Socialization is, in effect, encapsulating, providing few opportunities for most individuals to acquire more than stereotypes about ethnic groups other than their own. Therefore, many people tend to view other ethnic groups and life-styles as "abnormal" and/or "deviant." The multiethnic curriculum can help students correct these misconceptions by teaching them that there are other ways of living that are as valid and viable as their own.

The multiethnic curriculum should also promote the basic values expressed in the major historical documents of democratic nation-states. Each ethnic group should have the right to practice its own religious, social, and cultural beliefs, but within the limits of due regard for the rights of other people. There is a set of values that all groups within a society or nation must endorse to maintain societal cohesion. In democratic societies, these core values stem from a commitment to human dignity and include justice, equality, freedom, and due process of law. Although the school should value and reflect ethnic pluralism, it should not promote the practices and beliefs of any ethnic group that contradict the core values of a democratic nation. Rather, the school should foster ethnic differences that maximize opportunities for democratic living.

Ethnicity and/or ethnic group membership should not restrict an individual's opportunity and ability to achieve and to participate, but it is sometimes used by groups in power to the detriment of less powerful groups. Individuals who do not understand the role of ethnicity often find it a troublesome reality, one extremely difficult to handle. Multiethnic curricula should help students examine the dilemmas surrounding ethnicity as a step toward realizing its full potential as an enabling force in the lives of individuals and groups.

11. The Multiethnic Curriculum Should Help Students Develop Their Decision-Making Abilities, Social-Participation Skills, and Sense of Political Efficacy as Necessary Bases for Effective Citizenship in an Ethnically Pluralistic Nation

The demands on people to make intelligent decisions on ethnic issues are constantly increasing. When people are unable to process the masses of conflicting information—including facts, opinions, interpretations, and theories about ethnic groups—they are often overwhelmed.

The multiethnic curriculum must enable students to gain knowledge and apply it. Students need a rich fund of sound knowledge. Facts, concepts, generalizations, and theories differ in their capability for organizing particulars and in predictive capacity; concepts and generalizations have more usefulness than do mere collections of miscellaneous facts. Young people need practice in the steps of scholarly methods for arriving at knowledge: identifying problems; formulating hypotheses; locating and evaluating source materials; organizing information as evidence; analyzing, interpreting, and reworking what was found; and coming to some conclusion. Students also need ample opportunities to learn to use knowledge in making sense out of the situations they encounter.

When curricular programs are inappropriate, teaching inept, and/or expectations low for students of some ethnic groups and especially for students who are poor, the emphasis in class is likely to be on discrete facts, memorization of empty generalizations, and low-level skills. Though the names and dates and exercises in using an index may be drawn from ethnic context, such an emphasis is still discriminatory and inconsistent with the basic purpose of multiethnic education. All young people need opportunities to develop powerful concepts and generalizations and intellectual abilities in the multiethnic curriculum.

Students must also learn how to identify values and relate them to knowledge. Young people should be taught methods for clarifying their own values relating to ethnicity. Such processes should include identifying value problems, their own and others'; describing evaluative behaviors; recognizing value conflicts within themselves and in social situations; recognizing and proposing alternatives based on values; and making choices between values in the light of their consequences.

Determining basic ideas, discovering, and verifying facts, and valuing are interrelated aspects of decision making. Ample opportunity to practice is necessary—as often as possible—in real-life situations; such practice frequently requires interdisciplinary as well as multiethnic perspectives. Decision-making skills help people assess social situations objectively and perceptively, identify feasible courses of action and project their consequences, decide thoughtfully, and then act.

The multiethnic curriculum must also help students develop effective social and political action skills because many students from ethnic groups are overwhelmed by a sense of a lack of control over their destinies. These feelings often stem from their belief that, as in the past, they and other ethnic minorities have little influence over political policies and institutions. The multiethnic curriculum should help students develop a greater sense of political efficacy and become politically more active and effective. With a basis in strong commitments to such democratic values as justice, freedom, and equality, students can learn to exercise political and social influence responsibly to influence societal decisions related to ethnicity in ways consistent with human dignity.

The school, in many ways, is a microcosm of society, including the changing dynamics of ethnic group situations. The school can provide limitless opportunities for students to practice social participation skills and to test their political efficacy as they address themselves to resolving some of the school's ethnic problems. Issues such as the participation of ethnic individuals in school government, discriminatory disciplinary rules, and preferential treatment of certain students because of their ethnic backgrounds are examples of problems that students can help resolve. Students are applying social action skills effectively when they combine knowledge, valuing, and thought gained from multiethnic perspectives and experiences to the resolution of problems affecting ethnic groups.

By providing students with opportunities to use decision-making abilities and social-action skills in the resolution of problems affecting ethnic groups, schools can contribute to more effective education for citizenship.

12. The Multiethnic Curriculum Should Help Students Develop the Skills Necessary for Effective Interpersonal and Interethnic Group Interactions

Effective interpersonal interaction across ethnic group lines is difficult to achieve. The problem is complicated by the fact that individuals bring to cross-ethnic interaction situations sets and expectations that influence their own behavior, including their responses to the behavior of other people. These expectations are formed on the basis of what their own groups deem to be appropriate behavior and what each individual believes he or she knows about other ethnic groups. Much knowledge about ethnic groups is stereotyped, distorted, and based on distant observations, scattered, superficial contacts, and incomplete factual information. The result is that attempts at cross-ethnic interpersonal interactions are often stymied by ethnocentrism.

The problems created by ethnocentrism can be at least partially resolved by helping students recognize consciously the forces operating in interpersonal interactions, and how these forces affect behavior. Students should develop skills and concepts to overcome factors that prevent successful interactions. These skills include identifying ethnic stereotypes, clarifying ethnic attitudes and values, developing cross-ethnic communication skills, recognizing how attitudes and values are projected in verbal and nonverbal behaviors, and viewing the dynamics of interpersonal interactions from other people's perspectives.

One goal of multiethnic education should be to help individuals function easily and effectively with members of both their own and other ethnic groups. The multiethnic curriculum should provide opportunities for students to explore lines of cross-ethnic communication and to experiment with cross-ethnic functioning. Actual experiences can be effective teaching devices, for students can test stereotypes and idealized behavioral constructs against real-life situations, and they can make the necessary adjustments in their frames of reference and behaviors, especially when asked to reflect on their own experiences. In the process, they should learn that ethnic group members, in the final analysis, are individuals, with all of the variations that characterize all individuals, and that ethnicity is only one of many variables that shape their personalities. Students will be forced to confront their values and make moral choices when their experiences in cross-ethnic interactions produce information contrary to previously held notions. Thus, students should broaden their ethnic options, increase their frames of reference, develop greater appreciation for individual and ethnic differences, and deepen their own capacities as human beings.

13. The Multiethnic Curriculum Should Be Comprehensive in Scope and Sequence, Should Present Holistic Views of Ethnic Groups, and Should Be an Integral Part of the Total School Curriculum

Students learn best from well-planned, comprehensive, continuous, and inter-related experiences. In an effective multiethnic curriculum, the study of ethnicity should be integrated into all courses and subject matter areas from preschool through twelfth grade and beyond. This study should be carefully planned to encourage the development of progressively more complex concepts and generalizations. It should also involve students in the study of a variety of ethnic groups.

A comprehensive multiethnic curriculum should also include a broad range of experiences within the study of any group: present culture, historical experiences, sociopolitical realities, contributions to the nation's development, problems faced in everyday living, and conditions of existence in society.

Students should also be introduced to the experiences of persons of widely varying backgrounds. The curriculum should include study of ethnic peoples in general, not just ethnic heroes and success stories. However, the study of ethnic heroes and success stories can help students of an ethnic group develop greater pride in their own group. In addition, people outside of an ethnic group can develop greater respect for that group by learning about their heroes and successes. Moreover, in establishing heroes and labeling people as successes, teachers should move beyond the standards of the dominant society and consider the values of each ethnic group and the worth of each individual life. An active contributor to an ethnic neighborhood may be more of a hero to the local community than a famous ethnic athlete. A good parent may be more of a "success" than a famous ethnic politician.

For optimum effectiveness, the study of ethnicity and ethnic group experiences must be interwoven into the total curriculum. It should not be reserved for special occasions, units, or courses, nor should it be considered supplementary to the existing curriculum. Such observances as Afro-American History or Brotherhood Week, Chanukah, Cinco de Mayo, St. Patrick's Day, and Martin Luther

King, Jr.'s, birthday are important and necessary, but insufficient in themselves. To rely entirely on these kinds of occasions and events, or to relegate ethnic content to a marginal position in the curriculum, is to guarantee the minimal impact of ethnic content.

The basic premises and organizational structures of education must be revised to reflect ethnic pluralism. The curriculum must be reorganized so that ethnic diversity is an integral, natural, and normal component of educational experiences for *all* students, with ethnic content accepted and used in everyday instruction, and with different ethnic perspectives introduced when various concepts, events, and problems are being studied. Ethnic content is as appropriate and important in teaching such fundamental skills and abilities as reading, thinking, and decision making as it is in teaching about social issues raised by racism, dehumanization, racial conflict, and alternative ethnic life-styles.

14. The Multiethnic Curriculum Should Include the Continuous Study of the Cultures, Historical Experiences, Social Realities, and Existential Conditions of Ethnic Groups, Including a Variety of Racial Compositions

The multiethnic curriculum should involve students in the continuous study of ethnic groups of different racial composition. A curriculum that concentrates on one ethnic group is not multiethnic. Nor is a curriculum multiethnic if it focuses exclusively on White ethnics or exclusively on multiracial and non-White ethnic groups, such as Blacks, Latinos, Asian Americans, and Native Americans. Every ethnic group cannot be included in the curriculum of a particular school or school district. The number is too large to be manageable. However, the inclusion of groups of different racial compositions is a necessary characteristic of effective multiethnic education.

Moreover, the multiethnic curriculum should include the consistent examination of significant aspects of ethnic experiences influenced by or related to race. These aspects include such subjects as racism, racial prejudice, racial discrimination, and exploitation based on race. The sensitive and continuous development of such concepts should help students develop an understanding of the racial factor in the past and present of our nation.

15. Interdisciplinary and Multidisciplinary Approaches Should Be Used in Designing and Implementing the Multiethnic Curriculum

No single discipline can adequately explain all the components of the life-styles, cultural experiences, and social problems of ethnic groups. Knowledge from any one discipline is insufficient to help individuals make adequate decisions on the complex issues raised by poverty, oppression, powerlessness and alienation. Concepts such as racism and anti-Semitism have multiple dimensions. To delineate all dimensions requires the concepts and perspectives of such disciplines as the various social sciences, history, literature, music, art, and philosophy.

Single-discipline or monoperspective analyses of complex ethnic issues can produce skewed, distorted interpretations, and evaluations. A promising way to avoid these pitfalls is to use consistently multidisciplinary approaches in studying experiences and events related to ethnic groups. For example, ethnic protest is not singularly a political, economic, artistic, or sociological activity; yet, it is all of these. Therefore, a curriculum that purports to be multiethnic and is realistic in its treatment of ethnic protest must focus on its broader ramifications. Such study must address the scientific, political, artistic, and sociological dimensions of protest.

A nation's accomplishments are due neither to the ingenuity and creativity of a single ethnic group, nor to accomplishments in a single area, but rather to the efforts and contributions of many different ethnic groups and individuals in many areas. Members of many different ethnic groups within a nation contribute to the fields of science and industry, politics, literature, economics, and the arts. Multidisciplinary analyses will best help students understand them.

16. The Curriculum Should Use Comparative Approaches in the Study of Ethnic Groups and Ethnicity

The study of ethnic group experiences should not be a process of one-upmanship. It should not promote the idea that any one ethnic group has a monopoly on talent and worth, or incapacity and weakness, but, instead, the ideas that each individual and each ethnic group has worth and dignity. Students should be taught that persons from all ethnic groups have common characteristics and needs, although they are affected differently by certain social situations and may use different means to respond to their needs and to achieve their objectives. Furthermore, school personnel should remember that realistic comparative approaches to the study of different ethnic group experiences are descriptive and analytical, not normative or judgmental. Teachers should also be aware of their own biases and prejudices as they help students use comparative approaches.

Social situations and events included in the curriculum should be analyzed from the perspectives of several ethnic groups instead of using a monoperspective analysis. This approach allows students to see the subtle ways in which the lives of different ethnic group members are similar and interrelated, to study the concept of universality as it relates to ethnic groups, and to see how all ethnic groups are active participants in all aspects of society. Studying such issues as power and politics, ethnicity, and culture from comparative, multiethnic perspectives will help students develop more realistic, accurate understandings of how these issues affect everyone, and how the effects are both alike and different.

17. The Curriculum Should Help Students View and Interpret Events, Situations, and Conflict from Diverse Ethnic Perspectives and Points of View

Historically, students have been taught to view events, situations, and their national history primarily from the perspectives of mainstream historians and social scientists sympathetic to the dominant groups within society. The perspectives of other groups, such as Afro-Americans and Canadian Indians, have been largely omitted in the school curriculum. When the World War II Japanese-American internment and the Indian Removal Act of 1830, for example, are studied in U.S. schools, they are rarely viewed from the points of view of the Japanese Americans interned or the Indians forced to leave their homes and move to the West.

To gain a more complete understanding of both our past and present, students should look at events and situations from the perspectives of mainstream groups and also from the perspectives of people who are members of ethnic minority groups. This approach to teaching is more likely to make our students less ethnocentric and more able to accept the fact that almost any event or situation can be legitimately looked at from many perspectives. When using this approach in the classroom, the teacher should avoid, as much as possible, labeling any perspective as "right" or "wrong." Rather, the teacher should try to help students understand how each group may view a situation differently and why. The emphasis should be on understanding and explanation and not on simplistic moralizing. For example, the perceptions of many Jewish Americans of political events in the United States have been shaped by memories of the Nazi Holocaust—the attempt at extermination of European Jews—and the recurring anti-Semitism in the United States.

Ethnicity has strongly influenced the nature of intergroup relations in most Western societies. How individuals perceive events and situations is often influenced by their ethnic experiences, especially so when the events and situations are directly related to ethnic conflict and discrimination, or to issues such as affirmative action and busing for school desegregation. When students view a historical or contemporary situation from the perspectives of one ethnic group only—whether it is a majority group or a minority group—they can acquire, at best, an incomplete understanding.

18. The School Should Provide Opportunities for Students to Participate in the Aesthetic Experiences of Various Ethnic Groups

Ethnic groups should not be studied only at a distance. Although there is considerable value to incorporating statistical and analytical social science methodologies and concepts in the study of ethnic groups, an overreliance on intellectualism will miss an important part of the multiethnic experience — the participation in the experiences of ethnic groups.

A number of teaching materials can be used. Students should read and hear the past and contemporary writings of members of different ethnic groups. Poetry, short stories, folklore, essays, plays, and novels should be used. Ethnic autobiographies offer special insight into the experience of what it means to be ethnic in a modern society.

Ethnic music, art, architecture, and dance — past and contemporary — provide other avenues for experiential participation, as they interpret the emotions and feelings of ethnic groups. The arts and humanities can serve as excellent vehicles for studying group experiences by focusing on this question: What aspects of the experience of a particular ethnic group helped create these kinds of musical and artistic expressions?

In studying multiethnic literature and arts, students should become acquainted with what has been created in local ethnic communities. In addition, members of local ethnic communities can provide dramatic living autobiographies for students. Local people should be invited to discuss their viewpoints and experiences with students. Students should also have opportunities for developing their own artistic, musical, and literary abilities, even to make them available to the local community.

Role-playing of various ethnic experiences should be interspersed throughout the curriculum to encourage understanding of what it means to belong to various ethnic groups. The immersion of students in multiethnic experiences is an effective means for developing understanding both of self and others.

19. Schools Should Foster the Study of Ethnic Group Languages as Legitimate Communication Systems

A multiethnic curriculum recognizes the reality of language diversity and promotes the attitude that all languages and dialects are valid communicating systems among some groups and for some purposes. The program requires a multidisciplinary focus on language and dialect.

Concepts about language and dialect derived from disciplines such as anthropology, sociology, and political science expand the students' perceptions of language and dialect as something more than correct grammar. For example, the nature and intent of language policies and laws in the United States can be compared to those in nations officially bilingual. Students can also be taught sociolinguistic concepts that provide a framework for understanding the verbal and nonverbal behavior of other people as well as themselves. Critical listening, speaking, and reading habits should be nurtured, with special attention to the uses of language.

Research indicates that school rejection of the student's home language affects the student's self-esteem, academic achievement, and social and occupational mobility.[5] Research also indicates that school acceptance and use of the student's home language improves self-esteem, academic achievement, and relationships among students in a school.[6] In a multiethnic curriculum, students are provided opportunities to study their own dialects as well as others. They become more receptive to the languages and dialects of fellow students. Such an approach helps students develop concepts in their own vernaculars whenever necessary while it promotes appreciation for home language environments.

The multiethnic program should provide for literacy in at least two languages, develop respect for language and dialect diversity, and diminish language ethnocentrism.

20. The Curriculum Should Make Maximum Use of Local Community Resources

An effective multiethnic curriculum should include a study of ethnicity and ethnic groups not only nationally, but also in the local community. An effective multiethnic curriculum must expand beyond classroom walls. Teachers should use the local community as a "laboratory" in which students can develop and use intellectual, social, and political action skills in the local ethnic communities. Planned field trips and individual or group research projects are helpful. Continuous investigation of the local community can provide insights into the actual dynamics of ethnic groups. It can create greater respect for what has been accomplished. It can promote awareness of and commitment to what still needs to be done to improve the lives and opportunities for all local residents.

Every member of the local community, including the student's family, is a valuable source of knowledge. There are no class, educational, or linguistic qualifications for participating in the national culture of a democratic society, for having a culture or society, for having family or neighborhood traditions, for perceiving the surrounding community, or for relating one's experiences. Teachers should invite local residents of various ethnic backgrounds to the classroom. In this setting, community people can share their experiences and views with students, relate their oral traditions, answer questions, give new outlooks on society and history, and open doors of investigation for students. Special efforts should be made to involve senior citizens in school multiethnic programs both to help them develop a higher sense of self-worth and to benefit the students and the school community.

It is important that students develop a sensitivity to ethnic differences and a conceptual framework for viewing ethnic differences before interacting with ethnic classroom guests or studying the local ethnic communities. Otherwise, these promising opportunities may reinforce rather than reduce ethnic stereotypes and prejudices.

In sound study projects, students can consider such topics as local population distribution, housing, school assignments, political representation, and ethnic community activities. Older students can take advantage of accessible public documents, such as city council and school board minutes, minutes of local organizations, and church records for insight into the community.

To separate the local community from the school is to ignore the everyday world in which students live.

21. The Assessment Procedures Used with Students Should Reflect Their Ethnic Cultures

To make the school a truly multiethnic institution, major changes must be made in how we test and ascertain student abilities. Most intelligence tests administered in the public or state schools are based on a mainstream, monoethnic model. Since many students socialized within other ethnic cultures find the tests and other aspects of the school alien and intimidating, they perform poorly and are placed in low academic tracks, special education classes, or low ability reading groups.[7] Research indicates that teachers in these kinds of situations tend to have low expectations for their students and often fail to create the kinds of learning environments that promote mastery of the skills and abilities needed to function effectively in society.[8]

Standardized intelligence testing frequently serves, in the final analysis, to deny some ethnic youths equal educational opportunities. The results of these tests are often used to justify the noneducation of ethnic youths and to relieve teachers and other school personnel from accountability. Novel assessment devices that reflect the cultures of ethnic youths need to be developed and used. Moreover, teacher-made tests and other routine classroom assessment techniques should reflect the cultures of ethnic youths. It will, however, do little good for educators to create improved assessment procedures for ethnic youths unless, at the same time, they implement curricular and instructional practices that are also multiethnic and multiracial.

22. Schools Should Conduct Ongoing, Systematic Evaluations of the Goals, Methods, and Instructional Materials Used in Teaching about Ethnicity

Schools must set up attainable goals and objectives for multiethnic education. To evaluate the extent to which these goals and objectives are accomplished, school personnel must judge—and with evidence—what occurs in their own school in three broad areas: (1) school policies and governance procedures; (2) everyday practices of staff and teachers; and (3) curricular programs and offerings, academic and nonacademic, preschool through grade twelve. These guidelines will help schools in their evaluation programs.

Many sources of evidence should be used. Teachers, administrators, supportive staff, parents, students, and other people in the school community ought to participate in providing and evaluating evidence.

Evaluation should be construed as a means by which a school, its staff, and students can improve multiethnic relations, experiences, and understandings within the school. Evaluation should be oriented toward analyzing and improving, neither castigating nor applauding multiethnic programs. (See the Appendix.)

Notes

1. Manual Ramírez III and Alfredo Castañeda, *Cultural Democracy, Bicognitive Development and Education* (New York: Academic Press, 1974); Vernon L. Allen, ed., *Psychological Factors in Poverty* (Chicago: Markham Publishing Co., 1970); Roger D. Abrahams and Rudolph C. Troike, eds., *Language and Cultural Diversity in American Education* (Englewood Cliffs, N.J.: Prentice-Hall, 1972); Stephen S. Baratz and Joan C. Baratz, "Early Childhood Intervention: The Social Science Base of Institutional Racism," *Harvard Educational Review* 40 (Winter 1970), pp. 29–50; Frederick Williams, ed., *Language and Poverty: Perspectives on a Theme* (Chicago: Markham Publishing Co., 1970).

2. Ramírez and Castañeda, *Cultural Democracy*; Judith Kleinfeld, "Effective Teachers of Eskimo and Indian Students," *School Review* 83 (February 1975), pp. 301–344.

3. Susan S. Stodolsky and Gerald Lesser, "Learning Patterns in the Disadvantaged," *Harvard Educational Review* 37 (Fall 1967), pp. 546–593; G. S. Lesser, G. Fifer, and D. H. Clark, "Mental Abilities of Children from Different Social-Class and Cultural Groups," *Monographs for Research in Child Development* 30 (1965).

4. Ramírez and Castañeda, *Cultural Democracy*; Kleinfeld, "Effective Teachers"; Stodolsky and Lesser, "Learning Patterns."

5. United States Commission on Civil Rights, *A Better Chance to Learn: Bilingual-Bicultural Education* (Washington, D.C.: U.S. Government Printing Office, 1975), pp. 33–36.

6. Ibid., pp. 38–40.

7. Jane R. Mercer, "Latent Functions of Intelligence Testing in the Public Schools," in Lamar P. Miller, ed., *The Testing of Black Students* (Englewood Cliffs, N.J.: Prentice-Hall, 1974).

8. Ray C. Rist, "Student Social Class and Teacher Expectations: The Self-Fulfilling Prophecy in Ghetto Education," *Harvard Educational Review* 40 (August 1970), pp. 411–451; Eleanor B. Leacock, *Teaching and Learning in City Schools* (New York: Basic Books, 1969); United States Commission on Civil Rights, *Teachers and Students: Differences in Teacher Interaction with Mexican American and Anglo Students* (Washington, D.C.: U.S. Government Printing Office, 1973).

Multiethnic Education Inventory

School Structure Relating to Multicultural-Multiracial Education

A. Racial-Ethnic Balance of the Total Staff

1. List below percentages for the various racial and ethnic groups.

	American Indian %	Black %	Asian American %	Spanish speaking %	European American %	Others specify %
Administrators						
Classroom Teachers						
Guidance Counselors						
Media Personnel						
Health Services Personnel						
Specialists and Consultants						
Food Services Personnel						
Secretaries and Clerks						
Custodial and Maintenance Personnel						
Paraprofessionals						
Others						

*Reprinted from *Evaluation Guidelines for Multicultural-Multiracial Education*. Arlington, Virginia: National Study of School Evaluation, 1973, pp. 25–33. Used with permission of the National Study of School Evaluation. Not to be reproduced without permission.

a. How many of the non-White professional personnel in the school are under tenure?

b. What percentage is this of all tenured personnel in the school?

c. How many of the administrators are women?

Checklist*

1. Minority* personnel on the staff are more numerous now than five years ago. . . . .   na 1 2 3 4

2. The racial composition of the professional staff is in keeping with the racial makeup of the student body. . . . .   na 1 2 3 4

3. Minority* staff members have been given professional assignments other than that of classroom teachers. . . . .   na 1 2 3 4

4. The racial-ethnic composition of the professional staff fairly reflects the racial-ethnic balance of the community. . . . .   na 1 2 3 4

Evaluations

a) Are minority* personnel sufficiently represented on the school's teaching staff so as to provide a favorable setting for multiracial education?. . . . .   na 1 2 3 4

b) Are minority* personnel sufficiently represented on the school's administrative and other non-teaching professional staff so as to provide a favorable setting for multicultural-multiracial education? . . . .   na 1 2 3 4

c) Are minority* personnel on the school's professional staff represented to a degree that reflects the broad pluralistic society of the United States rather than the immediate community? . . . .   na 1 2 3 4

d) Are women sufficiently represented on the school's administrative staff to indicate the absence of sexual bias?. . . . .   na 1 2 3 4

e) In the general school structure, is there an effort to reduce sex stereotyping? . . . .   na 1 2 3 4

Comments

---

*4 = Excellent; 3 = Good; 2 = Fair; 1 = Poor, Missing; na = Not applicable. Wherever the word *minority* is asterisked, it refers to racial or ethnic groups that are the numerical minority within this particular school or district.

B. The Teaching Staff

Checklist

1. The staff is receptive to minority* colleagues......   na   1   2   3   4

2. Teachers attend in-service workshops or institutes on multicultural-multiracial education...........   na   1   2   3   4

3. Teachers recognize the need for multicultural-multiracial education in this school.............   na   1   2   3   4

4. Teachers search for ways to overcome the reluctance of students to recognize and discuss racial and ethnic questions.............................   na   1   2   3   4

5. Teachers are relatively consistent in expecting adequate classroom behavior of all students..........   na   1   2   3   4

6. Teachers establish legitimate standards for classwork, but also make special efforts to see that all students, despite any initial learning deficiencies, can reach those standards.....................   na   1   2   3   4

7. Teachers openly recognize racial and cultural biases in themselves and in students and attempt to overcome these................................   na   1   2   3   4

8. Teachers respect the cultural, racial, and ethnic differences of their students. ....   na   1   2   3   4

Evaluations

a) To what extent is the staff committed to multicultural-multiracial education in this school? .....   na   1   2   3   4

b) To what extent does the teaching staff make a consistent effort to promote sound multicultural-multiracial relationships in all their contacts with students in this school? ....   na   1   2   3   4

c) To what extent do the teachers practice sound interpersonal and intergroup relationships among themselves? ....   na   1   2   3   4

d) To what extent are all staff members required to have training in multicultural-multiracial education?.................................   na   1   2   3   4

Comments

C. The Principal and His or Her Administrative Staff

Checklist

1. Members of the administrative staff have participated in workshops, seminars, institutes, and so on, in human relations and minority issues........   na   1   2   3   4

2. The principal actively seeks and welcomes minority* group teachers.........................   na   1   2   3   4

3. The principal promotes better relations between faculty members from minority and majority groups..................................   na   1   2   3   4

4. The principal is accessible to minority* parents wishing to discuss racial, ethnic, and school issues..................................   na   1   2   3   4

5. The principal is accessible to minority* students wishing to discuss racial, ethnic, and school issues..................................   na   1   2   3   4

6. The principal regularly reports to the parents about the progress of the multicultural-multiracial education program in the school...................   na   1   2   3   4

7. The principal makes program and other recommendations to the superintendent for improving multicultural-multiracial education...........   na   1   2   3   4

8. The principal deals directly and openly with minority* groups.............................   na   1   2   3   4

9. The principal regularly works with the teaching staff to help them improve the quality of their efforts in multicultural-multiracial education......   na   1   2   3   4

10. The principal is committed to the need for multicultural-multiracial education in this school......   na   1   2   3   4

11. The administrative staff is committed to the need for multicultural-multiracial education in this school...............................   na   1   2   3   4

Evaluations

a) How effectively does the principal perform his or her duties in relation to multicultural-multiracial education?..............................   na   1   2   3   4

b) To what degree do the assistants to the principal support his or her policies and program relating to multicultural-multiracial education?............   na   1   2   3   4

Comments

D. School Organization and Grouping

Checklist

1. In organizing the school, consideration has been given to the subtle and overt effects of the schedule, grade placement, course requirements, and the like, on minority group students. . . . . na 1 2 3 4

2. Rules and regulations of the school relate strictly to the need for general control and not to nonessential culture differences and mores. . . . . na 1 2 3 4

3. The school recognizes the need among its students for self-segregation at times in the classrooms, in their leisure moments, and in their extracurricular activities . . . . na 1 2 3 4

4. The school is aware of the specific learning conditions in those schools previously attended by its students. . . . . na 1 2 3 4

5. The school has attempted to eliminate the negative effects on pluralistic education of formal tracking in student placement. . . . . na 1 2 3 4

6. The school has sought to reduce the negative effects on pluralistic education of informal tracking. . na 1 2 3 4

7. The only courses in the school for which prerequisites have been established are those of a strictly sequential nature, such as French I and II. . . . . na 1 2 3 4

8. Concern is given to having classes fully representative of the racial-ethnic, cultural diversity of the student body. . . . . na 1 2 3 4

9. Lunchroom facilities are organized to promote the free association of all students. . . . . na 1 2 3 4

Evaluations .

a) To what degree does the organization of the school provide a total experience promotive of multi-cultural-multiracial education? . . . . na 1 2 3 4 *b)* To what extent do the grouping, class scheduling, and student assignment policies and procedures in the school promote multicultural-multiracial interaction? . . . .   na   1   2   3   4

c) To what extent are the published policies of the board relating to multicultural-multiracial education observed in this school? . . . .   na   1   2   3   4

Comments

The Educational Program

A. The Formal Curriculum

Checklist

1. The English curriculum includes the writings and works of a wide range of ethnic groups. . . . .   na   1   2   3   4

2. The social studies curriculum purposely has been revised to include the historic, cultural, and intellectual contributions of American Indians, Blacks, Asians, Spanish-speaking people, and so on. . . . . . .   na   1   2   3   4

3. Special courses are provided in a broad spectrum of ethnic studies. . . . .   na   1   2   3   4

4. All students are encouraged to take special courses in ethnic studies. . . . .   na   1   2   3   4

5. Special help in basic skills is provided so that all students may succeed in all curriculum areas. . . . . .   na   1   2   3   4

6. All courses are readily available to students from all ethnic groups. . . . .   na   1   2   3   4

7. The school's curriculum provides genuine options for non-White students to pursue education beyond high school. . . . .   na   1   2   3   4

8. The school's curriculum provides worthwhile options for those non-White students who will enter the work force on graduation from high school. . . . .   na   1   2   3   4

9. Where pertinent, the content in all courses includes a focus on multicultural-multiracial education. . . . .   na   1   2   3   4

Supplementary Data

1. Describe the formal curriculum for the study of multiethnic and multiracial history and culture.
2. Explain in what other ways the curriculum facilitates multicultural understandings.
3. Describe how the curriculum supports equal power, prestige, and access to a full life in a pluralistic society for non-White students.
4. Describe the efforts made within the last two years to make the curriculum more pertinent to the needs and requirements of non-White students.

Evaluations

a) to what degree does the school's formal curriculum promote multicultural-multiracial education?..... na 1 2 3 4

b) To what extent is the school preparing every one of its students for a productive life in the pluralistic society of America? .... na 1 2 3 4

c) To what extent does concern for multicultural-multiracial education permeate the entire school program? .... na 1 2 3 4

d) To what extent are appropriate programs and teaching materials being developed for ethnic studies?...................................... na 1 2 3 4

Comments

B. Learning Materials

Checklist

1. There is in the school's professional library a good collection of multicultural-multiracial materials. .. na 1 2 3 4
2. There are in the media center current and pertinent books and other printed materials written by members of non-White groups................ na 1 2 3 4
3. There are in the media center nonprinted materials on non-White groups and diverse cultures........ na 1 2 3 4
4. The materials on multicultural-multiracial matters in the media center are readily accessible to all students...................................... na 1 2 3 4

5. Factual materials in the library have been evaluated for accuracy and authenticity as far as multi-cultural-multiracial concepts are concerned. . . . . . na 1 2 3 4

6. Textbooks are carefully selected for their equitable treatment of non-White and ethnic minority groups. . . . . na 1 2 3 4

7. Teaching materials for multicultural-multiracial education are available in a range of interest levels for students. . . . . na 1 2 3 4

8. Multicultural-multiracial teaching materials are provided at varying levels of difficulty. . . . . na 1 2 3 4

9. Curriculum materials are judged on their coverage and treatment of non-White group contributions, as well as on other criteria. . . . . na 1 2 3 4

10. Curriculum materials are continually being reviewed in relation to their impact on multicultural-multiracial relationships. . . . . na 1 2 3 4

11. No student is denied the learning materials he or she needs because of an inability to pay fees or charges. . . . . na 1 2 3 4

Evaluations

a) To what extent do the learning materials available to students contribute to and support the school's efforts towards multicultural-multiracial education? . . . . na 1 2 3 4

b) To what extent do the teaching materials available to teachers contribute to and support the school's efforts towards multicultural-multiracial education? . . . . na 1 2 3 4

Comments

C. Special Education

Note: Special education is generally accepted to mean education designed for and available to handicapped children and youth whose educational needs are different in part from those of most of their peers.

Checklist

1. The special education program is an integral part of the instructional program and operates on a nondiscriminatory basis. . . . .   na   1   2   3   4

2. Students are placed in programs for the mentally handicapped or for the mentally disturbed on the basis of learning or behavioral deficiencies alone, and not because of racially, socially, or culturally conditioned factors. . . . .   na   1   2   3   4

3. The special education staff is integrated racially and ethnically. . . . .   na   1   2   3   4

4. Students are provided special supportive services on an integrated basis, in accordance with individual needs. . . . .   na   1   2   3   4

5. In referring its handicapped students to supporting lay and professional groups, the school insists that all its students be treated equally. . . . .   na   1   2   3   4

6. Multicultural-multiracial programs are fully available to special education students. . . . .   na   1   2   3   4

7. Handicapped students, regardless of race or ethnic background, are encouraged to seek the highest levels of education and/or employment for which they are suited. . . . .   na   1   2   3   4

INDEX

N